EIGHTEENTH-CENTURY RUSSIAN MUSIC

Eighteenth-Century Russian Music

MARINA RITZAREV
Bar-Ilan University, Israel

ASHGATE

Published by
Ashgate Publishing Limited
Gower House
Croft Road
Aldershot
Hampshire GU11 3HR
England

Ashgate Publishing Company
Suite 420
101 Cherry Street
Burlington, VT 05401-4405
USA

Ashgate website: http://www.ashgate.com

British Library Cataloguing in Publication Data
Ritzarev, Marina
  Eighteenth-century Russian music
  1.Music – Russia – 18th century – History and criticism
  I.Title
  780.9'47'09033

Library of Congress Cataloging-in-Publication Data
Ritzarev, Marina.
  Eighteenth-century Russian music / Marina Ritzarev.
      p. cm.
  Includes bibliographical references and index.
  ISBN 0-7546-3466-3 (alk. paper)
  1. Music—Russia—18th century—History and criticism. I. Title.

  ML300.3.R58 2006
  780'.947'09033—dc22

                                                                    2005024441
  ISBN-10: 0754634663

Printed and bound in Great Britain by MPG Books Ltd. Bodmin, Cornwall.

Contents

List of Figures and Tables

Figures

Table

List of Music Examples

Preface

The wealth of available knowledge on the rich eighteenth-century Russian musical legacy has long begged to be made available to the English-speaking public. This knowledge, expressed mostly in Russian studies, is so extensive, however, that one medium-sized book can hardly cover even a small part of it. Realizing the weighty responsibility of setting out to provide the first general presentation of this topic in English, I chose to restrict myself in the provision of a great many fascinating facts and details, and instead determined upon a certain conceptualization of the material according to my personal perspective of eighteenth-century Russian music.

I developed this perspective over the course of more than three decades of work, beginning in Leningrad in the late 1960s and mainly accomplished in Moscow during the 1970s–80s. My work on the topic might well have been concluded then if not for my emigration to Israel, which somewhat obliged me to carry it westward with me. The final project turned out to be not quite as simple as merely revising and translating my existing works. Although significantly based upon them, it resulted in an entirely new book, written between 1998 and 2004 and targeted first and foremost at the non-Russian-speaking reader.

This new contribution will return to the Russian libraries, probably to be listed under the category of *Rossica* – the old St Petersburg Public Library department for Russian studies carried out by foreign scholars. Nonetheless, it is the product of a long-dreamed process of scholarly integration between Russia and the West, at a time when the post-Soviet release from former prejudices is happily coinciding with the development of Russian studies in the West and the new tempo of communication. This book, therefore, has been written free from fear of my being too Soviet for the West or too Western for Russia.

The century of Russian studies on eighteenth-century national music experienced a complicated historiography. I analyze this in the opening essay, which serves as the cornerstone of my conception. I also note that this period of Russian music cannot be understood outside the context of the Russian culture and history of previous epochs that combined to form the complex Russian identity. Regarding the structure of the book, I have chosen to follow a general chronological principle, attempting to cover each period with a cross-section of the various social milieus, and portrayals of the two leading musical figures of the period – the Russian composers Maxim Berezovsky and Dmitry Bortniansky. I present them as they appear within different aspects of the culture itself, in its dynamic development, highlighting in each particular period the most characteristic phenomena and protagonists.

The present text includes, partially or in full, a number of my earlier works. Material from my books *Kompozitor D. Bortniansky* (1979) and *Kompozitor M.S. Berezovsky* (1983) published in Leningrad: Muzyka, as well as from the forthcoming

Dukhovny kontsert v Rossii vtoroy poloviny XVIII veka (St Petersburg: Kompozitor) can be found in Chapters 4, 5, 6, 8, 10, 12, 13 and 14. My articles: 'Rethinking Eighteenth-Century Russian Music', (2003) and 'Russian Music before Glinka' (2002b) are used in Chapters 1–2; 'The Legacy of Late Eighteenth-Century Russian Spiritual Music: its Sources and Destiny' (2002a) – in Chapters 12–13; 'The Italian Diaspora in Eighteenth-Century Russia' (2001) – in Chapters 3, 4, 5 and 10; and 'Chant and Polyphony in Russia: Historical Aspects', (2000) – in Chapter 14.

Acknowledgements

Since this book is the result of many projects accomplished over the last three decades, dozens of my colleagues have given their help, support and encouragement at one time or another. During my years at the St Petersburg Conservatory, there were three persons to whom I am particularly grateful: Sergei Slonimsky, the supervisor for my MA and PhD theses – for his suggestion of the topic and utter hands–off of the contents; Mikhail Druskin, who taught us the history of West–European music and from whom I hope I learned to think historically; and Elena Orlova, who taught us Russian music and how to work with archival sources, and whom I seldom understood, but from whom, paradoxically, I believe I learned a multi–dimensional and systematic approach.

Among my Muscovite colleagues I recall with appreciation two major Russian music scholars, Yury Keldysh and Vladimir Protopopov, who supported my research with kind advice; and the former director of the Central Museum for Musical Culture, Ekaterina Alexeeva, who provided the museum archives with invaluable eighteenth–century sources and greatly encouraged studies in this field.

There were also many people whose kind assistance contributed so much in a variety of areas – references, library sources, comments, advice, reviews, editorial initiatives etc., over the years. Among them are my colleagues from Moscow: Boris Dobrokhotov, Galina Koltypina, Lyudmila Korabelnikova, Elena Dolinskaya, Lyudmila Rapatskaya, Irina Kosareva, Sophia Filshtein, Tatiana Vladyshevskaya, Alexey Naumov, Tatiana Lebedeva, Irina Medvedeva, Marina Rachmanova, Irina Vetlitsina and Galina Timoshchenkova; from St Petersburg: Alexei Vulfson, Lyudmila Kovnatskaya, Anna Porfirieva, Arkady Klimovitsky, Anatoly Milka, Natalia Seregina, Viktor Lapin, Vladimir Gourevich, Konstantin Malinovsky, Ol'ga Velikanova, Ol'ga Rodyukova, Konstantin Butz; from Vologda: Morris Bonfeld; from Nozhnii Novgorod: Larisa Krylova and Svetlana Sinitskaya; from Minsk: Ola Dadiomova; from Copenhagen Musikhistorisk Museum: Dr Ole Kongsted and from the United States: Margarita Mazo (Columbus), Malcolm Hamrick Brown (Bloomington), Richard Taruskin (Berkeley), Izaly Zemtsovsky (Berkeley) and Oleg Timofeev (Iowa). My special thanks to Mikhail Stepanenko from Kiev and Pavel Serbin from Moscow, who have contributed a lot in this field and generously shared with me their recent findings.

I am greatly indebted to Israeli Ministry of Absorption and Bar–Ilan University: without their support the continuation of my research in Israel would have been impossible. Among my Israeli colleagues I feel specially obliged to Bathia Churgin, whose encouragement kept me going as a musicologist during the early period of my immigration; and to Edwin Seroussi, who, as chairman of the Music Department of Bar–Ilan University, provided me with breathing space for my research. I am also grateful to linguists Paul Wexler and Arkady Burshtein for valuable bibliographical references, Bella Brover–Lubovsky, Atara Kotlyar and Igal Shuster for their help with library sources and to Morel Korn for technical support.

I cordially thank Uri Sharvit (Jerusalem), Danica Petrovich (Belgrade) and Isaac Lambertsen (New York) for their kind help with the translation of ecclesiastical matters.

The generous review of my proposal, written by an anonymous Ashgate reader, had particular significance in advancing my work and presenting me with valuable ideas.

Since I wrote this book in my "Russian" English, I clearly needed an editor. I am deeply grateful to Naomi Paz, my English editor, who far beyond formal corrections, in some incomprehensible way managed to fathom my philological intentions and suggest an effective articulation of my ideas.

A project of this kind usually involves a family: to my mother Sophie Zifkin, my sister Nina Libin, who made a camera–ready copy, and my husband–colleague Sergei Ritzarev–Abir, who made music examples, I express my deep gratitude for all kinds of moral and technical support; as I do to the person who has awaited this book most eagerly and who has heroically supported me in all my work – my father, Gregory Zifkin. He contributed to this endeavour in every possible way, and his extensive searches in the St Petersburg archives resulted in many of the fascinating findings presented here.

Abbreviations, Transliteration and Dates

Institutions

AVPRI	Arkhiv Vneshney Politiki Rossiyskoy Imperii, Moscow
BRAN	Biblioteka Rossiyskoy Akademii Nauk, St Petersburg
GIM	Gosudarstvenny Istoricheskiy Muzey, Moscow
GMMK	Gosudarstvenny Muzey Muzykal'noy
GMPI	kul'tury imeni Glinki, Moscow
	Gosudarstvenny Muzykal'no-Pedagogicheskiy
IRLI	Institut imeni Gnesinykh, Moscow
	Institut Russkoy Literatury (Pushkinskiy Dom), St Petersburg
RGADA	Rossiyskiy Gosudarstvenny Arkhiv Drevnikh Aktov, Moscow
RGAVMF	Rossiyskiy Gosudarstvenny Arkhiv Voenno-
RGB	Morskogo Flota, St Petersburg
	Rossiyskaya Gosudarstvennaya Biblioteka, Moscow
RGIA	Rossiyskiy Gosudarstvenny Istoricheskiy Arkhiv, St Petersburg
RIII	Rossiyskiy Institut Istorii Iskusstv, St Petersburg
RNB	Rossiyskaya Natsional'naya Biblioteka, St Petersburg
TsGIA SPb	Tsentral'ny Gosudarstvenny Istoricheskiy Arkhiv Sankt-Peterburga, St Petersburg

Bibliographical and Archival Sources

HLA	Haehne-Lehnhold Announcements (Catalogues of Russian spiritual
IRM	concertos, advertised by the book-sellers E.F. Haehne (known in Russia as Ch.B. Gene) and K.P. Lehnhold (known as Lengold) in the supplement to the newspaper MV) Istoria russkoi muzyki (History of Russian music in ten volumes; Yu.V. Keldysh, O.E. Levasheva and A.I. Kandinsky eds)
KFZ	Kamer-furiersky zhurnal (Eighteenth-century court chronicles, published in the nineteenth century)

KPN	Katalog pevcheskoy note, pisanny 1793 goda genvarya 16 dnya (Catalogue for Vocal Music written on 16 January 1793. GMMK, f 283, no 25)
LPC	Lvov-Prach Collection (A Collection of Russian Folk Songs by Nikolai Lvov and Ivan Prach)
MPES	Muzykal'ny Peterburg: Entsiklopedicheskiy Slovar' (Musical St Petersburg: encyclopaedic lexicon, eighteenth century, in five volumes. Anna Porfirieva ed. 1997–2002)
MV	Moskovskie vedomosti (Moscow newspaper)
PRMI	Pamyatniki russkogo muzykal'nogo iskusstva (Monuments of Russian music art, editions, Yury Keldysh Editor-in-Chief)
SPV	Sankt-Peterburgskie vedomosti (St Petersburg newspaper)
SRP	Slovar' Russkikh Pisateley (Lexicon of eighteenth-century Russian writers, A.M. Panchenko Editor-in-Chief)

In the references to Russian archival sources I have produced a transliteration of the Russian notifications. Consequently, the abbreviation of a depository is followed by 'f' (from the Russian *fond*, meaning collection), 'op' (from the Russian *opis'*, meaning one of the records of items within a huge collection), file number and 'L' or 'LL' (from the Russian *list*, meaning folio), with the addition of 'r' for recto and 'v' for verso as required.

Transliteration from Russian

I use a Russian transliteration currently accepted in contemporary English literature, in which 'y' has three main functions: 1) as 'ï' for the Russian 'ы', 2) as 'ïy' for the Russian 'ый' and 3) before a, e, o and u to achieve soft vowels: ya for 'я', ye for 'e', yo for 'ё' and yu for 'ю'. However in the spelling of some names I prefer to omit the 'y' and write Fedor and Peter rather than Fyedor and Pyotr. In other cases I have chosen the shorter and more familiar spellings like Alexander and Maxim rather than Aleksandr and Maksym.

The names of eighteenth-century musicians often had several variants of spelling in their own lifetime due their multicultural backgrounds. The twentieth century, in seeking the 'correct' variant, sometimes offers even more. Both approaches are a matter of identity or policy. This is why, although following the New Grove Dictionary 2001 for most of the names, I nevertheless express certain preferences that are closer to tradition. For example, I spell the name of one of my main characters, Dmitry Bortniansky, following his own signature (transformed during his lifetime from 'Bortnianskij' to 'Bortniansky') and tradition, and not Dmitro Bortnyans'ky as NGD suggests, stressing his Ukrainian identity. I do not ignore this element of his identity (though the man left the Ukraine at the age of six and spent 68 years of his life serving the Russian court, including eleven years in Italy). However, while articulating the great significance of Ukrainian music for Russian culture, I consider Bortniansky in the context of Russian culture and his contribution to it. Moreover, there is no single source in Russian historiography that definitely pronounces him in the Ukrainian way – a circumstance worth consideration without any relation to the 'Great-Russian chauvinism' that humiliatingly denominated the Ukraine (included in the Russian Empire on an autonomic basis) as Malorossiya (Little Russia). Several cross-references in the Index should solve the problem of variant readings.

Dates

Dates in Russian documents are given as they appear in originals, according to the Julian calendar practiced in Russia from 1700 to 1918. It lagged behind the Gregorian Style eleven days in the eighteenth century and twelve days in the nineteenth.

Chapter 1

Rethinking Eighteenth-Century Russian Music

Due to the events of history and their complex intertwining, it was only in the last third of the twentieth century that the artistic treasures of Russian pre-Glinka music began to attract broad public attention even in Russia itself, while outside Russia they have remained virtually unknown. Anyone studying this fascinating repertoire from a broad historical and cultural perspective must face intriguing questions. We know, for example, that in 1726 J.S. Bach wrote to his Lyceum friend George Erdmann, resident consul of Danzig at the court of Empress Catherine I (widow of Peter I), asking about a possible position (Pantielev, 1983). Similarly, Mozart, exhausted by the uncertainties of his freelance existence, authorized Count Andrey Razumovsky, Russian ambassador in Vienna, to start negotiations with Prince Gregory Potemkin about his possible employment in Russia (Mooser, 1951, II:466). What was it that attracted these eminent West-European composers? What prior knowledge would they have had concerning contemporary Russian musical culture?

The European-like infrastructure of the musical culture that coalesced in Russia in the eighteenth century was striking in its unevenness and the contradictory nature of its manifestations: the old and the new not only interacted with each other but sometimes became thoroughly mixed. Eighteenth-century Russia closed the socio-cultural gap between the isolated pre-Petrine Rus' and the remodelled strong Russian Empire that would successfully join European society at the beginning of the nineteenth century. Its culture in general, and music in particular, reflected the main social processes – secularization, Westernization and urbanization.

These processes, however, were of too dynamic and impetuous a nature to permit any smooth development of the accompanying culture, including the arts. The result was an uneven, frequently accelerated progress, without prior establishment of a solid base. The overall picture of eighteenth-century Russian fine arts is characterized by a quaint melange of copied foreign models and vernacular self-expression that appears naïve and unprofessional against the background of the centuries-old Western tradition of culture. Later, in the nineteenth-century Russian public consciousness, all this cast an odd light of condescending contempt toward the efforts of the eighteenth-century native Russian artists. The reputation of eighteenth-century culture suffered from two sides. On the one side, it was overshadowed by the glorious nineteenth-century accomplishments and considered as only an insignificant prelude to the real triumph. On the other side, it was also bereft of any national 'authenticity', unlike pre-Petrine culture, which was seen as having such authenticity. Contributing to this contempt was the fact that nineteenth-century musicians simply did not possess sufficient knowledge of the cross-cultural influences of earlier times to be able to assess the eighteenth century fairly.

Historiography in the Nineteenth and Twentieth Centuries

All this created tendentious overtones in the historiography of eighteenth-century Russian music. The moment that one tries to analyze stylistic features in order to separate the borrowed from the native (or what had become native by the eighteenth century), one becomes trapped either in exaggerated nationalistic pretensions or in a total rejection of native elements, throwing out the baby with the bath water. Sticking to the facts still remains the safest approach.

To this end, nineteenth-century studies are of little help, in that they mainly retell familiar legends in a nationalistic–romantic way. Twentieth-century studies, in contrast, have presented quite solid and reliable information on sources. They begin with research by the Russian historian Nikolai Findeizen (1868–1928), and the Swiss scholar Robert-Aloys Mooser (1876–1969). Both explored the Imperial archives. Findeizen's work was published in the two-volume *Essays on the History of Russian Music* (1928–9), in which the entire second volume is devoted to the eighteenth century. Mooser published two valuable major works: *Opéras, intermezzos, ballets, cantatas, oratorios joués on Russie durant le XVIIIe siècle* (1945; 3rd edn, 1964) and the three-volume *Annales de la musique et des musiciens en Russie au XVIIIe siècle* (1948–51).

Exploring the sources is an ongoing effort. Boris Volman (1957) has contributed with research into eighteenth-century Russian printed music, while an array of monographs on individual composers or genres, containing new sources, appeared in the 1970s and 1980s. The collective twentieth-century efforts culminated in the highly respectable five-volume encyclopaedia of eighteenth-century musical St Petersburg. *Muzykal'ny Peterburg: XVIII vek, entsiklopedicheskiy slovar'* (1997–2000) edited by Anna Porfirieva.

Although the above-mentioned publications are mainly devoted to sources, the tradition of interpretive studies developed in parallel, providing those viewpoints that reflected the ideological agenda at any given moment in twentieth-century Russia. For most of the period this was the viewpoint of Soviet Russia, where general humanistic values had often been replaced with unconcealed imperial nationalism, little differing from that of Nikolai I. It is thus hardly surprising that the nationalism inherited from the nineteenth century caused a strong bias in twentieth-century Russian music studies too.

The nationalism of Nikolaian Russia, flavoured with the general views of the romantic era, provoked the subconscious preference of Russian society to perceive its cultural heroes as victims of cruel fates. This phenomenon was not specifically Russian; rather, it developed all over Europe in the post-Beethoven era (Raynor,

1972:350–5).[1] A notable example of a biography turned into a hagiography was (and still remains) that of Maxim Berezovsky. Remarkably, sentimental fiction based on his biography appeared during the darkest, most chauvinistic periods of Russian history, those of Nikolai I and Stalin, and appealed to Russian nationalism at its worst. Berezovsky's myth began from the drama by P.A. Smirnov, *Maxim Sozontovich Berezovsky* (1841), which paralleled an episode from young Franz Liszt's life when he had fallen in love with his upper-class pupil and was thrown out of the house by her father. Continuing and contributing to this fiction at about the same time, closely following Berezovsky's biography (as it was known at the time) Russian writer Nestor Kukolnik succeeded in creating a hagiographical masterpiece (Kukolnik, *Maxim Berezovsky*, 1844). In the twentieth century, following M. Alexeev's drawing attention to the composer (1921) and Findeizen's hints at his mysterious fate (1929), the young writer Vera Zhakova composed a no less tragic novel – *Maxim Berezovsky*, although stressing other aspects of his life (between 1932 and 1936).

A nineteenth-century Russian romantically-nationalistic cliché retrospectively applied to Berezovsky, Khandoshkin and Degtyarev, made them the most precious cultural protagonists of Catherine's cosmopolitan and 'corrupt' age. Their biographies, indeed attracting sympathy, became flooded with moving details of their misfortunes and humiliations, justifying the 'pure Russian' abuse of alcohol and conveying the message of a national artist doomed to neglect in his own homeland. Degtyarev was the only serf among the three, but people tend to see serf in all of them. Interestingly, Andrey Tarkovsky, an avant-garde Soviet cinema producer, took Kukolnik's story as a base for his film *Nostalgia* in the early 1980s. When I wrote to tell him that Kukolnik's biography of Berezovsky is incorrect and that Berezovsky was not a serf, he changed the name of his protagonist to Sosnovsky (taken from the name of another tree; *bereza* means birch and *sosna* means pine) but did not change the fable, and Berezovsky's spiritual choral concerto *Ne otverzhi mene vo vremya starosti* [Cast me not off in the time of old age] remained as the background music. A serf as a symbol of Russian subjugation was incomparably more important than historical scrupulosity for such a great artist as Tarkovsky, who had suffered enough from the Soviet regime.

Two decades later, while two generations of Russian musicologists had in general accepted my documentarily proved version of Berezovsky's biography, another Russian artist, the composer Alexey Rybnikov, famous for his rock operas, announced his intention to write a musical based on the life of Maxim Berezovsky, as presented in Kukolnik's story.[2] His intention was to generalize the eighteenth-

---

1   Interestingly, the Bohemian composer Josef Mysliviček, who studied in Italy together with the Russian composer Maxim Berezovsky around 1770 and whose career afterwards was more successful than Berezovsky's, was for all that described in nineteenth-century Czechoslovakia in hagiographic tones.

2   'Berezovsky stanet geroem opery: neobychny teatral'ny proekt', Valery Kichin, interview with Alexey Rybnikov, in *Izvestia*, 16 January 2000. See also *Izvestia*, 16 November 2001.

century composer's image, calling his protagonist 'Berestovsky' (*beresta* means birch-bark, again a tree reference), furnishing additional proof that a myth will continue to live its own independent life.

Although scholars tend to resist the influence of fiction, the pressure of nationalism inevitably left its stamp, climaxing in Stalin's ideological terror in the late 1940s. The most telling example is the work of Moscow scholar Tamara Livanova (1909–86). In one study (1938), she diligently traced the features of western styles in seventeenth-century Russian music. However, in the Preface to her next, major work (1952–53), she repented having 'exaggerated' the alien influences in her earlier work. In 1948 she wrote denunciations of her Russian-studies colleagues – M. Pekelis and Yu. Keldysh – accusing them of cosmopolitanism. She seemed to have been neither regretful nor embarrassed by her actions, as evidenced by her leaving copies of these documents in her personal archive, which she sold to the State Museum of Musical Culture in 1980.

Yu. Keldysh, in contrast, having been forced to inflate the nationalistic traits in his *History of Russian Music* (1948), normalized his views as soon as possible after Stalin's death and wrote a fundamental study on eighteenth-century Russian music (1965). A major scholar, he became an official and central figure in Russian music studies, tutoring disciples, founding the series *Monuments of Russian Music Artl* and the ten-volume *History of Russian Music.* A former member of RAPM (Russian Association of Proletarian Musicians, 1923–32), he was equally tolerant of nationalist opinions and of those open to other cultures. What he did not revise, however, was what had become the traditional conception of Russian music since the nineteenth century, which implied opera as its main genre and sign of maturity.

The 'opera-centric' conception was in fact a continuation of the conventional Russian 'Glinka-centric' conceit. Since operas were considered to be Glinka's primary achievement, and Russian symphonic music had not yet been developed, opera was the only genre in which Russia could compete with the West. This idea was formed and promoted by the highly charismatic and influential critic Vladimir Stasov (1824–1906) and adopted by Boris Asafiev (1884–1949), a major Russian-Soviet scholar. Asafiev's scope was immeasurably broader than Stasov's. He realized that what might be true for nineteenth-century music was not fully compatible with eighteenth-century processes. In the early 1920s, influenced by a socio-anthropological trend in Russian arts and philology studies, he saw a major importance in researching Russian eighteenth-century popular genres beyond the Imperial court and estate cultural life. He supervised and edited Antonin Preobrazhensky's study of Russian cult music (1924), in which the truly mass role of popular spiritual genres in eighteenth-century Russia was articulated for the first time.

The upswing and ideological freedom in Russian humanities, and sociomusicology in particular, was short-lived however. Stalin's anticlassical and antireligious 'cultural revolution' ended it abruptly. The year 1927 witnessed a huge collection of eighteenth-century Russian sacred music being burned on the bridge connecting the building of the Imperial Court Cappella with the Palace Square (where a monument to three Russian religious composers – Bortniansky, Turchaninov and

Lvov – was planned to be erected, but never realized due to the outbreak of World War I). Opera offered a more ideologically pure and safe subject for research into the eighteenth-century Russian music legacy. The same year also witnessed publication of Asafiev's article *On Studying Eighteenth-Century Russian Music and Two Operas by Bortniansky*.[3] The cornerstone of Soviet studies on eighteenth-century music had been laid. The secular part had been given the arterial road, while the sacred sector was channelled into the periphery.

I by no means wish to belittle the quality or quantity of eighteenth-century Russian operas, which comprised a significant corpus of works and were widely circulated in the courtly, aristocratic and urban strata of Russian society in the last third of the eighteenth century. Moreover, opera had its own great attraction and importance. It dramatically helped to change values in Russian urban society at the end of the Enlightenment era and greatly promoted its secularization and democratization. It prepared the people for the art of theatre, which in the following century took upon itself the role of high art indeed.

One has to note, however, that what Russia really knew as opera in the eighteenth century was in fact a quite simple model of comic opera, which had only begun to develop as late as 1772. Russian operas of this kind were actually theatrical comedies, with the addition of folk songs, and sometimes even quite developed overtures and other operatic elements. Most of their composers were foreign kapellmeisters, such as J. Kerzelli, H. Raupach, J. Starzer, M. Stabinger, A. Bullant, V. Martín y Soler and C. Canobbio, although some native composers eventually appeared, among whom the skilful Vasily Pashkevich and Evstigney Fomin were the most notable. The repertory was mostly from French and Italian sources, sometimes translated, although comedies by Russian writers were also played.

It is no accident that Pashkevich was chosen by Empress Catherine II to set to music her own folksy librettos, in which she shrewdly manifested her policy of official nationalism. To be fair, comic theatre in the last third of the eighteenth century was so popular among the enlightened circles of St Petersburg and Moscow, and the public consciousness reflected by this theatre was so multicoloured and active, that the interweave between official nationalism and the revolutionary outlook expressed by Alexander Radishchev, whom the Empress had arrested, was sometimes quite subtle. The same was true concerning not only opera but also collections of folk songs as well as the activity of Lvov's famous late eighteenth-century salon, which anticipated Stasov's nineteenth-century circle that nourished 'The Mighty Five'. In

---

3   According to the list of Bortniansly's compositions given by his widow to the Imperial Court Cappella 'for eternal keeping', the scores of Bortniansky's operas that Asafiev studied were in the Cappella collection. They, among some other eighteenth-century scores, seem to have been saved from the fire by Mikhail Klimov (1881–1937), then director of the Leningrad Cappella, who apparently transferred some of them to the Institute of Art History (its musical section then headed by Asafiev, currently the RIII), and some to the Leningrad Public Library (currently the RNB).

the eighteenth century, like the century to follow, *Russian*, *Rus'ian* and *a là Rus* were not always interdistinguishable. These issues will be discussed in Chapters 7 and 9.

Among the defining features of eighteenth-century Russian culture was the purely Russian phenomenon of serf theatre. Serf actors/singers and musicians, sometimes highly trained, often directed by a foreign kapellmeister, staged a wide repertoire consisting mainly of French sentimental comedies, some works from the repertoire of the capital's public theatres and occasional works by serf composers (see Chapter 12).

Another kind of opera theatre altogether existed at the Imperial court, where generously paid Italian stars – composers and singers – reproduced the fashionable repertory of Italian opera, a necessary attribute of all major European courts. Accessible only to the nobility, the court stage was the only place where *opera seria* could be watched. However, these rare productions failed to inculcate a taste for this genre in Russian society elsewhere at the time. Four native composers who had been able to study in Italy and gain experience in *opera seria* – Maxim Berezovsky, Dmitry Bortniansky, Peter Skokov and Evstigney Fomin – could not fully apply their newly acquired skill in Russia upon their return. Berezovsky died soon after his return. Skokov wrote occasional cantatas and Fomin wrote comic operas and music for melodramas. The only opportunity Bortniansky was given was to create three French-language operas (one pastoral and two *semi-seria*) composed in a mixed French-Italian style and produced by the improvised cast of trained noble amateurs for the 'Young court' of Grand Duke Pavel Petrovich in 1786–7. These operas remained unknown outside the narrow circle of young courtiers, with the apparent exception of two aristocratic estates where the scores were later found. It was two of these operas that Asafiev discovered in 1927 and realized how rich the eighteenth-century Russian legacy must have been to have produced such brilliant scores by a native composer (see Chapter 8).

Asafiev's discovery was especially surprising because although the name of Bortniansky was very well known, it was exclusively as a composer of religious music and as the venerable director of the Imperial Court Cappella. This new revelation equally well suited both the traditional opera-centric conception of Russian music and the ideological limitations imposed by that critical period in Russian-Soviet historiography. It also indicated the safe direction in which Russian music studies were able to develop. Thus Bortniansky's historical reputation was saved, while his religious scores blazed at the stake of the Bolshevik inquisition.

To summarize this brief survey of eighteenth-century Russian opera, one can see that despite all its flourishing, achievements and the involvement of professional and public forces, opera was unable to satisfy eighteenth-century Russian society in its search for artistic expression of the noble emotions of compassion, confession, delight in the harmony of being, and so on. The question thus arises as to what, if not opera (and of course not instrumental music, which at that time was in its infancy) served as high art for the Russian people, or at least for the inhabitants of Moscow and St Petersburg and perhaps also such culturally developed towns as Yaroslavl or Kharkov? The answer is that the only genre that responded to their need was that of the spiritual concerto, offering King David's psalms performed by a mixed choir *a cappella* with a quite elaborate polyphony.

In brief, the choral concerto was a para-liturgical genre, which flourished in Russia from the middle of the seventeenth until the beginning of the nineteenth century – altogether a 'long eighteenth century'. Its very existence resulted from the peculiarity of Russia as an Orthodox state in Eastern Europe. While the Russian music mentality was suited to that of its European counterpart, its instrumental music remained undeveloped due to its prohibition by the Orthodox Church (see further in Chapter 2 'Pre-Petrine Legacy'). The *a cappella* spiritual choral concerto thus evolved in Russia as a kind of compromise, becoming a hybrid motet with miscellaneous elements from genres existing in Russia and the Ukraine: from the popular spiritual three-voiced songs *kanty* and *psalmy* to the later appearance of elements from *opera seria*, mass and oratorio which had been known previously only at court. It was the only genre in early and pre-Glinka Russian music to respond to the Russian people's desire for high art and had no substitute or alternative; and, of course, native comic opera, which had began to develop only in the 1770s and with other intentions and purposes, could not compete with it.

The first to write a thorough albeit brief study of Bortniansky's concertos was Sergei Skrebkov (1948). Considering the era, this was quite a feat, although despite all the Stalinistic obscurantism and censorship there still arose the occasional work that remained untouched by the negative spirit of the times. The topic was later picked up by Yuriy Keldysh. Giving all due credit to the role of eighteenth–century musical theatre, Keldysh was also fully aware of the role of the spiritual concerto. He gave it a respectable place in his own studies, supported the works of his colleagues in the field, and in the 1960s he completed a study begun by his late colleague Sergei Skrebkov.

The spiritual concertos seldom had scores and the preserved notes were normally in part books and written in vocal clefs, according to the old *partes*–singing tradition.[4] Their analysis involves the arduous work of first searching for them among the numerable archives and then assembling them into scores. The only easily available corpus of scores remains that of Bortniansky, who being both enlightened and wealthy had edited and published them at his own expense. Their very availability and popularity, however, turned against the composer. Glinka's malicious labelling of Bortniansky as 'Sakhar Medovich Patokin' [Mr Sugar Honeyevich Molassky] influenced public opinion, and one can only guess that he had expected Bortniansky to be another J.S. Bach. Bortniansky's spiritual concertos, moreover, were seriously misdated in the historiography, being related to the period at the beginning of the nineteenth century when he was appointed director of the Imperial Court Cappella. More recent findings in archival documents, however, now allow us to date their composition far earlier: mostly to the 1780s–early 1790s (Rytsareva, 1973). This

---

4   Although the term 'part-singing' is commonly accepted for Russian *partesnoe penie*, I choose the term suggested by Gerasimova-Persidskaya's (1994) translation as '*partes-singing*', which refers to the specific Polish-Ukrainian style.

completely justifies their classic style and helps to refocus the entire dating of this genre. Its half-century existence can be divided into three periods: 1760s–70s, baroque-preclassic style, produced by Berezovsky and Galuppi; 1780s, classic court fashion, dominated by Bortniansky; and 1790s–1800s, sentimental mode, expressed mainly by Bortniansky (changing his style), by the serf composer Stepan Degtyarev (who commercially Italianized its tone in response to the wave of Italomania in early nineteenth-century Moscow), and by the Ukrainian Vedel. (Their choral concertos will be considered in Chapters 5, 8, 10, 12 and 13.)

Another unique phenomenon of mid-eighteenth-century Russian music was the rise of the so-called horn music that filled the almost empty niche of instrumental music. However, the entire genre was considered as a kind of curiosity, and its significance in the context of eighteenth-century Russian musical culture has been underestimated (see Chapter 3). Its fundamental and indeed only researcher to date was K. Vertkov (1948). Remarkably, horn music existed within the same time framework as the choral concerto (including the first quarter of the nineteenth century), and continued to function until the conventional contemporary European forms of music-making became established, replacing the aristocratic estate culture.

This shared appearance and demise was no coincidence, for both resulted from the same reasons and circumstances. Both had arisen as a substitute for an insufficiently developed though much desired instrumental culture of the European tradition, and both ended up being displaced by this tradition when it took strong root in nineteenth-century Russia. This occurred about the time of Glinka, whose work is inscribed in the European cultural milieu not as a typical eighteenth–century wavering between imitation of Western models and immature native attempts, but as a self-sufficient national version of a familiar European style.

The twentieth-century perspective of eighteenth-century Russian musical culture has in general lacked an overall approach. Each genre or sphere has been analyzed separately and their coexistence and interaction have not been conceptualized.

The survey that I undertake here of the history and historiography of eighteenth-century Russian music raises several serious points that demand a thorough rethinking. Musical theatre, popular songs/romances, and classic instrumental music – the entire body of European genres that Russia familiarized, assimilated and eventually mastered – need neither be advocated nor impugned. However, for all their significance as an introduction to the world of nineteenth-century Russian music, they must also not overshadow in historiography what they did not overshadow in history: the importance, the creative potential, and the truly mass character of other major genres – horn music and the spiritual concerto, especially the latter, and not only because of its primacy and closeness to the Russian soil, but also for its original aesthetic and high ethical values. The peculiarity of eighteenth-century Russian music cannot be understood without analyzing its historical roots.

The Complexity of Russian Identity

In the tenth century, the Varangian Princes probably knew better than we do now what was Rus'. The Princes established themselves in the Khazar town of Kiev using the established social organization of the defeated Khazar Kingdom,[5] ruled over the Slavic tribes and accepted the religious institution of the Greek Church as a means of political protection and mercantile profit from the Byzantium superpower. Together, these factors constituted the complex foundation of the Russian nation that was to develop under the influence of new ethnic impacts over the following millennium.

Orthodox animosity towards Catholicism was not an isolated phenomenon in Russian history; rather it was part of Russia's more general negative attitude towards the West. The West, as noted by Y. Lotman and B. Uspensky, was perceived as much more than

> ... a specific political-geographical reality, but as an ideal, which was either adopted or rejected. Enthusiasm for such a position was based on the idea that it was not the real West being discussed but some concept in the system of values of Russian culture... According to the ancient Russian tradition, the concept of West as a part of the world had a most definite character: West is where hell is...[6]

The forming of a national identity accompanied the process of centralizing feudal principalities and mutual defence against external enemies. While Kievan Rus' was Byzantium oriented, the more lately established Muscovite Rus' sought independence from Byzantium, which had already lost its political power (over half a century earlier when conquered by the Latin Empire existing from 1204–61) and now looked westward. What remained of Rus'-Byzantium relations was Rus'ian economic dependence since the Rus'ian Church, which owned most of the land, continued to pay a golden tribute to Constantinople (Nikol'sky, 1983:96, 109). From the end of the fourteenth century, however, Moscow sought union with the Catholic Church. In 1492 Moscow was proclaimed 'the third Rome' and the ascent of Grand Duke Ivan III to the throne commemorated the end of dependence on Constantinople, which in 1453 was conquered by the Turks. The way to Westernization was open. No longer forced to supply gold to Byzantium, the Russian tsars could now approach the main internal problem – how to redirect this wealth to the Rus'ian secular establishment. Their answer was to expropriate church lands, in an act of 'secularization' that was to be fully achieved only three centuries later.

---

5   For an updated survey of Khazaria see, for example, Kevin Alan Brook, *The Jews of Khazaria*. Northvale, New Jersey: Aronson, 1999.

6   '...отношение к Западу не как к определенной политико-географической реальности, а как к утверждаемому или ниспровергаемому идеалу. Страстность такого утверждения или отвержения определялась тем, что фактически речь шла не о реальном Западе, а о некоторой ценностной характеристике внутри русской культуры... в древнерусской традиции понятие запада как стороны света имело совершенно определенную характеристику: на западе помещается ад...' (Yu. Lotman and B. Uspensky, 1974:277).

Westernization and secularization were thus in effect the two-fold process of the Rus'ian state's struggle for liberation from Byzantium and internal domination by the Church. This process occupied eight of the entire ten-century-long Russian history, indicating a power struggle between two equally powerful sides. While the secular forces governed by means of the State establishment, the Church's strength lay in its possessing both material resources and ideology, for which a suffering people always furnishes the best soil. The idea of theocratic absolutism, maintained by the Riurik dynasty and culminating in Ivan the Terrible's rule, crystallized Russian identity as inseparable from Orthodoxy and was personified in the Tsar, ordained by God to rule the land.[7]

This duality of Russian national identity became a matter of tradition, taken for granted by the secular authorities and eventually by the broad nationalist stratum of Russian society. The tradition succeeded in uniting the concepts of *sacred* and *national* into a single symbol of Russian genuineness, no matter how 'sacred' or 'national' a particular element actually was. With time, the rhetoric of *old* (canonized, stable) became a necessary proof of national authenticity. Subsequently, the symbols of *secular* and *alien* were regarded as Western evils, reinforced by linking them with *new* (changeable). This triad now comprised the social image of the enemy, projected and constantly reconfirmed by the Russian Church until its retirement from the political scene in the time of Peter the Great (1672–1725). Although Peter broke the church's dominance, he could not eradicate this thorny duality between *religious–national–old (stable)* and *secular–extraneous–new (changeable)*, and it was this antinomy that constituted one of the important factors that prevented Russia from completely joining Western Europe. Seen in this light, it is now clear that the notorious triad – *Orthodoxy, autocracy, nationality* – of Count S. Uvarov, the Minister of Education, did not in fact originate during the period of Tsar Nikolai I (reigned 1825–55), but rather reflected a well-formulated reinvention, or variation, of a doctrine that had crystallized in pre-Petrine Rus'. The goal of this pronouncement, which perpetuated old prejudices, was to divert Russian public consciousness away from *modern – outlandish – non-religious* ideas of liberation.

It is thus hardly surprising that two identities took shape long before Petrine Russia: the first – that of the Orthodox Church sanctifying the old Byzantium values, and the second – secular and/or Western-oriented. Their coexistence constituted a complex and dramatic rivalry in which neither side could win. However, they rarely manifested themselves in a pure form such as that of the Old Believers in the seventeenth to eighteenth centuries or the Russian philosopher, Catholic Providencialist and Social Christian Peter Chaadaev (1794–1856) in the nineteenth, but tended rather to interlace. Sometimes this happened for political reasons, as in the case of Catherine II who, despite being an atheist and an admirer of Voltaire, converted to Greek Orthodoxy, opened private home churches (previously closed by Peter III), strengthened the influence of the clergy in censure, and – after all these

---

7   See Michael Rywkin, 'Russia and the Former Soviet Union' in *Encyclopedia of Nationalism*, vol. I, San-Francisco, 2000:655.

manoeuvres – secularized church lands (Milov, 2000:199–200). More often, however, the two aspects are genuinely and inseparably combined within the same individual, both causing and reflecting the eternal schism in the Russian national identity. The particular dominance of one over the other has been determined by the fluctuations of Russian (or sometimes broader – pan-European) history. Consequently, it is not constructive to search for any single answer. Russian identity has always been two-fold, and the correlation is always changing, a dynamic system in modern terms.

The best-known chapter in this ancient and constant confrontation is that of the nineteenth-century polemics between Slavophils and Westerners, although other manifestations of this ongoing duality of Russian identity can be traced both before and after that period. It remains the best known merely because it has been well formulated and widely publicized. The polemics itself was anti-historical in nature because Slavophils have never taken pains to determine the origins of their spiritual symbols, or simply have no desire to know them. It might be very disappointing for them to learn that their main visual symbol – the old Muscovite architecture (including the Kremlin and old boyars' *palaty*) had been designed by Italian architects in the fifteenth to seventeenth centuries,[8] while church *partes*-singing in the seventeenth to eighteenth centuries had the same Italian source and Russia was its last stop after Poland and the Ukraine. It is the great age of these symbols that nationalized them, just as Byzantian chant and church painting had been nationalized a few centuries earlier. The same applies today to St Petersburg, whose age makes its foreignness forgivable and nationalizes its semantics. Alexander Solzhenitsyn, known for his Slavophilic stance, wrote about St Petersburg: 'What a blessing that no new building is allowed here. No wedding-cake skyscraper may elbow its way onto the Nevsky Prospect, no five-story shoebox can ruin the Griboedov Canal. … It is alien to us, yet it is our greatest glory!' (cited by Monas, 1983:37–8).[9]

Two Capitals

The post-Byzantium split in Russian identity could perhaps have been lessened had it not been enormously augmented by the coexistence of two capitals. In the thirteenth century Moscow had become a major new centre between Kiev and its northern rival, the free town of Novgorod (later a member of the Hanseatic Union). Located equally eastward of both, while it could centralize Rus' it could not solve the problem of access to a sea, without which successful trade and the eventual economic survival of the State was impossible. Ivan the Terrible was the first to realize this. He established trade with England and between 1558 and 1583 waged the Livonian war in an attempt to obtain access to the Baltic. However it was not until the beginning of the eighteenth century that Peter I successfully overcame the

---

8   See Ivan K. Kondratiev, *Sedaya starina Moskvy*. 2nd edn, Moscow: Citadel, 1999:28.

9   Monas quoted it from: Alexander Solzhenitsyn, *Stories and Prose Poems*. New York: Farrar, Straus & Giroux, 1974:252–3.

Swedes and gained the vital access. Thus he firmly and irrevocably plunged Russia into European affairs. In order to do so, however, he had to found a new, Western-oriented centre in the north-westernmost region of the country. This cost a new divide in Russian society.

Opposition by the Muscovite nobility to transferring their capital, to the north of nowhere moreover, was only natural. Whereas the 'Time of Troubles' in the 1650s had split the religious population into those who accepted Nikon's reforms and the Old Believers who did not, transfer of the capital in 1713–14 split the Russian aristocracy into those who accepted Peter's reforms and those who resisted them. Both Nikon's and Peter's reforms led to the westernization of Russia, but both were strongly opposed. Muscovite nobles, far from the lands and courts that supplied them with their livelihood, experienced difficulties in distant Petersburg and tried to return the capital to Moscow, first through Tsarevich Alexey in 1717 and then through Tsar Peter II in 1730.

Moscow culture was nonetheless becoming westernized, although at its own pace, due to the city's physical remoteness from the West, to which it was connected only by poor roads. There had always been a pro-Western sector in its establishment, albeit a minority. The city had ghettoized communities of foreigners, the so-called 'German Quarters', Chinatown and others. International connections developed, sometimes awkwardly, as well as the city's attempts to find its proper place in the European market and on the political map. Moscow's long struggle with the Polish-Lithuanian Commonwealth for Ukrainian and Byelorussian lands, resulting in Kiev being annexed to Great Russia, was accompanied by a powerful and westernizing Ruthenian cultural impact from these countries. Tsar Alexis (Alexey Mikhaylovich, 1629–76, reigned 1645–76), father of Peter I, and whose reign began in the most Church-dominated period in Russian history, was finally responsible for the dramatic strengthening of secular power and westernization, and his 'late years were profoundly revolutionary in the modern sense of the word' (Billington, 1970:149). The references of later Old Believers to Peter I as the Antichrist were in fact preceded by those regarding his father. It was Moscow that produced Peter I. Moscow *became* conservative *vis-à-vis* the rising Petersburg when it was deprived of the status of capital city.

Since foreigners dominated in Peter's establishment, the Russian nobility's dissatisfaction with the drastic changes taking place often expressed itself in xenophobia. 'Groups or individuals opposed to political or social innovation often denounce as alien those changes in the national life of which they disapprove. It is not necessary that the object of their protest be, in fact, foreign,' noted H. Rogger about the Petrine period, an observation that continues to be valid today (1969:8).

A strong element of nationalism is natural for any society suffering from socio–economic problems but unable to do without foreign experience. Nationalism always cultivates a bitter nostalgia for some vague and bountiful past, firmly ignoring its cultural complexity and troubles. While nationalists look to an idealized past and concentrate solely on present-day stability, being closed (or possibly marginally open) to the West, and firmly believing in sacred Christian values, Russian Westerners (in any epoch) strive for an ideal future, challenge the West and eagerly accept its challenges, being modern, dynamic, open and secularized. The former preserve, the latter build. In all cases, both attitudes crystallized their associations with either one capital or the other. The former kept Moscow on their banner, the latter – St Petersburg. St Petersburg probably cultivated its majestic grandeur to demonstrate its power not only to the West, but to the Muscovite tradition as well.

There was unevenness however in their interrelations. St Petersburg always respected the Muscovite tradition as of primary national value (all coronations of Tsars took place in Moscow). In St Petersburg ways were sought to amalgamate old and new, Russian and European. In contrast, it was only at the end of the eighteenth century that Moscow started to enjoy belonging to Europe, which eventually, by the end of the nineteenth century, found its expression in Russian culture. Skriabin and Rachmaninoff were the first Muscovites (not only living in Moscow, but inspired by her spirit) to join the list of great Russian composers, all of whom had previously been of St Petersburg stock or education. Both were products and stimulators of Moscow's creative musical milieu where such figures as Derzhanovsky, Yavorsky, Roslavets and many others played a significant role. Chekhov, Meyerhold, Stanislavsky, Bulgakov, Levitan, Kandinsky, Pasternak and many other remarkable artists of the time all contributed to the glory of Muscovite culture. It is no wonder that Prokofiev and Shostakovich finally settled in Moscow. By the beginning of the twentieth century Moscow had developed a culture of which any major capital could be proud, and the two capital cities had somewhat exchanged personalities: while St Petersburg acquired a touch of conservatism and developed a refined decadence, Moscow was fanned by the fresh breezes of renewal. Both capitals beautifully complemented one another in the creation of the Silver Age of Russian art.

The gulf that remained between the two cities was due to their entirely different socio-anthropological population structures. Whereas Moscow was dominated by clergy, gentry and merchants, St Petersburg developed wide circles of courtiers, foreigners, imperial bureaucrats, military and naval elite, intelligentsia and proletariat. Despite all their differences, the two capitals nonetheless constructed cultural traditions rather than cultures as such. These traditions clearly dominate either as Muscovite or St Petersburgian, and each has its own clearly distinguishable elements of the Russian identity.

The real need for construction of a national identity arose as the Russian Empire matured and Russia began to integrate into the European world, when *Rus'* became *Rossia, Rossiyskaya Imperia* – in the eighteenth century.[10] The facts revealed by the eighteenth-century scholars in the course of studying the national history were intended to provide a strong foundation for such an identity. Instead, however, the

---

10   See Michael Rywkin, 'Russia and the Former Soviet Union' in *Encyclopedia of Nationalism*, vol. I, San-Francisco, 2000:656; O.N. Trubachev, 'Russky – rossiysky: istoria dvukh atributov natsii', in *E.R. Dashkova i rossiyskoe obshchestvo XVIII stoletia*, ed. L.V. Tychinina and I.V. Makarova. Moscow: Moskovskiy Gumanitarny Institut im. E.R. Dashkovoy, 2001:13–21.

disclosure of their national history posed quite a problem to Russian society due to the ethnic complexity of the Russian people.

> The middle decades of the century, almost entirely taken up with disputes on the origins of the Russian state, illustrate the degree to which academic and personal issues had become questions of national pride and integrity. The Bironovshchina had made Russians particularly sensitive to any real or presumed slight to the national honor, with the result that history as scientific pursuit became almost an impossibility. It was this period which left to later generations the irritating legacy of the 'Norman controversy'. It also produced the first projects for the institutional approach to the study of history. (Rogger, 1969:189–90)

The uncomfortable truth about the Varangian origins of the first Russian rulers, as well as pre-Petrine Rus' being less civilized than contemporaneous Europe, also noted by Muller and Schlözer (Russian scholars of German origin), drastically clashed with the concept of Russian national pride, so ardently defended by Mikhail Lomonosov. By the end of the eighteenth century, due to the serious intervention of Catherine II, some compromise was achieved: recognition of the Norman origins of the Russian State but mythologization of pre-Petrine Russian culture can be traced in the views of I.N. Boltin, M.M. Shcherbatov and N.M. Karamzin (Rogger, 1969:221, 223, 247). Since in post-Byzantian and especially Petrine Russia, the West as a cultural symbol had been reinterpreted from evil to ideal, the Russians began to adjust their history to European standards and to learn to feel a part of Europe.[11] This adjustment was not for the sake of scientific history but for the construction of a belief that would reconcile Muscovite and Petersburgian outlooks. Enhancing the civilized traits of old Moscow, by presenting it as Europeanized rather than Byzantized, brought it closer to St Petersburg, releasing Peter from the 'sin' of denouncing traditional national values, and mitigating the current inferior relations with the West. Finally, every national identity rests on myths, and the border between interpretation and mythologization of any event (usually manipulated by a few select individuals) is always too subtle for the public/mass consciousness.

Since this search for a national identity was widely publicized, it permeated the various intellectual and artistic circles and found its expression first of all in the creation of a national language, which is always a matter of identity, and generated both deliberately and spontaneously. While the development of the new Russian language – secular, colloquial and open to borrowings – started in the 1710s as one of Peter's reforms, the corresponding processes in music developed at random and became especially notable in the second half of the century. Eighteenth-century Russian music, whatever the sources that had nourished it, actively participated in constructing the national identity and basically accomplished its task, as the following chapters will show.

---

11 See Yu.M. Lotman and B.A. Uspensky, '"Pis'ma russkogo puteshestvennika" Karamzina i ikh mesto v razvitii russkoy kul'tury', in N.M. Karamzin *Pis'ma russkogo puteshestvennika*. Leningrad: Nauka. 1984:562.

Chapter 2

Pre-Petrine Legacy

The musical culture of Ancient Rus' developed in the three directions usual for most European countries: folklore, church music, and urban entertainment performed by minstrels generally known as *skomorokhi*.

Folklore

Russian musical folklore (usually perceived as peasant folklore) is famous for its inspirational effect on Russian art music. It is rich, multigeneric, tough and vital as a result of the centuries-long dominance of agrarian feudal life. Early folklore originated in pagan rites. Indeed, it was the rites rather than the beliefs themselves that were denounced by the Church from the twelfth to the seventeenth centuries (Keldysh, 1983:46).[1] The six-century record of prohibitions is in itself evidence of their vitality. As late as 1806, the Wilmot Sisters, British collectors of Russian folk songs, noted how elements of pagan superstitions were organically interlaced with Orthodox rites (the Marchioness of Londonderry and H.M. Hyde, 1934:238; Cross, 1988:32). With the suppression of these rites and the passing of time, ritual music eventually became dissociated from functionality and gained elements of folk games related to agrarian cycles and Christian festivities. The rituals of marriage and burial however, like those of other peoples, have remained distinguished in their stability.

The development of social and political life in the tenth to thirteenth centuries generated the evolution of the epos; and later, in the fourteenth to seventeenth centuries, lyrical – including the so-called *protyazhnaya* [protracted] – songs emerged, reflecting individual experience and emotions as a subject for artistic expression. The rise of this latter genre has been associated with the crisis of medieval consciousness (Keldysh, 1983:126), as well as with the formatting of the Great-Russian ethnos. Neither the Ukraine nor Byelorussia possesses this genre, unlike the ancient ritual songs that are shared by all the Slavic peoples (Zemtsovsky, 1967:14). Diatonic and modal (with characteristic mutable mode), with free rhythm and melismatically developed melody, lacking any hint of dance rhythms, the lyric songs are often heterophonic and embellished with highly variable subsidiary voices – altogether a quite unique and specifically Russian phenomenon. The term *protyazhnaya* is sometimes translated as 'melismatic' song. This definition articulates monody as a

---

1   See also Dmitry S. Likhachev, 'Russkoe narodnoe poeticheskoe tvorchestvo', in *Ocherki po istorii russkogo narodnogo poeticheskogo tvorchestva X–nachala XVIII vekov*. Moscow, 1953:238.

basis of melodic structure and, consequently, the linear character of polyphony. That such a genre exists in Russian folklore indicates how inherent multi–part singing is to the Russian musical mentality.

Many other genres developed in later periods in Russian folklore. Among them were historical songs (whose texts first appear to have been transcribed by the Oxford scholar Richard James who visited Russia in 1618–20 as chaplain to the British Ambassador Sir Dudley Digges; see Cross, 1988:21). Humour, love, the military, spiritual verse (*dukhovny stikh*) and other genres also emerged. Other traditions contributed to expanding the repertoire, such as those of the Cossacks, Gypsies, Ukrainians (Little Russia), Polish (sometimes implying Byelorussian when Byelorussia was part of Poland), and Kalmucs. The repertoires vary from region to region in the vast Russian lands, but in general they all seem to contain the entire progression from ancient ritual and epic to the latest limericks.

The Rise and Fall of *Skomorokhi* Culture

From its inception at the end of the tenth century the Orthodox establishment in Kiev had waged a constant and ruthless war against *skomorokhi* – folk musicians, particularly instrumentalists – since they represented the stronghold of paganism and its ritual aspect.[2] Equally significant was the fact that *skomorokhi* were bearers of urban culture, which always tended to multicultural contacts and constituted a natural link connecting Rus' with the Latin West condemned by the Church.

In Kiev the Orthodox Church implemented its policies by pressurizing the local secular authorities, which, however, remained fond of secular music-making and practised it at the courts in the usual way. Nevertheless, regulated by the political situation, the grand dukes were often dependent on the church authorities and forced, at least in public, to subject their interests to the religious dictates. Privately, they continued to enjoy secular music in closed court circles. At least two Russian chronicles in the eleventh and twelfth centuries, and *Pateric Kievskogo Pecherskogo monastyrya* in the thirteenth century, mention one popular and much quoted episode, which describes the saintly monk Feodosiy Pecherskiy's visit to Prince Svyatoslav II of Kiev in 1073:

---

2   The Russian Orthodox Church persistently condemned the pagan *Satanic games* often associated with rituals and entertainment accompanied by instrumental music. These condemnatory texts mentioning *Satanic games*, *Rusaliyas*, and *gusli* in Kievan Rus', are exactly the same as those known from Bulgaria. Bulgaria had converted to Christianity almost a century earlier than Kievan Rus', and had also retained its pagan culture in a similar way to that of Kievan/Muscovite Rus' (see V. Krastev, *Ochertsy po istoria na bolgarskata muzika.* Sofia, 1970). It was thus not only Orthodoxy that appeared to have spread from the Byzantine Empire; rather, as a centre of world culture Byzantium also served as a model for a secular culture that appealed to the pagan or recently pagan population. The Orthodox encounter with pagan culture, therefore, was not entirely a new problem in the lands of Kievan Rus' or in Bulgaria.

Once the Holy Father Feodosy came to Prince Svyatoslav Yaroslavich. Entering the hall where the Prince sat, the Father saw in front of him many musicians playing *gusli* [a kind of zither or *kantele*], organs, and other instruments and enjoying themselves as usual. The Holy Father, sitting at the side, looking down, lowered his head, and bowing slightly, said to him: 'Will it be so in the future age?' The Prince, immediately touched by the words of the holy man, shed a small tear and ordered the musicians to stop playing. Afterwards, whenever listening to music, if he became aware of the Holy Father visiting him, he would stop the music.[3]

Thus, as early as the twelfth century, the ruling classes demonstrated a hypocritical tradition. Formally, they observed the official ideological constraints, while informally they continued to enjoy the forbidden pleasures.

Pre-Christian Rus' used typical medieval European musical instruments, including the *gusli, svirel* – a woodwind instrument similar to an oboe; *gudok*, similar to a fiddle; and also horns, and so on, as well as shamanic accessories like drums, small bells, tambourines and noise-makers. Such instruments were typically used during rites, entertainment, court ceremonies, and probably in pagan temples. The *skomorokhi* played instruments at the weddings they organized in Kievan and later in Muscovite Rus'. These musicians also engaged in clowning, acrobatics, puppet shows, juggling and performing animals, and so on – perpetuating the traditional medieval popular culture. The source for both the term and the phenomenon of the *skomorokhi* remains unclear. It could be of Byzantine, Western European (Famintsyn, 1995:1), or Eastern (possibly Syrian players) root (Findeizen, 1928: I, 53–7). Zguta suggests that it may be of native origin, but resulting from foreign influence (1978:14–15). There are about twenty versions of its etymology (Belkin, 1975:23–7; Koshelev, 1994), although none are recognized as definitive.

The various approaches to the origin of *skomorokhi* might not be as contradictory as they seem. The lack of any available evidence for the ethnic and cultural complexity of the population of Kievan Rus' in the tenth century does not imply that this area was homogeneous or isolated. The proximity of the Khazar Empire to Rus' from the seventh to the tenth centuries (and whose very existence on pre-Rus'ian territory remained a traditional taboo in Russian historiography until the post-Soviet era) stimulated connections that affected the population of the future Kievan Rus'. Rus'ians absorbed not only the town of Kiev (the word itself means

---

3   'Однажды пришел к нему блаженный и богоносный отец Феодосий, и войдя в палату, где сидел князь, он увидел многих играющих перед ним: одни играли на гуслях, иные на музыкальных инструментах, иные же на органах – и так все играли и веселились перед князем по обычаю. Блаженный же, сидя с краю и опустив глаза, поник и, слегка наклонившись, сказал ему: "Будет ли так в том будущем веке?". И князь сразу же умилился слову блаженного, и немного прослезился, и повелел игру с тех пор прекратить. А если он когда-либо и приказывал играть, то когда узнавал о приходе блаженного Феодосия, повелевал им [музыкантам] остановиться и молчать' (Rogov, 1973:49). This text was extracted from the edition of *Paterik Kievskogo Pecherskogo monastyrya* (St Petersburg, 1911:50) and translated from Church Slavonic by A. Rogov.

'lower settlement' in the Khazar language), but many of its social characteristics as well. These included its entire system of government, legal procedures and military organization, as well as certain crafts, costumes, coiffures and a partial lexicon, including such words (known as 'pure Russian') as *bogatyr* ('brave warrior'), *telega* ('wagon, chariot'), *bayan* or *bojan* ('singer'), and many others.[4] Finally, Khazarian and Rus'ian populations conjoined to form a single super-ethnos.[5] Khazaria, a multiethnic state connecting West and East, had intercultural contacts with the Byzantine Empire, the Arab Caliphate, Persia, the Caucasus, and East and West European countries. The difference between the multi-religious establishment of Khazaria (Judaism, Islam, Christianity, not to mention the obviously strong pagan substratum) and the late paganism of the Rus'ian Eastern Slavs, did not exclude possible cultural interrelations. Since Khazaria was a strong Empire and therefore a cultural centre for at least two centuries, it accumulated various contemporary trends. Its musical culture must certainly have enjoyed some minstrelsy. Whatever the sources of Rus'ian *skomorokhi* may be, certain elements could have been transmitted via Khazarian culture and inherited by Kievan Rus'.[6] Novgorod, an ancient North Rus'ian town and one of the centres of *skomoroki* art, was a member of the Hanseatic union and had its own connections with medieval urban European culture.

The study of Rus'ian music culture began in the nineteenth century, but little mention was made of the Khazar kingdom. The development of Khazar studies by the 1940s, however, prompted Joseph Yasser (who contributed to Russian and Jewish studies in the USA from 1930 to the 1950s) to analyze references to Hebrew music in Russian medieval ballads and to conclude that

> ... through all sorts of channels – secular, sacred, social and professional, Hebrew chants and songs, doubtless well-assimilated by the upper classes of the Khazars, also found their way into the musical practice of the same classes of the native population of Kiev, and to all appearance remained with them long after the Khazars had been banished from Russian soil. (1949:44)

The texts of Russian *byliny* usually mention a repertoire performed by *skomorokhi* and grand-ducal singers – *bayans* – active at the banquets of Kievan dukes between

---

4   See Julius Brutzkus, 'The Khazar Origin of Ancient Kiev', in *Slavonic and East European Review* XXII, 1944:108–24; Max Vasmer, *Russisches etymologisches Wörterbuch*, vols I–III, 1953–8; 2nd edn 1976–80. Heidelberg: Winter.

5   I follow Gumilev's definition of super-ethnos as an ethnic system, comprising several ethnic entities that arose simultaneously in a specific geographical area, and which display themselves in history as a mosaic whole (Lev N. Gumilev, *Etnogenez i biosfera Zemli*. Leningrad: LGU, 1989:499).

6   Paul Wexler provided a bibliography relating to the possible Jewish (Khazar) impact on Slavic literature and culture and the possible Khazar contribution to the East Slavic pantheon (*The Ashkenazic Jews: A Slavo-Turkic People in Search of a Jewish Identity*. Columbus, Ohio: Slavica Publishers, 1993:249).

the tenth and twelfth centuries. They invariably also included miscellaneous tunes: *evreysky, po umil'nomu* ('Hebrew, touching'); *igrishche ot Erusolima* (minstrel performance of Jerusalem songs, which Yasser tends to refer to contemporaneous Jewish music); songs from the lands of the Saracens, which Yasser interprets as typical for medieval Europe reference to the entire range of Moslem music (1949:36–41), *igrishche drugoe ot Tsarya–grada* ('another piece, Constantinoplian'), also Venetian or Italian, and Kievan music.[7] Sharing Yasser's hypothesis regarding Rus'ian-Khazarian musical connections, I might add that Chernihiv, considered to have been a Khazarian town, and Tmutorokan, another town under Khazar possession between 704–988 and under Rus'ian control between 988–1094, were the centres of the south-Rus'ian rhapsodic epos – *byliny*, sung by *bayan* and narrating the deeds of *bogatyri*.[8]

Considering that the *skomorokhi* existed as an already established Kievan socio-cultural institution before Rus' Christianization, alongside the pagan priests *volkhvy* (Zguta, 1978:3, 6), we should also bear in mind the coexistence of East Slavs and Khazar Jews living in Kiev and presumably in other locales too. While Kiev was being transformed into a Slavic centre, Kievan Jewry must have experienced acculturation, shifting from Khazar cultural sources and language to Slavic ones and maintaining cultural interactions with the changing residents.[9] The preoccupation of Kievan Rus' Jewry with particular professions and institutions is indicated by the widespread family names derived from Rus'ian professional nomination. The Jewish family name *Skomorovsky*, as well as other names related to the instruments played by the *skomorokhi* such as *Dudnik* or *Tsymbal'nik*, speaks of Kievan Jewry's

---

7   J. Yasser cites many collections of *byliny* written in various regions of Russia.

8   Chernihiv's belonging to Khazaria also casts another light on the well-publicized archeological finding – a gigantic pair of horns from a now-extinct wild ox / tau discovered in *Chernaya mogila*, 1873. Its silver ornamentation, featuring oriental motives on one horn, and northern barbarian hunting birds, a dragon and griffons on the other (Findeizen, 1928, I:26–7), might be related to the Khazarian culture. For linguistic data showing interrelations between the Khazar and Russian languages see N. de Baumgarten, *Aux origines de la Russie*. Roma: Pont, Institutum Orientalium Studiorum, 1939:69; J. Bruckus, 'Istoki russkogo evreystva', in *Evreyskiy mir* I, 1939:22; G.Y. Shevelov, *A Historical Phonology of the Ukrainian Language*. Heidelberg, 1979:211; Omeljan Pritsak, 'The Pre-Ashkenazic Jews of Eastern Europe in Relation to the Khazars, the Rus' and the Lithuanians', in *Ukrainian-Jewish Relations in Historical Perspective*, ed. Howard Aster and Peter J. Potichnyi, 3–21. Alberta, Canada: Canadian Institute of Ukrainian Studies Press, 1988:9; V.Ja. Petrukhin, Comments in his Russian translation of Norman Golb and Omeljan Pritsak, *Khazarian Hebrew Documents of the Tenth Century*. Ithaca – New York – London: Cornell University Press, 1982: *Khazarsko-evreyskie dokumenty X veka*. Moscow-Jerusalem: Gesharim, 1997:398–9; Paul Wexler, *Two-Tiered Relexification in Yiddish: Jews, Sorbs, Khazars and the Kiev-Polessian Dialect*. Berlin: Mouton de Gruyter, 2002, chapter 4.4; N.V. Shlyakov, 'Boyan', in *Izvestiya po russkomu yazyku i slovesnosti AN SSSR*, I/1, Leningrad, 1928, I: 483–98.

9   See Kevin Alan Brook, *The Jews of Khazaria*. Northvale, New Jersey: Aronson, 1999: 302–3.

active involvement in this profession.[10] Folk fiddlers are still called *skomorokhi* in Byelorussia (*skamaroxi*) and the Kursk area (with a mixed Russian-Ukrainian-Jewish population). The name *Skomorokhov* appears in Ukrainian families too, though noticeably less so. (Wexler notes that one should always consider the conversion of a significant number of Slavs to Judaism and of Khazar Jews to Orthodoxy, especially at the end of the First Millennium and the early Second Millennium.)[11] These occupations were still identified with Ashkenazi Jewish customs, based, however, on their own minstrelsy institution of *badkhanim*, which served as a counterpart to the Rus'ian *skomorokhi*.[12]

While the practice of *skomorokhi* could have sprung up in ancient times within syncretic pagan rites, the word itself became known in Russia only during the twelfth century, from an officially ideologized document, the Russian (Primary) Chronicle, which related to the events of 1068.[13] By the time of the Primary Chronicle, in the course of the Christianization of Kievan Rus', the *skomorokhi* institution had become a marginalized social group of itinerant actors (Keldysh, 1983:60). The term itself only appeared later, and could have been in accord with the still unclear sociolinguistic phenomenon of a constant Hebrew-Greek component in all European jargons – the secret languages of marginalized groups, including the secret language of the Ukrainian minstrels, *lirniki* (Kononenko, 1998:72).[14] Its existence in the Russian language demonstrably preserves the original ecclesiastic disapproving overtones.[15]

---

10 A. Beider in his *A Dictionary of Jewish Surnames from the Russian Empire* (Teaneck, N. J.: Avotaynu, Inc. 1993) gives Skomorovsky as derived from the Ukrainian village in the Zhytomir district called Skomorokha (Skomoroxa).

11 See Paul Wexler, *Explorations in Judeo-Slavic Linguistics*. Leiden: E.J. Brill, 1987; *The Ashkenazic Jews: A Slavo-Turkic People in Search of a Jewish Identity*. Columbus, Ohio: Slavica Publishers, 1993, Chapter 6.

12 Regarding the enigmatic etymology of the word *skomorokh*, I would like to suggest associating it with the phonetically close and logically connected Latin term *humor*, which has been adopted by many European languages as well as the Hebrew ('khumor') and Russian ('yumor'). There is also the Russian word *umora* (dying from laughter) with its connotation to *skomoroki* as the principal bearers of the laughter culture, and the *s-m-kh* root of the word that comprises the Russian *smekh* ('laughter'). As so often happens with adopted alien words, their phonetic closeness to the vernacular language serves to ensure their smooth absorption. *Skomorokh* was neither the sole nor the first word for Rus'ian minstrels. They were often called by the Rus'ian terms *glumets* (he who sneers), *igrets* (he who plays), *poteshnik* (amuser) *gusel'nik* (playing *gusli*) and others of similar ilk. However, there was also the popular German word in use – *spielmann*, which was substituted by the term *skomorokh* (Belkin, 1975:46) and whose appearance in the Kievan Rus' context poses a serious challenge to researchers.

13 Belkin associates its appearance with the first translation of biblical texts from Greek into Old Church Slavonic, and as coming from Bulgaria where he traces it to the ninth–tenth centuries (Belkin, 1975:40–1).

14 See also Wexler, 1993:43, 234–5.

15 S.I. Ozhegov and N.Yu. Shvedova, *Tolkovyi slovar' russkogo yazyka*. Moscow: Nauka, 1999:724.

Figure 2.1   Performance of *skomorokhi*. **Drawing from Adam Olearius'**
Journey to Muscovy **(seventeenth century)**

Forced to exist as a counter-culture yet enjoying great popularity, the *skomorokhi* represented an ideological threat to both sacred and secular authorities, and this was to cost them their very existence as a cultural institution. Between the fourteenth to seventeenth centuries Muscovite Rus' experienced the painful processes of centralization and secularization of the State, which led to the long period of the 'Time of Troubles'. During this period, whether perceived as a threat to the regime, or perhaps merely sacrificed in the political game between Church and State, the activities of the *skomorokhi* were totally banned. The interdiction issued by Tsar Alexey Mikhaylovich in 1648, under pressure from the Church, was strongly enforced. The *skomorokhi*, whose art had been the most beloved constituent of Russian culture for seven centuries, were deported to Siberia and the northern parts of Russia; and their musical instruments were broken, burned, or otherwise destroyed.

The *skomorokhi* culture, however, which had developed in Rus' over such a long period of time, could not be so easily destroyed. Their instrumental music-making was preserved in folklore. The jester's tradition continued to entertain courts during the eighteenth and nineteenth centuries, as well as *balagan* (folklore theatre) performances given by travelling actors at fairs and puppet-shows, etc. The enormous popularity of balladry in the former Soviet Russia cannot be understood without relation to the *skomorokhi* culture. The very existence of this phenomenon as a counterculture, including the 'double-standard' relationship with the authorities, is part of its tradition. The most famous singer-songwriter and actor Vladimir Vysotsky (1938–80), who actually became a folk-hero, and was ignored by the official culture, was often invited to the highest circles of the Soviet establishment.

Seeking an Art-Music Tradition (Seventeenth Century)

One cannot predict how instrumental music-making would have developed in Russia if the *skomorokhi* had not been repressed. However, the reasons for its demise went beyond their good or ill fortune. While in European countries minstrels participated in creating popular urban music, they were not the only necessary contributors to professional instrumentalism. The key to the situation in Russia lay in the establishment of the Orthodox Church. Throughout those seven centuries the secular and sacred art music traditions maintained a strictly parallel but segregated existence, completely lacking the fruitful interaction that generated universal (that is, not confined to either secular or sacred) musical instrumental genres in the West. For example, in 1648, the year of the *skomorokhi* suppression, G. Frescobaldi died, leaving behind a sophisticated organ legacy. During his lifetime he had tutored disciples in many European countries. Other instrumental genres, such as the *sonata da chiesa*, spread competitively and challenged German, French and English suites. These forms failed to take shape in Russia, however, due to the absence of instrumental music in the Church.

One can claim that there were other complications in Russian history that delayed the progress of Russian art music, including the Mongol yoke that eventually arrested Russia's economic and cultural development. I would argue, however, that although it may seem far-fetched to accuse Orthodoxy of being the ultimate cause of all of Russia's misfortunes (as proclaimed by Peter Chaadaev), this conception does help us to understand the following facts:

a) The boundaries between the suppression of instrumental music in Russia and the beginning of its development were exactly the same as those between pre-Petrine (Orthodox dominance) and Petrine (downplaying of Orthodoxy) Russias.

b) Other Orthodox countries, such as Greece, Bulgaria, Romania, Serbia, Armenia and Georgia, which had not experienced the Mongol yoke and whose minstrelsy had not been eliminated, have no early instrumental music traditions of which to be proud.

Religious Chant

The Russian Church's crusade against secular instrumentalism may have resulted from its failure to develop a proper form of religious music in its own domain. The ancient Byzantine chant had been introduced by the Greek Orthodox Church in the eleventh-twelfth centuries and was canonized by the Russian Orthodox Church in its

Byzantium monodic version. The chant was notated in neumes but its earliest form – *kondakar* notation – still resists deciphering. Only in its later form, developed in the thirteenth century, has *znamennaya* or *kryukovaya* notation (*znamya* = sign and *kryuk* = hook, as a typical form of Russian neumes) yielded to deciphering.

Like other Christian religious music, the Russian one too was influenced by the folk tradition (N. Uspensky, 1971:61–7), which, being modal, was generally compatible with the chant. But the prohibition of instruments (as a result of purism and fidelity to the ancient Jewish tradition by the Greek Orthodox Church), and polyphony in the church services, caused an essential aesthetic conflict, which deepened as folk polyphony developed. Russian church music thus experienced pressure from two sides, suffering from the prohibition of both instruments and polyphony. Chant and polyphony interrelations were always dramatic in Russia. The history of Russian church music during the thirteenth to seventeenth centuries is indeed the history of singers struggling for their artistic right to multi-part singing. With the development of the polyphonic protyazhnaya song in Muscovy folklore the Church finally lost its chance to preserve znamenny chant as the only form.

The first scores of multi-part church singing were written in the same notation as chant – *znamyona* – and only appeared in the seventeenth century, although there are sources indicating that scores may have existed in the sixteenth century. Russian scholars believe that this tradition goes back even earlier, as well as that specific Russian polyphony using subsidiary voices was not recognized by singers as multi-part singing but considered monophonic instead (in some places it still is) (Skrebkov, 1969:50). The deciphering of these scores created a puzzle. Since direct deciphering presents a very dissonant sound, Sergei Skrebkov has suggested that certain parts or fragments most probably required 'correction' with the help of transposition at certain intervals. The compositions deciphered by using this method sound reasonably organized acoustically and are based on thirds. However, there are no marks on the scores themselves, and Skrebkov believed that knowledge of the proper intervals for transposition was an oral tradition only, not shown in the scores[16] (1969:51–3).

What actually took place in the church up to the sixteenth century was not even a parody of the music that was once introduced by the Greco-Byzantine missionaries. It was not a monodian chant but, still in neumic notation, a multi-voiced linear polyphony, termed *strochnoe penie*, completely lacking an acoustical harmonic basis, and, in addition, having multiple versions in various areas of Russia. A revolt appears to have broken out against the musical confines established by the Church. The Russian Orthodox Church understood the situation but could do nothing about it. It first needed to reconstruct its own institutions and to create a new, more realistic attitude to church music in order to preserve its prestige.

---

16 Since Skrebkov's original suggestion of this hypothetical method of deciphering, his colleagues have still been unable either to completely rely on it, or to suggest anything more convincing.

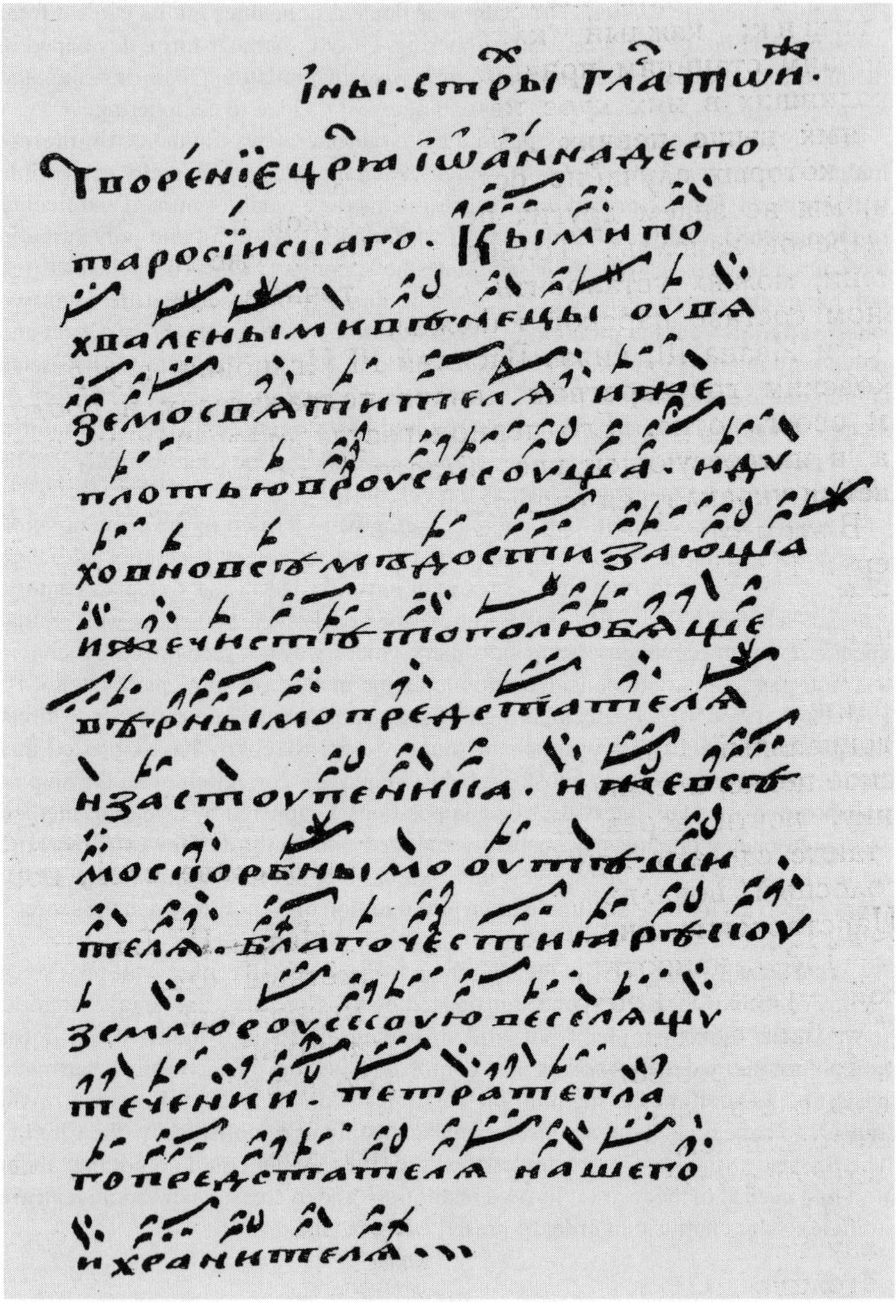

Figure 2.2   **Sticheron by Tsar Ivan the Terrible. Early type of score. End of the sixteenth/beginning of the seventeenth century**

In the course of the centralization of secular power in the mid to seventeenth century there was also a campaign for the centralization and standardization of the Orthodox liturgy in all of its components. The procedure began without any intention to introduce dramatic changes. Setting up a printing press in Russia made it possible to correct and standardize the handwritten liturgical books, which were full of mistakes and variants. However, upon studying the contemporaneous Greek sources it was apparent that these had undergone serious reforms since the tenth century. In the course of this campaign it became clear that the entire choice of the proper authentic model on which to base corrections had been ambiguous and now demanded a more considered flexibility as well as more time. Incidentally, the newly-appointed Patriarch Nikon (1605–81, presided from 1652–9), working amicably with Tsar Alexey Mikhaylovich and known as a man who would conclude any task he undertook, vigorously pushed this campaign. Finally, the Tsar and Patriarch Nikon decided to take as a source the Greek and Slavonic books of the Orthodox Church in the Russo-Lithuanian Uniats, all printed in Venice. The result of these corrections was both unexpected and undesired. Since every local version had inevitably undergone some corrections, such changes were perceived as destroying the base of its spiritual existence, equal in enormity to changing the ritual of signing the cross from two to three fingers. In addition, the association with Venice was interpreted by the masses as going over to Catholicism, despite the prayer books being printed on Venice's Greek presses, which belonged to the only community still faithful to the Orthodox Church (besides Muscovy) during the time of Turkish Byzantium.[17] The upheaval that these reforms produced, also touching upon music as one of its most important elements, coupled with great socio-economic disorder, resulted in a highly tragic situation, the so-called *raskol* (schism, dissidence) in Russian society (Nikol'sky, 1983:129–32). This initiated the self-imposed exile of the *starovery* (Old Believers), who emigrated to the outlying regions of the country in order to maintain their traditional ritual. The Old Believers' liturgical practice continues to preserve the tradition of ancient Russian chant to the present day.

Since church polyphonic singing was chaotic, Nikon, at the first opportunity (in his position as Bishop of Novgorod, 1649–50), undertook some regulatory measures like banning dissonant linear polyphony and *homovoe penie* [singing with the addition of the particle *homo* to every word of liturgical texts] and establishing harmonic three-voiced *partes*-singing on the Kiev model. He charmed the Novgorodians with this music and pleasantly surprised even Moscow itself (Kartashev, 1959:II, 136; see also N. Uspensky, 1976:15).[18]

Thus, after centuries of the musicians' struggle, it was the Russian Church itself, through its own political intentions and reforms, that officially introduced Western

---

17   See Philip Longworth, 'Russian-Venetian Relations in the Reign of Tsar Aleksey Mikhaylovich', in *Slavonic and East European Review*, vol. 64, 3, 1988:387, 391.

18   Nikolai Uspensky, however, referred to the later event of 1653 when Nikon demanded that the Abbot of the Valdaysky-Iversky monastery send him copies of multi-voiced *kanty* and concertos.

polyphony organized in the ready-made form of *partes*-singing (*partesnoe penie*). The introduction of this music presented the most revolutionary changes in the course of Russian music history, including the acceptance of the five-line (though square) notation and the major-minor harmonic concept, though still with a strong prevailing tendency toward modality (see Gerasimova-Persidskaya, 1983).

The encounter of chant with polyphony was defined with remarkable ambiguity. Chant was performed by the tenor voice, like *cantus firmus*. However, there was no trace of the Italian imitative polyphony or rhythmic development characteristic of the German *Tenorlied*. In Russian polyphonic settings the rest of the voices presented mono-rhythmic, often *organum*-like parallel movement, with limited linear freedom of voices, while the bass fulfilled a harmonic function and was only rarely figurative. The whole texture gave a harmonic – rather acoustic – interpretation to the tones of the chant, a kind of fusion of modal and functional elements, which one can find in Italian vocal music of a century earlier.

Settings of this kind dissolved modality and submitted it to harmony, which basically was already functional. The process was haphazard, hard-line and European in essence. Polyphony and harmonic functionality were an aspect of power. The monody of ancient chant was curtailed and deprived of its melismatics, submitted to the demands of vertical organization. Even if this initial seventeenth-century effort was a 'legal marriage' (using Glinka's expression of his hope to unite the conditions of Russian music with western fugue by the bounds of legal matrimony, see Glinka, 1977:180)[19] it was nonetheless a 'patriarchal wedding'. If there was any ideological trend behind this it could only have been that of westernization.

The *partes*-singing developed in two genres: the above-mentioned settings of the chant, and the concerto *a cappella* that was dissociated from the chant and usually based on the psalms. Having a common stylistic background and developing in parallel, the genres at times brought together and complemented one another, as they did in the eighteenth century; whereas in the nineteenth century they drew apart, with public consensus considering them as opposed. While chant settings were always a part of the liturgy, concerto was both an element of liturgy as its climax (not obligatory), and a para-liturgical (spiritual) genre often performed during secular ceremonies or entertainments. It lent the liturgy its attractiveness; while in secular ceremonies *partes*-singing lent the court an atmosphere closer to the majestic beauty of the European courts. The evidence of its polyfunctionality can be seen in the existence of two major choirs: that of the Patriarch – the Choir of Patriarchal Singing Clerks, and that of the Tsar – the State Singing Clerks, with a total of 300–350 singers between the two (Moleva, 1971: 145).

The genre of Russian *partes*-singing concerto was borrowed from the Venetian Andrea Gabrieli's school of the spiritual concerto. It was successfully adopted and took root in Russia as had happened previously in Poland and the Ukraine. However, the organ accompaniment to polyphonic singing applied in Italy, Poland and West Ukraine

---

19   Glinka wrote this in a letter to his friend K.A. Bulgakov in 1856.

was not allowed to cross the border into the Orthodox countries.[20] In the rest of the Ukraine (and later in Russia) *partes*-singing existed solely as an *a cappella* genre. With the introduction of *partes*-singing many Ukrainian singers migrated to Muscovy, becoming traditional members of the court choir.

The huge amount of material preserved, mostly from monasteries, contains no scores but only manuscript sets of parts. Singers were supposed to memorize the whole. Concertos were usually composed for four to six and sometimes twelve-voice choirs. There are however a few rare sets of twenty-four voice *partes*–singing concertos and even a unique example of a forty-eight voice one. Many notes have the composers' names but many others are anonymous. Among the composers are such famous names as Vasily Titov, Nikolai Bavykin and Vasily Redrikov. The notes often also bear the names of their owners, as well as the fanciful insignias of copyists or their humorous inscriptions. The mere sight of all this mass of music inside the archival depositories is in itself a most impressive experience. There are hundreds of slightly damaged brown leather covers (approximately 20×23 cm) with metal fasteners, usually broken. Inside are the endless square notes written in slightly faded ink; the most popular compositions tend to have grease spots in their lower right corners as a result of the singers thumbing the pages and of wax dropping from the burning candles. The pervasive acrid smell of the old leather and paper adds to the sense of authenticity and vitality of the repertoire. This culture was indeed a massive one, embracing the widest layers of Russian society from the second half of the seventeenth century for the course of at least a hundred years. Disclosed by musicologists, it is currently used in beautiful performances and studiously examined. Although its plain harmony may not fire the imagination of modern listeners familiar with the more developed contemporaneous West-European harmonic successions, it captures one with the sophistication of its texture and iridescent play of timbres of voices and registers, associated with the architectural complexity and charm of late seventeenth- and early eighteenth-century Moscow baroque (the so-called Naryshkin baroque) characterized by secularly elegant multi-tiered buildings adorned with white-brick fretwork.

The genre of *partes*-singing concerto would never have taken root in Russia had it not been theorized and developed in schools of composition. The key figures in this were Ioanniky Korenev (d. *c.* 1680), clerk of the Sretensky Cathedral in the Kremlin and author of the polemical treatise *Musikia* (1671), targeted at the conservative defenders of monodian chant; and Nikolai Diletsky (*c.* 1630, Kiev – *c.* 1680, Moscow), theoretician, composer and teacher, whose own life story reflects the transition of *partes*-singing from the Ukraine to Russia. His main work, *Grammatika musikiyskaya*, was published in four editions, three of them during his lifetime: 1675, Vilno, in Polish; 1677, Smolensk (an ancient Kievan-Rus' town, twice under Polish-Lithuanian control) translated into Church-Slavonic and revised; 1679, Moscow, in Russian; and 1681, Moscow, probably posthumous, opening with the second edition of Korenev's

---

20 The predominant denomination in the West Ukraine was defined as the Uniate Church, uniting Orthodox and Catholic churches in recognizing the authority of the Pope, although preserving Orthodox customs and observations.

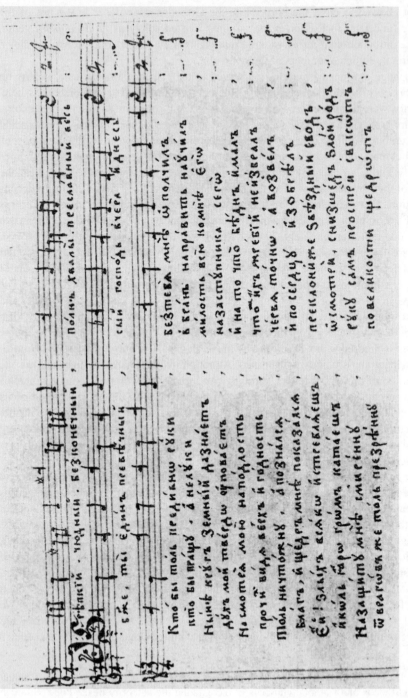

Figure 2.3 Kant 'Krepky, chyudny, beskonechny'. Text by V. Trediakovsky (versification of Psalm 144:2 'My goodness, and my fortress; my high tower, and my deliverer'), 1744

treatise[21] (Protopopov, 1989:44–65; Jensen 1987, 1992).

Kanty and *Psal'my*

The popularity of the *partes*-singing concerto among audiences could not have developed if it had not been strengthened by the appearance and active existence of new, popular semi-secular genres: Polish *kanty* and *psal'my*, which sounded like three-voiced songs – bass and two upper voices in third. *Kanty* and *psal'my* were widely adopted in urban music-making and became the primary source for development of the functional music mentality among the growing urban population of Russia. (Although both terms traditionally exist, their difference in music is indistinguishable: while *psal'my* indicates the use of spiritual texts of psalms, there are also many spiritual *kanty*. Since *kanty* dominated in history, this term has remained more widespread, sometimes also implying *psal'my* in Russian writings on eighteenth-century music.) The popularity enjoyed by *kanty* made them the flesh and blood of Russian music of the 'long eighteenth century' (Livanova, 1938, 1952, I; Keldysh, 1965, 1969, Dolskaya-Ackerly, 1983).

Kanty usually appear in handwritten music books (approximately 20 cm wide × 17 cm long), incorporating a significant number of items. Each page has a three-system line in its upper part (written in square notation, of course) with the poetic text below. Two pages of the open score provide the exact space needed for one *kant* or *psal'ma*. *Kanty* were sung in homes (with family members being among the singers as well as in the audience). They were also performed at celebrations of public events and official State ceremonies commemorating important dates. 'Singing a *kant* then was like playing a waltz or polka today' – wrote Danilevsky a century later.[22]

Since *kanty* were based on the tonic and dominant chords of relative keys they became the best vehicle for establishing a West-European harmonic mentality in Russia. One should bear this in mind in order not to accuse the (quite tactful) composer Ivan Prach of thrusting harmonic leading tones upon 'innocent' or 'authentic' minor-mode Russian folk songs in his arrangements of the famous *A Collection of Russian Folk Songs* (by Nikolai Lvov and Ivan Prach) in the late eighteenth century. The Russian ear had already lost its modal chastity a century earlier, no later than during Tsarevna Sophia's 1680s Moscow culture, which in no way disturbed the peaceful coexistence of both harmonic functionality and modality in the urban repertoire.

A classic example of an art-music version of the new Ruthenian style was *Psaltyr' rifmovannaya* – a collection of 150 of King David's psalms. The psalms were rhythmetized by the Byelorussian, Simeon Polotsky (*en monde* Samuil Emel'yanovich Petrovsky-Sitnianovich, 1629–80), Tsar Alexey Mikhaylovich's leading cultural authority, 'an aggressive spokesman for new, Western art forms'

---

21   There is a huge historiography on eighteenth-century Russian and Ukrainian theoretical works, including evaluation of Korenev's and Diletsky's contributions summarized in Protopopov's 1973 and 1989 studies.

22   G. Danilevsky, *Ukrainskaya starina*, Kharkov, 1866:332.

(Billington, 1970:146), the court poet and tutor to the Tsar's children. Polotsky's book was set to music after his death, presumably after 1682 (but in any case during the reign of Sophia), by Vasiliy Titov, mentioned above as a highly prominent composer of *partes*-singing concertos.

Ukrainization

The role of *kanty* cannot be overestimated. In general, they contributed the notable Ukrainization of Russian musical culture. Russian and Ukrainian folk music differ in part due to the ethno-cultural environments and influences under which they developed and evolved. Russian music of the sixteenth and early seventeenth centuries was exceedingly modal, and its polyphony lacked harmonic definition (in folk as well as church music), while Ukrainian music preserved these East-Slavic traits only in its south-eastern and north-central regions close to Kiev. The folk music of the larger, 'right-bank' Ukraine, bordering with Poland, Austria–Hungary and Bessarabia, has a strong major-minor base, reflecting its cultural ties with central Europe. Moreover the entire Ukraine was affected by a noticeable Turkish influence, expressed in the special 'pitiful' augmented second, inherited from the songs of captured Turkish women and applied in lyrical folklore. Lastly, the rich Gypsy involvement in Ukrainian life made its powerful impact, just as it had in Bessarabia and Austro-Hungary. Ukrainization of Russian music had thus become a necessary stage of its westernization, making this process more natural and easily absorbed. The previously lacking sustenance from the European musical environment now became available to the Russians through the channel of popular urban and art music. Neither Glinka nor Tchaikovsky could have become what they were without the Ukrainization of Russian music that continued throughout the long eighteenth century.

The impact of Ukrainian music generated a new musical mentality including a semantic system and rhetorical tradition, and created a western-oriented cognitive base among a wide stratum of Russian society.[23] It was welcomed and traditionally enjoyed by the urban population in Russia from at least the mid-seventeenth century, comprising the basis for two equally developed eighteenth-century genres: sacred *partes*-singing and popular song.

---

23   The young Italian singer Philipp Balatri from Pisa, visiting Russia in 1698–1701, was the first to witness the readiness of the Russian public to appreciate quite complex contemporaneous vocal works, dramatically differing in style from Russian church music. His ms. autobiography (1725–32) is found in the RGB presented as gift by the Chechen National Library (Moleva, 1971:143).

Instrumental Music

In contrast to vocal culture, Russian seventeenth-century instrumental music left behind neither compositions nor names of composers. There is also little evidence of repertoires and genres, either native or borrowed. The consequence of the many centuries of anti-instrumental-music policy was obvious. Instruments were played nonetheless, including the timpani, trumpet, flute, oboe, horn and organ. Lute and violin as instruments accompanying songs praising Tsar Mikhail Fedorovich, were mentioned by the German scholar Adam Olearius travelling in Russia in the 1630s (1986:299). The old folk instruments *gusli* and *rozhki* (corns) were also in demand, though by the 1660s these musicians had become less well paid and notably ousted by the oboists and horn players. Trumpet players were especially popular and well paid and even had their own school 'Trumpet court'; one of the Moscow streets in the vicinity still retains the name 'Trubnikovsky pereulok' (Trumpet lane). Timpani and wind instruments were broadly used in the military and on all kinds of civilian occasions. Muscovite citizens particularly enjoyed the fanfares that accompanied ceremonies. However, no mention is found of the popularity of contemporaneous string instruments; even the folk prototype of the violin – the *gudok* – disappeared with the destruction of *skomorokhi* culture.

Many instrumentalists were of Polish origin. Foreign musicians were especially esteemed, as expressed in two extremes: either generous reward or violent measures to keep them in Russia. There were negotiations concerning the invitation of Danish singer Mme Paulsen and some lute players (Findeizen, 1928, I:315, XXVIII; Moleva, 1971:149–50).

The special popularity of the organ among the Moscow population, deduced from household and Kremlin *palaty* inventories, is rather unexpected.[24] For example the *palaty* of Prince V. Golitsyn contained several positive organs, *tsimbaly* (formerly interpreted as cembalo, although more probably folk cymbals), *oktavki* (clavichords) and *bass domra* (folk instrument of Eastern origin played with a plectrum). This combination of European and native folk instruments speaks for the repertoire, reflecting the epoch's openness to both the traditional native and the new imported, essential for the development of Russian culture.

The emergence of organ production (in modern sense) used to be interpreted by scholars as linked to the Moscow 'German quarter' population. However, there are also indications of the opposite: organists were often invited by foreigners to play in their homes. Moreover, the development of organ production began in the historically obscure period of the first half of the seventeenth century. Both approaches show that the source of the idea itself was not from the West. Rather, for Russians the organ was associated primarily with Byzantium and, endowing itself with the ambitious mission of becoming heir to Byzantium after its fall, Muscovy saw the organ as

---

24 In ancient Russian sources 'organ' or 'argan' meant any musical instrument except the organ as a key wind instrument in the modern sense of the word. Other nominations of instruments also differ from the modern (Roizman, 1979; Protopopov, 1989).

an important element of its own identity. Documents show that in the 1650s the manufacture of key instruments (organs and harpsichords) was under the supervision of the Chancellery of the Big Palace (Moleva, 1971:153). Thus, while looking back to Byzantium, Russia found itself closer to the West.

The organs in Moscow ranged from portable to the more massive positives with their complex mechanisms, many registers and large number of pipes. They became highly fashionable in the second half of the seventeenth century and the demand for organists grew. The appearance of Polish and Byelorussian musicians was a timely one. One can assume that they imported not only their knowledge, but their repertoire as well. The high point of the organ industry was the production of a four-register instrument as a gift for the Persian Shah, Abbas II (completed in 1662). It was followed a few years later by the twenty-register organ with more than 500 pipes, commissioned by the same addressee. In 1675, the Khan of Buchara expressed his desire to possess a Moscow organ and organist, thereby contributing to normalization of diplomatic relations. In 1701 a fire in the Kremlin destroyed the factory and since the priorities of young Peter I did not include organs, it was never rebuilt (Orlova, 1979:143–4; Moleva, 1971:153–4).

Music in the Theatre

The picture of late seventeenth-century Moscow musical entertainments is not complete without the mention of theatre. In 1672, when Peter was born, an all too brief period of new style began in court life. The spectacular performances presented at court were 'school dramas', the most popular being the well-known old Russian *Peshchnoe deistvo* [Drama of the Stove]. The principal authors of the time were Johann Gregory, pastor of the Saxon Church in the German quarter of Moscow, Simeon Polotsky and Dmitry Rostovsky. The actors comprised members of the German community (Findeizen, 1928:I, 317)[25] and professionals who had survived from the *skomorokhi* and become legalized with the lifting of the ban (Moleva, 1971:148). The texts of Polotsky's works usually indicate the participation of an organ. One of the spectacles, Gregory's ballet *Orpheus and Euridice*, used music by H. Schutz. There are also indirect data relating to music by J. Sweelinck, S. Scheidt, and Polish composers M. Mielczewski (whose *partes*-singing concertos were also performed in Russia), M. Zieleński and others (Moleva, 1971:153). In 1672 and 1674 groups of musicians were commissioned from abroad (Findeizen, 1928, I:315–6). The entire arsenal of musical instruments – mainly trumpets, organs, choirs performing *kanty* – was activated, thus bringing together sacred and secular, vocal and instrumental, national and western and presenting it before the multiethnic Moscow public. This natural Russian blend sowed the seeds of a national culture, for whose mature shape the coming eighteenth century would be mostly responsible.

---

25   See also N.S. Tikhonravov, *Russkie dramaticheskie proizvedenia 1672–1725 godov.* 2 vols, St Petersburg, 1874.

Figure 2.4 Scene from the comedy *Parable on the Prodigal Son* by Simeon Polotsky from the 1685 edition, Moscow

Figure 2.1 ...

Chapter 3

Toward the New Russian Idiom:
Between Germans and Italians;
Between Italians and Russians

Peter the Great – Pro-German and Anti-Italian

Peter's birth appears to have served as a trigger for his father's abrupt switch toward westernized-secularized entertainments. His childhood and adolescence, spent in Moscow, were surrounded by sound as modern as possible in the context of late-seventeenth-century Russia. Peter also spent much time in the German Quarter, an influence that contributed to the new aesthetic orientation. By the time of his first journey abroad therefore, in 1697–8, he was fully prepared to evaluate the new realities. As his familiarity with the various musical genres grew, the young Tsar Peter quickly defined his sympathies. Russian music unquestionably remained in the forefront. The *partes*-singing concerto that Peter loved and knew had by that time become an indispensable and basic part of Russian music, both sacred and secular. Despite his secular orientation, in order to inculcate in the public the custom of standing in silence during the Divine Liturgy, Peter introduced a fine for anyone found talking.[1] The Tsar himself often participated in the singing and took pleasure in visiting the homes of the court singers. *Kanty* and *partes*-singing concertos were also the form of music used at the time to commemorate Russian military victories (Example 3.1).

Military music underwent an especially intensive development, proportional to Russia's militarization. As Stählin noted, oboes, horns and trombones were the most popular instruments and probably familiar to Peter from his travels in Germany and Holland. He maintained an ensemble of this kind from Riga, which usually played *tafel musik* (its musicians were also accomplished in violin and contrabass). On particularly merry occasions the Emperor would order his ensemble of Polish pipers, with the addition of reed pipes and muted drums (Stählin, 1769, 1982:79–80).

What remained was the choice of which European model to follow and Peter chose the German one, having a personal dislike for Italian and French music (Stählin, 1830:II, 55; Porfirieva, III:361). German music, along with other German

---

1   Edict of Peter I from 18 December 1718. The effectiveness of this edict, however, does not appear to have lasted long, since it was repeated in 1742.

cultural realities, thus established itself in Russia as one of the main elements of court entertainment in the first quarter of the eighteenth century. German music also became a regular element of the environment. In 1710 Silesian master Johann Förster installed a Glockenspiel in one of the church towers, which reproduced pieces from the organ repertoire. In 1720 the first chamber music ensemble, imported by Duke Karl Ulrich Holstein-Gottorp, Peter's future son-in-law, was taken under the patronage of the court. Its repertoire eventually became popular throughout St Petersburg. German musicians, headed by kapellmeister Johann Hübner, took on Russian pupils with professional aims as well as pupils from the aristocracy, among whom music became a widespread and prestigious pastime. From then on, for more than two hundred years, German musicians traditionally constituted the personnel of St Petersburg's court orchestra.

Example 3.1   Kant *Dnes'orle rossiysky*, **anonymous (eighteenth century)**

Among the first measures taken by Peter in the late 1690s was the introduction of organized social gatherings (*assamblei*) with music and dances. New musicians were invited from abroad and a city theatre was opened in Moscow under the management first of Johann Kunst and then of Otto First. Its repertoire included contemporary French and German pieces, Molière's comedies and the Russian beloved sacred 'school dramas' (Findeizen, 1928:I, 342–344). Staged serenades and other ceremonies accompanied by instrumental music increasingly became the practice. An engraving depicting Peter's wedding banquet in 1712 shows musicians playing violas and oboes. The demand for musicians for both court and city life began to increase. This, however, did not happen all at once. Peter's long years of camp life during the military campaigns and the construction of St Petersburg did not allow him to maintain the usual forms of court music-making, which demanded settlement first of all. What those years did contribute was the collection of silver trumpets used in the court and probably taken as trophies along with the 279 Swedish musicians captured in the battle of Poltava in 1709.[2]

Only after establishing *his own* new capital, St Petersburg, did he begin to create a court and its milieu and to develop modern forms of social life. His orders regarding the tutoring of musicians and forming of orchestras were followed by directives strictly obliging the nobility to serve as an audience for the concerts; disobedience could lead to exile from the capital. Enforced participation in aristocratic entertainments continued throughout the first half of the eighteenth century (Stolpyansky 1989:5–8). This eventually turned into a habit and way of life, strengthened by the development of domestic music–making. In the course of time this practice of concert-going became an integral part of court social life, and the process continued throughout the nineteenth and twentieth centuries among the mixed-caste intelligentsia, becoming a sign of *bon ton* among the St Petersburg population.The course of development established by Peter I continued throughout the eighteenth century but it is a little difficult to assess his true achievements in the field of musical culture. The genre most indicative of a "level of Europization" was opera, and Peter did not establish opera as an institution, though he would have probably considered it to be a suitable European genre for his country. Had Peter lived for another few years, he would perhaps have been given credit for installing the Italian opera and other forms of concert life, with all their relevant institutions. Opera would then have been associated with his name and the grand scale of his reforms. But this only occurred somewhat later, after his death in 1725.

What Peter I did succeed in was to establish the public forms of secular life, for which the nobility perceived music as one of its principal elements. St Petersburg became firmly placed on the map of the European musical market. The stream of German and other European musicians into Russia became so notable that it was little wonder that in 1726, J.S. Bach also contemplated such a possibility[3] (Pantielev, 1983:74–6). Coincidentally or not, in the same year, 1726, the nineteen-year-old Leonhard Euler accepted an invitation from the St Petersburg Academy of Sciences and in May 1727 he started his work there on physiology as a junior scientific

---

2   The collection is housed in the GMMK, Moscow.

3   Georg Erdmann (1682–1736), with whom Bach studied from 1698–9 at the Ordruf lyceum, after which both moved to Lüneburg, was accepted into the service of the Russian court in 1714 and worked as the Court Counsellor and resident in Danzig (Poland). Erdmann enjoyed the patronage of Prince Anikita Ivanovich Repnin (1668–1726), General Field-marshal and Peter's comrade-in-arms. On 26 July 1726 Bach wrote to Erdmann asking about a possible position at the Russian court. Erdmann's reply is not known.

Figure 3.1   Leonhard Euler (1707–83), St Petersburg, 1768

assistant. This great multidisciplinary scholar whose spectrum included mathematics, mechanics, astronomy, geography, physics and music, lived in Russia from 1727–40 and again from 1766–83, working for Frederick II (the Great) in between. His musical-theoretical works were not numerous but they were fundamental, and most of them were published in Russia. They include *Tentamen novae theoriae musicae, ex certissimis harmoniae principiis dilucidae expositae* (1739) and *De harmoniae veris principiis per speculum musicum repraesentatis* (1773) (Gertsman MPES, III:293–8). Considering that in 1729 the Russian court had made an (unsuccessful) effort to invite George Telemann, one must conclude that a small but firm ground for European-type court music already existed in Russia.

Empress Anna – Pro-Italian

Peter's immediate successors continued his policy in musical entertainment, but his niece Anna Ioannovna (1693–1740), reigning from 1730–40, in addition to the established German tradition of instrumental music also solidly initiated the Italianating of Russian court music, which was continued by all the following eighteenth-century Russian rulers. Empress Anna is unfortunately associated in Russian history with the Kurliandian Count Ernst Johann Biron (1690–1772), effectively the true ruler at the time – in a period of cynical and aggressive corruption known as *bironovshchina*. Historiographically this has cast something of a shadow over everything Anna accomplished. An objective overview of this period in relation to the development of Russian musical culture is thus both necessary and informative.

The 1730s was the decade when the Italian *commedia dell'arte*, musical interlude, ballet, *opera seria* and Italian musicians, along with other theatre specialists, were invited to St Petersburg. At first, Russian diplomats borrowed them from the courts of Saxony and Germany but later also from Italy itself. A precedent for Russian musicians being sent abroad for study was established. The first such was the Ukrainian *bandurist* Timofey Belogradsky, in the service of Count Keyserling, the Russian ambassador in Saxony. Belogradsky was sent to Dresden in 1733 to study the lute with Silvius Weiss. At around the same time kapellmeister Reinhardt Keiser arrived from Hamburg; violinists Giovanni Verocai and Bindi and cellist Gasparo Janeschi were sent by the Polish King Augustus II and contrabassist Eisel arrived from Bohemia. Noted virtuosi such as the cellist Giovanni Piantanida and violinists Luigi Madonis and Pietro Mira arrived with a group of players, probably headed by the eminent Harlequin Antonio Sacco. In 1734, Mira was sent to Italy to engage the best possible Italian opera cast. After unsuccessful attempts to court Nicola Porpora, Mira's mission resulted in an invitation to Francesco Araja, who became the first Italian kapellmeister at the Russian court, the composer of the first Italian opera seen by the St Petersburg public and, later, of the first opera with a Russian text.

By the time of Pietro Mira's mission, Araja's reputation in Italy was already evident. His *Il Cleomene*, staged in Rome in 1731, was a sensational success. From 1730 to 1735 his oratories and operas were being produced in Rome, Venice and Milan. In summer 1735 Araja arrived in St Petersburg with the large Italian Company, consisting of first-rate singers (Caterina and Filippo Giorgi, Caterina Mazani, Pietro

Figure 3.2   Francesco Araja (1709 – after 1775), portrait by unknown artist

Morigi, Domenico Cricchi, and others), eleven comedians, dancers, painters, producers and set builders. Together with other musicians who were already serving in the Russian court, the Italian Company gave the composer the freedom to pursue fascinating theatrical ideas. As court kapellmeister, Araja was required to produce operas for the major Imperial ceremonies. During Anna Ioannovna's rule, spectacles were produced not only for her birthdays but sometimes also for the anniversaries of her coronation. New intermezzi were also commanded for every Friday at the Court Theatre; ballets too were often requested. The same epoch saw the introduction of the custom of embellishing as many events as possible with Italian music, from commemoration days (usually cantatas) to the regular entertainments and formal receptions given on Thursdays and Sundays and accompanied by chamber vocal and instrumental music.

Following the model of European courts, Italian opera became a centre of Russian court musical life. Budget, manpower, aesthetics, education, architecture, ballet – everything revolved around the opera theatre and subsequently established a structure of main art–music institutions. It is thus hardly surprising that Russian opera, the pride of national culture, counts its beginnings from Araja's opera *La forza dell'amore e dell'odio*, originally composed for Milan (1734) and staged in St Petersburg in 1736. The only Russian thing about this opera, however, was the fact that the production had been commissioned by Russians for a Russian audience. All 'the rest' was Italian: music, text and performers. Over the course of the eighteenth century Russia began to develop its national opera, subsequently Russifying all these components. However, just as it did in other European countries, local musical theatre advanced here too in the direction of comic opera, never rivalling the Italians in the genre of *opera seria*. It was not until exactly a century later, in 1836, that the first Russian national serious opera, Glinka's *A Life for the Tsar*, was written.

The appearance of an Italian cast at the court of Empress Anna Ioannovna has been traditionally perceived as pure extravagance on her part, something exotic and irrational, not conforming to any Russian cultural background of the time. Indeed, it must have looked undeniably funny and clumsy, this presentation of a traditional Italian spectacle, for the local courtiers at the time had indeed little more than a vague idea of European secular music. Undoubtedly, any implantation of a cross–cultural experience always feels artificial at first, but the fact does not lessen its stimulating significance. Moreover, both Germany and France – the main influences defining eighteenth-century Russian culture – were themselves quite Italianated by that time and, thus, indirectly affected Russian music too.

Music in Russia would in any case have developed in its own way, but we would have known much less about its development if, in the same year as Araja's arrival, Jacob von Stählin (1709–85) would not have also arrived in St Petersburg. A student of the humanities at Leipzig University from 1732, he had also learned engraving and music. He played the flute and could conduct an ensemble. Stählin participated in the *Collegium musicum* concerts led by J.S. Bach and was a friend of Bach's sons. In 1735 he obtained the position of junior assistant in eloquence and poetry studies at the St Petersburg Academy of Sciences and in 1737 became a professor. His record, in addition to his academic work and teaching, includes the position of inspector at an engraving workshop (from 1738); chair of the Artistic Department of the Academy (from 1747); librarian and tutor to Grand Duke Peter Fedorovich (1744–62); manager of court fêtes and fireworks, composer of odes and translator of

Figure 3.3   Jacob von Stählin (1712–85), St Petersburg

libretti (1738–76); and honourable member of the Madrid and London Academies, Göttingen Institute of History and Leipzig Society of Free Sciences.

Stählin's name has been preserved in history due to his writings on various subjects, in which music had a respectable place. He was music correspondent for the newspaper *St Petersburg Vedomosti*, author of the first Russian column (in 1738) popularizing the art of opera (printed twice weekly over four months, timed to the production of Araja's spectacles); and author of the first book on the musical history of Russia (1770), from which our knowledge of the time primarily originates.

Stählin was a witness and participant at every ceremony or event associated with music, he socialized among court, academic, literary, art and music circles, knowing and consulting all and sundry on many topics. The information he provided may occasionally be erroneous or incomplete regarding dates or names in connection with those events that he had not witnessed himself, but most of it is highly accurate and important. Presented from a global view, it comprises a multitude of details skilfully organized into a comprehensive and easily-readable whole. The scholar continued his record right up to his death in 1783, but only part of it, completed in 1769, has been published and is known. It contains essays on the history of the theatre and the arts of dance, ballet and music in Russia (*Zur Geschichte des Theaters in Russland; Nachrichten von der Tanzkunst und Balletten in Russland; Nachrichten von der Musik in Russland*).[4] The rest of the material exists in catastrophically unreadable microscopic Gothic German handwriting. Had his Essays been translated into Russian not in 1935, but, say, in 1835 or 1885 – Russian historiography might well have been different.

During the same period, Empress Anna also realized several highly important projects in the foundation of national music institutions. These included the establishment of music printing at the Academy of Sciences Printing Press, invitations to famous Italian musicians to play with the Court Orchestra, construction of the Opera House at the Winter Palace (a project by the Italian architect Bartolomeo Rastrelli), installation of an organ in St Petersburg's Lutheran St Peter Cathedral (1737) and others.

Her most significant project, however, was the School for Court Singers, opened in 1738 and providing the Imperial court with child singers and musicians, because at that time neither St Petersburg nor even Moscow had an educational framework for professional musicians. The Ukraine still remained the main source for training specialists in *partes*-singing and instruments. 'Everything sings, plays and dances in this land. The most widespread instrument is the *bandura*, with which skilful

---

4   Stählin's 'Nachrichten von der Musik in Russland' were originally published by the historian August Ludwig Schlözer (1735–1809) under the pseudonym Magister Johann Joseph Haigold in: *Beilagen zum Neuveranderten Russland*, Riga-Mietau, 1769. The edition was reprinted in 1982 as a facsimile, with research, commentaries and index written by Ernst Stöckl (Leipzig: Edition Peters). There are three Russian translations: two published in 1935 in Moscow (Livanova ed.) and in Leningrad (Asafiev ed.), and a new one, by the leading specialist in Stählin – Konstantin Malinovsky (Moscow: Iskusstvo, 1990).

Ukrainians play the finest Polish and Ukrainian dances and accompany their numerous and quite gentle songs,' noted Stählin (1769, 1982:72). The school was founded in the town of Glukhov, the then residence of the Ukrainian Hetman.[5] Enlarging and improving the old Imperial Choir became of special concern and pride to the eighteenth-century tsars. Throughout the middle of the eighteenth century, when the desire for contemporary European sound preceded any real possibility of achieving it, the huge reverberation provided by a large and magnificent choir not only compensated for a lack of instruments, but also lent a special grandeur and sanctity to the whole atmosphere of the Imperial court. Singers, primarily trained in the performance of Russian spiritual music, were also taught contemporary Italian music, and it was from this choir that the first Russian professional composers were to come. Court Choir singers were widely used in ensembles for everyday court entertainment and in opera productions. If choruses in Italian *opera seria* were normally performed by a modest ensemble of soloists, then the St Petersburg court custom brought the entire choir onto the scene. The expanded role of the choir, constituting a kind of oratorical bias within an opera spectacle, became traditional for St Petersburg grand opera and was to influence even the nineteenth-century style of classical Russian opera (Porfirieva, MPES, I:59).

This serious development of native musical life made Araja's endeavours highly welcome and enthusiastically accepted by increasingly wider circles of the Russian public. During Anna's reign, however, Araja produced only three operas. In addition to *La forza dell'amore e dell'odio*, with which he debuted in 1736 and repeated on 30 April 1737, he also wrote *Il Finto Nino, overo La Semiramide riconosciuta* (29 January 1737 specially for St Petersburg). His third production was *Artaserse* (30 April 1737 and 29 January 1738). By the year 1739 grandiose spectacles had vanished from the scene, probably marking the decline in court entertainments followed by Empress Anna's death and the so-called 'period of *coups d'états*'. During this period, 1740–41, Araja was sent to Italy to engage new musicians for the Russian court. The period of uncertainty ended when Peter's daughter Elizaveta Petrovna (Elizabeth) ascended the throne on 25 November 1741 and Araja was reassured that his new musicians would be highly in demand.

The successful development of Italianate music-making would have remained within the narrow court sphere if not for the development of Russian popular music, which bridged between the court, the wider aristocracy and urban society. The first five years of Araja's service in Russia were the five last years of Anna's reign, and a time when the most important process in Russian musical life was taking place. This was the significant Europization of the musical environment, which expressed itself in the 'minuetization' of *kanty*. Three-voice singing of *kanty* remained traditional, but whenever there was a three-beat metre, the inner rhythmical division became

---

5   Hetman (Polish from the German *Hauptmann* – chief) was the position appointed by the Russian tsars from 1648–1764 (with intervals) of Russian governor-general in *Malorossia* (Little Russia, the Imperial denomination of the Ukraine from the mid-seventeenth century until 1917).

increasingly reminiscent of the minuet. The process was inspired by the development of lyrical poetry in Russian *belle lettres*, which not only stimulated the appearance of a new style in popular music but also influenced the style of courtly behaviour, adding an elegance and graciousness (Example 3.2).

The development of popular music was usually connected with the developing technology and commerce, as exemplified by the inauguration of the printing press at the Academy of Sciences in St Petersburg (1727). One of its first examples of 'mass' production was a Russian translation of Paul Tallement's book *Le Voyage à l'île de l'amore à Lycidas*, 1663 et 1713 (1730, commissioned from Vasily Trediakovsky by Prince A.B. Kurakin). Attached to the book was a sheet of music (large format, 41.5 × 32 cm) and on it was printed the kant: Pesn' sochinennaya v Gamburge k torzhestvennomu prazdnovaniu koronatsii Ee Velichestva Gosudaryni Imperatritsy Anny Ioannovny, samoderzhitsy Vserossiyskoy, byvshemy tamo avgusta 10, 1730 [The Song Composed in Hamburg for the Coronation Festival of Her Majesty the Sovereign Empress Anna Ioannovna, Autocrat of all Russia, which Took Place on 10 August 1730].

This early attempt to promote popular music would not have succeeded without a patron and additional support. Trediakovsky probably had good reason to attempt the commercial production of this official piece. There were already many official *kanty* associated with Tsar Peter I and the various historical-political events, which

Example 3.2   Kant *Ah, svet moy gorky*, **anonymous (eighteenth century)**

were later depicted in manuscript collections.[6] Moreover, Trediakovsky was already a popular poet. After spending some years in Paris he had introduced Russia to a new style of poetry, one flavoured with eroticism and noticeably more refined and flexible in rhymes, and which found an immediate setting in *kanty*. But the rigid hand of autocracy came down hard. Trediakovsky had problems with the censor of the Secret Chancellery for his spelling of 'Imperatrice' as 'Imperatrix'. All the copies were collected and destroyed (Volman, 1957:27).

One person who did enjoy unclouded success was Ernst Biron, a favourite of Anna Ioannovna. Biron published *Aria or Minuet* (1734) as a gift from his four-year-old son Carl Ernst to the Empress on the anniversary of her coronation. The sheet is full of signs of the new period, and their combination provides telling evidence. The music itself is a typical two-voice minuet of the time in a baroque clavier style. The engraver seems to have lacked experience, because all the stems are formed from the right side of the note whether up or down. The text is in German and Russian. The margins of the sheet are richly decorated with both imperial and musical symbols. Along with trumpets and horns one can see an organ, which perhaps suited the ceremonial character of the event but clearly contradicted the genre of the minuet. The explanation for this probably lies in the excitement caused by the first grand organ ordered for St Peter's Church in St Petersburg, and which was then in the process of being assembled (it was installed in 1737).

The appearance of the minuet constituted a turning point in eighteenth-century Russian music, very much like the introduction of the *kant* in the seventeenth century. The *kant*, however, with its canzone-like style, was new only to Russia; in the European context it was already out of date. Nonetheless it narrowed the gap between Russia and Western Europe. In contrast, the minuet linked the Russian musical environment directly with contemporary European music. This precedent opened the way for the powerful impact of the new idiom in the Russian court, estate and urban soundscape. It also confirmed the association between *popular*, *modern* and *coming from the West*, a western *Other*, strongly appealing to the adventurous spirit of rebuilding Russia, and remaining of prime significance for Russian popular culture up to the present time.

Araja in the 1740s

Starting his work in Russia in Anna Ioannovna's epoch, Araja, however, spent much more time accompanying Empress Elizabeth's (1709–61) rule that lasted from 1741–61. This Empress contributed much to the development of all the fine arts in Russia in general and music in particular. Well-educated, supported by enlightened favourites and with a taste for European styles, she, unlike her father, was very fond of Italian and French music. Among her major concerns was that of music and

---

6   The tradition of domestic performance of songs with such content remained alive throughout the long nineteenth century; even the 1950s witnessed the singing of political-slogan songs, for example 'Moskva-Pekin' [Moscow-Peking], composed by the official ode writer Vano Muradeli.

musicians and especially of Italian instrumental and vocal music. One of her first commands was to introduce regular Wednesday performances of various kinds of music, including Italian.[7]

Araja's return to Russia in 1742 with a superb team, including the castrati Lorenzo Saletti and Carlo Farinelli, violinists Tito Porta, Giuseppe Passarini and Angelo Vocari, poet Giuseppe Bonechi and theatrical painter-perspectivist Giuseppe Valeriani, was timed for the preparation of Elizabeth's grand ceremonial coronation in Moscow. The highest standard for court musical entertainments had now been established, and Araja was eminently suited to the task. He was fully occupied with operas, cantatas, numerous court spectacles and shows, musical fêtes and all kinds of chamber music for court festivities and pleasures. His opera productions, restarted in 1744 with *Seleuco* (Moscow), continued in 1745 with the particularly representative spectacle *Scipione* (for the marriage of Grand Duke Peter Fedorovich to Sophie Friederike Auguste Prinzessin von Anhalt-Zerbst, future Empress Catherine the Great), and went on to *Mitridate* (1747), *L'asilo della pace* (1748), *Bellerofonte* (1750), *Eudossa incoronata, o sia Teodosio* (1751) and other productions. Normally every year was marked by a new Araja's opera.

While Araja was proceeding with his Italian Augustan entertainment, three notable figures of the time, Gregory Teplov, Count Kirill Razumovsky (through his Cappella) and Count Semen Kirillovich Naryshkin (through his kapellmeister Jan Maresh), all in the early 1750s, each contributed in his own way a great deal to the process that had matured in the 1740s, and dramatically galvanized the *Other*'s idiom into becoming *Ours*.

Gregory Teplov and Russian Song

The two decades following Biron's *Aria et Minuet* (1734) constituted the period of 'minuetization' and 'erotization' of popular vocal music in Russian society, more specifically in high society. By the early 1750s the new rhythms had become highly popular, as follows from the publication of a collection of songs entitled *Mezhdu delom bezdel'e* [Idleness Midst Labor or Collection of Various Songs with tunes attached for three voices/music by G.T.],[8] a well-researched compilation whose songs established the new style of the sentimental gallant *lied*/romance (Swan, 1973; Brown, 1983; Mazo, 1987). The significance of this collection for the development of the Russian idiom is, nonetheless, not obvious at first glance.

The non-Russian reader might be amused to see that the edition contained songs very much in the tradition of contemporary French, German and English collections. Levasheva points to such possible models as 'Recueils d'airs serieux et à boire' published by J.B.C. Ballard in the first half of the eighteenth century, 'Singende Muse an der Pleisse' by Sperontes, 'Augsburger Tafelconfect' (1733–37), 'Berlinische Ode und Lieder (1756–63), 'Musicalische Zeitvertrieb' (1743–51) and

---

7   RGIA, f 466, op 1, no 81, L 50.

8   This translation of the title is borrowed from Brown (1982); there are others, however, such as that offered by A. Swan as 'Between Work a Bit of Leisure' (1973:54–5).

others (1984:196–7). The tunes are typically European arias in dance rhythms of the *tambourin* (see Example 3.3), *siciliana, minuet, branle, rigaudon, courante, sarabande* and *rondeur*. Sometimes the composer has written 'Minuet' or 'Siciliana' in the left margin as an instruction in regard to tempo or type of movement. This led their first researcher, Findeizen, to the conclusion that the minuet and siciliana predominated in the collection and in all the Russian songs/romances that followed it (1929:II, 287–8). More than a third of the songs are indeed in three-quarter beat, although in some cases their rhythm is closer to the sarabande or chaconne. What is of real importance, however, is that these terms indicating fashionable genres could have actually been meant to serve as an additional element to attract them to the public.

The author of the above-mentioned collection, hidden behind the initials G.T., was well known – Gregory Nikolaevich Teplov (1711, in some sources 1717, to 1779). One might have imagined the songwriter to be a bohemian-type poet strolling about the court, but the man familiar from the portrait painted by the finest court painter of the time, Dmitry Levitsky, appears otherwise. Teplov, indeed a high official and senator, was the illegitimate son of Pheophan Prokopovich, (1681–1736, a remarkable cultural figure of Petrine times and the possible author of *The Lay of Igor's Host*).[9] He had received a refined education abroad in the mid–1730s, and was recognized as a scholar, writer and musician (fine violinist, highly trained singer, clavecinist and conductor) contributing much to Russian culture in the Elizabethan and Catherinian periods. He was also tutor to Count Kirill Grigorievich Razumovsky, who was the brother of Alexey Grigorievich (Elizabeth's favourite and/or secret husband) and the father of Andrey Kirillovich Razumovsky, well known in the West from the biographies of Haydn, Mozart and Beethoven.

Example 3.3   **Rossiyskaya pesnya** *Dlya tovo l'ya v dni razluki* **from the Teplov's Collection** *Mezhdu delom bezdelie*

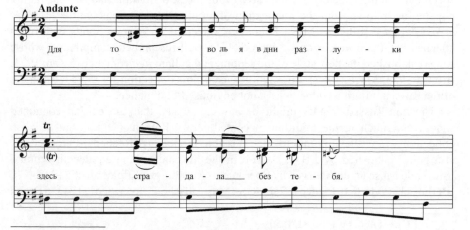

---

9   See Tatiana Fefer, 'Did the 'Heretic' Feofan Prokopovič Write the Slovo o Polku Igoreve?' in *Russian Literature* XLIV, 1998:41–115.

The use of initials rather than his full name was not intended to hide Teplov's identity, for otherwise he would have used a pseudonym or anonym as he did in his literary polemical discourses. Everybody who was supposed to know – knew, for high society was composed of a relatively small number of people. The use of initials was mandated by the social codex, according to which a professional occupation with music was incompatible with high rank or noble title.

Considering that the volume consists exclusively of love songs, this publication was a clear and logical embodiment of Teplov's aesthetic ideas. In 1755 the academic journal *Monthly Works* anonymously published his 'Thoughts on the Beginnings of Poetry', in which – following the trend of contemporaneous ideas on the origins of music[10] – the author argues that the amorous song reflects the earliest kind of poetic creative work, serving as a source for all other forms of 'educated' poetry:

> One has to give respect to the passion of love as more enrooted in humankind than any other... It inspired the language of love, which, combined with singing, reduced the significance of the words... This seems to be the origin of poetry by nature, which afterwards gained its importance among enlightened people.[11]

In Teplov's collection the lyrics were anonymous. Again, however, interested parties were aware of the authorship because such poems were already circulating in handwritten copies, sometimes with tunes attached in the oral tradition or – more often – without tunes.[12] Among the authors were aristocratic writers constituting the cream of the court's intellectual milieu. These included, first and foremost, the poet Alexander Petrovich Sumarokov (1717–77), who dramatically modernized Russian literary language, introduced classicist norms into poetry and drama and elevated song-poetry to high classicism, thus sharing Teplov's aesthetic approach. Another writer of note was Ivan Perfilievich Yelagin (1725–93), member of a noble-military family, a state and public figure and an inexhaustible Freemason functionary; there were few social activities in which he did not involve himself. The third probable composer of some of the songs in Teplov's collection was the youngest, Nikita Afanasievich Beketov (1729–94), also of noble origin, a handsome court dandy and a constant participant in poetry gatherings among the aristocratic youth (Stepanov, SRP, 1988:75). Caught

---

10 See Francesco Algarotti's Essay on Opera (1755); John Brown's Dissertation on the Rise, Union, and Power, the Progressions, Separations, and Corruptions, of Poetry and Music (1763) and Rousseau's Essai sur l'origine des langues (1781) in Enrico Fubini, *Music and Culture in Eighteenth–Century Europe. A source book.* Chicago: The University of Chicago Press, 1994:235, 161–9 and 92–3.

11 'Почитать следует страсть любовную больше вкорененну в род человеческий, нежели многие другие страсти... Она родила любовные речи, которые, когда соединялись с голосным пением, произвели падение слов... Сие мнится быть происхождение от начала стихотворства в натуре своей, которая после обратилась в великую важность между учеными людьми' (quoted by Keldysh, 1984:68).

12 The tradition of handwritten copying of poetry and song lyrics is very strong in Russia. 'Copy the words!' – the expression still exists as a Russian colloquialism.

up in court intrigues as the Empress's supposed favourite, Beketov's court career was ruined and he was forced to quit the social scene of the capital.

Teplov, Sumarokov and Yelagin all belonged to the same stratum of eighteenth-century Russian intellectuals whose classical cultural background, refreshed by the Petrine spirit of building the new Russia, inspired their lifestyle as passionate idealists striving for the universal good, which became a fundamental facet of Russian social consciousness. This elite group even belonged to the same social milieu. Young Yelagin had worked for some years in the office of the Life-Guardian Department under the supervision of Sumarokov and helped him in publishing his tragedies. His sincere admiration for his spiritual mentor did not prevent him however from publicly criticizing some of Sumarokov's ideas on cultural policy; this was a polemic that in fact expressed the struggle between the pro-German and pro-French influences in the Russian national consciousness, and one that involved almost the entire literary establishment of St Petersburg in the 1750s.

Yelagin replaced Sumarokov after the latter's resignation from his post as director of the court theatres. Teplov and Yelagin were also strongly connected in the late 1750s by their mutual closeness to the heir to the throne, Grand Duke Peter Fedorovich. Both were skilfully and effectively manipulated by his wife, Grand Duchess Ekaterina Alexeevna, who later became Empress Catherine the Great, not without their collaboration. Teplov, Sumarokov and Yelagin were key figures (among others) in the cultural milieu of Berezovsky and Bortniansky. Their names will appear often in the following chapters.

The eighteenth-century reader of the Russian newspaper *Sankt-Peterburgskie vedomosti* would have read an advertisement on 20 August 1759 that an edition of Teplov's collection had been published by the Academy of Sciences as a second printing, that its price was three roubles and that it could be purchased in Moscow as well (Findeizen, 1929:II, 282–3). There is much to be learned from this announcement. The fact that it was a second printing raises questions about the first one.[13] Stählin mentioned the first edition as appearing, among other events, 'at some time' after the Grand Duke's wedding in 1745, (1769, 1982:100–01), allowing us to relate it to the late 1740s. Volman considered that the first edition could have appeared no earlier than 1751 since documents dated to that time and preserved in the Academy of Sciences made no mention of this edition (1957:42). One can safely establish the time of the first edition, therefore as *c*. 1750.

The appearance of the second edition of the collection suggests that it had been a commercial success that the publisher wanted to exploit further. The reprint of Teplov's collection does not appear to have sold well however. Three years later, in 1762, there was a new advertisement for the same edition, with its price reduced to two and a half roubles (Findeizen, 1929:II, 283). Although the peak of its popularity

---

13 N.A. Ogarkova, ignoring both the note about a new print of the songbook in the newspaper announcement as documental evidence and indirect information from Stählin, therefore questions the existence of an edition earlier than 1759 (MPES, III:149–150).

Figure 3.4   Gregory Teplov (1717–1779) Portrait by D. Levitsky, oil

seems to have passed by then, a third edition was published in 1776 (45 copies, probably not for profit, since it was not advertised).

The special significance of the collection is reflected in the reprinting of its songs (with the same innocent piracy characteristic of the time and place that Teplov himself practised) partly or fully throughout the entire second half of the eighteenth century. Every new appearance demonstrated a widening circle of consumers: from the narrow high society in St Petersburg of the 1750s to the broad urban population of the entire country at the end of the century.

Kirill Razumovsky and Russian Opera

A certain wave of mode *à la russe* can be traced in the 1730s–40s. In 1731 Reinhardt Keiser visited Russia, where he composed *Russian songs with variations* for two violins and bass. Two Italian violinists and composers who had been working in Russia since 1735 – Domenico Dall'Oglio and Luigi Madonis – later continued the trend. The former wrote *Sinfonie alla Russa* and the latter – a pair of sonatas on Ukrainian themes. Even the court balletmaster Fusano composed contradances on Russian tunes for court balls and an 'Italian Russian' ballet. None of these pieces are known today and it is impossible at present to determine their exact dates. The existence of Dall'Oglio's and Madonis's works is only known from Stählin's having mentioned them together, emphasizing their enthusiastic reception, in relation to the late 1740s (1769, 1982:100).

In this context Teplov's songbook might be seen in another light: not 'Russian lyrics with *European-like* tunes' but '*Russian lyrics* with European-like tunes' – with the emphasis on the nationalistic aspect. This seems to be precisely what Stählin had in mind when describing this edition in connection with the compositions on Russian/ Ukrainian themes. Moreover, this was followed by a paragraph describing the private cappella of Count Kirill Razumovsky (created with Teplov's participation), which eventually led to the 'Russian' opera by Araja.

During the 1750s, the hetman of the Ukraine, Count Kirill Grigorievich Razumovsky, was one of Russia's most influential and wealthy figures, a man of European education, and president of the Academy of Sciences. His taste in music, although nurtured by an innate love, was conveniently in accordance with court fashion. In 1751, following the edict creating the post of hetmanship, he left for *Malorossia* accompanied by his inseparable escort Teplov, numerous carriages, saddled horses, cooks and musicians, by *haiducs* and footmen, by sergeants of the Ismail regiment and even a troupe of actors. He also had with him Andrey Andreevich Rachinsky (1729–*c*. 1800), a professional precentor who had previously held a position in Lvov under Bishop Lev Meletsky and from 1753 had served as kapellmeister to Razumovsky's house capella. Banquets with instrumental music, balls and even French comedies were constant entertainments at the hetman's palace (Vasilchikov, 1869:487, 491).[14] Stählin, who gave Razumovsky's cappella a respectable place in his essay, noted that with the assistance of Teplov Count Razumovsky had provided his hetman's palace with a first-rate private choir and some forty extremely skilled chamber musicians (mostly Russians and a few foreigners). In 1753, when this choir made its first appearance in Moscow at the hetman's house in front of a sizeable audience of courtiers and other notables, it was a deserved success. Describing the choir, Stählin in particular mentioned one young Ukrainian singer Gavrila [Marcinkevich] who could sing the most difficult Italian operatic arias with the most sophisticated cadenzas and refined embellishments. Gavrila was often in demand at the Court, together with the usual musical accompaniment provided for the regular receptions (*kurtagi*), and he acquired complete and constant success. Together with others of his compatriots, almost his equals in singing, they served as an incentive for the Empress's venture. She ordered the staging of a full-scale opera in Russian, which, known for its softness, many vowels and its own euphony, is closer to Italian than other European languages and suits singing very well. The poet and then colonel Alexander Petrovich Sumarokov, from whom the new opera was commissioned, chose Ovid's story of Cephalus and Procris. Araja, to whom this felicitous opera was explained word by word, successfully set it to music, according to all the passions and tender expressions, despite the fact that he did not understand Russian[15] (Stählin, 1769, 1982:101–03).

It was staged and repeated several times with complete success, in honour of the Empress who had initiated the idea of this 'singspiel', and for her special pleasure. Its music was light and tender, as can be seen from Tsefal's aria, which is similar to the siciliane from Teplov's collection (Example 3.4); and the singers, of whom the oldest could have hardly been more than fourteen: Mlle Belogradskaya, Gavrila Marcinkevich (called 'Gavrilushka'), Nikolai Klutarev, Stepan Rashevsky and Stepan Evstafiev – attracted great sympathy. The audience and connoisseurs marvelled at the articulate pronunciation, fine performance of long arias and skilful cadenzas of these young as well as inexperienced opera singers, not to mention their natural, unexaggerated and extremely appropriate gestures. At the end of this 'singspiel', the Empress, the entire court and the overcrowded pit applauded enthusiastically. Further expression of approval was given a few days later when all

---

14 Later on, at the beginning of the 1760s, or possibly earlier, Razumovsky retained Franz Kerzelli (brother of Joseph Kerzelli) as his choir conductor; Kerzelli, who came from Vienna with his sons, also musicians, played a significant part in Moscow's musical life in the last third of the eighteenth century.

15 Appreciating Araja's music, but seemingly unaware of *opera seria* rhetoric, Sumarokov wrote some admiring verses, published in the journal *Ezhemesyachnye sochinenia* [Monthly works], March, 1756: 'Арайя изъяснил любовны в драме страсти / И общи с Прокрисой Цефаловы напасти / Так сильно, будто бы язык он Руской знал / Иль паче, будто сам их горестью стенал.' [Araja narrated love passion / And the sorrows shared by Prokris and Tsefal in drama / So powerfully as if he knew Russian / Or even as if he himself had experienced this bitterness.] Cited by Kryukov, MPES, III:111.

Figure 3.5　　Tobacco box made in Imperial porcelain factory depicting music
　　　　　　　from Araja's *Tsefal i Prokris*, 1750s

Example 3.4   Araja: Tsefal's aria from the opera *Tsefal i Prokris*

the young opera singers were presented with beautiful fabric for new dresses, and kapellmeister Araja was given a valuable sable coat and 100 golden half–imperials (500 roubles) (Stählin, 1769, 1982:104).

Araja's *Tsefal i Prokris* [Cephalus and Procris] (1755) indeed deserves special mention as an important event in Russian music history. The event paralleled other

European aspirations to nationalize operatic and other Italian genres, usually inspired and in a large part performed by the Italians themselves. Considering the appearance of the above-mentioned 'Russian' instrumental works, in Russia this aspiration had clearly been preceded by the desire to attempt such an experiment.

Semen Naryshkin and Russian Horn Music

The 'minuetization' of popular music stimulated the use of instruments. By the late 1740s, many households interested in performing music had a contemporary keyboard instrument. The importation of instruments, and their later production in Russia itself from the late 1720s, increased with each decade in an attempt to keep up with consumption. In 1733 the court musician and bell master Johann Christian Förster advertised two *clavicembali* for sale in St Petersburg, but this was only the beginning of his successful business (Findeizen, 1929, II:30). Performances by virtuosi and salon music-making on various levels, along with the invention of new instruments or appendages to the old ones, became especially intensive in the 1740s. Music-making in circles close to the court was provided by instrumentalists from the court orchestra (mostly foreigners settled in St Petersburg), who also had pupils among the nobility as well as teaching their own children. Thus every professional musician constituted a microcosm of music-making.

The dissemination of European keyboard instruments in Russian society would probably have developed much faster, however, had it not been for the powerful influence of Ukrainian culture, with its widespread use of two string-pluck instruments, the *gusli* and the *bandura*. Although Stählin noted that in wealthy households over the course of the 1750s–60s these instruments were being replaced by the clavier, violin, traversflute, horn and a love of Italian music in general (1769, 1982:74), they still remained greatly popular. *Bandura* and *gusli*, looking and sounding much more familiar to the Russians, were sometimes a good substitute for the clavicembalo, enabling the playing of much of its repertoire. For instance, when Timofey Belogradsky, the Ukrainian singer, composer, *bandurist* and lute player (a virtuoso performer of concert repertoire) was appointed in 1739 to Imperial court service after studying in Dresden (the lute with S.L. Weiss and voice with Domenico Anniballi and Faustina Bordoni-Hasse), he replaced the clavicembalist Gertruda König (Findeizen, 1929:II, 25). Parallel with the main court musicians there were also the personal musicians of the future Empress Elizabeth, who, besides having her own cappella of eight musicians playing European instruments, also had four soloists: two *guslists* and two *bandurists* (Findeizen, 1929:II, 27). The last *Kammerguslist* at the Russian court, Vasily Trutovsky, was appointed in 1761, the year of Empress Elizabeth's death, and he then went on to serve Catherine II. *Gusli* continued to be widely used in the 1760s, during Catherine's rule, especially in *plein air* entertainments.

This spread of contemporary European music was naturally accompanied not only by the introduction of foreign instruments but also by an intake of foreign musicians. A foreign instrumentalist who had found a position in Russia, evidently

Figure 3.6   Russian horn band of the late eighteenth century

with better conditions than those prevailing in Central Europe at the time, was the most typical constructive element of eighteenth-century Russian musical culture. These musicians usually reproduced European forms of music-making, exactly as demanded by their employers. Sometimes they involved themselves in the adaptation of European forms to local realities, which in many ways were dramatically undeveloped compared to the West European tradition. The foreign musician was thus a key figure linking his employer with the majority of other performers, usually serfs, who comprised the bigger ensembles: opera casts, choirs and orchestras. Foreign kapellmeisters trained Russian musicians and created repertoires, produced the instruments and worked as music copyists, engravers, etc. in St Petersburg and in Moscow. They provided Russian musical culture with the infrastructure necessary for domestic music-making.

There are two main collections of the instruments used in eighteenth–century Russia. The Muscovite one (belonging to the State Museum of Musical Culture and until 1983 located in the sixteenth-century *palates* of boyar Troekurov, connected to the Kremlin by an underground passage) begins with the Petrine collection of silver trumpets mentioned earlier. The St Petersburg collection (now located in the palace of Count Sheremetev and belonging to the St Petersburg State Museum of Music and Theatre Arts) is dominated by the luxurious and exquisitely decorated keyboard instruments of the Catherine period, distinguished by the artistic richness of their wood and mother-of-pearl incrustations. Differing in every possible way, these two exhibitions reflect the dramatically divided poles of Russian culture as a whole. One, the Muscovite, opens the eighteenth century; the other, the St Petersburgian, closes it. Both collections however feature sets of unique Russian instruments, those of the *rogovoy orkestr* ('horn orchestra' or 'horn band').

The horn orchestra was invented by a Czech, Jan Maresh (Hoteshov, Czechia, 1719 – St Petersburg, 1794), who was a horn player, cellist and kapellmeister. Educated in Hoteshov, Drezden and Berlin, Maresh found work in Russia, where he had lived from 1748. He was employed in the private orchestras of Count Alexey Petrovich Bestuzhev and of Elizabeth's favourite Count Semen Kirillovich Naryshkin and also in the Imperial court orchestra. In 1751 Count Naryshkin, who loved both hunting and music and whose taste could not bear the cacophony produced by the sixteen horns of his huntsmen, ordered Maresh 'to accord all the horns of his hunters in harmony' (Vertkov, 1948:21). The industrious musician solved the problem and created a kind of ensemble whose potential appeared to realize the immediate aesthetic demands of Russian society, to its great delight, and lasted throughout the entire second half of the long eighteenth century. Ranging from the way the sound is produced to the repertoire itself, the horn orchestra displays all the complexity of Russian musical culture in the cross-section of its national, social and historical aspects.

Technically, the horn orchestra could be compared to the organ, with the principal difference being that the air enters the pipe not via some mechanical means but from human lungs. It consists of a maximum set of 91 pipes of sheet copper – in some cases several pipes for the same note in order to achieve a balance of sound – in the form of horns of various sizes (95 mm for the *d* of the third octave and 2250 mm

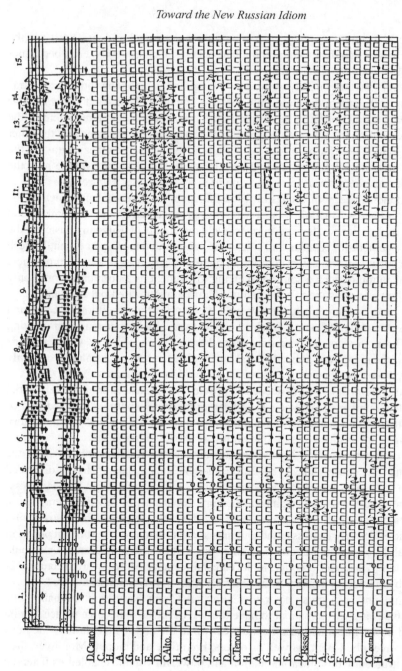

Figure 3.7   A score for horn band (with piano reduction) from J.C. Hinrichs, *Entstehung, Fortgang und jetztige Beschaffenheit der russischen Jagdmusik*, St Petersburg, 1796

for the *a* of the counter-octave), each one producing a sound of definite pitch in the chromatic scale extending to four and a half octaves. Consequently, each performer functions like one key of an organ.

There are two frequently reproduced engravings showing horn orchestras performing at the end of the eighteenth century. The horn players and *Kapellmeister* are dressed in what appear to be military uniforms. In one engraving some of the players are holding the score of their part in one hand and the instrument in the other hand; the longer, heavier horns are supported on stands. In the other engraving the scores lie on a diagonal stand, so that both hands of the player are free to hold the horn. Here, too, the heavier horns are supported by stands (see Figure 3.6).

The sound of the horn orchestra filled the spacious outdoor landscapes of the Russian court and aristocratic estates with its unprecedented timbre – a combination of power and delicacy. Its repertoire was characteristic of Russian music of the time: arrangements of Russian and Ukrainian songs and dances, pieces that Maresh himself or other kapellmeisters composed, popular overtures and even symphonies.

The invention of such a sound-producing instrument as a horn band could only have resulted as a substitute for something familiar and desired but unattainable. It could not have appeared in a country with a centuries-long tradition of court and urban music-making. If Count Naryshkin had had available trained musicians playing European brass instruments producing more than one pitch, or a good German-made organ, or if the manpower at his disposal had been more limited, he almost certainly would have been satisfied with a conventional outdoor brass band.

The large numbers of serfs needed to provide such music were paid very little, if at all. The number of participants in horn orchestras sometimes reached two or three hundred. The technology constantly improved and by the end of the century the playing of up to four notes on one horn was already possible.

Horn orchestras became highly popular among the Russian nobility until the 1830s, when the more widespread European-style music-making finally displaced them. The 1830s was the period associated with Glinka. Pre-Glinkian Russian music of 'the second half of the long eighteenth century' could aptly be called 'the era of horn music', not only because other genres were insufficiently developed, but also because horn music effectively expressed the longings and aspirations of the Russian public in its musical tastes within the musical framework that existed at that time. One could even say that *Naryshkin baroque* in seventeenth-century Moscow architecture was followed by eighteenth-century 'Naryshkin baroque' in Russian horn music.

It would not be a gross error to claim that Count Naryshkin, probably like others of his class, was impatient to have the sort of music in his own palace that he had heard at the Imperial court. In the meanwhile the happy invention of the horn orchestra saved the Count, as well as others, both time and money. Moreover, they had an instrument whose ideal intonation and powerful volume enabled its listeners to stroll at leisure around the landowners' large estates while continuing to enjoy the music. Serfdom indeed determined the development of horn bands: the players were mere serfs or soldiers, both of whom shared the same subservient position. The physical effort involved in horn orchestras was an exhausting one.

The spread of the horn orchestras in the 1750s–1760s provided only a temporary substitute for the symphony orchestra, but it gave the nobility, who loved music and the prestige derived from it equally, the necessary time for the training of musicians and acquisition of the required instruments and repertoires.

Horn music should be seen not just as a curious or strange amusement of the Russian aristocracy, but as a historically justified means to achieve aesthetic goals. The entire experience of the horn-music period, paradoxically combining pristine technology with advanced Central European-oriented tastes, suggests that Russia's aesthetic acceptance of the European style preceded its material and institutional possibilities. Understanding this aspect is instrumental in comprehending the essence of eighteenth-century Russian music processes.

The impression made by this sound was so exciting that it was enthusiastically remarked upon in the notes and memoirs of contemporaries of the period, including foreigners. Information about this music therefore, also reached European music lovers, initially through J.C. Hinrichs' book (1796 and facsimile, 1974; see also Seaman, 1959; Ricks, 1969:364–71; Zielinsky, 1917:59–69). It could be tentatively suggested that Johann Nepomuk Maelzel constructed his Panharmonicon, a gigantic organ-like instrument (1805), under the influence of Russian horn music. He could have been made aware of it from Count Andrey Razumovsky, who was residing in Vienna.[16]

Both the material culture and frequent mention of horn music in eighteenth-century documents speak for its enormous popularity and extremely wide audience. By the end of the long eighteenth century, however, discarded like the white wigs of the Catherinian grandees, horn music had lost not only its audience and prestige but also its place and reputation in Russian music history. Perhaps not entirely forgotten or erased, it was nonetheless minimized and marginalized, with a consequent neglect of its music material, which has been quite poorly preserved. The repertory of horn music, moreover, was not exceptionally innovative or stimulating and the material was clearly not original.

Finally, only Vertkov himself seemed to know how to decipher its peculiar notation. The phenomenon itself as a substitute for a desired but non-available sound may be compared to the twentieth-century Trinidad steel-pan bands. Both share the same type of repertoire: arrangements of light popular pieces; similar pitches produced per instrument – first one pitch, later more; untrained performers specializing only in this music; and even a similar kind of notation.[17]

---

16 This invention, among Maelzel's other creations and innovations, reflected the flourishing automaton production at the time, originating in contemporary France. (See Paul Metzner, *Crescendo of the Virtuoso: Spectacle, Skill, and Self-Promotion in Paris during the Age of Revolution*. Berkeley: University of California Press, 1998:183.)

17 See Tom Chatburn, 'Trinidad All Stars: The Steel Pan Movement in Britain', in *Black Music in Britain: Essays on the Afro-Asian Contribution to Popular Music*. Ed. Paul Oliver, Milton Keynes – Philadelphia: Open University Press, 1990:118–36.

Araja's Rise and Fall in the 1750s

The year 1755 was especially productive for Araja. In addition to *Tsefal i Prokris* he also wrote *Amor prigioniero* (1755) and *Alessandro nell'Indie* (1755, 1756, 1759). As one can see from the above list, he was intensively occupied until 1755, constantly collaborating with the Italian librettist Giuseppe Bonechi (or Bonecchi, in Russia from 1742–52) who enjoyed the patronage of both Araja and the Empress. The arrival of Giovanni Carestini in 1754 and his singing the role of Poro in *Alessandro nell'Indie* a year later, can only have added to Araja's prestige. In the same year, 1755, Grand Duke Peter Fedorovich completed construction of the Opera House and another stage was opened for Araja. On 16 June his theatrical dialogue based on Metastasio's text *Amor prigioniero* was played there, most probably as the inaugural performance. Nothing forecasted decline.

The climax of Araja's activity in 1755, however, seems to have been followed by enforced idleness. After that year, except for two reproductions of *Alessandro nell'Indie*, his name stopped appearing in connection with notable events. The explanation probably lies in unexpected changes on the Russian scene. In 1757, taking refuge from his creditors, Giovanni-Batista Locatelli signed a contract with the Russian court, which guaranteed a subsidy and indeed supported him until 1761.[18] The great success of his enterprise and the powerful impact of the opera *buffa* genre (reinforced by the dynamic flourishing of comedy in Russian theatre of the 1750s) captured the attention of the Court, not to mention the wider circles of Russian nobility in St Petersburg and Moscow. The Empress herself, incognito, used to attend every spectacle. The composer of most of the operas in Locatelli's repertoire was Baldassare Galuppi. For the Russian public this music was a marvellous revelation. From then on, the idea of hiring Galuppi as court kapellmeister haunted the Russian court, until they were finally able to do so in 1765.

Beaten by the genre of *opera buffa*, Araja also met an unexpected rival in his own field of *opera seria*. Russian national opera, which he had so successfully founded with *Tsefal i Prokris*, was usurped by Hermann Raupach (1728–78). This young German harpsichordist was appointed to the Court Orchestra in 1755, and it must have been a blow for Araja when, in 1758, the next Russian-language opera, *Altsesta* [Alceste], also with Sumarokov's libretto, was commissioned from Raupach, who had only recently made his debut as a composer. All these events of 1757–58 drew the Court's attention away from Araja, leaving him inactive and lacking support. His relations with Grand Duke Peter Fedorovich remained good, however, although the latter was not actually able to help Araja until he became Emperor, two and a half years later. Meanwhile, on 27 July 1759 Araja resigned. The thread that continued to link Araja with Russia was the young cellist Thomas Überscheer from the Young court of Grand Duke Peter Fedorovich, whom Araja had taken with him to study in Italy.

---

18 Documents concerning the hiring of the manager of the Italian comic opera, Locatelli, and his troupe into service in Russia can be found among documents concerning the diplomatic relations between Russia, Austria and the German Empire in RGADA, f 32.

Upon ascending the throne, Peter III restored the authoritative kapellmeister to his former position. Araja, however, had barely arrived for his reappointment on 28 May 1762, when on 5 July his patron was assassinated and a week later the new Empress, Catherine II, appointed Vincenzo Manfredini to compose the music for her coronation ceremonies. This time Araja truly had nothing left to wait for in Russia and quit its soil forever. His date of death is usually assumed to be *c.* 1770. However, the mention of his name as a living maestro by Manfredini in his treatise *Regole armoniche, o sieno Precetti ragionati* (1775) demands a re-examination of this assumption (Porfirieva, MPES, II:61).

Chapter 4

At the Court of Grand Duke
Peter Fedorovich

Grand Duke Peter Fedorovich (1728–62), son of Peter the Great's daughter Anna
and Karl Ulrich, Duke of Holstein-Gottorp, ascended the Russian throne after the
death of his aunt Elizabeth. Unpolished and brutal, he acquired a strong enemy in
his wife, Grand Duchess Ekaterina Alexeevna, the future Catherine the Great, who
was not prepared to either forget or forgive his endless humiliations. Planning the
coup against him, she successfully disseminated his image as that of an idiot, a
miscarriage of Russian history, to which his behaviour indeed contributed a great
deal. However, in truth he was a much more complex figure, initiating many positive
reforms including annulment of the Secret Chancellery.

Oriented on the taste and style of the Prussian court and tutored by Stählin, Peter
Fedorovich turned his estate at Oranienbaum (now Lomonosov) into a cultural
centre. Built by Peter I, Oranienbaum was one of the most beautiful of the palaces
and gardens. Its main architectural structure is the Grand Menshikov (Imperial)
Palace. A cool and shady English garden with an artificial brook winding through
the landscape complemented the scenery. Receiving the estate as a gift from his aunt
Elizabeth in 1744, the Grand Duke built the *Kamenny zal* [Stone Hall], also known
as *Kartinny dom* or *Kartinnaya palata* [The Picture Pavilion] and *Byvshy Operny
Dom* [Old Opera House]. The latter structure housed the theatre, which was called
the 'opera', as well as a collection of curiosities, the library and the picture gallery
with 400 canvases on display.

The Grand Duke was a passionate music lover and violinist. The eighteen-year
history of his court was filled with musical entertainments, of which, naturally,
Stählin was the closest participant and witness, giving a detailed account of them
in his chronicles. Another witness to the era was Gabriel Misere, who succeeded
Stählin as librarian, fireworks technician and medal collector, and so on (although
officially registered as a 'buffoon') and who remained constantly at the side of Peter
Fedorovich for the last eighteen months of the Grand Duke's life.[1] Peter Fedorovich's
contemporaries were divided in their opinion of his skills as a violinist. The Grand
Duchess, with an equally strong distaste for both her husband and violin music,
naturally regarded his performance as unbearable. Fully aware of her increasing

---

1   The contemporary Stählin scholar Konstantin Malinovsky stated (in conversation
with the author in April 2005) that Misere as a writer had never existed, and that this was a
pseudonym of Stählin. He came to this conclusion after comparing texts by the two.

annoyance, the Grand Duke missed no opportunity to upset his spouse and succeeded particularly well on one of her birthday celebrations, 21 April 1762, when he played the violin in concert for three hours without intermission, little suspecting that it was his last opportunity of this kind and that he had only two months left to enjoy his life.[2]

Stählin appreciated his pupil's sincere dedication to music and described him with diplomatic delicacy. He mentioned the Grand Duke's ability to easily fit into an orchestra or play ritornellos to Italian arias, and so on but also marked a notable incongruence between what his taste expected and what his hands produced, even on instruments made by the great Cremonians Amati and Steiner (of which he had a rare collection and whose cost often exceeded 500 roubles). The Italian musicians solved the problem with his intonation – by interrupting his wrong notes and crying 'Bravo, Your Grace, bravo!'

The Grand Duke held weekly concerts from four in the afternoon to nine in the evening. Among the performers that Stählin recollected were the Italian singers Maria Camati (nicknamed La Farinella) and Maria Monari, two German singers – Eleonore Brihan (or Brian) and Sophie Niederstedt, the Bolognian violinist Caselli and musicians from St Petersburg – the violinist Onezorg, traverso player Koster and young cellist Überscheer. Numerous Italian, Russian and German musicians serving at the Imperial court, as well as *castrati*, were also sometimes called upon to perform. His Royal Highness himself enjoyed acting as concertmaster for the entire concert, and in order to please him, court cavaliers, officers and other amateurs of various ranks (including such skilled musicians as Lev Alexandrovich Naryshkin, Adam Vasilyevich Olsufiev, Gregory Nikolaevich Teplov and Jacob Stählin himself) participated on the various instruments, bringing the number of performers up to 40 or 50 (Stählin, 1769, 1982:107–8; 1868:101).

In his diary Misere gives brief accounts of the musical events that featured regularly in the Grand Duke's everyday court life. His entries for January 1761 read as follows:

> 10. A grandiose dinner accompanied by music and cannonade. The garden and the big Palace were lit. After dinner there was pipe smoking with military music. The musicians were served during breaks.
>
> 13. A big table for lunch and dinner. Music in the evening. After dinner – pipe smoking at Prince Menshikov's.
>
> 14. Morning at the church. A huge lunch with court music. After lunch the Grand Duchess Catherine drove in the small sled. The Grand Duke visited the stables.
>
> 15. Morning hunt for wild fowl... A walk to the farm of the Grand Duchess Catherine for a superb lunch served by the obliging hostess. Before lunch, His Royal Highness and his entourage were in unusually high spirits. A ball [took place] in the small room, with no other music except the human voice, with a hat in hand instead of a violin and with a sword instead of a bow. In the evening, the Grand Duchess Catherine returned to Oranienbaum, where mountains of ice were piled up and everybody played *barry*... .

---

2 Gabriel Misere, 'Dnevnik', in *Russkii arkhiv*, 1911, no 2, kniga 5:15–16.

17. The usual evening reunion, concert and fireworks. After dinner, pipe smoking in Chamberlain B's quarters, and a few additional small fireworks.[3]

Opera productions also held a significant place at the court. The special Opera House – a wooden two-storey structure with an attic – was built in 1755. Its pit had 24 seats and the stage was fully equipped. The two levels of spectator boxes and most of the walls were covered with bleached canvas. Many of the boxes had painted ceilings, created between 1757 and 1761 by the Italian master Francesco Gradizzi.[4]

The sets at the Oranienbaum theatre, designed by the famous perspectivist painter Giuseppe Valeriani, grew in extravagance with each year. The troupe included an increasingly large number of performers and, typically for Russian culture of the time, was multinational. Most of the singers were Italian, the musicians were mostly German, and the ballet dancers (of whom there were approximately twenty-four) were Russian, with the exception of seven French and Italian soloists. Temporary players and singers were sometimes employed from among the pupils of the Cadet Corps, who received training in music and fine arts.

In order to provide future native performers (who were paid much less than their foreign counterparts), Peter Fedorovich founded a music school for the children of German soldiers of the Holstein regiment, which was in his service. In 1755 he also opened a ballet school, recruiting 'children of the gardeners and peasants, who are aged ten to thirteen, and having a pleasant appearance' (Gozenpud, 1959:101).

The Grand Duke often organized parties and even orgies in the presence of his opera troupe and gave lavish presents to the prima donnas. He fraternized with the musicians on some occasions and ignored them on others. The following is the expense sheet for one performance of Araja's *Alessandro nelle Indie:*

---

3   10 [Апреля]. Большой ужин, стол в зале с музыкой и пальбой. Иллюминация в саду и на большом дворце. После ужина внизу курили трубки при военной музыке. Угощение музыкантов для отдыха. Прекрасная погода до самой полуночи. 13 [Апреля]. Большой стол к обеду и ужину. Вечером музыка. После ужина трубки у Кн. Меншикова. 14 [Апреля]. Утро в церкви. Большой обед с придворной музыкой. После обеда Великая Княгиня ездила кататься на маленьких санях. Великий Князь посетил конюшню. 15 [Апреля]. Утро на охоте за лесными пулярками... Оттуда пешком на ферму Великой Княгини, где она угостила великолепным обедом с любезностию хозяйки. До обеда странная веселость Его Императорского Высочества и всей компании. Бал в маленькой комнате и никакой другой музыки, кроме человеческого голоса, со шляпой в руке вместо скрипки и шпагой вместо смычка. Вечером Великая Княгиня воротилась в Ораниенбаум, где стояли ледяные горы и общество занялось игрою в барры... 17 [Апреля]. ...Вечером обыкновенное собрание и концерт (фейерверк). После ужина трубки у камергера Б., маленький фейерверк' (Misere, 1911:7).

4   The building of the Opera House was moved from Oranienbaum to St Petersburg in 1824 and was later destroyed by fire. It has since been restored on its original site in Oranienbaum.

tinsel and copper foil from the Cabinet's office	1071 roubles,	05 kopecks
miscellaneous acquisitions	577 roubles,	58 kopecks
decorations and machinery	592 roubles,	11 kopecks
payment for the artists	388 roubles,	30 kopecks
total	2628 roubles,	04 kopecks

Generally, the repertory at the Oranienbaum theatre reflected the taste and tradition of Elizabeth's Court. For a lengthy period the theatre was supervised by Araja, after whose retirement young Manfredini was appointed, with the same duties.

Vincenzo Manfredini at the Oranienbaum Court

Vincenzo Manfredini (born in Pistoia near Florence in 1737 to a family of musicians) studied in Bologna with G. Perti and in Milan with G. Fioroni. He arrived in Russia with his brother, the castrato Giuseppe Manfredini, both as members of Locatelli's Italian comic opera troupe. The brothers separated in 1760 due to the company's dwindling fortunes, and Guiseppe left to work in the Moscow branch of Locatelli's troupe.

Vincenzo Manfredini's direction of Peter Fedorovich's musical and theatrical ensembles won him his patron's favour. His first *opera seria, Semiramide riconosciuta* with Metastasio's libretto (1760), must have been a success, for only two days after Elizabeth's death on 25 December 1761, and having just become Emperor, Peter Fedorovich appointed Manfredini to the position of kapellmeister of the Court's Italian Company. He replaced Hermann Friedrich Raupach, who had briefly held the position after Araja's departure. The new Emperor, however, also hurried to reinstate Araja and planned to get Galuppi as well, but this demanded more time. Meanwhile, patronizing the Italian Company, the Emperor terminated his subsidy of the French Court Opera Troupe, which had entertained the Russian court for almost twenty years, from the beginning of Elizabeth's rule.

During this period Manfredini had succeeded in becoming the musician most in demand. His requiem for the dead Empress Elizabeth, a two-hour piece for four soloists with orchestra, was performed in February 1762, captivating the audience with its sublime beauty. Soon after this he wrote the heroic pastoral *La pace degli eroi* for the celebration of the peace treaty with Prussia (3 June 1762). Generally, the year 1762 was one of official mourning for Elizabeth and all musical events were forbidden. However, the entertainments described by Misere suggest that the profound silence that was supposed to rule the court was often noisily broken.

When Araja indeed arrived and was commissioned to write a new opera for the summer entertainments at the Ropsha Palace, Manfredini must have felt uncertain at best. However the young composer seemed to fit well into the circle of people close to the Grand Duchess and the events that followed the Palace coup appeared to promote his career (possibly with the help of Teplov, who supported Manfredini and continued to patronize him later into the 1760s).

Figure 4.1   **Vincenzo Manfredini (1737–99)**

When Catherine II revised her court staff, upon ascending the throne, the names of many musicians, first and foremost those who had been close to the late Emperor – Nunciata Garani, Maria Camati, Catarina Brigonzi and Ignacio Dol, and Pietro Peri, the leader of the Italian Company – disappeared from the court records. They left immediately upon receiving their September wages, but Manfredini and his bride Maria Monari stayed on.

Maxim Berezovsky's Early Career

Oranienbaum of the 1750s was where young Maxim Berezovsky, later to become the pride of eighteenth-century Russian music, began his career. His affiliation with the Grand Duke's court was not always clear. Berezovsky's traditional biography associates him with the Imperial Court Cappella and facts such as his participation in two opera productions at the Oranienbaum theatre – *Alessandro nelle Indie* by Araja (1759) and *Semiramide Riconosciuta* by Manfredini (1760) – have been interpreted as reflecting an occasional event. However the printed libretti containing the affiliation of each performer tell us otherwise: 'Mr. Maxim Berezevsky in the service of His Imperial Highness'.[5] This brief description presents a key to Berezovsky's biography, although it still has many lacunas.

The place and time of his birth are unclear, but his social status is now considered as gentry.[6] His first biography was content to describe him as a 'native of *Malorossia*' (Bolkhovitinov, 1805, II:224). Later biographies began to mention a precise location, Glukhov, perhaps because of the stereotyped notion that one had to be born in Glukhov in order to become a pupil of the Glukhov School for Court Singers and/or to be noticed by the hetman Razumovsky. However its archives hold no record of his family's existence. The traditionally accepted date of his birth, 1745, only appeared in the literature much later and demands re-evaluation, as the following will show. The circumstances of his early education and eventual arrival in St Petersburg are also unclear. All these issues interact with the question of his age, and should thus be considered together.

According to Bolkhovitinov's biography, Berezovsky was educated at the Kiev Ecclesiastical Academy.[7] The author's relative proximity to the eighteenth century notwithstanding, he has not proven to be the most reliable source, particularly in regard to the education of various personalities at the ecclesiastical academies. A typical example of his unreliability can be found in his biography of the architect Vasily Ivanovich Bazhenov, in which he claims that Bazhenov studied at the Moscow *Slavonic-Greek-Latin Academy*, a claim later refuted by A.I. Mikhaylov (1951), who provided facts and dates.[8] It may be that in his eagerness to enhance the prestige of the old ecclesiastical academies in the eyes of both his contemporaries and future

---

5   'Г-н Максим Березевский в службе Его Императорского Высочества'. Berezovsky's family name evidently had two spellings, including Berezevsky as in this libretto; the composer himself signed with both. The version with an 'e' sounds more Ukrainian.

6   M. Stepanenko informed the author about finding Berezovsky family arms (in conversation on 4 September 2005).

7   Evfimy Al. Bolkhovotonov (monastic name Evgeny, 1767–1837), Russian historian, Kievan metropolitan from 1822.

8   A. Mikhaylov, *Bazhenov*. Moscow, 1951.

Figure 4.2   Mikolaivs'ka tserkva (St Nicolas Church) in Glukhov, 1693

generations, Bolkhovitinov fabricated stories in which such figures as Bazhenov and Berezovsky attended these schools. The Kiev *Academy Acts and Documents* indeed mentioned five pupils named Berezovsky but their first names were Vlasey, Gregory, Stepan and two Ivans.[9] Nevertheless, on the chance that Maxim Berezovsky may have been educated at the Academy, a few colourful details of the life of its students will not go amiss. For example, the pupils spent their summer vacations without any financial support, touring villages in groups, earning money by singing, performing in salons and officiating at parish church services.

When the town of Glukhov began to feature in biographies written in the mid-nineteenth century, the version that claimed Berezovsky as a pupil of the Glukhov School for Court Singers naturally acquired verisimilitude, without necessarily contradicting the other biography since he could have spent time in both institutions, one after the other. Regardless of the legitimacy or significance of such accounts, it is highly possible, retrospectively, that he had received musical training prior to his arrival in St Petersburg. If he did not attend either the Glukhov School for Court Singers or the Kiev Ecclesiastical Academy, Berezovsky may have been tutored at hetman Razumovsky's court cappella. Let us consider this latter possibility.

The celebrated event through which Count Kirill Razumovsky's cappella introduced young musicians to the Imperial court was the production of *Cephalus and Procris* in 1755. Although Berezovsky's name is not mentioned among the young singers participating in it, this does not exclude his connection with this ensemble: Stählin mentions only five of the approximately 40 musicians (Stählin, 1769, 1982:103). On the other hand, Count Razumovsky visited the capital later too, providing other opportunities to introduce the young musicians. Longing to return to the stimulating life of St Petersburg, he used every excuse to escape Glukhov and deluged the Empress Elizabeth with letters begging her permission to return: 'I won't survive Glukhov's humid and putrid air in the coming fall and winter',[10] which was somewhat ironical in view of the dry and healthy Ukrainian climate *vis-à-vis* the truly humid and putrid air of the North Russian capital. On 12 December 1757, having finally been granted permission, the hetman headed for the capital. This matches the beginning of Berezovsky's work at the Grand Duke's theatre and the year of 1758 as the commonly accepted, though not documented, date of his arrival in St Petersburg (Ginzburg, 1968:7).

In all cases the earliest known document of Berezovsky's biography, dated 26 September 1758, was found in the accounts ledger of the future Emperor: 'The singer Maxim Berezovsky is to receive an annual wage of one hundred and fifty roubles, of which, for his service since 29 June, he has been paid twenty-five roubles and eighty-two kopecks – 25.82.'[11]

---

9   *Akty i dokumenty, otnosyashchiesya k Kievskoy dukhovnoyi akademii, s vvedeniem i primechaniami N.I. Petrova.* Kiev, 1904–06, vol 1:6.

10   'Не снесу в наступающия осень и зиму Глуховскаго сыраго и гнилаго воздуха' (Vasilchikov, 1869:545).

11   'Певчему Максиму Березовскому в определенное ему годовое денежное жалование во сто пятьдесят рублев: заслуженного им июня с 29 числа сего году

The 26 September payment was thus for the period that had begun in May. In eighteenth-century Russia employees were paid three times a year (each payment being for a period of four months). In May they were paid for January–April, in September for May–August and in January for September–December. A third of Berezovsky's annual wage of 150 roubles would have been 50 roubles, but the period from 29 June to 1 September covered only two months and two days, resulting in a payment of 25 roubles and 82 kopecks. This was also the occasion of the first-known signature of the future composer, on a salary receipt: '*Maxim Berezovsky* received the twenty-five roubles and eighty-two kopecks and signed'.[12] There are ten such signatures: three times a year, until January 1762. One can follow the change in Berezovsky's handwriting over the period. Diligent and accurate on the first receipt, it became increasingly hasty and careless. Sometimes he wrote his name as 'Massimo', in the Italian manner.

Berezovsky was thus hired as a singer in the service of the Grand Duke on 29 June 1758, with a wage far exceeding the usual payment received by Russian musicians. Peter Semenov, a singer hired earlier than Berezovsky, received only 100 roubles annually, but even he was not the lowest paid of the musicians. The reason for Berezovsky's preferential treatment could of course be explained by his talent alone, but there were also other possible circumstances, including the matter of his lineage. The higher the original social status of a person in service – the higher the salary. Berezovsky's background in the gentry, rather than an upper or lower societal standing, matches the socio-cultural context of eighteenth-century Russian culture. (The vital stereotype regarding eighteenth-century Russian musicians coming from the serf class inspired by nineteenth-century historiography does not even take into consideration the fact that a serf could not be accepted into court service because he had an owner who would first have been required to liberate him.) Finally, since Count Kirill Grigorievich Razumovsky frequented the circles close to the Grand Duke, he could have provided Berezovsky with an opportunity for exposure to him.

It is the accepted opinion that Berezovsky sang in Araja's *Alessandro nelle Indie* (1759) and in Manfredini's *Semiramide riconosciuta* (1760), as an unbroken soprano voice (that is. at the age of fourteen and fifteen respectively, since the date of his birth as 1745 is unquestioned). Stählin, however, a direct witness to these productions, noted that the leading parts were played by 'Ein vortrefflichen Bassist aus der Ukraine Berezovskij' [perfect bassist from the Ukraine, Berezovsky] (1769, 1982:110). Had the scores of these operas been available of course, there would be no question as to the facts, but they are not; and what remains is to hypothesize, based on the printed libretti of both operas and on the piano reduction of *Alessandro nelle Indie* made for its earlier production in 1755.

жалования выдано денег двадцать пять рублев восемьдесят две копейки – 25.82' (Kniga prikhoda i raskhoda za 1758 god. RGADA, f 1239, op 144/3, no 61550, L 63).

12 'Оные деньги двадцать пять рублей восемьдесят две копейки *Максим Березовский* принял и росписался.'

The two versions (1755 and 1759) of *Alessandro nelle Indie* reveal different distributions of voices: in the former the roles of Alexander and Timogen were played by the tenors Filippo Giorgi and Pietro-Constantino Compassi and that of the antagonist Poro – by the famous male soprano Giovanni Carestini. In 1756 two of the leading soloists, Giorgi and Carestini, left Russia. The 1759 version had thus to be adjusted for a different cast, which consisted almost totally of female singers plus a castrato, Giuseppe Millico, who had just entered the Empress's service and was immediately incorporated into this spectacle, and Berezovsky, whose voice is now in question.

In the new casting – in contrast to the previous one – Alexander and Timogen were played by female performers, Elizabeth Zampra and Catarina Brigonzi. Following the desirable contrast in vocal range between the protagonists and the antagonist in the earlier performance, it would be logical to assume that if, in the later version, the protagonists were now intended for high voices then the antagonist Poro must have been played by a masculine voice, otherwise the range of sound would have been quite monotonous. Even had it still been decided to cast a male soprano as Poro, the role would have been given to the castrato Giuseppe Millico rather than to Berezovsky. But there is Berezovsky's name in the role of Poro.

The libretto of Manfredini's *Semiramide riconosciuta* also indicates that all the participants were either women (Maria Camati, Nunciata Garani, Maria Monari and Catarina Brigonzi) or one male soprano (Millico), with only one 'unclear' Berezovsky cast in the role of Ircano. Both Berezovsky's roles – Poro, the king of a province in India, and Ircano the barbarian, a Scythian – were exotic characters similar in many ways, probably making masculine appearance preferable. Of course in the eighteenth century it did not really matter because even the most mannish roles in *opera seria* had been sung by *castrati*. Yet, considering the above reflections, Stählin's mention of Berezovsky as a bass voice would seem to be accurate.

Additional support for the theory that Berezovsky played these roles in a masculine voice can be found in an article on Russian cultural life in *Sankt-Peterburgskie vedomosti* (1855:3), though without reference to the source: 'We owe to the collector P.S. Shishkin the information that Berezovsky performed the leading tenor role at the Oranienbaum Theatre with an Italian troupe.'[13]

Shishkin's 'tenor' or Stählin's 'bassist' show that one of them was not entirely accurate, but there is no doubt that both were referring to a masculine voice. The above arguments thus suggest that by 1759 Berezovsky's voice had matured and that he had already reached the age of at least seventeen to eighteen. Consequently, 1745 loses its validity as the year of his birth. It is a known fact that a singer, even

---

13 'Благодаря коллекционеру П.С. Шишкину мы узнали... что Березовский пел вместе с итальянской труппою первую теноровую партию на ораниенбаумском придворном театре' (Sankt-Peterburgskie vedomosti, 1855, no 63). P.S. Shishkin was a Petersburgian merchant and a participant member of the Imperial Russian Archeological Society. After his death in 1869 his collection of Russian portraits and rare books disappeared.

though trained from childhood, is required to retrain his voice after it breaks. This may have been the period (in 1758) when Berezovsky began training with Nunciata Garani – one of the finest singers of the Italian Company, working in Russia in 1750–62 (Gozenpud, 1959:100–02). Having come to Russia from Bologna in 1758 in order to enter Elizabeth's service, this famous singer frequently performed at the Oranienbaum Theatre, being known for her mastery of both *seria* and *buffa* operatic roles.

As noted above, Bolkhovitinov's biography of Berezovsky (1805) had not attempted to solve the riddle of the composer's real date of birth. The year 1745 was first mentioned in V. Askochensky's book *Kiev s drevneishym ego uchilischem Akademieiu* [Kiev with its oldest school, Academy] (1856). A comparison of certain passages from several biographies of Berezovsky that preceded Askochensky's book reveals the latter's thinking. According to the earlier work by Bolkhovitinov, Berezovsky had left for Italy to study 'some time around 1765'. A pseudo-documentary novel written by N. Kukolnik (1844), undoubtedly known to any author writing about Berezovsky, noted that the future composer had left for Italy at the age of twenty. $1765 - 20 = 1745$. This simple calculation of figures from these two sources may thus have prompted V. Askochensky to determine Berezovsky's year of birth as 1745. This misguided conclusion, however, cannot be considered a reliable source.

Further endeavours to establish the exact date were undertaken, first by N. Lebedev, who in a booklet (1882) claimed the month of birth to be October; and, finally, by F. Soloviev, who in an entry in the dictionary compiled by Brokhaus and Efron (1891: vol. 6), combined Askochensky's 1745 with Lebedev's 16 October and deduced 'the exact date' to be 16 October, 1745, probably, like Lebedev, having based his assumption on the fact that the Name Day for 'Maxim' is October 16.

Such misleading data were unfortunately a common occurrence in nineteenth–century reference books, being based on legends, doubtful sources and anecdotes. Present-day studies of eighteenth-century Russian artists often cite up to four different dates of birth, each based on a different nineteenth-century source. What we can tentatively assume, however, is that Berezovsky was born no later than 1740 or 1741.

Following the Oranienbaum period, Berezovsky's life can be traced at the Imperial court. After Peter III ascended the throne, Berezovsky was assigned by Imperial Order (15 January 1762) to the Italian Company as a singer, with an annual salary of four hundred roubles.[14] This occurred as the result of a reassessment of servants' wages, including those of the Italian Company. Therefore, in the early 1760s his career was also associated with the opera and not with the Court Choir as has been traditionally believed, probably retrospectively, in view of what were to be his future achievements in the genre of choral concerto.

Despite Berezovsky's affiliation with the Italian Company he did not appear in any further opera productions and his career as an opera singer came to a halt. Indeed, such an affiliation was sometimes purely formal – not connected with opera as such, but paid from its budget, such as was the *Kamer-guslist* Vasiliy Trutovsky. The most

---

14 *Imennye ukazy Petra III*, RGIA, f 466, op 1, no 103, L 11.

probable scenario is that Berezovsky was occupied as an instrument player. He had mastered the harpsichord, violin and possibly also the contrabass.

Documents from this period also include information on his marriage. The following is an excerpt from an edict issued by Catherine II on 11 August 1763:

> Her Imperial Majesty kindly decreed in an Edict of Her Imperial Majesty that the singer Maxim Berezovsky from the Italian Company in the service of Her Imperial Majesty may be united in matrimony with the dancer France Überscheer from the same company and has deigned to order that the bride be presented with a dress. Seeking to execute this Edict of Her Imperial Majesty the Court office ordered in the name of Her Imperial Majesty to announce this Edict to the said Berezovsky and the said Überscheer and to order them to appear at once to receive that dress.[15]

This edict presented a major problem for the church officials: in order to officiate at an interfaith marriage – in this case between a Catholic (the bride) and a Russian Orthodox (the groom) – dispensation from the St Petersburg religious consistory was normally required. In the case of Berezovsky, the dispensation came from the Empress herself, who simply ignored the religious institution. Her solution was wise and diplomatic, as recorded in the Inventory of Files of the St Petersburg religious consistory.[16] The document shows that on 16 October 1763 (two months after Catherine's edict) a file was opened for 'Dispensation for the court dancer of Catholic faith to enter into marriage with the court singer Berezovsky'.[17] Unfortunately, the twelve-page document itself, which presumably included important biographical data on Berezovsky and his fiancée, has not been preserved.

The 'dancer France Überscheer' was first mentioned as Franzina in Stählin's chapter on ballet at the court as one of the best performers among the Russian dancers around 1760 (Stählin, 1769, 1982:21). Later her name appears in one of the first edicts of Catherine II with regard to the personnel of the Italian Company. The Empress ordered a number of performers from the Oranienbaum Theatre 'to enter the service of Her Imperial Majesty in the Italian Company with due payment'. These included the dancers Peter Patepa, Trofim Melnikov and Timofey Bublikov

---

15 'Ея Императорское Величество изволила указать имянным Своего Императорского Величества указом находящемуся в службе при дворе Ея Императорского Величества при итальянской компании певчему Максиму Березовскому дозволить жениться той же компании на танцовальной девице Франце Ибершерше и притом соизволила указать пожаловать ей платье. Того ради придворная контора во исполнение оного Ея Императорского Величества Имянного указа приказали сея Имянной Ея Императорского Величества Указ оному Березовскому, и той Ибершерше собъявить и для получения платья велеть Ем явится Итого надлежит немедленно' (*Imennye ukazy Ekateriny II*, RGIA, f 466, op 1, no 110).

16 *Opisi del Peterburgskoy dukhovnoy konsistorii*, TsGIA SPb, f 19, op 1, no 5485, L 238.

17 'О дозволении придворной танцовальной девице, состоящей в католицком законе вступить в брак с придворным певчим Березовским.'

and the musical apprentice Ivan Khandoshkin.[18] The artists were to receive payment and housing as of 1 July 1762 (see details in Rytsareva, 1983:44). In a list of dancers at the Court Theatre in 1768 Stählin again mentioned Franza Berezovskaya along with Marfa Khandoshkina (Chandoschkina, probably Ivan Khandoshkin's sister) and Timofey Bublikov (called Timoshka) – the outstandingly talented pupil of Franz Hilverding (Stählin, 1769, 1982:34).

The German spelling of Francina's maiden name – Überscheer – matches that of the cellist who 'pleasantly accompanied' Peter Fedorovich (Stählin, 1769, 1982:109) and whom Araja took to Italy. His full name was Thomas Friedrich Überscheer. Although his name had been Russified to Thomas Nozhnitsov, which originates from the noun meaning *scissors*, he continued to sign himself as 'Überscheer'. He was first employed in 1757 as 'a musical apprentice' in the service of Peter Fedorovich, being paid the meagre sum of 24 roubles per annum (the most modest of the court salaries, with the exception of the scribe, who received 22 roubles). In 1759, the year in which he left for Italy together with Araja, his salary rose to sixty roubles. There are documents dated 15 January and 7 June 1760 regarding money transfer to Italy to the kapellmeister Araja for the upkeep of the musical apprentice Thomas Überscheer, 250 and 375 roubles respectively.[19] Tomas Überscheer returned to Russia in 1762 together with Araja, two weeks before the coup (Stählin, 1769, 1982:159).

The ledgers of Oranienbaum also mention a certain Madame Maria Ivanovna Überscheer who was 'with the dance apprentices'. Thomas and France (Francina) may have been brother and sister, born to Maria Ivanovna Überscheer, with young France being among the 'dance apprentices'. Their father could have been Friedrich Überscheer, who played *waldhorn* in the court orchestra from 1731. The various individuals thus bearing the name Überscheer in all likelihood belonged to the same branch of the Russified German family involved in musical life at the court, and they are of interest to us here as possible in-laws of Berezovsky. This covers all the known sources on Berezovsky up to the early 1760s.

The period of the late 1750s – early 1760s also seems to be the most appropriate one for his study of composition and counterpoint. According to Bolkhovitinov Berezovsky's teacher was Francesco Zoppis (1715 – after 1781), an Italian musician from Venice, who worked in Russia from 1757 to 1781. Zoppis arrived in Russia as a kapellmeister for the Locatelli Company in 1757. After the company disbanded he is believed to have conducted the theatre orchestra and the court choir (Findeizen, 1929, II, 49), though this is not documented (Porfirieva, MPES, 1999:250–51). Considering Berezovsky's contacts with Manfredini, who in the 1760s revealed himself as a composer of several choral compositions, including the Russian ecclesiastic ones for the Imperial court choir, it is also possible that Manfredini was among Berezovsky's instructors.

---

18 Among the Oranienbaum dancers included in the Italian company were Vavila Medvedev, Avdotia Stepanova, Agrafena Ignatieva, Praskovia Mikhaylova, Anisia Churbanova, and among the singers were Fedosia Nikanova and Natalia Churbanova.

19 *Kniga prikhoda i raskhoda za 1760 god*, RGADA, f 1239, op 144/3, no 615569, L 19.

Chapter 5

The 'Thaw' of the 1760s

The thirty-four year reign (1762–96) of Empress Catherine II was rich in events and controversial in the successes and dramas that were a consequence of the enlightened absolutism with which she ruled.

Catherine's dynamic rule, following the thirty-five year period of post-Petrine reaction and stagnation, restored the spirit of rejuvenation established by Peter I. Every decade of her reign was characterized by its own particular spirit. The enthusiasm and liberalism of the 1760s were followed by the crises of the 1770s. The self-confidence and firm tread of the 1780s were shaken by the French Revolution of 1789 and led to the wary 1790s.

Music in Catherine's time flourished freely as never before, paralleling the development of social life, broad cultural exchanges and technology. All the principal forms of contemporaneous European music-making became firmly established and the social circles of its consumers widened considerably. An almost instantaneous interweaving of the borrowed and the native took place, and by 1800 the ground had been laid for nineteenth-century Russian music to join the European community.

Each period naturally expressed itself in generic and stylistic preferences in music, following the dominating mood in the country. The 1760s in Russia, like every period heralding a liberal epoch (and in many ways forecasting the 1860s and the 1960s), can indeed be called a 'thaw' (in analogy with the post-Stalin decade), creating a highly stimulating ambience for the new generation. In music the genre of the spiritual choral concerto *a cappella* was the only one with a long national tradition, and so it naturally became the first to bear native fruits. Berezovsky was the leading figure among the local composers during these years, and his compositions will constitute the focus of this chapter, along with Manfredini and Galuppi, who in many ways defined the level and style of culture in St Petersburg. The same decade also saw the musical beginnings of the young Dmitry Bortniansky, whom we shall meet in the last part of this chapter.

Manfredini in the 1760s

Due to the circumstances of his overthrow, no requiem was composed for Peter III. Rather, an *opera seria* in three acts based on Metastasio's libretto *L'olimpiade* and ballet-pantomime *Amore e Psiche* were commissioned from Manfredini, and both were performed in Moscow (on 20 October and 24 November) during Catherine II's coronation celebrations. The grandiose coronation ceremony and other spectacular events demanded the creation of musical spectacles. *L'olimpiade* was followed by the *Carlo Magno* (for the first anniversary of the coronation, 24 November 1763). This latter opera, however, was felt by the court to be too learned and – with Manfredini's knowledge or not – by 31 March of the same year the Empress had already sent for the 'famous *Kapellmeister* Galuppi Buronelli' to enter the Court service.[1] Even though Galuppi was not expected immediately, Manfredini was dismissed from *opera seria* productions and the following year, 1764, the court restored Hermann Raupach's *Alcesta* as the annual serious spectacle. Over the next two years Manfredini's name appears only on the scores of two pasticcio intermezzi, *La pupilla* (1763) and *La finta ammalata* (1764). In order to fill the gap until Galuppi's arrival the Empress ordered the reinstatement of the former French Opera Troupe, which her husband had closed.

With Galuppi's arrival Manfredini was finally relegated to a secondary role and from then on he kept a low profile. Between 1765 and 1767 he became vice-kapellmeister and his compositions included masses upon the deaths of the Roman Emperor and the French Dauphin, ballet divertimentos for Galuppi's operas and cantatas. Among those are *Le rivali* and the *drama per musica Minerva e Apollo*, which, as Zolotnitskaya suggests, could be two versions of the same work (MPES, II:169) as well as cantata for the foundation of the new building of the Academy of Arts, St Petersburg. His other duties included writing religious works for the Court Choir. In 1765 Manfredini was appointed to the additional position of musical instructor for Grand Duke Pavel Petrovich, son of Catherine II and Peter III. On this occasion he wrote *Sis Sonate da Clavicembalo* and dedicated it to the Empress, being rewarded with 1,000 roubles.[2]

Manfredini maintained connections with the aristocratic music lovers who used to frequent Oranienbaum, primarily Teplov, Olsufiev and Lev Naryshkin. Mooser has suggested that Manfredini also tutored Elizaveta, daughter of Gregory Teplov, basing his claim on Manfredini's dedication of his *harpsichord concerto* to her. Teplova and her sister were both good musicians and belonged to the circle of youthful courtiers surrounding Grand Duke Pavel Petrovich. Manfredini was clearly popular enough to have had other students too. Levashev hypothesized that Manfredini taught the young Russian musician Vasily Pashkevich (1973:262).

In the meantime Manfredini cooperated with Teplov in a successful albeit brief experience of organizing subscription concerts (on 25 February and 17 April 1769) at the house of Prince Baryatinsky[3] in St Petersburg, with the participation of Adam Olsufiev and Lev Naryshkin who were now joined by Elizaveta Teplova.

Ignoring Galuppi's initial success, Manfredini patiently bided his time, assessing

---

1   *Imennye ukazy Ekateriny II*, RGIA, f 466, op 1, no 110.

2   The following year the same opus was severely criticized; the German composer A. Huller accused Manfredini of being illiterate, unmelodic, unharmonious, and so on (Mooser, 1948–51, II:39).

3   The same house was also known and mentioned in some sources as belonging to Ivan Ivanovich Shuvalov (Petrovskaya, MPES, III:288).

his own situation. In the summer of 1766 (20 June / 1 July) he was joined by his nephew, thus confirming his intention to remain in Russia.[4] Galuppi was supposed to return to Italy at the end of his contract, and Manfredini probably hoped to be fully reinstated then to his former position. However, the court was already negotiating with the famous Italian composer Tommaso Traetta, who arrived in St Petersburg at the beginning of September 1768, only one month after Galuppi's departure. It seems to be at this point that Manfredini saw no option but to resign, and was granted a pension upon doing so. His position of vice-kapellmeister passed to Hermann Raupach, whom in 1761 he himself had replaced as kapellmeister, and who was waiting in Paris, maintaining relations with Prince Dmitry Alexeevich Golitsyn and Count Andrey Kirillovich Razumovsky. The circle was closed and Manfredini departed in summer 1769, with his singer wife and their little son.

Manfredini's Russian chapter did have an epilogue, somewhat similar to Araja's epilogue during the short rule of Peter III. Grand Duke Pavel Petrovich, remaining faithful to his teacher Manfredini, three decades later invited him to court upon his ascent to the throne as Emperor Pavel I (see Chapter 10).

Baldassare Galuppi

Galuppi's engagement in St Petersburg followed growing agitation around his name and drawn-out diplomatic negotiations before the Venetian Senate would consent to let him sign a three-year contract with the Russian court. According to the contract, Galuppi was to compose and produce operas, ballets and cantatas for ceremonial banquets. His salary was to be 4,000 roubles plus rent and carriage. Galuppi crossed the Russian border on 15 July 1765, bringing with him the virtuoso Josef Bianin, the tenor Gianfrancesco Sandali, his son and a servant.[5] Galuppi wrote two operas in Russia: *Il Re Pastore* (1766) and *Ifigenia in Tauride* (1768) and two cantatas, *La virtù liberata* (libretto by Lazzaroni, performed on 24 and 26 November 1765) and *La pace tra la virtù e la bellezza* (libretto by Metastasio, performed on 26 June 1766).

Most of his works performed during that period had been written much earlier.[6] Ten days after his arrival in St Petersburg, on 22 September 1765, Galuppi received an order from Her Imperial Majesty to compose and to produce the opera *Didona*[7] for

---

4   AVPRI, Vnutrennie kollezhskie dela 1762–76, op 2/6, no 3638, L 17v.

5   AVPRI, Vnutrennie kollezhskie dela 1762–76, op 2/6, no 3638, L 14v. (The date in the document appears as 15/26 July, reflecting the difference in the Russian and European calendars).

6   By the time of Galuppi's arrival, the Russians were already familiar with his comic operas from the repertoire of Locatelli's troupe: *Il mondo della luna* (Venice, 1750), *Il filosofo di campagna* (Venice, 1754), *L'Arcadia in Brenta* (Venice, 1749), *I'bagni d'Abano* (Venice, 1753), *Il conte Caramella* (Venice, 1751), *La calamita de' cuori* (Venice, 1752), *Il mondo alla roversa, ossia Le donne che comandano* (Venice, 1750).

7   There was no need to compose since the score of *Didone abbandonata* to the libretto by Metastasio was already long in existence and had been staged in 1741 in Modena; 1750 Venice; 1764 Naples.

24 November. This could have been quite realistic within the context of regular on-going productions. However, considering that no new *opera seria* had been staged in St Petersburg since Manfredini's *Carlo Magno* in 1763, and that the micro-world of the Italian opera troupe was quite isolated in the Russian musical domain, it was impossible to finish it in time to contribute to the Empress's coronation anniversary. Moreover, Galuppi planned the production with incredible pomp and the court had to meet his high standards of performance (eloquently expressed by him in a less than gentlemanly form). Altogether, it took until the beginning of February 1766 to complete. Relating to the situation quite equably, the Empress presented the composer with a golden tobacco-box embellished with brilliants and 1,000 ducats accompanied by a coquettish note saying that this gift had been bequeathed him in Dido's will (Stählin, 1769, 1982:173). Galuppi also did quite a lot beyond his contractual obligations. He gave weekly concerts as harpsichordist or sometimes conductor and instructed the brilliant young Ukrainian court singer Dmitry Bortniansky in composition. All these extra activities were of course most generously rewarded by H.I.M. The Court chronicles recorded a number of Galuppi's performances:

> 26 November 1765 …In the evening Her Majesty graced the audience hall with Her presence and indulged in a game of cards with the cavaliers. Then His Highness [Grand Duke Pavel Petrovich] emerged from his chambers and joined them. Her Imperial Majesty bestowed Her Royal approbation upon a new composition of Italian instrumental and vocal music with choir written by the *Kapellmeister* Galuppi [*La Virtù liberata*]. Then, honouring the said composer by offering him her hand, Her Majesty returned to Her private chambers.

> 11 April 1766 …And in the afternoon at about five [the Empress] came to the Big Palace Church to hear the singing by the Court Choir of the concerto written for Good Friday by the composer Galuppi. (KFZ, 1765–8)[8]

Galuppi's compositions for the Imperial Court Choir mentioned in the Chronicles were not isolated cases. The choir was the subject of the often-cited exclamation of delight from Galuppi: 'Un si magnifico coro, mai non sentito in Italia!' [I have never heard such a magnificent choir in Italy!] (Stählin, 1769, 1982:58). We will probably never know precisely what the music was that Galuppi was hearing, but this compliment was no mere polite lip service. Rather, it appears to be the result of an impression that would stimulate him to write choral compositions and to work

---

8   '26 ноября 1765. …А в вечеру Ея Величество изволила выходить в аудиенц-залу и с кавалерами забавляться в карты, куда из своих аппартаментов изволил прибыть Его Императорское Высочество; при чем капельмейстер Галупи получил от Ея Императорского Величества Высочайшую апробацию новаго его сочинения Итальянской инструментальной и вокальной музыки с хором певчих. При сем Ея Величество удостоя помянутого капельмейстера к руке, изволила возвратиться в свои покои. 11 апреля 1766. …А пополудни в 5-м часу изволила проходить в большую придворную церковь слушать пение придворными певчими сочиненнаго капельмейстером Галуппи, на день Великого Пятка, концерта.'

out a style that would reveal a tactful interaction with local tradition and develop into an early-classic technique. Considering the special importance of this genre for eighteenth-century Russian society, Galuppi's contribution was a significant one and deserves a more detailed examination.

In the traditional view of the history of eighteenth-century Russian choral music, Galuppi was considered the founder of the new – Italianated – style. However his appearance in the mid-1760s fell upon well-prepared soil. Raupach had set Psalms translated by Lomonosov and Sumarokov for the Court Choir as early as 1760 (Porfirieva, MPES, III:13). Manfredini's work as well as Berezovsky's rise as a composer must have preceded Galuppi's compositions. Since Raupach's and Manfredini's choral compositions remain unknown, it is thus hard to judge precisely whether Galuppi's choral style was a dramatic innovation or a powerful and welcome accelerator in the Russian context. Only a few of Berezovsky's and Galuppi's works have remained from the 1760s and, based on them, we can tentatively speculate about a certain mutual orientation between the two.

Berezovsky would have undoubtedly wanted to study closely the works of the maestro, full of admirably elegant counterpoint; while Galuppi for his part would have needed to find a key to his new audience's popular taste for the Orthodox liturgy, which was unfamiliar to him. Berezovsky's works and other pieces from the Imperial Court Choir repertoire were almost certainly the point of departure for Galuppi. For example his Liturgy, of which only one part is known, *Slava Ottsu* [Bless the Lord], obviously indicates his familiarity with Berezovsky's Liturgy, written most probably in the early 1760s and bearing traces of *partes*-singing style. Additional details on Berezovsky's Liturgy will be given later in this chapter, but we can already note that Galuppi used the same devices as Berezovsky: 3/2 proportions (already rare in Italy) in the first section, strict choral texture and the unwavering character of the psalmodic tune. Furthermore he applied the same *C major* key and bare harmony (even simpler than Berezovsky's), containing elements of modality; and last but not least, a very precise prosody, which obviously preoccupied the composer. Galuppi demonstrably succeeded in creating an accurate representation of the Russian liturgical style (Examples 5.1a, b).

Example 5.1 (a) Berezovsky: *Edinorodny syne* **(twentieth-century arrangement for male choir)**

Example 5.1 (b) Galuppi: *Edinorodny syne*

Another contribution was his simple, *gallant* and slightly sentimental manner as applied, for example, in the trio *Da ispravitsya molitva moya* [Let my prayer be set forth]. This manner was later picked up by his student Dmitry Bortniansky and developed in the 1780s. Comparison of their pieces on the same text clearly points to their connection (Examples 5.2a, b).

Example 5.2 (a) Galuppi: *Da ispravitsya molitva moya*

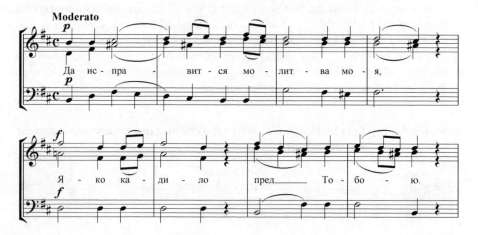

Example 5.2 (b) Bortniansky: *Da ispravitsya molitva moya*

The specifically Galuppian style of his other choral works, highly appreciated by his contemporaries, synthesized a rich and sophisticated polyphony of motet writing with the graciousness and simplicity of gallant early classicism. His technique included a broad use of complex and detailed rhythmic patterns and an engaging elaboration of texture, making voices shine with free diversions of registers. He had a particular fondness for echo-like antiphons, light and energetic motifs of the horn calls and fanfares with dotted rhythms, changing dynamics, and thickness of sound. The multiplicity of registers, rhythmic diversity and rhythmic organization of the small sequential structures together created the concertos' festiveness, ceremonial grandeur and baroque density of contrast and detail.

Example 5.3   Galuppi: Concerto *Uslyshit tya Gospod'*

About fourteen of Galuppi's Russian choral works are known today, including three concertos (*Uslyshit tya Gospod'* [The Lord hear thee in the day of trouble], *Gotovo serdtse moe* [My heart is fixed] and *Sudi, Gospodi, obidyashchi mya* [O Lord, judge those who wrong me]) and two minor pieces (motet *Blagoobrazny Iosif* [Joseph was a goodly person] and motet with fugue *Plotiu usnuv* [After sleeping in the flesh as dead]).[9] Half a century after being written they were edited by his former student Dmitry Bortniansky, who had become a leading eighteenth-century Russian composer and practitioner of the genre of choral concerto, and director of the Imperial Court Capella. They were published by the Russian music publisher J. Fuchs in 1816. The misattribution (in a manuscript collection) to Galuppi of the choral concerto *Gotovo serdtse moe*, actually written by Bortniansky in the 1780s, serves as evidence of the former's popularity in the repertory of the following decades.[10]

Galuppi's intensive dealings with the Court Choir may have determined his choice of Coltellini's libretto *Ifigenia in Tauride* for his St Petersburg opera of 1768, which contained ten choruses. The plot had no love intrigue and instead concentrated on ethical conflicts in the strict spirit of ancient classicism. The choral episodes appeared naturally, were full of action and logically strengthened by Angiolini's ballet directly associated with the plot (Porfirieva,I:232). Although this was in accord with the Russian ideals of the Enlightenment, the opera bored its audience. This trend took root nonetheless and Tommaso Traetta, known as a master of scenic and orchestral expression, and a successful and fashionable composer who had collaborated with Coltellini and shared Gluck-Calzabigi's ideas of reform, was Russia's next choice as Court Kapellmeister.

Berezovsky: Choral Work of the 1760s

Although Berezovsky's general creative path reveals his talent as a universal composer, he is known to have produced only choral work in the 1760s. At the time this was the only genre in which Russian musicians felt secure, following the firmly established tradition. Opera and instrumental music were still out of the question for them.

At the Kievan Ecclesiastic Academy, or indeed elsewhere, Berezovsky might have been trained only in the *partes*-singing tradition, with its modality and Renaissance rhetoric. Yet his compositions were entirely contemporaneous in their harmonic and thematic style, typical of the 1760s transitional period that produced the baroque – early classic style. The missing link, therefore, probably lay in choral

---

9   Galuppi's other Russian Orthodox compositions are the trio *Da ispravitsya* [Let my prayer be set forth], concertos *Vsi yazytsy vospleshchite* [O clap your hands, all ye people], *Na Tya Gospodi upovakh* [In thee, O Lord, do I put my trust], *Preobrazheniyu Gospodnyu* [To the transfiguration of the Lord], *Priidite Presvetloe Khristovo* [Come ye, the all-radiant of Christ] and *Vozneseniyu Gospodnyu* [Onto the ascension of the Lord], Liturgy and Cherubic Hymn (HLA in MV 1804, no 80).

10   *Sbornik dukhovnykh kontsertov XVIII veka*, score, ms. RNB, f 1021, op 3 (1), no 2.

works composed in the transitional late *partes*-singing style. Some of the possible composers in this possible style could have included Mark Poltoratsky (1729–95), from 1753 precentor and from 1763 director of the Imperial Court Choir, or Andrey Rachinsky (1729–*c*. 1800), from 1753 kapellmeister of Razumovsky's house cappella and in the late 1750s chamber musician to the Grand Duke Peter Fedorovich.

Unfortunately, none of their compositions are known today. Generally, singers of the Court Choir, participating in Italian opera productions and absorbing the musical environment of the capital, had a wide stylistic experience. In all probability attempts to modify the church style were made but were discouraged by the Empress Elizabeth because, as Stählin asserted, in order to preserve genuine and more ancient Russian church music, she did not allow newly composed church motets to contain any touch of the Italian style so beloved by her in other music (Stählin, 1769, 1982:54). Whatever the reasons for her policy – clerical influence, to which she was susceptible, the wave of nationalism that had emerged in the late 1740s, or simply personal predilection (she was a well-trained *partes*-singer herself) – it resulted in stagnation of the choral concerto during the 1740s–50s.

In contrast, the new Empress, Catherine II, was both anti-clerical and anti-musical and – accordingly – indifferent to stylistic processes in spiritual music. Thus, new perspectives opened up in the early 1760s and native musicians began to generate a novel style of sacred choral music *a cappella*, much closer to the contemporary musical reality than the old Renaissance-like style. Stählin, whose Chronicles are revealing in this matter, called the new music 'improved' and related that from 1762 this music began to occupy an increasing place in the Court Choir, with the most impressive church concertos being performed by the full choir not only on occasions of major festivities, but at minor ceremonies and on Sundays too, and that even the regular mass was accompanied by so-called *figurative* singing (a German term for the expressive baroque style widely using rhetorical figures). Moreover, such church concertos spread out from the Court across the entire country, where they were performed in cathedrals and other big churches by volunteers and talented amateurs of the vocal art in town churches where singers were not employed. Enthusiastic young people, especially from the merchant classes, formed choral societies in Moscow and St Petersburg and collected a repertoire of spiritual music in the old, the newer, and even the newest styles (p. 60). Stählin related the emergence of this new style not only to the court kapellmeisters Manfredini and the respected Galuppi, but also to the Ukrainian composers who were former church singers.

§7 ...The most remarkable of the latter is *Maxim Berezovsky*, a court chamber musician of great talent, taste and skill, who excels in writing refined church compositions. He knows how to combine in the best manner the fiery Italian tune with the gentle Greek one. In the past few years he has written splendid church concertos for the Court Choir, with such taste and exceptional harmony that their performance has won him the acclaim of the connoisseurs and of the Court. The most important were based on the text of the Psalms of David, for example: 1) *Gospod' votsarisya v lepotu oblechesya* [The Lord reigneth; he is closed with majesty], 2) *Ne otverzhi mene vo vremya starosti* [Cast me not off in the time of old age], 3) *Khvalite Gospoda s nebes* [Praise ye the Lord from the heavens]. Then the angelic doxology *Slava v vyshnikh* [Glory to God in the Highest] and the Ambrosian chant *Tebe Boga khvalim* [Te Deum].

§8 ...Those who have not heard these works will never be able to imagine how rich and sumptuous this music can be when performed by a large, skilled and select choir. The testimony of the famous Galuppi speaks better than any praise. When this great master of musical art heard the performance of that full spiritual concerto at the Imperial Court Cappella in St Petersburg for the first time, he said in complete surprise: 'I'd never heard such a magnificent choir in Italy'... (Stählin, 1769, 1982:57–8)[11]

These laudatory comments on the subject of Berezovsky attest to his overall skill as a composer. In 1769 Stählin noted that the above-mentioned choral concertos were written over a period of a 'few years', indicating that by the mid-1760s Berezovsky's career was on the rise. During this period his compositional output was in accordance with public tastes and was appreciated for its beauty and, furthermore, for its unique blend of formally opposing styles: the contemporaneous European ('fiery Italian') and the native Ukrainian-Russian ('soft Greek church'). Stählin's compliment was obviously derived from Quantz's theory of blended styles, with which he must have been familiar. By the end of the 1760s Berezovsky had thus written numerous ecclesiastical choral compositions and achieved fame and wide recognition.

About twenty scores and the same number of various other sources, giving only titles, together provide about 40 of Berezovsky's compositions including liturgical chorals, Communion verses and concertos. About a third of the scores, mostly liturgical pieces, are reliably attributed, while a few still remain arguable and can be attributed to Berezovsky with a greater or lesser degree of probability. Titles of Berezovsky's unknown compositions can be found (besides those mentioned by

---

11 §7... 'Unter den lesstern befindet sich einer, der nun Hof-Kammer-Musikus ist, Namens *Maxim Berezovskij*, der ganz besondere Gaben, Geschmack, und Geschicklichkeit in der Composition nach dem feinsten Kirchen-Styl besisst, worinn er das feurige der Italienischen mit der sanften Griechischen Kirchen-Melodei glücklich zu vereinigen weiss. Seit etlichen Jahren hat er in solchem Geschmack mit einnehmendster Harmonie die vortrefflichften Kirchen Concerte für die Kaiserl. Hofkapelle gesesst, und mit so viel Bewunderung der Kenner als Beifall des Hofs aufgeführt. Die vornemsten davon sind biblische Texte, meist aus den Psalmen Davids, als: 1. der Herr steht an der hohen Stätte, * 2. Herr verlass mich nicht, wenn ich alt werde, * 3. Lobet den Hernn ihr Himmel, * Ferner den englischen lobgesang, Ehre sen Gott in der Höhe *.: und den Ambrosianischen, Herr Gott dich loben wir *. §8 Wie pompös und einnehmend nun solche Kirchen-Musik von einem so zahlreichen als geübten Chor auserlesenster Stimmen klinge, ist sich kaum einzubilden, wenn man es nicht selbst gehöret hat. Das Zeugnis des berümten *Galuppi* kann indessen statt aller Lobes-Erhebung gelten. Als dieser grosse tonkünstler das erstemal ein solches vollständiges Kirchen-Concert in der Kaiserl. Hofkapelle zu Petersburg aufführen hörte, sagte er in voller Verwunderung: *un si magnifico coro mai non ho sentito in Italia!* The same text, with slight variation, is found in a letter by D. Hohnbaum published under the title "Noch etwas über russische Kirchenmusik" [A little more on Russian church music] in the *Allgemeine musikalische Zeitung* no 21, 1806 and attributed by V. Gourevich (2003a) to August Ludwig Schlözer, a Russian historian of German origins, who published Stählin's work under the pseudonym Johann Joseph Haigold.

Stählin) mostly in the announcements of the music-sellers Haehne and Lehnhold (hereafter referred to as HLA) in MV 1804, no 80, which includes Communion verses *Blazheni izhe izbral* [Blessed is the man whom thou choosest], *Vsi yazytsy vospleshchite* [O clap your hands, all ye people], *Znamenasya na nas* [It hath been signed upon us], *Raduitesya pravedni* [Rejoice in the Lord, O ye righteous]; four-voice concertos *Slava v vyshnikh Bogu* [Glory to God in the Highest], *Sudi Gospodi obidyashchi* [O Lord, judge those who wrong me], *Khvalite Gospoda s nebes* [Praise ye the Lord from the heavens], *Tebe Boga khvalim* [Te Deum], *Milost' i sud vospoyu* [I will sing of mercy and judgment: unto thee, O Lord, will I sing], *Ne imamy inyya pomoshchi* [For he shall deliver the needy when he crieth], *Priidite i vidite* [Come, behold the works of the Lord] and double-choir concertos *Vkusite i vidite* [O taste and see that the Lord is good], *Uslyshi siya vsi yazytsy* [There is no speech nor language, where their voice is not heard], *Vnemlite lyudie* [Take heed, O ye people], *Vskuyu mya otrinu* [But thou hast cast off and abhorred] and *Nyne sily* [Now the heavenly powers]. Some of these titles are mentioned in other sources too. There is also mention of a four-voice concerto *Otrygnu serdtse* [My heart is inditing a good matter] (Askochensky 1851:277 and Metallov 1914). The Catalogue for Vocal Music written in 1793 (hereafter referred to as KPN) contains incipits of two of Berezovsky's works (Examples 5.4 and 5.5).

Example 5.4   Berezovsky: Concerto *Ne imamy inyya pomoshchi* **(incipit from an eighteenth-century catalogue)**

Example 5.5   Berezovsky: *Tebe Boga khvalim* **(incipit from an eighteenth-century catalogue)**

The known compositions are uneven in style. The liturgical works and ten Communion verses are written in a typically reserved and neutral style, leaving little room for individuality.[12] Naturally, concertos characterized by a developed

---

12 There are four well-known Communion verses: *Tvoryay angely svoya dukhi* [Who maketh his angels spirits], *Vo vsyu zemlyu* [All the ends of the world shall remember and turn unto the Lord], *V pamyat' vechnuyu budet pravednik* [The righteous shall be in everlasting remembrance] *and Chashu spaseniya priimu* [I will take the cup of salvation], published by

polyphonic texture and contrasting sections offered Berezovsky much more freedom in devices, which the young composer duly exploited. To take as an example only three of his concertos whose attribution is not in doubt, these vary from the modest *Gospod' votsarisya* [The Lord reigneth; he is clothed in majesty] to the German-motet-style *Unser Vater* to *Ne otverzhi mene vo vremya starosti* [Cast me not off in the time of old age], which is rich in devices, monumental and melancholic. It is this latter piece that established Berezovsky in the Russian classical legacy.

This very variety was typical for the transition from the baroque to the early classical styles in 1760s in Europe in general, and indeed legitimate for the experimental period of new styles in Russia in particular. When many standardized works by one composer are available, it makes a stylistic definition possible. But this is not the case with Berezovsky. Hence, any discourse on the attribution of three other concertos (*Bog sta v sonme bogov* [God standeth in the congregation of the mighty], *Dokole, Gospodi* [How long wilt thou forget me, O Lord?] and *Da voskresnet Bog* [Let God arise]) must be especially tentative, as all the available data are indirect.[13] In the following, Berezovsky's Liturgy and some of his actual and possible concertos are considered in a relatively chronological order – from the dominating *partes*–singing to the mature baroque and classical traits. An exception is made for the concerto *Da voskresnet Bog*, which will be analyzed in Chapter 6

Jurgenson in 1887, and another six, preserved in the publisher's archives, having been edited but not printed for some reason (Yurchenko, 1986).

13   There is a late nineteenth- or early twentieth-century score of the concerto *V nachalyakh Ty Gospodi* [For he hath founded it upon the seas], found within a handwritten private collection in Zagorsk and known to me through the conductor Valery Poliansky who widely performed it in Moscow in the early 1980s. On the score the composer is indicated as 'M.S. Berezovsky', which in itself is not a warranty of correct attribution regarding eighteenth-century Russian choral music. Moreover, there are other versions of its attribution. For example, M. Yurchenko told me of the existence of a printed edition of the same concerto under the name Stepan Degtyarev from the beginning of the twentieth century and, according to an anonymous source, there is also a nineteenth–century handwritten copy of the same concerto under the name of Artemy Vedel. Such confusion is typical for the eighteenth-century Russian choral legacy and will be discussed in Chapters 10 and 11. However, the high quality of the music and the lack of similarity of its style to any other eighteenth-century writing, including Degtyarev and Vedel, made me tentatively admit at the time that it could indeed belong to Maxim Berezovsky (Rytsareva, 1983:125–6). With time, however, I increasingly realized that the style of this piece differs too greatly from Berezovsky's other works. Its polyphonic elements, which are significantly fewer than in his other compositions, previously served me as an indication of late baroque – early classic, but their proportions are also characteristic of nineteenth-century Russian choral music. Finally, the composition itself is too different. Whereas in Berezovsky's other compositions the texture and rhythmic pattern are fairly stable within one section, somewhat following the structure of eighteenth-century motet, in this concerto they frequently change every four measures or so, which is indeed more characteristic of Degtyarev or Vedel, though this concerto does not fit their styles in other respects.

in comparison with another concerto written on the same Psalm by his younger contemporary, Dmitry Bortniansky.

Liturgy

Berezovsky's Liturgy or *Obednya* has reached us in an early twentieth-century edition in a version for male choir.[14] Most probably written in the early 1760s,[15] the Liturgy became very popular in Russia, integrating innovative classic harmony with the *partes*-singing tradition. One of its pieces, *Veruyu* [The Creed], was especially popular and was printed and included in numerous nineteenth-century manuscript collections, as well as a bass part in an eighteenth-century manuscript copy.[16]

There are seven chorals to the cycle, all maintaining the same strict style characteristic of *partes*-singing settings of plainchant, which in general corresponds to the German motet or choral. The metric pulse in the first and last choruses of the Liturgy is proportional – half-notes in a 3/2 meter, typical of *partes*-singing compositions, but which was soon to became anachronistic, and which disappeared entirely from choral music from the late 1760s. The choral phrases here either follow one another or interchange with short imitative episodes. What distinguishes Berezovsky's Liturgy from *partes*-singing settings is harmony. While *partes*-singing settings are based mainly on four chords (tonics of relative keys and their dominants), Berezovsky's harmonic process heavily exploits secondary dominants and elongations, as well as the use of seventh chords of fourth and second degrees. Harmonies change every half or whole note. Voice-leading is extremely accurate and smooth. Diatonic sequences, sometimes coloured with suspensions, would have been perceived as a special attraction. What might also have been fascinating for the listeners was the typical harmonic dramaturgy: alternation of intensive changes in harmonic successions and sudden protraction of tonic chord (emphasized by plagal cadence and contrasting dynamics). The latter received a particular significance, lending the music a specifically 'authentic' church trait. It was Berezovsky's playing with his listener's expectations that probably gave his music that special charm, noted by Stählin as a blend of fiery Italian harmony and soft Greek melody (Example 5.6).

---

14 Sbornik dukhovno-muzykal'nykh sochineniy i perelozheniy raznykh avtorov dlya 4-kh muzhskikh golosov. Arr. and ed. by E.St. Azeev, St Petersburg, Kireev, 1914.

15 There are two indirect circumstances: the watermark of the paper indicates its production in Italy in the early 1760s (see M.P. Kukushkina *Filigtrani na bumage russkikh fabrik XVIII–nachala XIX vekov*, Moscow-Leningrad, 1958); and Galuppi's possible acquaintance with the Liturgy.

16 GMMK, f 283, no 25.

Example 5.6   Berezovsky: *Priidite poklonimsya* **(twentieth-century arrangement for male choir)**

Bog sta v sonme Bogov [God standeth in the congregation of the mighty]

Choral concertos were mostly written for the Psalms or other biblical texts, and certain psalms were set more often as well as there being more than one concerto with the same title. Among the rare and even unique settings is that of *Bog sta v sonme Bogov*. As far as can be told from the known data on eighteenth-century Russian choral concertos, this title is found only in Stählin's account of Berezovsky's works and in the HLA of 1804.[17] The score indicating Berezovsky's authorship has not been found, but there does exist an anonymous concerto bearing the same title, although this in itself is insufficient evidence for attribution. However, the style of this concerto does reveal certain traits that, even if not allowing firm attribution to Berezovsky, at least indicate the direction in which he or his fellow composers could have been working in the early 1760s in search of a new style.

The score was found in one of the few collections of four-voice choral concertos from the end of the eighteenth century, which included among the attributed works of the late eighteenth century (mostly by Bortniansky and Degtyarev, as usual), twelve anonymous concertos that differ from the rest stylistically.[18] The difference lies in their obvious *partes*-singing style, so closely reproduced that it would even have seemed quite natural had they been written in the 'Kiev square' notation. At the same time they also incorporate – non-organically – devices from instrumental baroque music. They are five- or four-voiced, indicating a tendency to the new style (in contrast to the multi–voiced scores more typical to *partes*-singing). Their

17   MV, 1804, no 80.

18   Sbornik khorovykh dukhovnykh kontsertov Yaroslavskogo Kazanskogo zhenskogo monastyrya. Part books 'абвг' and 'дежз'. GMMK, f 283, ns 918–21 and 903–6.

composers, however, were definitely native Russo-Ukrainian. In other words, these concertos represent that same transitional style that would have reflected works just preceding or contemporaneous with early Berezovsky (early 1760s), in the period when the death of Elizabeth put an end to stylistic constraints. The presence of these concertos in this late eighteenth-century collection attests to their having traditionally belonged to the particular repertoire of a Kazan nunnery (see note 18).

The concerto *Bog sta v sonme Bogov* has a typical *partes*-singing structure, based on alternation of 3/2 chordal sections with 2/2 lighter and more spirited polyphonic sections. The best-known model for this is the *Voskresensky kanon* [Eastern Canon] by Nikolai Diletsky.[19] The prevailing harmonic successions of both, however, are functional and not modal, and the voice-leading is still unskilled and full of parallel fifths and octaves (Example 5.7). In other fragments it shows opposite traits, being quite learned and resembling Berezovsky's Liturgy (Example 5.8) with piquant sequences of seventh chord inversions and suspensions in middle voices.

Example 5.7   **Anonymous concerto** *Bog sta v sonme bogov*, **section 1**

Rather than short imitative motet-like sections, there is a notable *fugato* in one of the middle sections, which is not only untypical of *partes*-singing concertos but also has obvious contemporaneous instrumental reference, and could even be a citation of some European work. *Fugue* and especially *fugato* would become characteristic of the mature new concerto only a few years later, and Berezovsky would prove to be its remarkable master (Example 5.9).

---

19 Diletsky's *Voskresenskiy kanon* [Eastern Canon] is an extended multi-sectional work for an 8-voiced choir *a cappella* on the text by John of Damascus (Published in *Mikola Dilets'ky, Khorovi tvori*. Compilation, ed., research and comments by N.A. Gerasimova-Persidskaya, 1981:23–81).

Example 5.8　**Anonymous concerto** *Bog sta v sonme bogov*, **section 2.**

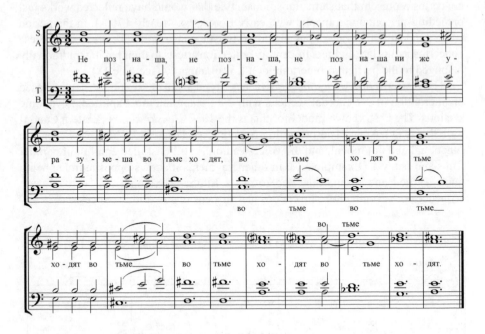

Example 5.9　**Anonymous concerto** *Bog sta v sonme bogov*, **finale**

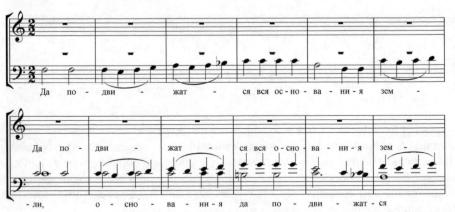

Despite its interest and importance in itself, this concerto is nonetheless inconclusive regarding any attribution to Berezovsky and thus must remain anonymous. Considering the eighteenth-century tradition of free treatment of musical texts, one could also speculate on Berezovsky's redaction of a certain popular *partes*-singing concerto through the insertion of new sections, and a consequent possible association of this concerto with his name.

Dokole, Gospodi, zabudesh' imya moe [How long wilt thou forget me, O Lord?]

This concerto was found in a manuscript collection of choral concertos from the end of the eighteenth century and beginning of the nineteenth.[20] Berezovsky's name, followed by a question mark, appears to have been added to the manuscript at a later date, although no known list of his compositions mentions this title. The concerto is not lacking in quality. Its style is less connected with the *partes*-singing tradition and seems more addressed to the new audience. The rhythmic organization is modern and free from the old 3/2 proportions. The music possesses a strong lyrical and dramatic nature, uses baroque rhetoric of prayer and torment, and motifs gleaned from the *kanty*, wailing songs, and lyrical folk songs, the combination of which would tend to assign it to the 1760s or even the 1770s (Example 5.10). Remarkably, despite the wide popularity of the minuet at the time, no trace of this genre can be found in the concerto, in contrast to the 1780s when the minuet rhythm would become widespread.

Example 5.10   **Berezovsky: Concerto** *Dokole, Gospodi, zabudesh imya moe?*, **section 1**

While the composer of this concerto was evidently occupied with harmonic successions, his attention to the melodic expressiveness of each voice recalls *partes*-singing in its linearity. This appears to have resulted in the parallel fifths and voice-crossing (natural in *partes*-singing, where the large number of parts, usually between eight to twelve, often made it unavoidable). The reduced number of voices in the concerto must have posed a special problem to musicians trained in *partes*-singing. They had to sacrifice melodic value in each part for the sake of vertical evenness. The first attempts were awkward and coarse. Generally, however, the voice-leading of this particular concerto is overpowered by the vertical harmonic relationships.

---

20 *Sbornik khorovykh sochineny kontsa XVIII veka* from the Collection of S. Smolensky. RGIA, f 1119, op 1, no 80.

It concludes with a remarkably good *fugue* in the finale, suggesting that a fugue, being a highly formalized and theoretically defined genre, was an easier task for composers in that particular era.

The attribution of this concerto to Berezovsky is less problematic than that of *Bog sta v sonme Bogov* because of its masterful technique, quality and modernity of material. Irrespective of the composer's identity, however, it would still be safe to assume that Berezovsky's first attempts would have been similarly directed. He could not possibly have ignored the incompatibility between the old compositional techniques and the new requirements imposed by harmony and polyphony in a four-voice choir. At this stage, the developing genre of concerto had not as yet assimilated the principles of fully functional harmony. On the other hand, while perfecting his professional skills, the composer would have gradually discovered the much-needed flexibility, universality and infinite possibilities of expression made possible through polyphonic techniques.

Gospod' votsarisya [The Lord reigneth; he is clothed in majesty]

This concerto is known as Berezovsky's only from its early twentieth-century publication.[21] The edition looks reliable and – according to its date – could be based on the eighteenth-century manuscripts from the Imperial Court Capella collection. In addition, a similar title is included in Berezovsky's list in HLA (1804, no 80). The problem is that in two Moscow collections (as reflected in KPN 1793 and the Collection of 1806–10)[22] this music is attributed to Tommaso Traetta – a fact that compliments both men: Berezovsky for his public recognition and Traetta for his delicate grasp of Russian music and his popularity in Russia. Hence, although it cannot be stated unequivocally that Berezovsky was the composer, we can at least be sure that the period coincides – from the late 1760s to the mid-1770s.

The ambiguity of attribution and existence of different versions speaks for the concerto's popularity. A comparison of two versions – printed in St Petersburg in 1903 and handwritten in Moscow around 1800 – reveals a rare identity of the scores, with the few slight variations inevitable in redactions in the live praxis of the time. The three-section concerto is as compact as Psalm 93 itself, composed masterly and for easy performance. The composer reveals much experience in choral writing. The first section (Example 5.11) is written in a somewhat light and playful baroque polyphonic style with certain references to *partes* concerti. The Finale (fugue) is similar in character. The real gem is the middle section of the concerto. It not only exemplifies a contemporary Russian song style featured in a spiritual concerto, but this song-like theme is also outlined in choral polyphony in the most organic way (Example 5.12). Its tender and melancholic 3/8-time theme is quite similar to the wedding songs presented in LPC in 1790, (Example 5.13) but with a slight touch of siciliana, more typical of the 1760s.

---

21 The concerto was published by M. Lisitsyn in the *Istoricheskaya khrestomatia tserkovnogo penia* (St Petersburg, 1903, vol. VI).

22   *Sbornik khorovykh kontsertov*. GMMK, f 283, ns 4, 48, 51.

Since there is no Russian choral concerto by Traetta known today, we have nothing to compare this concerto with and no idea of what his style might have been. Berezovsky, therefore, remains the most plausible candidate for its authorship, particularly as its elements well match certain of the stylistic features of his Communion verses and concertos *Ne otverzhi mene* and *Da voskresnet Bog*.

Example 5.11   Berezovsky: Concerto *Gospod' votsarisya*, **section 1**

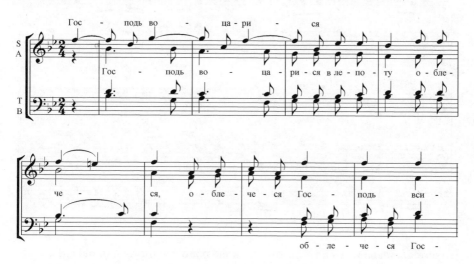

Example 5.12   Berezovsky: Concerto *Gospod' votsarisya*, **section 2**

Example 5.13   Russian wedding song *Chto ne Pava* **from the Lvov-Prach Collection of Russian folk songs**

Ne otverzhi mene vo vremya starosti [Cast me not off in the time of old age]

This concerto is the only one of Berezovsky's works with no problems regarding attribution, date of composition (late 1760s), public recognition and preservation of the score. Although there is no autograph score, there is a good commercial copy from the end of the eighteenth century (currently in the British Museum) and three nineteenth-century editions were also produced.[23] The only mystery surrounding this concerto is the general lack of creative context of the time in Russian music, except for Berezovsky's own Liturgy, most probably written several years earlier, and Galuppi's concertos. Berezovsky's other concertos mentioned by Stählin, as well as the compositions of his Ukrainian fellow-musicians written around the same time, remain unknown.

---

23 The first edition of the concerto *Ne otverzhi* relates to the beginning of the nineteenth century (Ginzburg, 1968:468), probably edited and published by Bortniansky (see Chapter 14); the second was made by the Imperial Court Cappella in 1844; and the third was released by Jurgenson in 1890. There is a modern edition of the concerto prepared by V.M. Ikonnik: *Khorovye kontserty XVIII–nachala XIX vekov: M. Berezovsky, D. Bortniansky, A. Vedel*. Kiev: Muzychna Ukraina, 1988:6–31.

The other works closest to Ne otverzhi... in style are the only known part of the German liturgy Unser Vater, traditionally attributed to Berezovsky24 and the concerto Da voskresnet Bog.25 Neither of these have any indication of when they were written. The first corresponds to Ne otverzhi... in the reserved character of its expression, thematic material and wide use of polyphony, although not in the form of fugue or fugato, but in numerous motet-like short imitative sections. The second is a large-scale concerto, rich in contrasting images and developed polyphony.

Ne otverzhi... is an almost monothematic concerto with a relatively simple cyclic construction. Its two main sections – the first and the third – consist of *fugues* on related themes, while the middle, contrasting section is built of intense harmonic movement. The overall structure is based on the development of these themes, whose rhythmic and harmonic possibilities are imaginatively exploited. The significance and potential of each motif within the themes generates an inner impulsive charge that nurtures the entire cycle.

The melodic value of the themes is characterized by a close alliance between the musical expressiveness and the semantic content of the text. The main theme has a structure resting on first and fifth degrees of minor mode with undulating gestures filling the gap as typical or even quintessential for protracted folk songs (Example 5.14). While Levashev and Polekhin (1985:156) noted its similarity to the Russian song 'Ne shumi, mati, zelenaya dubravushka' [Don't rustle, mother – green leafy grove] collected by N. Lopatin and Prokunin (Example 5.15a) and the Ukrainian duma 'Gei, yak na slavniy Ukraini' [Hey, as in the glorious Ukraine]

Example 5.14 **Berezovsky: Concerto** *Ne otverzhi mene vo vremya starosti*, **section 1**

---

24 *Unser Vater* was published by Breitkopf und Härtel, Leipzig, 1813. The new edition prepared by V.M. Ikonnik can be found in *Poet Kievsky kamerny khor* (Kiev: Muzychna Ukraina, 1977).

25 *Sbornik khorovykh sochineny kontsa XVIII veka* from the Collection of S. Smolensky. RGIA, f 1119, op 1, no 80.

Examples 5.15 (a) Russian folk song *Ne shumi, mati zelenaya dubravushka* **from the Lopatin-Prokunin Collection and (b) Ukrainian folk song** *Oy, nas brattsy pyat'*

collected by K. Kvitka, Vytvyts'ky (1974:51–2) noted it regarding the Ukrainian song 'Oy, nas brattsy pyat'' [Oh, brothers, we are five], (Example 5.15b), and Yurchenko (1985:22) found a closeness with the Russian protracted song 'Ne odna vo pole dorozhen'ka' [There is more than one path in the field]. However, there are no intrasyllabic expansions in Berezovsky's theme, making it strict and simple. It achieves an altogether folk-like quality with a complete absence of affectation. There are highly impressive contrasts between this intimate melodic speech and the explosions sounded in a *tutti* that reverberates with the chill of damnation. Berezovsky skilfully manipulated the typical baroquesque suspension-resolution idiom. He inverted the common suspension-as-dissonance and resolution-as-consonance order by shifting the consonance to the weak beat, thus further emphasizing the dissonance. The consonant thirds and sixths are 'resolved' to extended dissonant tritons, thus intensifying the rhythmic piercing quality of the suspension. This intensification of the theme from the outset permeates the entire harmonic framework of the concerto, creating a dense, dissonant texture. The triton, which appears in the first section, occurs mostly in its vertical form, but in the Finale (the counter-subject) it appears and persistently recurs in horizontal melodic constructions.

The potential of this masterpiece has motivated some interesting research. Levashev and Polekhin found a certain correspondence between the structure of this concerto and the Passion genre (1985:159), while Katz emphasized Berezovsky's attempt to underscore the rhythmic qualities of the prosaic text through musical means (1994).

Ne otverzhi... as a classic polyphonic work was important for the developing nineteenth-century musical aspirations. Russian composers were familiar with this music and its sound could have served as a point of departure for the attempts by Glinka and Taneev to combine Russian folk melody with classical counterpoint. The concerto may have served as a remote source of inspiration for Musorgsky's theme and its polyphonic development in the Introduction to *Boris Godunov*.

Berezovsky Leaves for Italy

Returning to Berezovsky's biographical data, his whereabouts in the 1760s requires some clarification. Stählin's text serves as the only evidence of Berezovsky's position as court *chamber musician* by 1769, otherwise not documented. There is also an earlier mention of Berezovsky in the Court Chronicles, stating that on 22 August 1766, in the Amber Chamber of the Tsarskoe Selo Palace, 'for approbation, a concerto, composed by *musician* Berezovsky was performed by court singers' (KFZ, 1765–8). Finally, there is the above-mentioned manuscript copy of Berezovsky's Liturgy, probably written between 1762 and 1765, noting him as the Court kapellmeister. In the mid-1760s, therefore, *musician, chamber musician* and *Kapellmeister* were probably interchangeable titles indicating some position that Berezovsky held at Court after (or at the same time as?) being recorded as a singer in the Italian company. In 1770s documents he is already mentioned as a composer.

It is also important to note that no other native composer was ever mentioned in the Court Chronicles. Even Galuppi was mentioned only three times during his three years in Russia. Hence the importance of the above note is no less significant than Stählin's paragraphs in defining the extent of Berezovsky's recognition. Everything combines to indicate that Berezovsky had become an excellent candidate to be granted the privilege, established by Peter I, of being sent abroad as a young and talented Russian, at the State's expense, in order to perfect his knowledge and skill. This practice became especially popular during the reign of Catherine II. Among those who enjoyed it were the scientist Lomonosov, the writer Radishchev, the architect Bazhenov, the actor Dmitrevsky, the sculptor Martos, the dancer Bublikov, the violinist Pomorsky, the cellist Überscher and the composers Berezovsky, Bortniansky, Skokov and Fomin. These artists returned to Russia with broadened knowledge and life experience, some with foreign diplomas and accreditations, and many of them went on to contribute to Russian culture.

Traditionally, the date of Berezovsky's departure is considered to be 'around 1765', as noted by Bolkhovitinov in 1805. This conflicts, however, with Stählin's mentioning Berezovsky (in 1769) as 'the current court chamber musician Maxim Berezovsky', implying his presence in St Petersburg. But Stählin's essay seems to have been effectively forgotten by the nineteenth century, and before it was rediscovered and introduced into Russian historiography in 1902[26] a certain tradition of Berezovsky's hagiography had emerged, in which the concerto *Ne otverzhi* played a significant role.

When in the 1830s–40s, on the wave of romantic nationalism, Berezovsky's personality began to attract attention, the tragic circumstances of his life were heavily played up and began to form a myth around Bolkhvitonov's brief and somewhat approximate account of the composer's life. The artistic maturity and dramatic power of this concerto were related to the unfortunate end to Berezovsky's life

---

26 In 1902 Findeizen edited and published in *Russkaya muzykal'naya gazeta* Antonin Preobrazhensky's translation of Stählin's paragraphs related to the Court Cappella.

(Vorotnikov, 1851).[27] Meanwhile the version of his biography in which he was born in 1745 and sent to Italy in 1765 (eventually without 'around') had been established. It was as if he was considered to have been too young to write such perfect and tragic music before his years of study in Italy. An emotional link between this concerto and Berezovsky's tragic life has continued to dominate his biographers until now. The desire to prove by any means that Berezovsky wrote the concerto at the end of his life appears to have forced such a solidly institutionalized scholar as Levashev to have consciously distorted Stählin's listing of Berezovsky's concertos, omitting the title of *Ne otverzhi*, not referring to the source, using the incorrect Russian translation by Zagurgsky (Stählin, 1935), and not bothering to look at Stählin's German original or at least at the accurate translation offered by Preobrazhensky (Levashev and Polekhin, 1984:141).

My own search for documentary confirmation of Berezovsky's departure for Italy around 1765 was unfruitful. The standard procedure for sending a student abroad in the 1760s was first and foremost by order of Catherine II. The formal decree was then presented to the Cabinet and the Court Administration by the Imperial secretaries (Yelagin and Count Sivers were in charge of actors and musicians). The orders for financial remittance were given to Olsufiev and those for issuance of passports – to the vice-Chancellor, Prince Golitsyn. The final document required before the actual departure was the daily report sent from Riga by the Governor of Livonia, Count Yury (George) Brown,[28] to the Board of Foreign Affairs. This report noted every individual crossing the border in either direction.

However, even these routine procedures are, in the case of Berezovsky, not documented. Mention, full or partial, is made of certain of the students at every stage of the process. Berezovsky, however, is not alluded to in any of the procedural documents of the 1760s. His name does not appear in any of the imperial edicts, nor is it mentioned in Yelagin's papers, in the registry of newly issued passports, in the expense book of the accounting office, or recorded in the reports of the Governor of Livonia.

It is also true, however, that not all the sets of documents were properly kept and preserved. Among them, the best maintained are the imperial edicts, Golitsyn's passport records, and the border reports from Riga. The lack of continuity in the catalogue numbers recorded in the nineteenth-century office book in RGIA is an indication that only a small portion of Yelagin's original records have survived, similar to the state of the treasurer's accounts. Furthermore, the ledgers of the

27 Berezovsky's biography by Vorotnikov was evidently influenced by the prevalent fiction about the composer, whose tragic image met romantic ideas of the time. Two works preceded it: a play by P. Smirnov *Maxim Sozontovich Berezovsky* (1841, see M. Rytsareva, 'Maxim Berezovsky i zabytaya russkaya drama', *Teatral'naya zhizn'* 1984, 24:26–7) and a story by N. Kukol'nik *Maxim Berezovsky*, (1844, 2nd edn 1852). It is also most probable that Vorotnikov was not aware of the existence of Stählin's *Nachrichten...* However this notion still has its adherents even in our time (E.M. Levashev, A.V. Polekhin, 1985:132–60).

28 Field-marshal Yury (George) Browne was the father of Ivan Yurievich Browne, known as one of Beethoven's admirers and patrons (Klimovitsky, MPES, I:126).

Solyanaya kontora, [Salt office], which paid the salaries of the musicians of the Italian Company and the Court Choir singers, have no record of payments for 1765. According to the archivists, this information had already been removed from the books in the eighteenth century, leaving us only with the registration notes in the internal accounts office book.

One exemplary file is that of a dancer from the Italian Company, Timofey Bublikov. For the years 1764–5 all the relevant books show the preparations for his departure.[29] Bublikov is also mentioned in the papers of Yelagin and vice-Chancellor Golitsyn. In addition, the ledgers of the *Solyanaya kontora* registered 'the release of funds for the voyage of Timofey Bublikov' on 14 January 1765.[30] Bublikov was apparently an outstanding dancer just as Berezovsky was an outstanding musician. It is interesting that the former left Russia at the same time as the latter's presumed departure. However no known imperial edict, passport or border document exists to support this date in Berezovsky's biography.

While some of these departments often lack records there was one that was always particularly accurate – the Board of Foreign Affairs. What remained was thus to make a thorough examination of the border reports up to the year when Berezovsky became affiliated with the Bologna Accademia Filarmonica – 1771. The result was unexpected and not only concerning the date of Berezovsky's departure. The note on those leaving St Petersburg reads: 'On 26 May, to Vienna, for the plenipotentiary minister, Prince Golitsyn, Maxim Berezovsky, as a courier.'[31] It can now be confirmed that Berezovsky left Russia in 1769, the same 'spring 1769' when Stählin finished his essay, mentioning Berezovsky's presence at the time at Court. This note, however, generates a number of puzzling aspects, which for the present must remain unsolved.

The mere mention of Berezovsky as a courier is in itself puzzling. Could there have been another individual named Maxim Berezovsky? Extensive research of the border reports reveals a constant mention of the same two persons serving as official

---

29 On 17 December 1764, an imperial edict ordered the release of the dancer Timofey Bublikov for superior dance study abroad for two years, along with a departure remittance of 150 roubles. In addition, for his daily expenses there and till his return there were to be added 200 roubles plus another 300 roubles, a total of 500 roubles per annum. See *Vysochayshie povelenia*, 1763–64, RGIA, f 466, op 1, no 106.

30 *Delo o vydache deneg na dorozhny proezd Timofeyu Bublikovu*. RGADA, f 355, no112, L 73. Along with Bublikov's name, the set painter Ivan Firsov and the music student Nikolai Pomorsky are often mentioned as receiving an annual allocation of 500 roubles. Timofey Bublikov was Berezovsky's fellow artist at the court of Grand Duke Peter Fedorovich. His name appears on the list of performers at the Oranienbaum Theater and in one of Catherine II first edicts (1 June 1762, with regard to court personnel and salaries).

31 '26 мая в Вену находящемуся тамо полномочному министру князю Голицыну курьером Максим Березовской' (Raporty v Kollegiu Inostrannykh del iz Lifliandskoy General Gubernskoy Kantseliarii o proezzhayushchikh v Rossiyu i ot'ezzhayushchikh za granitsu raznogo zvania lyudyakh. AVPRI, Snoshenia Rossii s Lifliandiey i Estliandiey, 1769, op 64/1, no 1, Ll 59, 69).

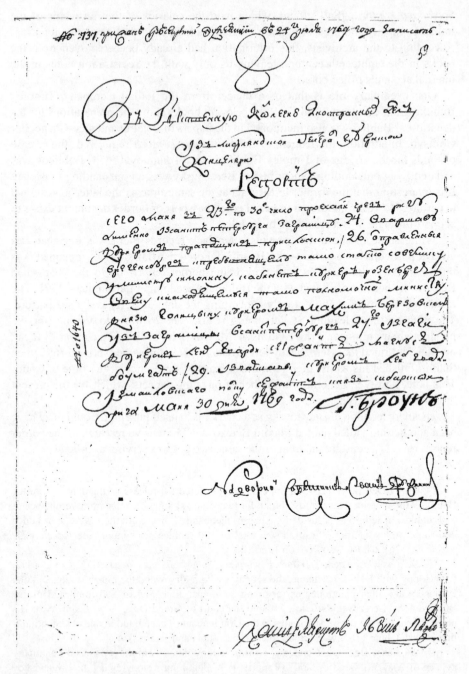

Figure 5.1   **Report of Count George Brown, Governor of Livonia on border crossings from 23–30 May 1769, Riga**

couriers: Pavel Yulenets (sometimes spelled Yelenets) and Vladimir Fedorovsky. What was Maxim Berezovsky doing in this capacity, and why was he on his way to Vienna to the plenipotentiary minister Golitsyn while his destination was Italy and the Bologna Accademia Filarmonica? There could of course have been prosaic circumstances, such as the regular courier having fallen ill, or an opportunity for economy by the court office (being in chronic budget deficit). An indirect possible explanation for this mysterious circumstance is also to be found in the international political situation of the time, which will be dealt with in the next chapter.

The date of Berezovsky's departure from Russia is perhaps less important in itself than the fact that it provides strong confirmation of Stählin's account of Berezovsky, who by the time of his departure from Russia was already the accomplished and renowned composer who had written *Ne otverzhi*. The goal of his stay in Italy was thus to broaden his musical horizon, to receive additional training in counterpoint and to prove himself as a composer of international calibre. This might also have been considered a necessary stage for further promotion in his service to the Empress.

The Young Dmitry Bortniansky

The 1760s also saw the beginning of the career of Dmitry Bortniansky, Berezovsky's younger fellow-composer. Bortniansky, like Berezovsky, was a native of the Ukraine and had begun his career as a court singer. These were the parallels that provoked nineteenth-century writers to extrapolate facts from Bortniansky's biography to that of Berezovsky in order to fill in the missing details. Bortniansky was indeed born in Glukhov, as confirmed by various documents. His great-grandfather came from the kingdom of Poland. His father, who had served as a Cossack under hetman Razumovsky (Ivanov, 1980:3, 1995), had married a widow, Marina Dmitrievna Tolstaya, and they had had one daughter, Melania, and two sons – Timofey, who died at a very early age, and Dmitry. The year of Dmitry's birth is accepted as 1751, although 1752 and even 1753 are also occasionally given in biographical references.

The main source of Bortniansky's biography is an essay written by his grandson Dmitry Dolgov (1857). According to it, Bortniansky was a pupil at the Glukhov School for Court Singers (where not only singing but also violin and *bandura* were studied). In 1758, at the age of seven, he qualified among the top ten vocal students and was sent to St Petersburg Imperial court. Considering Razumovsky's direct involvement with sending musicians from the Ukraine to the Court, it is likely that Bortniansky reached the capital under his supervision during his 1758 trip.

Becoming a court singer was an attractive prospect. Among the privileges enjoyed beyond those granted to all court servants was an exemption from taxation for the singers and their families. On 18 November 1759, after Bortniansky had left home, the governor of Malorossia, hetman Razumovsky, decreed that 'the homes of underage court musicians in Kiev and *Malorossia,* where their fathers, mothers, brothers and sisters still reside, will be exempt from billeting, services and duties' (Gusin and Tkachev, 1957:20).

The head of the Imperial Court Choir from 1745 was Mark Fedorovich Poltoratsky, a friend of the Razumovsky brothers. Alexey Grigorievich Razumovsky himself had served as a court singer in the 1740s, and thus the Court Choir was connected to Elizabeth's court not only professionally (through religious services, opera performances or routine chamber concerts) but also personally. Famous for her lack of royal decorum, Elizabeth enjoyed singing with the choir during private services in her chambers, for which occasions a smaller ensemble would gather.

In the life of the court singers their privileges were intertwined with uncertainty and difficulties. Although they were tutored in foreign languages, arithmetic and geography, were clad in uniforms and fur coats, and received bonuses on Christmas and Easter, nothing was guaranteed. The possibility of being suddenly relieved of their duties loomed constantly, often under unclear circumstances. They were paid on an irregular basis and were frequently ill and hungry, as documented in the court archives.

In 1758 the choir received new quarters, possibly due to the recruitment of additional singers, making their former home at the Main Postal Office too small. Their new residence was in the house of Lieutenant Peter Nashchyokin ('close to the Admiralty Channel... near the house of State Counsellor Ivan Pugovkin'), not far from their former quarters, specially rented for this purpose. The new quarters were under the administration of Mark Poltoratsky and the owner had a contractual obligation to keep the place well-maintained and clean. Nashchyokin failed to fulfil his obligations and Poltoratsky had to complain repeatedly, and ineffectually, to the Cabinet, requesting its intervention. On 22 February 1760, he sent a particularly expressive report, writing that the stoves and everything else need repairing, the house had not been cleaned for a long time and that with the coming of the spring the stench would become unbearable and even dangerous. He disclaimed any responsibility if singers fell sick in a possible epidemic in the spring as a result of the lack of hygiene and the stench, and demanded that urgent measures to be taken to repair and clean the residence.[32]

Bortniansky's life with the court choir can be reconstructed from known facts about the general conditions governing its activity during the 1750s and 1760s. There was no systematic education. The adult singers were assigned to teach the younger ones *partes*-singing with style and to thrash the lazy. Only those who had already fully mastered *partes*-singing were to be taught reading or other disciplines, each according to his inclinations (Vsevolodsky-Gerngross, 1913, I: 409–11).

For the child Bortniansky the hardships of duty may have been outweighed by the more positive elements. Bortniansky's grandson wrote that, charmed by the child's looks and innate talent, the Empress Elizabeth had cared for him as she would have for her own son. After concerts, when the little boy was leaving the palace, the sovereign herself would sometimes tie her own scarf around his neck. One particular and possibly anecdotal episode, which became a family legend, related that after a

---

32 *Delo o pridvornykh pevchikh*, RGADA, f 14, op 1, no 96, L 92.

Bright Christ's Sunday morning mass, little Bortniansky was so exhausted by the lengthy religious service that he fell asleep in the choir loft. Upon noticing this, the Empress ordered that immediately following services the boy should be taken to her own chambers and put to bed quietly. When Bortniansky woke up he couldn't believe his eyes. Thinking that he was still dreaming, he remained in a drowsy state, amusing his benefactor with his childish apprehensions and shyness (Dolgov, 1857:18).

The court singers led full and diversified professional lives. They performed regularly at religious services in the main church of the Winter Palace (sometimes also in the small church and quite often in the private quarters). Musical events at the Court also involved performances of secular music – Italian arias and Russian and Ukrainian folk songs as well as instrumental pieces. (The choristers were sometimes also trained in playing instruments.) Unfortunately, although there are occasional records of the performers' names, there is no documentation on the repertory performed. The court chronicles of the mid-1760s mention *Yantarnaya komnata* [Amber Chamber] and *Kartinnaya komnata* [Picture Chamber] as the places where in the evenings the young singers would perform Italian arias accompanied by violins, often as background music for 'Her Majesty amusing herself by playing cards with the cavaliers' (KFZ, 1765–8). During the summer the court musicians and singers enhanced the beauty of the parks with their performances. They serenaded Her Majesty's approaches to the palaces, accompanied her and her son, the Grand Duke, when sailing in their boat on the pond, performing on the other vessels behind them or standing on the island and so on.

Because performing in the opera productions was among the duties of the young choristers, they were sometimes selected to perform solos in these productions. In 1764, at the age of thirteen, Bortniansky was listed as playing the lead male soprano (King Admet) in a renewed production of *Alcesta* by Hermann Raupach, with libretto by Alexander Sumarokov, the second Russian-language opera after Araja-Sumarokov's *Tsephal i Prokris*. This was Bortniansky's only known performance and the one that later served as an analogy to Berezovsky's performances in Oranienbaum (for those scholars who were certain that Berezovsky had a soprano voice at the time).

In the 1760s, court singers demonstrating acting potential were sent to the elite Cadet Corps (*Shlyahetsky* or *Kadetsky korpus*) to learn the art of acting. Among them was Bortniansky.[33] Dramatic art was taught by the young Ivan Afanasievich Dmitrevsky, the future great Russian actor, and the Italian language by the Turk Fedor Alexandrovich (Magometh-Ali) Emin. Emin had lived an adventurous life in Turkey, Italy and England before his arrival in St Petersburg in 1761 and his transition to Russian writer, translator and journalist. From an early age therefore, moving in the Imperial Court circle and enjoying the patronage of Empress Elizabeth and probably also of Kirill Razumovsky, Bortniansky would have been in contact with the intellectual elite, who contributed to his development into a polished gentleman

---

33 Bortniansky returned to the Cadet Corps 40 years later, as the conductor of its student choir. (See Faddey Bulgarin, *Vospominania*. St Petersburg, 1846. part II:50–2.)

and a learned courtier, making him a popular figure and welcome in high circles throughout his life.

Bortniansky received his initial training in composition and counterpoint from Mark Fedorovich Poltoratsky, an expert in choral performance and composition, as well as from Hermann Raupach and Josef Startzer (Dobrokhotov, 1950:5). The latter worked in St Petersburg as a ballet composer with Franz Hilverding from 1760 to 1768, where he successfully promoted the music of Gluck, Telemann, Wagenseil, Graun and other German masters at the court performances (Findeizen, 1929, II:125). Having acquired this rich background, Bortniansky then became Galuppi's student and accompanied him to Italy. They crossed the border on 2 August 1768 – almost a year earlier than Berezovsky.[34]

---

34 *Vnutrennie kollezhskie dela*, AVPRI, op 169, years 1763–65, no 3510, L 320.

Chapter 6

Lessons of the 1770s:
Berezovsky and Bortniansky in Italy

Berezovsky and Bortniansky, each following his own path, appeared in Italy during the same period. Their sojourn there coincided with the Russian-Turkish war of 1768–74, during which Venice and Livorno became strategically important for the Russian forces. Many Russian high-ranking military officials (among them Count Panin, Prince Repnin, Count Vorontsov, Count Ivan Chernyshev) arrived there on special missions, accompanied by their entourages. Count Alexey Orlov, the Commander-in-Chief of the Russian navy and Marquise Pablo Maruzzi, the Russian chargé d'affaires in Venice from 1762–83, were the key figures around whom the temporary Russian community gathered.

Little evidence remains of the young musicians' activities during their studies in Italy. What there is, however, suggests that they spent time not only confronting sheets of music paper, but that their lives also pulsated with the dynamic historic, and sometimes fabulous, events afforded them by being abroad during this time of war. While Bortniansky arrived in Venice, the home town of his maitre Galuppi, Berezovsky went to Bologna, to his maitre, Padre Martini. There is no evidence that they met in Italy, but they would have visited the same places and people, making it convenient to unite their Italian experiences into a single chapter, as well as to include the Italian composer Tommaso Traetta, who – in contrast – spent the same years (1768–75) serving the Russian Empress in St Petersburg.

Bortniansky's Missions

In Bortniansky's traditional biography his Italian period has been represented by the list of compositions he wrote under supervision of the venerable Galuppi, and on account of the cities he visited. However, a later document – a routine form concerning his service – filled out by Bortniansky in 1805, contains an unexpected record in a standard paragraph asking: 'Whether or not [you] have participated in [military] campaigns and in the battles themselves and when precisely?' Bortniansky's answer reads:

> [I] didn't take part in any battles, but during the advancement of the fleet in the Archipelago, [I] was often used by its Commander-in-Chief Count Orlov, then in Venice, for negotiations

with the Greeks, Albanians, and other peoples regarding military preparations, facing
great danger from the local government.[1]

This remarkable account can be clarified within the context of the Russian–Turkish
war. The Russian strategy was to distract the Turkish fleet from the Black Sea by
opening a second, southwestern front. Since the occupied Greeks, Albanians and
Montenegrins were Russia's natural allies, Russia dispatched a fleet of warships
to the eastern Mediterranean (Aegean) Sea to support the national liberation
movements against Turkish rule. Catherine II appointed Count Alexey Orlov to
command the entire Aegean fleet and coordinate all military action in the region.
The tactical support provided by the local rebels was coordinated by General Prince
Yury Vladimirovich Dolgoruky and it was under his immediate command that
Bortniansky participated in those expeditions.

The Prince and his entourage left Russia incognito. The check-point in Riga
recorded the crossing on 28 April 1768 of Prince Eria [Yury] Dolgoruky accompanied
by persons bearing the names of Russian subjects, merchants and three servants.[2] He
arrived in Venice, where Marquise Maruzzi was handling all the financial and currency
operations, knew the whereabouts of all the Russian subjects and was working in
cooperation with Count Orlov. With their help Dolgoruky organized the expeditions.
By the beginning of August, a first military mission had been assembled. It included,
according to Dolgoruky, all the Russians of various ranks and professions who were
present at the time in Italy, some thirty people altogether. After crossing the Adriatic
Sea, the mission made an incursion into Montenegro. Despite the instability and
internal strife there, the group accomplished its mission and Dolgoruky established
contact with Stephen the Small – Montenegro's ruler from 1767 to 1773. During this
expedition, the detachment came under fierce attack from opponents of the rebellion,
but miraculously survived.

Unfortunately, no known source gives the list of participants. Although
Bortniansky's evidence of his service record matches this event, his participation in
this particular mission is somewhat unlikely. He crossed the Russian border between
26 July and 2 August 1768 and may have arrived in Venice after the expedition's
departure or immediately prior to it. However, his comment that he 'was often used
... for negotiations' indicates that there were several similar missions around 1770–
71. Indeed, later diplomatic records of Prince Dolgoruky mention him briefly as
having stirred up the Montenegrins in 1770 and the Albanians in 1771.[3]

---

1   'В походах против неприятеля и в самых сражениях были или нет и когда
именно?' 'В сражениях не бывал, а во время шествия флота в Архипелаг часто был
употребляем главнокомандующим оного графом Орловым в бытность его в Венеции
для переговоров с греками, албанцами и другими народами касательно до военных
приготовлений с великою опасностию от тамошнего правления' (RGIA, f 1349, op 4, no
1, 1805. Quoted by Filshtein, 1980:23).

2   AVPRI, Snoshenia Rossii s Venetsiey, op 41/3, no 41, Ll 24–7.

3   See 200–letie Kabineta E. I. V. 1704–1904. St Petersburg, 1911.

Berezovsky's Studies

Since Maxim Berezovsky was also in Italy during the same period, there exists a possibility that he too may have taken part in Dolgoruky's missions. The account of Berezovsky's known compositions written in Italy is definitely a modest one and leaves plenty of room for other musical and/or non-musical occupations. Berezovsky's departure from Russia as a courier might have meant his involvement in a conspiracy, while both his and Bortniansky's being sent to Italy to study at the time of the Russian–Turkish war could have afforded good cover, cleverly veiling the true interest in having there as many young Russians as possible (especially those knowing Italian).

The only relatively clear aspect of Berezovsky's Italian years is the framework of his studies with Padre Giovanni-Batista Martini, due to the accuracy of the latter's archive. From Martini's papers it appears that Berezovsky reached him in Bologna some time prior to April 1770, and without any letter of recommendation or introduction, which indicates that his journey from St Petersburg to Bologna may have been spur of the moment. The lapse was corrected either in Vienna by Prince Dmitry Mikhaylovich Golitsyn or in Venice by Marquise Maruzzi who sent a request to the administrator of the Imperial Theatres, Ivan Yelagin, to write such a letter, which he did on 12 February 1770:

Reverend Father!

There are people who are known throughout the world for their rare talent. You, my Reverend Father, are one such. Please do not be surprised to receive this letter from an inhabitant of the North, who, although not being personally acquainted with you, greatly admires and esteems you. Mr Berezovsky, already among your students in Bologna, is a musician from my country, affiliated to the Imperial Theatres, for which I have the honour to be the Director-General. It is on his behalf that I write you these lines. I would be most grateful, Reverend Father, if you could extend your guiding hand so that the ground upon which you sow your seeds of instruction will bear fruit and truly justify the efforts of his illustrious tutor. This will but serve to increase your fame and reputation. We, the inhabitants of this icy land, will owe a debt of gratitude that on my part will be boundless. Finally, Reverend Father, you would eternally oblige me if you could advise me as to whether this man indeed possesses sufficient abilities in the art that you have perfected and rendered illustrious…

Reverend Father!
Your very obedient servant
I. de Yelagin
12 February 1770.[4]

---

4   'Mon reverend Pere! Il y a des hommes qui par leurs rares talents sont connus dans tous les pays. Vous, mon reverend Pere, etant de ce nombres ne devés pas [Vous?] etonner firons reccriés cette lettre d'un habitant du Nord qui, sans vous connaitre, vous admire et vous estime. Un Musicien de mon pays appartenant aux Spectacles de notre Souveraine dont j'ai l'honneur d'étre le Directeur general, me procure la satisfaction de vous écrire ces lignes, c'est le S.-r Beresousky qui est actuelle ment à Bologne parmis vos Elèves. Ayés la bonté

The letter must had been delivered to Berezovsky via Marquis Maruzzi, who added his part to Yelagin's request on 21 April 1770:

> ...For some time now, following the order of the Imperial court, Mr. Berezovsky has been here to study counterpoint. I consider myself greatly fortunate and satisfied to be distinguished by your favour and great kindness, which encourage me to apply to you for your help. I assure you that I shall do everything in my power to ensure the success of this endeavour...[5]

Within three days, on 24 April, the disciplined Martini had already responded to both addressees:

To Maruzzi

> ...The singularly sincere motivation of Your Excellency as demonstrated by your note regarding Mr. Berezovsky particularly obliges me to pass on to him that small degree of knowledge in counterpoint that I possess. I hope that he will cultivate his talent and natural abilities, a prerequisite for such a profession, and will indeed deserve the approval of Her Majesty, the Empress of Russia...[6]

To Yelagin:

> ... Mr. Maxim has indeed the necessary skills to study the art of counterpoint and to become an outstanding composer. If he continues thus to develop his talent, and I will

---

mon reverend Pere, de lui tendre votre main secourable et l'instruire, autant que la terre où vous jetterés les semenees pour à produire du fruit. Si après le retour de l'Eléve nous voyons on lui son digne. Maitre, cela servirá à l'augmentation de votre renommée; et comme nous autres habitants de ce pays froid cherissons la reconnaissance, la mienne sera pour vous sans bornes. Aurest, mon reverend Pere, vous m'obligerés infiniment, en m'instruissant de cet homme a asséz de Capacité pour un art que vous avès perfectionné et rendu illustre... / Mon reverend Pere ! / Votre très obeissant serviteur / J. de Yelagin / le 12 de Fevrier 1770.' This and the following letters are quoted by N. Fanti, *Manoscritti dei musicisti russi e sovietici nella Biblioteca Communale, annessi all Conservatorio musicale 'G.B. Martini' di Bologna*, Bologna, 1963. This correspondence was republished and translated into Ukrainian by M.Yurchenko (1989:67–79), from whose work the following letters are quoted here.

5   '... È qualche tempo, cheil Sig. Berezowski s'attrova costi d'ordine della mia Imperial Corte per apprendere il Contrapunto. Esse si chiama di molto fortunato e contento per essere distintamente favorito dalla di Lei insigne virtù, lo che m'impegna di vie più raccomandando alla di Lei assistenza. Assicurandola, che mi farò un pregio se le (?) potro essere utile negli incontri...'

6   'La signolara degnazione di V.E. di dimostrarmi le premesse che ha per il Sig. Berezowski sempre piu m'impegna a comunicarli quel poco nell arte del contrapunto, che potra darle la mia debole capacità, e voglio sperare che coltivando egli il talento e disposizione naturale che ha per tale professione possa mettersi in stato di servire con aggradimento a sua maestà imperatrice della Russie...'

teach him everything I know, upon his return it is hoped that he will be truly satisfied with the results of his long sojourn in Bologna...[7]

Once settled in Bologna, Berezovsky was to become involved in various negotiations between the Russian court and Italian artists.[8] A draft of a letter from Martini to Yelagin, dated 12 June 1770, reveals that Berezovsky, commissioned by Yelagin, had attempted to find a librettist for the Russian court. Martini, however, appears to have suggested himself as the most appropriate agent for this task.

Berezovsky's study with Padre Martini coincided with the same period as the Bohemian Josef Myslivíček, as well as with Mozart's presence there when the latter took his entrance test for the Bologna Accademia Filarmonica on 8 July 1770. However, the Mozarts do not seem to have made any mention of Berezovsky, whereas their references to Myslivíček are well known. The following year, on 15 May 1771, Berezovsky passed the standard entrance procedure, including writing of an excellent ten-bar polyphonic composition, and was unanimously accepted to the Academy.

Among the scattering of information available to us about Berezovsky's Italian years, there is some value to an undated letter written by the music copyist Antonio Cima to Padre Martini. In it he seeks advice with regard to some confusing remarks in Berezovsky's instructions for delivering a finished score to Signora Brigonzi in Florence. Catarina Brigonzi had been Berezovsky's fellow-performer in the Oranienbaum spectacles and also among those who had left Russia after the *coup d'état* in 1762, and it is quite natural that he would have used this connection to assist his promotion in Italy. Berezovsky's eighteen psalms and his eight-voice Mass mentioned in this note also constitute evidence of his professional activity during this period (Yurchenko, 1989:79).

Membership in this most prestigious academy appears to have been not the only goal of Berezovsky's studies. Rather, it comprised one more part of the necessary experience on his personal record. Opera production was a no less important requisite of the Italian curriculum for foreign students. Myslivíček, for instance, had become a member of the Academy two years after his opera *Demofoonte* (1769) had been produced in Venice.

After completion of his studies with Padre Martini and his admission to the Academy, Berezovsky presumably left Bologna. It is commonly assumed that he relocated to Livorno, where his own opera *Demofoonte* was staged in 1773. However, his Sonata for Violin and Harpsichord in C Major (*Sonata per Violino / e Cimbalo Del Sig.-re / Massimo Beresowskoy Russo / Accademico Filarmonico / al servizio di S:M: L'Impe / ratrice di tutte le Russie. / Pisa, 1772*), discovered by V. Vytvytsky (1974) and published by Stepanenko[9] indicates that Berezovsky had also spent some time in Pisa. This can

---

7   '... Sta il Sig. Massimo tutta la capacità per apprendere l'arte del contrapunto, e rendersi non ordinario compositore di Musica sicchce coltivando egli il suo talento, e comunicandarli io tutti quei pochi lumi, che mi da la mia debole capacità, spero ritornarà, a tempo opportuno in stato die esser contento del lungo viaggio intrapreso e dimora fatta in Bologna...'

8   Bologna was the city where Nunciata Garani, Berezovsky's former vocal instructor, had been born and was probably there at the time.

9   Maxim Berezovsky, *Sonata dlya skripki i chembalo*. Ed. M. Stepanenko. Kiev: Muzichna Ukraina, 1983.

probably be explained by the fact that Pisa (located not far from Livorno) also hosted one of the residences of Count Alexey Orlov. Pisa is mentioned too in a rather unclear context in the above-mentioned letter from Cima to Padre Martini.

The above violin sonata is the only one of Berezovsky's known today, although J. Engel, who wrote an article on Berezovsky for Granat's Encyclopedia in 1899, mentioned several of his works in this genre. Its music attests to Berezovsky's perfect command of early 1770s elegant instrumental writing, familiar from Mozart's early works as well as those of dozens of other European composers. The sonata consists of three contrasting movements. The first, *Allegro*, is lively and animated, whereas the second, *Grave*, is deeply lyrical. The third, *Menuetto con 6 variazioni*, is a traditional final dance movement.

The first two parts reveal a very compact and similarly constructed sonata form. Their melodic structures are extended and filled with inner motivic development as a continuous monologue, which organically, intelligently and logically renews itself, apparently maintaining the principles of the baroque melodic approach. The entire form is greatly lacking in development and the recapitulation skips the first theme, repeating only the second. The material is standard. However, the second movement, of true value, is a beautiful cantilena reminiscent of most of the romantic operatic arias of the time (Example 6.1). Examination of this sonata suggests that it was too skilful to have been Berezovsky's first attempt at writing chamber music and that it must have been preceded by years of dealing with this kind of material, if not solely as a composer, at least as a performer.

The score of Berezovsky's *opera seria Demofoonte* on a popular libretto by Metastasio has not been found in its entirety and not all is clear about its music. Studies of its Italian production were first initiated in the twentieth century. An early indication of such an attempt, with a less than successful outcome, is found in a letter sent by Alexander Cherepnin to Victor Belyaev in 1927 for publication in the typed Bulletin of the Commission for Research on Russian Music affiliated with the State Academy for Art Sciences.

> In Italy, I have combed the libraries of Venice, Bologna and Milan, using the letters of reference most kindly given by Malipiero, who hosted me in Azolo. His letters opened all the necessary doors for me, but alas, there wasn't much behind those doors.
>
> It is true though that I located a trace of Bortniansky's opera, but this would have required a trip to Palermo, which I unfortunately couldn't afford to make.
>
> As for Berezovsky, I was able to discover here that our Russian historians had over exaggerated his fame and significance... his opera *Demofoonte*, which was always believed here to have been a tremendous success, not only was not such, but did not even bear his name, rather like the works compiled from different arias by famous composers...[10]

---

10 'Находясь в Италии, я порыскал по библиотекам Венеции, Болоньи и Милана, воспользовавшись сопроводительными письмами милейшего Малипьеро, у которого в Азоло я был в гостях. Его письма открыли мне все двери. Но за дверьми не так много, как я ожидал, оказалось. Правда, я нашел след оперы Бортнянского, но за ней пришлось бы ехать в Палермо, чего я, к сожалению, сделать не мог. Что же касается Березовского,

Example 6.1   Berezovsky: *Sonata for Violin and Cembalo*, **second movement**

The fact that Cherepnin did not refer to any source indicated that he, probably in consultation with his Italian colleagues, had deduced that Berezovsky's *Demofoonte* was nothing more than a *pasticcio*. This could well have been the truth. The meticulous and fruitful searches undertaken by Mooser disclosed the four arias unequivocally written by Berezovsky himself. Whether this was all that Berezovsky wrote and all the rest was a *pasticcio* is still unknown, but Mooser also found two notations mentioning Berezovsky as a composer. One was the Directory of Theatre Productions for 1773 in Milan: '*Demofoonte*, dramma seria. Musica del Sig. Maestro *Berezowskoy*'. Among the cast were male singers: *Giacomo Verdi, Francesco Porri, Giuseppe Afferi* (tenor) and *Vincenzo Nicolini*; and two female performers: *Camilla Mattei* and *Caterina Spighi*. The ballets were choreographed and directed by the *Turchi* brothers. The second was the Livorno gazette *Notizie de mondo* of 27 February 1773, in which Berezovsky's opera, performed during the last carnival, was mentioned as a musical opera of remarkable quality, combining liveliness and good taste with a mastery of musical science. The same Livorno gazette mentioned a performance of *Demofoonte* (omitting the name of the composer) at the Florence theatre *Di via del Commero* on 16 November (Mooser, II:116). This bears some links with Mooser's location of four arias in the library of the Florence Conservatory.

то здесь я мог обнаружить, что наши русские историки славу и значение его много преувеличивают... его опера «Демофонт», о которой у нас пишется как о громогласном его успехе – не только такового не имела, но даже не была под его именем, но так: музыка, составленная из арий известных композиторов...' A. Cherepnin. 'Novoe o Bortnyanskom i Berezovskom' (Biulleten' Komissii po izucheniu russkoy muzyki Gosudarstvennoy Akademii khudozhestvennykh nauk, no 2) GMMK, f 340, no 1945.

In Cima's letter to Padre Martini, Florence was also referred to as where a score was delivered to Catarina Brigonzi (Yurchenko, 1989:77–8). Keldysh suggested that copies of arias from *Demofoonte* could have been made at the initiative of the male soprano Francesco Porri, an inhabitant of Florence, who sang one of the main roles (1978:119). In any event, the inclusion of Milan, Livorno and Florence tends to indicate both the quality of the score and the success of Berezovsky's public relations.

The proof of attribution to Berezovsky of the preserved four arias is that the first page of each score, in addition to the title of the aria, bears the note 'In Livorno, 1773. Del Sig. Massimo Beresowsky, Russo'. These arias illustrate the composer's mastery of the Italian *opera seria* genre, which is quite natural considering that by that time Berezovsky had had at least 15 years of performance experience with this genre (Example 6.2).

The faint hope that the score of *Demofoonte* exists somewhere is based on Sergei Prokofiev's brief comment that in 1922 Sergei Diaghilev entertained the idea of producing the opera in Paris.[11] Whether Diaghilev saw the score or had just read about the existence of such an opera is unclear. He certainly did not possess it: or at least the auction catalogue of his personal archives does not include any such title.

Bolkhovitinov's version of Berezovsky's biography was thus correct concerning his composing for local theatre and the approval of connoisseurs. Bolkhovitinov also stated that the Livorno production was associated with the Russian fleet staying there and that it was with such successes and the honour that Berezovsky had thus gained that he returned to his fatherland with Count Orlov in 1774 (1805:224). Since Count Orlov was a notable historical figure of Catherine's time, all existing accounts of Berezovsky's life diligently repeat this statement. Some even claim the opera to have been commissioned by Orlov – a suggestion quite probable, but for which no documentation has been found (Keldysh, 1973:116).[12]

Developing Bolkhovitinov's framework, the Russian fiction writer Nestor Kukolnik, in his tale of Berezovsky, played up the *Demofoonte* production and Berezovsky's return home soon after with such elegant verisimilitude that it fully deceived not only Findeizen (1929, II:n. 280, XXXVIII), but partly also even such an insightful and careful scholar as Keldysh. The latter, despite commenting ironically on Kukolnik's romantic invention of a singer named Matilda who had supposedly performed in *Demofoonte* and was ready to accompany the composer to Russia, nonetheless swallowed Kukolnik's version of Berezovsky's return to Russia on a ship in Count Orlov's fleet, where Berezovsky's brothers, Ivan and

---

11 Mentioned by I. Nestiev in his book *Zhisn' Sergeya Prokofieva* (Moscow: Sovetsky Kompozitor, 1973:235), referring to Serge Lifar' *Diaghilev: His Life, His Work, His Legend* (London: Putman 1940, 2nd edn London: Constable, 1953).

12 Alexey Orlov was not particularly knowledgeable in music, but had been fond of theatre since his youth. It is known that his brother, Gregory, when on diplomatic service in Königsberg in 1758, had the intention of staging Metastasio's *Demofoonte* at the local theatre (see A. Golombievsly, *Biografia knyazya G.G. Orlova*, Moscow, 1904).

Example 6.2   Berezovsky: Timanthes's aria from the opera *Demofoonte*

Terentiy, had served in the navy (Keldysh, 1973:116). This could have constituted an important connection, which, if substantiated, could have served as a possible source for additional information concerning Berezovsky's origins. A check of the documents, however, shows that the name 'Berezovsky' appears only once in the *Collection of Record of Service Lists* containing the names of those who served in Count Orlov's fleet. The Berezovsky listed there was Vasily Vasilievich, who served later, from 1777 to 1780, first as sergeant and then as second lieutenant.[13] The crucial point of associating Berezovsky with Count Orlov on their way home is that the

---

13 Shkanechnye zhurnaly 1773–75 gg. korabley, vkhodivshikh v sostav eskadry konr-admirala S. Greiga – linkorov 'Dmitriy Donskoy', 'Alexander Nevsky', 'Isidor', 'Mironosetz'; fregatov 'Pavel', 'Natalia'. RGAVMF, f 870, ns 1240, 1242, 1299, 1342, 1207, 1211.

circumstances of the Count's return to Russia had a very special significance in Russian history because of the part this episode played in the abduction of Princess Tarakanova. Princess Tarakanova (*c.* 1745–75) was an impostor, declaring herself to be the daughter of Empress Elizabeth and the Empress's favourite/secret husband Count Alexey Razumovsky, thus contending she had a legal claim to the Russian throne. Terminating her activity was one of Catherine's primary concerns.

Noting the growing recognition of Tarakanova in Paris and the support given her by the Polish nobility, Catherine II decided to put an end to Tarakanova's claims in 1772. The Empress waited for the right moment, which came shortly after Princess Tarakanova lost her Polish patronage and moved to Italy. Residing there, Count Alexey Orlov was an ideal person to carry out the plan to foil the impostor Princess. He was to conspire with the Marquise Maruzzi to become her apparent ally, and even make her believe that he was interested in her romantically and was actually making preparations for a 'wedding' which was to take place aboard a Russian naval ship. This was, however, an exquisitely designed trap (the plot, probably prompted by the *Iphigénie en Aulide* myth) to get her on board the ship, then quietly arrest her and have her brought to Russia for imprisonment. This plot, recounted very accurately in a historical novel by Danilevsky,[14] helped Findeizen to complete Kukolnik's version. Following the logic of the scenario, he 'corrected' Bolkhovitinov and redated the *Demofoonte* performance from 1773 to 1775, interpreting it as a commission by Count Orlov for the wedding ceremony and, consequently, Berezovsky as an involuntary participant in Orlov's deception, which somewhat contributed to Berezovsky's tragic end (Findeizen, 1929, II: n. 280, XXXVIII).

The actual documented chronology of the whole operation, however, completely separates it from Berezovsky. The abduction of Princess Tarakanova in which the Navy took part was referred to as 'The Nameless Expedition' or 'The 5th Archipelago Expedition' and lasted more than two years. It began with a special order from the Empress to Count Chernyshev to send 'reliable' ships for 'the nameless expedition' (28 March 1773, the month after the *Demofoonte* performance). Five months later, on 24 August 1773 – an order for the immediate preparation of four battleships and two frigates for the Archipelago Expedition was issued. Within two weeks, 7–9 September 1773 – Rear-Admiral Samuel Greig reported to the Empress that his fleet was ready for departure. On 14 September 1773 Count Alexey Orlov arrived in St Petersburg from Pisa. On 22 October 1773, the flotilla of the Archipelago Expedition, comprising four battleships and two frigates under the command of Rear-Admiral Greig, left Kronstadt and on 13 February 1774 arrived in Livorno.

For ten months, from February to December 1774, the flotilla patrolled the waters between Livorno and the islands of the Aegean Sea. Meanwhile, on 23 May 1774, Count Orlov crossed the Russian border on his way back to the 'Archipelago Expedition'.

---

14 G. Danilevsky, *Knyazhna Tarakanova*. St Petersburg, 1876. See also P. Mel'nikov (Andrey Pechersky), *Knyazhna Tarakanova i printsessa Vladimirskaya*. Polnoe sobranie sochineniy, vol. 11. St Petersburg-Moscow, 1898.

The operation itself, staged as a wedding ceremony, took place on 12 February 1775. At 16:00 h signals were given in the squadron for the preparation of a ceremonial cannon salute. At 16:30 h Count Orlov, the Lady (as Princess Tarakanova was referred to) together with a servant-girl and two gentlemen arrived at the flagship 'Isidor'. At 18:00 h the ceremonial cannon salute from the two squadrons of Greig and Bazbal ceased. At 21:00 h Count Orlov left his ship. The Lady and her entourage were arrested upon Orlov's order.

The Journals of the 'Archipelago expedition' reveal that the commander-in-chief, Count Orlov, had travelled by land only. Admiral Samuel Greig's squadron, with Princess Tarakanova, anchored at Fort Krasnaya Gorka on 12 May 1775 and awaited further instructions. The passengers, except for 'the persons under arrest', disembarked there on 13 May 1775. On 25 May, Princess Tarakanova and her entourage were transferred to a yacht dispatched from St Petersburg and transported to the Peter and Paul Fortress.[15]

Although Berezovsky could have participated in entertaining the circles of Count Orlov and Princess Tarakanova during 1772–3, by 1775 he was already far from Italy. It can now be determined that his return to Russia in fact took place on 19 October 1773, as documented in the archives of the Board of Internal Affairs, showing a record of all persons entering Russia: 'From Italy, the Russian *Kapellmeister* Maxim Berezovsky and the attendant Arkhip Markov'.[16] This official documentation of the composer's date of return puts a final end to the various speculations based on fictitious accounts.

Tommaso Traetta at the Russian Court

Traetta's work at the Russian court during 1768–75 has surprisingly left neither documentation nor any personal references, leaving quite a long period of his short life a blank.[17] This might be explained by the coincidence of several circumstances. First, the main source – the published part of Stählin's chronicles, ended with spring 1769. In this he managed to describe (with much delight) only the first of Traetta's productions in St Petersburg (January 1769), his recently written *azione drammatica L'isola disabitata* (Bologna, 1768). From then on, information becomes rare and fragmentary, unless some pearls will be found in the illegible continuation of Stählin's notes. The years spent by Traetta in Russia, moreover, were replete with

---

15 Flagmansky zhurnal kontr-admirala S. Greiga, vedenny na lineynom korable 'Isidor', RGAVMF, f 870, no 1300, 1775.

16 'Из Италии Российский капельмейстер Максим Березовский и служитель Архип Марков' (AVPRI, Raporty v Kollegiu Inostrannykh del iz Lifliandskoy General Gubernskoy Kantseliarii o proezzhayushchikh v Rossiu i ot'ezzhayushchikh za granitsu raznogo zvania lyudyakh. 1773. Snoshenia Rossii s Lifliandiey i Estliandiey, op 64/1, no 1, L 115).

17 The report on persons crossing the border between 30 August and 6 September 1768 registered Traetta's transit from Vienna. AVPRI, *Vnutrennie kollezhskie dela*, op 2/6, no 3502, L 141.

crises. In addition to the Russian-Turkish war, they included the epidemics of plague in Moscow in 1771–2, the major peasant uprising headed by Yemelian Pugachev (the pretender Emperor Peter III) in 1772–4, the affair of Princess Tarakanova, and others. The instability of the Empress's rule generated a somewhat nervous atmosphere at Court and the aspect of entertainment subsequently received much less attention in the regular Court Chronicles.

Traetta's next production (for the Empress's fortieth birthday, 21 April 1769) was *Olimpiade* (Verona, 1758) with the same libretto by Metastasio with which Manfredini had celebrated her coronation in November 1762, and which can probably be explained by her special partiality for this drama. His next spectacle, *Antigono,* also composed earlier (Padua, 1764, libretto Metastasio), was followed by a two-year lacuna. The entire season of 1770/71 produced no spectacles and the season of 1771–72 was filled with English comic opera performances. In August 1772 the comic opera *Anyuta* by Mickhail Popov (based on folk melodies) was presented at the court summer residence Tsarskoe selo, providing a cultural event of special significance that marked a new phase in the development of Russian national opera.

It was not until November 1772 that the Russians were treated to Traetta's first newly written opera, *Antigona*. By this time two highly important members of Traetta's team had arrived: the librettist Marco Coltellini (probably through the good offices of Padre Martini who had released Berezovsky from this task) and the soprano Caterina Gabrielli. Generally recognized as a gem of eighteenth-century opera classics, the work indeed struck the audience with the dramatic power of its action and wealth of ideas. Considering ballet to be a dramatically equal element of the spectacle, Traetta wrote the ballet episodes himself and imbued them with an expressiveness unusual for ballet music at the time. The opening scene, for example, featured two ballet dancers in the roles of the brothers Polynices and Eteocles, who kill each other, and upon whose actions the choir comment. The composer minimized the difference and blurred the border between airs and recitatives, as well as omitting large *arias da capo* in favour of short cavatina-like forms. The combination of this highly appealing opera and the extraordinary performance of Caterina Gabrielli made this spectacle a great event in both Traetta's creative path and Russian cultural life.

Traetta's next Russian scores were *Amore e Psiche*, created for the wedding ceremony of Grand Duke Pavel Petrovich and his first wife Natalia Alexeevna, 29/30 September 1773 (and repeated several times) and the *opera seria Lucio Vero* (libretto by Zeno, première on 24 November 1774) – one of his most original orchestral scores, with obvious bias in the direction of classicist declamation, which predominated over melodic warmth.

In addition to his duties at the Court, Traetta worked as a kapellmeister at the Smolny Institute for Noble Maidens. As director of its musical troupe, he introduced into its repertoire numerous French operas and the French version of Pergolesi's *La serva padrona*. The latter's *Stabat Mater* was also constantly heard in St Petersburg during the 1770s, probably due to Traetta's work (Porfirieva, MPES, III:162–3). The composer was known for his choral Orthodox music too, although no score of any sort has been found so far. However, there are sources that attribute to him the choral concerto *Gospod' votsarisya* [The Lord reigneth; he is clothed in majesty] also known as Berezovsky's, confirming Traetta's contribution to this genre.[18]

In 1775, the Imperial court moved to Moscow for a grandiose celebration of the Peace Pact with Ottoman Porte. Traetta was then in ill-health. It is not known whether he accompanied the Court or not, but on 30 June 1775 a Moscow newspaper informed its readers of his departure from Russia and on 15 August he crossed the border accompanied by the Neapolitan cellist Cicio Pollarisi.[19]

Bortniansky's Ordeal by Opera

Knowledge of the tremendous success of Traetta's *Antigona* in St Petersburg must have reached Italy via the intensive travels of Russian high-ranking officers between the two countries at the time. Traetta's activity was probably subjected to close attention by both Berezovsky and Bortniansky, whose aspirations to become a *maitre de chapel* someday would have been only natural.

Whereas Berezovsky spent four years in Italy, Bortniansky spent almost eleven – much more than any of his fellow students. Although he wrote three operas there as well as a few minor pieces (at least from what is known), this could have been accomplished within a much shorter period. The fact has never been commented on but it demands an explanation: who else (among Russians) could have afforded such luxury in the eighteenth century? Another question that arises is that of why he should have written three operas and not just one, as had been sufficient for the others? A possible answer relates to the above-mentioned expeditions, obviously distracting him from his music studies, which he had to make up for later. Yet another good question is under whose supervision he spent more time: Galuppi or Count Orlov?

Bortniansky's closeness to Count Orlov is revealed through his name appearing in a number of documents from the latter's expense books, where remittances to Bortniansky are noted, for example: 'Note on money that I paid out for J. Ex Mons' Count Alexis d'Orloff, Lieutenant-General of the armies of Her Imperial Majesty of all Russia. 1769. 6 June, "paid to Demetrio Bortniansky at the order of J. E., in payment for his paintings... 6 zecchins."'[20]

The composer seems to have provided various services to the Count, and it is this that appears to have gained him Orlov's recognition, in addition to his participation in Prince Dolgoruky's missions. An interesting testimony to his relationship with Count Alexey Orlov is to be found in a letter written many years later, in 1787 in Moscow, by the Count's brother, Vladimir Grigorievich Orlov, to his friend in St Petersburg, Ivan Avtonomovich Fursov. (Prior to this letter, V.G. Orlov had requested

18 KPN and *Sbornik khorovykh kontsertov*. GMMK, f 283, ns 4, 48, 51.

19 AVPRI, *Vnutrennie kollezhskie dela*, op 2/6 no 3511, L 259.

20 'Note de l'argent que j'ay journi à J. Exll Mons' Le Comte Alexis d'Orloff Lieutenant Général des Armées de Sa Majesté Imperiale de toutes Les Russies. 1769 6 juin "payés à Demetrio Bortniansky d'ordre de J. E. pour les fraix de ses tableaux... 6 zecchini"' (AVPRI, *Kollegia inostrannykh del*, op 41/3, no 45, L 93)

a full list of Bortniansky's choral compositions with the intention of purchasing all of the scores.)

> Please let D.S. Bortniansky know that I have received his letter and shown it to my brother Alexey. My brother was delighted by the feelings expressed in the letter and has asked me to send him his gratitude. In his own words: 'While abroad, I knew D.S. [Dmitry Stepanovich] as a very good-natured man, and apparently he hasn't changed. This pleases me. I would like you to thank D.S. on my behalf for his kind letter.'[21]

As can be seen from the above receipt, Bortniansky was dealing with the acquisition of paintings as early as 1769, which suggests that his well-known expertise in painting had already been acquired prior to his arrival in Italy and not during his stay there as is usually considered, although it is also obvious that he did not miss any chance to develop his knowledge there. This knowledge was to become very useful in his later years when, for several decades, he advised Maria Fedorovna (second wife to Paul I and mother of Alexander I and Nikolai I) and amassed his own art collection.

After the end of the war and Count Orlov's departure from Italy, Bortniansky had finally to dedicate himself entirely to music and to complete his studies. The production of an *opera seria* was on the agenda. Indeed, in winter 1776/7 Bortniansky appeared at the Venetian *Teatro di S. Benedetto* with *Creonte*. Its printed libretto indicates the date of the première as 26 November 1776, although the copy of the score deposited in Lisbon Biblioteca da Ajuda has the date 1777, added much later as a substitution for the missing title (probably torn out by someone who smuggled the score across the border when escaping from the Bolsheviks).[22]

The libretto was discovered by Mooser, who also established that it had been based on another libretto not mentioned by Bortniansky as a source – Marco Coltellini's *Antigona*, written in St Petersburg for Tommaso Traetta and published there in two languages (translated from Italian into Russian by the celebrated actor, Ivan Dmitrevsky). Bortniansky probably chose it for his opera having received it from his compatriots and relying upon its proven success. In addition to changing the title, the young composer also simplified the libretto and reduced it from three to two acts, inserting the third act (a short festive finale) into the second. The abridged text would have served the opera well, since the original had abounded in recitatives in order to accommodate the full plot.

Although the score looks fully professional, (see Antigone's aria, Example 6.3) there was no mention of the opera in the newspapers. One source casts new light on

---

21 Д.С. Бортнянскому прошу сказать, что я его письмо получил, казал оное брату Алексею; изьявляемыми в нем чувствами брат был очень доволен и поручил мне сообщить ему свое признание. Речи его были такия: знал я Д.С. очень добрым человеком в чужих краях, да и теперь кажется он таков же, чему я искренно радуюсь. Прошу от меня поблагодарить Д.С. за его ласковое письмо (Orlov-Davydov 1878, I:325).

22 According to Pavel Serbin, who compared the scores of *Creonte* and Bortniansky's later Italian opera *Quinto Fabio*, they were made by the same copyist.

the event however, as well as on Bortniansky's entire Italian epic. On 17/28 May 1777 Maruzzi wrote to Yelagin:

Monsignor,

I received in good time the three letters that Your Excellence honoured me by writing, of 4 February, 8 March and 10/21 April last. I have received for Mr. Bortniansky a note to change 500 roubles for his allowance, which I have sent to his address, and helped him to obtain. As for the rest, my zeal for service to her Imperial Majesty forces me to bring to Your Excellence's notice that it would be better for this young man if you were to put an end to his regular receipt of the mentioned allowance and make him earn his living, since its continuation makes it too easy for him to neglect his studies. He did not do well with the opera whose commission I produced for him for the last carnival, on the understanding that it would be revised by Maitre Galuppi. Nonetheless, he did not presume to consult on any matter, making a sad figure of it, of which I was extremely sensitive... [23]

Whatever reasons for the fiasco, the quality of music or merely of the performance, the failure of the opera made it impossible for Bortniansky to finish his studies in Italy on such a note. At the least a reasonable success was expected. While Maruzzi merely informed Yelagin and suggested what might be done, the final decision could only have been that of the Empress, since it was she who had sent him. There were three possibilities: to terminate his allowance and recall him; to terminate and, following the Marquis's advice, leave him in Italy to earn his own living; or to continue to pay. It is not possible to know what influenced the St Petersburg decision and exactly what decision was taken, but Bortniansky remained in Italy in order to work on achieving acceptable opera productions. The leniency was probably in consideration of his services during the war. It might also have been in part because two months earlier, on 24 March 1777, Berezovsky had died an untimely death.

23 Monseigneur, J'ai reçu en leurs temps les trois lettres, que Votre Excellence m'a fais l'honneur de m'écrire, du 4 Février, 8 Mars e 10/21 Avril dernier. J'ai remis au Sieur Demetrio Bortniansky la lettre de change de roubles 500 pour la pension, qu'elle m'a envoyé, à lor addresse, en l'aidans d'en toucher le montans: au reste, mon zèle pour le service de la Majesté Impériale me dicte d'assujettir à son égard aux lumières de Votre Excellence, qu'il conviendrais au bien de ce jeune homme, que la dite pension fois fixée à un terme, a fin qu'il prenne les mesures pour commencer a gagner la vie, la continuation ne le rendans que trop commode pour négliger les études, il s'ess assez mal conduis dans l'Opéra, que je lui ai procuré a écrire ici le Carnaval passé, fous la confiance es condition de faire revoir le tous à son maître Galuppi, néanmoins il ne l'a voulu par présomption consulter en rien, aussi in'a-t-il fais une triste figure, dans j'ai eté extrênnement sensible... *Kniga teatral'noy direktsii*, RGIA, f 468, 1777, op 399/511, no 34b, part I, L 202.

Example 6.3   **Bortniansky:**   **Antigone's aria from the opera** *Creonte*, **act 1, scene 3**

The Moral of Berezovsky

Little is known about Berezovsky after he arrived back home in the winter of 1773. His first biography, in Bolkhovitinov's biographical lexicon, reads:

> By his arrival in St Petersburg, he hoped to deserve the same respect from his compatriots as he had from foreigners. However, he was appointed only to the Court Choir, while the leading positions were occupied by foreign virtuosi. Prince Potemkin wished to

encourage him and following his intention to found a Musical Academy in Kremenchug, he was going to make Berezovsky its director. However, since this intention did not come through, Berezovsky remained with the Court Choir. The coincidence of these and other unpleasant circumstances drove him to hypochondria, of which he finally fell into delirium tremens and slashed his own throat in March 1777.[24]

Leaving aside the interpretive and nationalistically coloured speculations regarding Berezovsky's aspirations and motivation, the above paragraph approximates to what is also confirmed by documents. They attest that his annual allowance (500 roubles each for 1772 and 1773) had not been received until 22 February 1774, when he was already in St Petersburg. The funds, originally sent to Venice, did not reach Berezovsky and were returned to Russia, with a loss of some 50 roubles in the transaction. Berezovsky thus appears to have been able to support himself on his earnings as a musician during his stay in Italy (perhaps with the assistance of Count Orlov) and had enough money for his return journey.

Upon his return, Berezovsky continued his post as a composer, again affiliated to the Imperial Theatres Office (and not the Court Choir as Bolkhovitinov had written) with a yearly salary of 500 roubles. The records of his payment are consistent for this time, covering the three-year period from 1774 until 1777, when a salary payment was made posthumously to cover his funeral expenses. The salary was more than modest. In 1774 he was already forced to request an advance, a not infrequent practice at the court (for example, Sumarokov, who had an annual salary of 1,000 roubles, also received it and also died penniless).

During the same period, the theatre's account ledgers show that the composer's wife, the 'dancer France Berezovskaya', was fired on 30 April 1774 and that 55 roubles were retained from her salary for hospital fees. She had been hired by the Italian Company in 1763 with a yearly salary of 120 roubles, which increased at some time since the dancer continued to be paid 165 roubles annually even after termination of her employment.[25] France's dismissal was probably associated with the 'other unpleasant circumstances' at which Bolkhovitinov had hinted.

Upon Berezovsky's return his duties remained similar to those of five years earlier, and most probably included composing for the Court Choir (the reason for Bolkhovitinov's mistake in linking Berezovsky with the Choir). The approaching

---

24 По приезде своем в Петербург надеялся он лично заслужить такоеж уважение от соотечественников, какое заслужил он от иностранцев. Но его приняли только в Придворную Капеллию, в которой первые места заняты уже были чужестранными Виртуозами. Князь Потемкин, желая ободрить его, когда намеривался в 1776 году завести в Кременчуге Музыкальную Академию, то хотел определить его Директором оныя. Но поелику намерение сие не исполнилось, то Березовский остался по прежнему в Придворной Капеллии. Стечение сих и других неприятных обстоятельств ввергло его а ипохондрию, от коей впадши наконец в горячку и в безпамятство, он зарезал сам себя в Марте 1777 года... (Bolkhovitinov, 1805:224–5).

25 *Grossbukh teatral'noy kontory*, RGIA, f 468, op 36, no 40, 1774, Ll 16–18, 26–8, 51.

festivities furnished an additional significant demand for choral concertos. There was now much to celebrate in the Russian court, which had come out of the long period of crises caused by the war and serious internal complications.

On 10 July 1774 the treaty of Kuchuk-Kainarzh with The Ottoman Porte was signed and celebrations were planned to take place in Moscow in July and August 1775. The Court left for Moscow in January and was followed with considerable delay by the musicians; consequently the first events took place without music. Performances by the court singers began at the end of May, often accompanying the Empress on her visits to her courtiers' country estates and intermingled with the dancing of peasants, fishing trips for the maids-in-waiting and cavaliers and fish-soup picnics. According to the Court Chronicles, musicians playing the 'usual Italian music' returned to the palace in the evening to provide further entertainment.

Large-scale preparations were made for the main celebration. The festive opening was typically opulent and grand: 'In the Red Square, the letting off of a rocket signalled the choir to begin singing *Te Deum*. This was followed by the firing of cannons and bell-ringing from all the churches.'[26] On this festive occasion, a 3,500 *poods* (56 tons) bell was installed in the Ivan Tower of the Kremlin.

The mention of a choral performance of *Te Deum* is of particular importance. According to eighteenth-century tradition, such a consequential event warranted a specially commissioned opus. It is highly probable that this was written by Berezovsky, particularly because he has at least one known work with this title, while no such composition appears among Traetta's Russian ecclesiastical chorals. Traetta is also the least likely of the composers to have written it since he was preparing to leave Russia at the time. The composition performed at the celebration can thus in all probability be attributed to Berezovsky.

Due to the coincidence of these extraordinary events and Traetta's departure, for the next two years, 1775–76, there were no opera premières in Russia. During this period Yelagin actively sought to hire some renowned Italian composer to fill the position of first *Kapellmeister*. He first offered the position to Niccolò Piccini, who turned it down in favour of another post. Subsequently, Yelagin made contact through diplomatic channels with Giovanni Paisiello, who clearly hesitated for a while before finally accepting the lavish offer and arriving in autumn 1776.[27]

In all these arrangements to hire a new kapellmeister, Berezovsky's name naturally never came up. Irrespective of the quality of his music in any genre, he by definition did not belong to the calibre of world celebrities whose very names would add lustre to the Russian court. He could hardly have been so naïve as not to realize this, which his artistic ambitions and ego would have found hard to accept. Thus his hypochondria and its cause, as described by Bolkhovitinov, appear likely.

26　'На Красной площади пели Тебе Бога хвалим по сигналу ракеты, потом пушечная пальба и у всех церквей колокольный звон' (KFZ of 1775, 1889:475).

27　Yelagin's correspondence with different people concerning Paisiello, including Prince Golitsyn in Vienna and B. Marchetti, can be found in: RGIA, f 468, 1777, op 399/511, no 34b, part I. *Kniga Teatral'noy direktsii*, Ll 124–38.

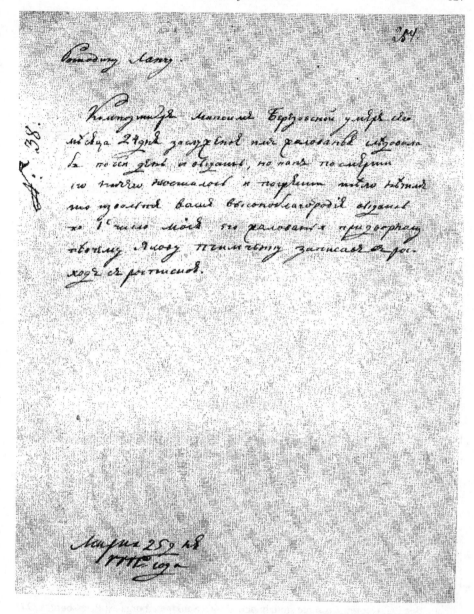

Figure 6.1   Ivan Yelagin's note concerning Berezovsky's death, 25 March 1777

Likely too is Bolkhovitinov's reference to Prince Potemkin and his good intentions toward Berezovsky. A remarkable personality, volunteer in the war, the newest (and longest-lasting) of the Empress's favourites, the Prince had unlimited power and was famous for the magnitude of his projects. Potemkin promoted a number of brilliant ideas, among them the founding of the town of Ekaterinoslav, which was to include the opening of a new university and a music academy. This would have been widely discussed in the mid-1770s, probably raising Berezovsky's hopes, but its realization, however, came only in the late 1780s, in Kremenchug – another town developed by Prince Potemkin (on the banks of Dniepr). Meanwhile, neither the plan for the town Ekaterinoslav with its records of construction estimates (1775), nor any other of Potemkin's papers, mentions this institution.[28]

Regarding Berezovsky's suicide – that crucial point of his biography, which turned it into a hagiography, there is no documentation. The only evidence to be found lies in a note sent by Yelagin to the treasurer of the theatre company, Peter Lang:

> The composer Maxim Berezovsky died on the 24th day of this month; he has earned his salary up to this day, but since he left nothing upon his death, there are no funds for the funeral. Your Highness is kindly requested to pay his salary up to the first day of May, to the court singer Yakov Timchenko against receipt.
>
> March 25th, 1777.　　　　　　　　　　[*Ivan Yelagin*][29]

The available statistics of the time offer little help. They mention that the number of suicides was extremely small in the 1760s–80s, but this clarifies nothing regarding a specific individual.[30] The Court Chronicles too are silent. Lack of documentation in such a special case as a sudden and untimely death is not always worse than its overwhelming presence, as in the case of Tchaikovsky.[31] Once rumours start it is almost impossible to stop or refute them. On the contrary, the more the official media ignore the discussion, the more the rumours grow. There are always some parties interested in exaggerating the matter and others in avoiding publicity. Nothing persists more than legends of suicide or murder.

The question of the composer's burial is also unclear. At the time of his death Berezovsky's salary was 500 roubles per year, paid in three annual instalments. In May he should have received his salary for January to April. At the time of his death however the composer had earned only about 120 roubles (for almost three months).

28　Bumagi Potemkina o Ekaterinoslavle, RGADA, f 16, op 1, no 690.

29　Композитор Максим Березовской умер сего месяца 24-го дня заслуженное им жалованье следовало б по сей день и выдать, но как по смерти его ничего неосталось, и погрести тело нечим, то извольте ваше высокоблагородие выдать по 1-е число майя, его жалованье придворному певчему Якову Тимченку, записав в росход с росписикой. / [Иван Елагин] / Марта 25 дня 1777 года' (RGIA, f 468, 1777, op 399/511, no 34b, part I. *Kniga Teatral'noy direktsii*, L 254).

30　See I.G. Georgi, Opisanie stolichnogo goroda Sanktpeterburga. St Petersburg, 1794.

31　The polemics around the legend of Tchaikovsky's suicide: legend as presented by Alexandra Orlova, ('Tchaikovsky: The Last Chapter', in *Music and Letters*, no 62, 1981, pp 125–45) and refutation offered by Alexander Poznansky (*Samoubiystvo Tchaikovskogo: mif i real'nost'*. Moscow, 1993), Richard Taruskin ('Pathetic Symphonist', in *The New Republic*, vol. 212, no 6:4, 177. 1995. February 6:26–40) and N. Berberova, M. Brown, S. Karlinsky, ('Tchaikovsky's "Suicide" Reconsidered: a Rebuttal', in *High Fidelity / Musical America*, USA, vol. XXXI/8, 1981. August: 45, 85) may have served as a certain parallel to Berezovsky's case.

Figure 6.2   Apocryphal portrayal of Berezovsky

Yet Yelagin ordered payment of the entire third, for otherwise there would not have been enough money to cover the funeral. The point is, however, that in the 1770s in Russia a simple burial cost only about 2–3 roubles. Thus, if Berezovsky owed no large debt to any creditors, or for other unknown circumstances, and the entire four-month period of salary was requested for burial, this suggests that the funeral must have been at a high ceremonial level. Mention of the court singer Yakov Timchenko as recipient of the money allows speculation that he was Berezovsky's closest friend and had supported him in the final period of his life. When Bolkhovitinov's biography of Berezovsky was published Timchenko was still alive and may well have been the source of information for the writer.[32]

Of course it does not take too much to realize that if Berezovsky, who was after all already recognized and known as a famous composer, had died in his thirties leaving no financial means to provide for his own burial – something must have been wrong. Indeed, the fact that Yelagin does not mention the reason for Berezovsky's death does not exclude suicide; there could always have been reasons not to mention it. In any case, even if it had not been suicide but the natural, miserable, death of a talented composer in ultimate despair and indigence, they would not have wished to deal with another such questionable death. Perhaps the lesson learned from Berezovsky saved the career of Bortniansky, who in the meanwhile had gained another two years to mature in Italy.

Bortniansky's Redemption

Maruzzi's letter to Yelagin clarifies why Bortniansky's stay in Italy had been so prolonged and why he had had to write more than one opera. After his failure, Bortniansky desperately needed to restore his reputation. His strategy was to find a commission, to write a good composition and to receive a positive press. For the first part he had to activate all his connections, while for the second he needed closer connections with Galuppi in order to make up for lost time. In any event, he obtained two commissions for the same year and devoted his entire time to answering this challenge; indeed, he wrote two good scores: *Alcide* (Venice, 1778) and *Quinto Fabio* (Modena, 1778).

Alcide was written for one of Metastasio's less popular librettos. At the time the only operas on *Alcide* were those by Stefani, Hasse, Heffner and Righini. A year later, in 1779, Paisiello's opera *Alcide al bivio* was performed in St Petersburg. The myth of *Alcide* conveys the idea of a choice of life-path: whether to dwell in the tranquil harbour of pleasure (Edonida tries to seduce Alcide) or to undergo initiation into the life of a hero (the challenge by Aretrea). The protagonist chooses the second option and fearlessly enters the kingdom of the Furies. Edonida, entranced by his courage, joins Alcide on his path of heroic deeds.

This briefest of plots, unburdened by secondary characters, furnished the composer with an opportunity to create a dynamic score with clear-cut classicist affects (only three of which, alas, are to be found here: heroic, pastoral and infernal) and their interaction. Bortniansky used typical tonal semantics and the tonal plan of the entire score makes it a good example of application of sonata tonal relations to musical drama. The infernal scenes, which seemed to have been the main attraction for the audience, were performed with the entire arsenal of harmonic and orchestral techniques of the 1770s: *C minor* as a mainstay among ongoing tonal instability, chromatic passages, tremolos and so on (see Danza delle Furie from Act II,

---

32   More on Timchenko can be found in Rytsareva 2000.

Example 6.4   Bortniansky: 'Danza delle furie' from the opera *Alcide*, act II

Example 6.4). Only the trombones are lacking for some reason. The accompanied recitatives are dramatized with strong rhythmic pulsation. As a whole, *Alcide* reflects an intelligent assimilation of the achievements of the Italian opera school of the 1770s as found in works by Piccini, Paisiello, Bertoni and others.

Quinto Fabio is a different type of opera. The lengthy but uncomplicated libretto, based on an historical plot, has commonly been considered to be identical to Apostolo Zeno's *Lucio Papirio dittatore*. *Quinto Fabio*, whose author remains unknown, was set to music by several composers, the earliest of whom seems to have been the experienced Ferdinando Bertoni (1725–1813). His *Quinto Fabio* premièred in January 1778 in Milan at the *Interinale*. (There are also data on a Padua production in December of the same year.) Bertoni's opera was probably a success and the libretto became fashionable, followed by Bortniansky's version (Modena, December 1778) and that of young Cherubini who was studying at the time in Bologna (Alexandria, 1780; a second version – Rome, 1783). Later, Marinelli (Rome, 1790) and G. Nicolini (Vienna, 1811) also wrote versions.

While Zeno's play obviously served as a source for *Quinto Fabio*, a deeper comparison however reveals significant discrepancies. In a preface to the libretto, Zeno referred to an episode from the eighth book of Titus Livius' *First decade*. This is the story of a confrontation between two military leaders during the Second Samnite War in 328–290 BCE. The dictator Lucio Papirio Cursor, having to leave the camp temporarily, named the cavalry commander, a young patrician, Quinto Fabio Rulliano, as his deputy, with firm orders not to engage in battle. Quinto Fabio, however, displeased by the restraint and lack of confidence displayed by the dictator, and enjoying broad support from the troops, seized the opportunity and attacked the Samnites, catching them unprepared and killing 20,000. Upon his return, Lucio Papirio was forced to react, and chose as a model Torquato Manglia, who in a similar situation had executed his own son for disobedience. The Senate, the people, the tribunal and the discontented troops, however, all supported Quinto Fabio. This forced Lucio Papirio to entrust the fate of the young man to the people, thus remaining loyal to Roman Law and military discipline.

We cannot know whether the choice of libretto was Bortniansky's or not, but it contains an interesting allusion to a recent episode in the Russian–Turkish war, of which Bortniansky was probably aware. In 1773, when Count Peter Rumiantsov gave Alexander Suvorov the order to withdraw, the latter disregarded it, deftly seizing a strategically important communications point between Silistra and Rushchuk. He reported the action to Rumiantsov in two humorous verses: 'Bless the Lord and blessed be you / Turtukai's taken and I'm there too.'[33] Rumiantsov conveyed this

---

33 'Слава Богу! Слава Вам! / Туртукай взят и я там.' Bortniansky's probable special reverence for Generalissimo Alexander Vasilievich Suvorov was later reflected in lines from the verses by the poet Khvostov, dedicated to Bortniansky: 'О Суворове хлопочешь' ([You] plead for Suvorov), probably hinting on Suvorov's being disgraced by Paul I.

Example 6.5   Bortniansky: Quinto Fabio's aria from the opera *Quinto Fabio*,
    act II

report, in the original, to Catherine II and arrested Suvorov for disobedience. The Empress, however, replied that the conqueror should not be court-martialled and rewarded Suvorov with the Order of the Second Rank.

The change in the title of the opera reflects the change of protagonist. The new libretto focused on Quinto Fabio's tormented self, his pride and honour. He would rather die than resort to dishonourable recantation. The earlier text lauded the rational behaviour and steadfastness of the dictator, which reflected the moral values in Italy at the beginning of the eighteenth century, a time when *secentismo* was rampant. The newer text, however, celebrated a more human, dramatic, impetuous and extreme character, evoking an individualistic quality much closer to the *Sturm und Drang* drama of the 1770s.

Bortniansky's score, like his previous one, reveals his following the contemporaneous operatic trend. To overcome the monotony of the noble and exalted style demanded by the overall positive tone of the libretto, having no villain or adversary, he widely employed a *chiaroscuro* of contrasting nuances to create depth for his characters. Thus, of the five, mostly heroic, arias of Quinto Fabio, the most interesting seems to be *Cara deh torna in pace* from the second Act (Example 6.5), which was so popular that a copy of it can be found in an album from Yusupoff's collection, among arias by G. Paesiello, A. Sacchini, F. Bertoni and others.[34] The highlighted roles of Quinto Fabio and his fiancée Emilia are the most stylistically defined. Only these two main characters have entire scenes to themselves and benefit from the accompanied recitatives preceding their most dramatically important arias. The boundaries of the arias are often broken, in both the vocal and orchestral writing Bortniansky also used a *leit-timbre* – bassoon – to identify with Quinto Fabio's disconsolate love for Emilia (in his arias, a duet and a recitative); its solo phrases maintain a dialogue with the singer. The autograph score of the opera reveals, among the few corrections, one interesting detail. Two measures containing one of Emilia's phrases have been erased and the phrase has been transferred four measures ahead, specifically to protract the bassoon line and render it more audible (in vol. III, f 5^v).[35]

Interestingly, in the same year 1778, when that most talented Russian composer was demonstrating his complete command of contemporaneous Italian *opera seria* style abroad, another young Russian man abroad was conspicuously using his brochure (*De la musique en Italie* published in the Hague) to support the Piccini party in the Gluck-Piccini rivalry.[36] This was Prince Alexander Beloselsky-Belozersky, who was travelling in France and Italy from 1775–8 and in 1779 replacing his deceased brother, Andrey Beloselsky, as Russian ambassador to Dresden. A disciple of Diedonne Tiebaut (Frederick II's secretary), as well as a correspondent of Rousseau, Beaumarchais, Marmontel, Grétry, Saint-Pierre, de Ligne, La Harp and others, Prince Beloselsky-Belozersky was a well-known poet. He was the author of *Poésies*

---

34   RNB, f 891, no 10, Ll 73–84.

35   The autograph score of *Quinto Fabio* is in GMMK.

36   This brochure was reviewed in *Journal encyclopédique*, 1778, t 7, pt 2:305–18.

françaises d'un prince étranger (published in Cassell, 1784 and 2nd edn Paris, 1789 with the support of Marmontel) and the philosophical etude *Dianyologie, ou Tableau philosophique de l'entendement* (Dresden, 1790; London, 1791; Freyberg, 1791 receiving high praise from Immanuel Kant), as well as, later in Russia, an erotically charged libretto for the comic opera with music by Joseph Kozlovsky, *Olinka, or the Initial Love* (1796).

Shortly after the première of Bortniansky's *Quinto Fabio*, an item appeared in the newspaper *Messagero* (no 52, 30 December 1778) describing every element of the spectacle but its music. The production nonetheless apparently redeemed him in the eyes of the Russian court and in April 1779 he received an important letter:

> Mister Bortniansky!
>
> You have been residing in Italy for ten years now. You have proved yourself as an artist, and you are no longer in need of the guidance of your teacher. Therefore the time has come for you to return to your homeland. For this purpose, I would recommend that you waste no time and prepare for your departure, taking all your compositions with you. You will receive a one-time salary of 200 *tchervonts* [2000 roubles]. A remittance of 150 *tcherv* [1500 roubles] for travel expenses will be delivered to you by Marquis Maruzzi. Should you decide to return to Italy for new inspiration, I assure you that you will be allowed to do so. Notwithstanding, I insist that you depart without delay: firstly – because you are greatly needed here, and secondly – because this will undoubtedly serve your personal well-being and serve to establish your good reputation. Assuring you that I am pleased to remain at your service,
>
> *Ivan Yelagin*   10 April 1779.[37]

From the letter, it is quite clear that a reasonably significant position was being prepared for Bortniansky. In any case this letter can hardly have been interpreted as the 'insistent reminders and hidden threat' (Levasheva, 1984:265) that made Bortniansky return to Russia. The sum mentioned in the letter was generous – two thousands roubles, which was equal to four years of his allowance in Italy. However, either the Court listened to the voice of Maruzzi and postponed sending the money

---

37 Господин Бортнянский! / Как уже десять лет прошло бытности вашей в Италии, и вы опытами доказав успехи вашего искусства отстали уже от мастера: то теперь время возвратиться вам в отечество: для чего и рекомендую вам как можно скорее отправиться, взяв с собою все ваши сочинения. На жалованье ваше при сем прилагается вексель в 200 червоных; а на проезд 150 черв.: получите от Маркиза Маруция. Ежели же вам надобно будет впредь для новаго вкуса еще побывать в Италии, то можете надеяться, что отпущены будете. Но вас повторительно прошу, немедля [нисколько], сюда ехать; первое, что в вас настоит великая нужда; второе, что сие послужит ко всегдашнему и непременному вашему счастию и к основанию чести Вашей навсегда; впротчем, будьте уверены, что я вам охотливый слуга. Иван Елагин. / 10 Апреля 1779 года.' According to Yurchenko (1989:72) the autograph of the letter is in the Central Music Library of the State Mariinsky Theatre, VII 2E47, it was published as facsimile in *Avtografy muzykal'nykh deyateley* 1839–89 in Supplement to the journal *Nuvellist* and in *Russkaya muzykal'naya gazeta*, 1900, no 40.

to Bortniansky as a measure of reprimand, or there was a delay due to the routine disorder in payments sent to those studying abroad, as known from biographies of other Russian artists.

The biographical notes written by Bortniansky's grandson reveal that he had spent time in Venice, Livorno, Pisa, Modena and Naples, as well as Bologna, Milan and Rome. Of all the music written by him in Italy, the only pieces known are the three mentioned operas and some minor pieces: *Ave Maria*, a composition for soprano, contralto, strings and horns composed in 1775 in Naples; *Salva Regina* for soprano, strings, horns and oboe, 1776; several motets and canzonet 'Ecco quell fiero istante' on Metastasio's text, discovered by M. Pryashnikova and M. Stepanenko in an album from the Alupka Collection of Vorontsovs and possibly relating to Count Simon Romanovich Vorontsov's stay in Italy in 1774–6 (Pryashnikova, 2001:182; Stepanenko, 2003:15–16).

Bortniansky's contacts with the Russian nobility could contain important clues to his biography. There is one family – that of Count Skavronsky – whose later connections with Bortniansky suggest that they may have begun during his time in Italy. The family's origins dated back to Catherine I, wife of Peter the Great. After the death of her husband, the Empress conferred the rank of Count upon several of her relatives. In 1776, Maria Nikolaevna Skavronskaya, née Stroganov, widow of Martyn Karlovich Skavronsky, and her son, Pavel Martynovich (born in 1757), left Russia and settled in Italy for an indefinitely extended period. Due to either his education or his personal inclinations, Pavel Skavronsky grew up to be a music-lover who, at least in the 1770s, constantly sought to surround himself with musicians, to attend musical performances and to engage in music discussions, often to the point of absurdity. Pavel Skavronsky's cousin, the historian V. Mikhnevich, wrote:

> Skavronsky's love for music is that of a nobleman's frivolous wilfulness and caprice ... Always surrounded ... by artists, singers and musicians, always concerning himself with music ... he ordered his attendant to speak to him in recitative, according to exact pitch. His footman, trained according to a score written by his master, would announce the carriage's readiness in a pleasant alto. The head waiter would call out in a festive tune. The coachman would communicate with the Count in *basso profundo*. During festive lunches and receptions, all the servants were organized in duets, quartets and choirs, imparting the atmosphere of an opera house. His Highness himself gave instructions to his servants in musical form, singing his orders.[38]

---

38 'Меломания Скавронского носила характер какого-то барского самодурства и баловства... Вечно окруженный... артистами, певцами и музыкантами, постоянно занимаясь музыкой... приказал своей прислуге разговаривать с ним речитативами, по нотам. Выездной лакей, приготовившись по партитуре, сочиненной барином, докладывал приятным альтом, что карета его сиятельства подана. Метрдотель извещал господ торжественным напевом, что кушать готово. Кучер объяснялся с графом густыми октавами *basso profundo*. Во время парадных обедов и раутов графские слуги составляли дуэты, квартеты и хоры, так что гостям казалось, будто они едят и пьют в оперной зале. Сам Его Сиятельство отдавал приказания слугам в музыкальной форме...' (Mikhnevich, 1879:267–8).

Bortniansky could have met Pavel Skavronsky under various circumstances. The Russian students, travellers and officials sojourning in Italy were generally in contact with each other. Many travelled across the country to study classical sculpture, architecture and painting. Although it is quite probable that Bortniansky would have encountered the musical fanatic Skavronsky, his contacts with this family in Italy remain mere speculation. However, the fact that the two families later developed very close ties (documented well into the nineteenth century) reveals that such contact must have been initiated at some point.

After receiving Yelagin's letter of 10 April 1779, Bortniansky still remained in Italy for several months. It was only on 26 November that the Riga border service recorded that 'the composer of court music Dmitry Bortniansky crossed [the border, arriving] from Warsaw, with the butcher Efraim Tornau, native of the town of Tilzit.'[39]

Soon after, in 1780, the Skavronsky family too returned to Russia.

---

39 'Проехал из Варшавы придворной музыки композитор Дмитрей Бортнянский, с находящимся при нем, уроженец города Тильзита мясник Эфраим Торнау' (AVPRI, *Vnutrennie kollezhskie dela*, op 169, 1779, no 3504, L 84).

Chapter 7

The City in the 1770s

Paisiello at the Russian Court

Unlike Traetta, of whose time in Russia so little is known, Paisiello's activity was well reflected both in the court documents and in his autobiography, which served as an excellent source for twentieth-century studies, including a special book on Paisiello in Russia (Panareo, 1910). Not only was he very active and skilled in establishing public relations, but the period of his work in Russia, from 1776–84, was a fortunate one for music. Having overcome the crises of the early 1770s, the Imperial court had every reason to celebrate and Paisiello's arrival coincided with (or perhaps even demarcated) a period when the entire atmosphere of the capital was focused on entertainment.

The genre of *opera seria* still remained in the spotlight of music as a fine art. In 1777 alone Paisiello wrote and produced five scores (only one of which was a one-act!). Opening his first season with *Nitteti*, followed by *Lucinda ed Armidoro* (both with the participation of the Imperial Court Choir), Paisiello immediately conquered the hearts of the Russian audience and continued to do so not only throughout his stay in St Petersburg, but far into the end of the century. Empress Catherine's former favourite Count Gregory Orlov and current favourite Prince Gregory Potemkin both commissioned small scenic works and cantatas from him to enhance the celebrations and receptions at their palaces.

Opening the 1778 season with a production of *Achille in Sciro*, Paisiello then switched to *buffa* (probably *Le due contesse*, later translated into Russian and staged by the Free Russian Theatre in 1782). Guest performances by M. Mattei and A. Orecia's Italian troupe in autumn of the same year (1778) acquainted the Russian public with Paisiello's *La frascatana* (1774, Venice). This opera, much loved by the Empress, was later frequently performed by the court Italian Opera Troupe. Then came *I filosofi immaginari* (the *Socrate immaginario* version, Milan, 1775). The Russian public went wild over it, the Empress more so than any, and it was played twenty times during the summer of 1779 alone. The same year saw the première of *Il matrimonio inaspettato* (better known as *Il marchese villano*); and the following year (1780) saw another four operas: the new *La finta amante* (especially successful and a constant presence in the Russian repertoire until 1799), *Il duello comico* (*Il duello*, Naples, 1774), *La finta ciarlatana* (or *La finta maga per vendetta*?, Naples, 1768), and the new serious opera *Alcide al bivio*.

By this time, however, *opera seria* was beginning to lose its charm for the Russian public. Tired of its pathos, society sought pure entertainment. Such an enjoyable genre as Paisiello's comic operas proved exceedingly suitable for the new atmosphere at court and the wider aristocratic circles. These works by Paisiello are known for their greater compactness, a result of the Empress's command (probably in 1778) to shorten spectacles to an hour and a half. (Panareo, 1910:41–2). This trend, however, might also have been due to the general tendency of the time, noted by Mozart in 1777 (letter dated November 4), in his account of musical life in Mannheim.[1]

During his next term of office (renewed contract from April 1781) Paisiello not only did not write any further *opera seria*, but wrote much less in general, paying more attention to enjoying the dividends from his earlier scores. One extraordinary episode took place when the Empress ordered that he be paid 10,000 roubles (around three times his annual salary) 'for copying his various operas and other works' (Porfirieva, II:326).[2] Since there was a rule that kapellmeisters must give the Directorate of the Imperial Theatres copies of the scores written under contract, it is probable that Paisiello had produced more than was required (usually two productions per year, and he had certainly done much more).

His next productions were three earlier Neapolitan operas, *La serva padrona* (1781) *Il duello comico* and *Dal finto il vero* (1782), and the new *Il barbiere di Siviglia, ovvero La precauzione inutile* (15 September 1782). It was at this point that the routine course of Paisiello's service at the Russian court ceased and the conflict began to develop, eventually leading to his abrupt departure from Russia. The entire intrigue associated with his departure, and with his serving two courts at the same time, has been described in detail by Mooser (II:355–62).

As a result of reorganization in the Directorate of the Imperial Theatres, Paisiello was given the additional responsibility of 'an inspector of the Italian opera seria and buffa'. As this was beyond his contractual obligations, he tried to assert his rights, and probably not in the most courteous form. The aristocratic functionaries of the Directorate responded in a manner that humiliated the composer, and were even about to arrest him. However, by temporarily hiding out at Angiolini's house,[3] Paisiello won that round. Only the intervention of Her Majesty herself and the certified illness of his wife finally settled the matter. The composer was now free to depart on vacation with an obligation to compose and send the scores of scenic productions and to recommend singers and comic actors suitable for the needs of the Russian court. Paisiello, however, sent no scores, nor did the Empress continue paying him after realizing that he had been accepted into service at the Neapolitan court. Using his personal acquaintance with Emperor Joseph II (made during their meeting with Empress Catherine the Great in Mogilev, 29 May 1780), Paisiello managed to

---

1   'They can produce fine music, but I should not care to have one of my masses performed here. Why? On account of their shortness? No, everything must be short here too' (quoted by Einstein, 1945:39).

2   RGADA, *razryad* 14, op 1, no 31, ch. 4, L 290v.

3   Gasparo Angiolini (1731–1803), the famous dancer, choreographer, composer and teacher known as a reformer of the ballet in the eighteenth century, worked in Russia from 1766–72, 1776–79, 1782–86, a total of fifteen years. See G. Dobrovol'skaya, MPES, I:40–2.

negotiate with the Emperor's brother, King Ferdinand of Naples, presented him with his scores, and eventually achieved the position he desired.

His final year in St Petersburg saw the productions of *Passione di Gesù Cristo*,[4] with Metastasio's text, the cantata *Efraim*, with Locatelli's libretto (3 January 1783) and the comic opera *Il mondo della luna*, which was possibly a version of *Il credulo deluso* (Naples, 1774) but this remains to be checked.

Paisiello's activity during his service at the Russian court went far beyond opera scores and productions. He was a constant participant in court chamber music-making. His chamber works in St Petersburg include 24 divertimentos for winds, two canzonets with Metastasio's lyrics and a collection of sonatas for violin and harpsichord (all presented to different European royal music lovers).

A significant part of his time was devoted to work at the Young court, where he served as music instructor to Grand Duchess Maria Fedorovna, the Empress's daughter-in-law. For this advanced student Paisiello composed a two-volume piano album, *Raccolta di Vari Rondeaux, Capricci e Sinfonie per il Fortepiano*, containing 31 pieces (original and arrangements of fragments from his operas); *Raccolta di vari Rondeaux e Capricci con l'accomp. Di Violino per il P.-fte*, which should be compared with the very similar *Twelve Capriccios and Rondos* (published in London at the end of the eighteenth century), a piano sonata *L'Addio della Gran Duchessa*, some harp sonatas, and two cembalo concertos (one for her and another for the Empress's lady-in-waiting Ekaterina Alexeevna Sinyavina, who used to play piano duets with Paisiello at the court musicales and was married to Count Simon Romanovich Vorontsov, see Pryashnikova 2001:174). In 1782 he also wrote *Regole per bene accompagnare il partimento, o sia Il basso fondamentale sopra il cembalo* for her.

Paisiello was to maintain his connections with Russia until the end of his life. Count Vorontsov's archive contains seventeen letters from him dated between 1780 and 1813.[5]

From Song to Song-Opera

Princess Ekaterina Dashkova (1743/4–1810, née Vorontsova), or the 'minor Catherine' (as compared to Catherine II, of whom she had once been a close friend and helped ascend the throne), was a woman of great intelligence, knowledge, dignity and ambition. Feeling insufficiently rewarded by her exalted friend she voluntarily exiled herself from the court and shared her time between her estates in Moscow and Byelorussia and travelling abroad, except for a short period in the 1780s (referred to in Chapter 9). She spent much time in Paris and Edinburgh (while her son was

---

4   This composition was commissioned from Paisiello by the King of Poland, Stanislas Poniatowsky, and performed for him in Warsaw in 1784 (Hunt, 1975:28–9).

5   RGADA, Count Vorontsovs' collection. These letters are currently being prepared for publication in parallel by M. Pryashnikova in Moscow and by E. Khodarkovskaya in St Petersburg.

studying at Edinburgh University), being a guest of honour at the gatherings of the aristocracy and intellectuals.

A great music lover and possessor of a beautiful voice, she would sing while accompanying herself on the harpsichord. Her repertoire comprised songs and arias, including some Russian folk songs of her own arrangement, which offered a special attraction when performed at the European salons. Diderot, visiting St Petersburg in 1773–4, wrote her a letter to her estate, vividly recalling his delight and asking the Princess to send him the music of Russian songs that she had sung during their meeting in Paris (Pryashnikova, 2000:21). We cannot know what particular songs had captured his imagination, but what is important is that by that time Russian songs were no longer merely an exotic element but had become a natural component of the aristocratic repertory.

In 1772 Reverend William Coxe visited Russia (in the course of his travels in north-east Europe, including Poland, Sweden and Denmark) and was greatly impressed, if not so much by the folklore itself as by its functioning in public life. His oft-quoted passage reads:

> The postillions *sing* from the beginning of a stage to the end; the soldiers *sing* continually during their march; the countrymen *sing* during the most laborious occupations; the public houses re-echo with their carols; and on a still evening I have frequently heard the air vibrate with the notes from the surrounding villages. (Reverend William Coxe, *Travels into Poland, Russia, Sweden and Denmark*. London, 1792, vol. II, p. 210. Quoted by Alfred Swan, 1973:52)

Indeed, according to the wealth of evidence, all the Russian estates and cities resounded with the sounds of folk songs. The process of urbanization had drawn vast masses of peasants to the cities. Singing in the open air became a custom among coachmen, oarsmen and people of other professions working in groups. Peasants arriving from the different regions brought with them their own repertories and the open air became a living laboratory where traditions interacted and the peasant songs, detached from the ritual, became urbanized. Moscow, surrounded by large populated territories, was richer than St Petersburg in the variety of repertories. The two cities absorbed folk songs in different ways, each imprinting its own tradition (Keldysh, 1984:216–19). The ubiquitous folklore also inspired poets, who wrote numerous songs, many of which quickly gained popularity and became in turn part of the anonymous urban folklore.

Influenced by this reality in the 1760s–70s, the Russian littérateurs were inspired to collect all the genres of oral folklore: not only song texts, but legends, proverbs, superstitions and so on. A broad movement of Enlightenment-oriented culture united intellectuals of various socio-political views. The central figure in this was the great Russian enlightener Nikolai Novikov (1744–1818), the writer, editor and publisher, a man of outstanding stature. A Freemason-mystic, belonging to a Masonic Rosicrucian lodge, constantly working for the common good and fighting against serfdom, he published books in all fields, edited his own journal and opened bookstores in sixteen Russian towns.

It was Novikov who called upon his colleagues to edit and publish the treasures of oral folklore. Among the first to respond was Mikhail Dmitrievich Chulkov (1743/44–92), writer, historian, ethnologist and journalist. He undertook the first Russian collection and publication of a four-volume poetic anthology of song texts: *Sobranie raznykh pesen* [Collection of Various Songs], which appeared in 1770–73. The broad title of this anthology deliberately avoided a national definition, which was in any case self-evident. All the songs were Russian in origin but only half of them were folk. This was not a scientific selection but a repertory reflecting live urban practice.

Urban absorption of folklore accompanied the development of Russian theatre, which at the time meant mainly comedy. Eighteenth-century Russian comedy provided a rich field in which society both learned and shaped its identity. The three-fold process (secularization, urbanization, westernization) experienced by Russian society throughout the eighteenth century was an unnaturally accelerated one, conducing to many incongruities that were noted not only by intellectual circles but by wider social circles too. The newly emerging middle class presented a vast amount of material for satire and parody, which nurtured not only eighteenth-century theatrical comedy but also the later and more widespread Russian culture of laughter in general, including literature, anecdotes and the urban ballads of singer-songwriters. The adjustment of country folk to the big city (urbanization) and the superficial imitation of the external signs of western life (westernization) have remained objects of laughter in Russian urban culture to this very day.

The late 1760s were also years of intensive politization for Russian society. Established in 1767, the Legislative Commission aimed at reorganizing the State structure. The Empress herself boldly initiated public discussion on social problems, inviting debate with all – from Voltaire and other figures of the French Enlightenment to Russian peasant deputations. As a result, the question of serfdom, which was the most painful of all the Russian problems, came forcefully to the fore. Initial discussions of the problem quickly turned into rumours about immediate liberation, and peasant uprisings began to flare up. Catherine sought the most appropriate way to back down from the campaign, which had gone much further than she had wished. She gradually moved the debates back from practical to theoretical discourse until she was fortunately 'saved' by the war with Turkey, which furnished a good pretext to stop it. The issue nonetheless remained alive and for almost a century, until the peasants' liberation in 1861, it was at the core of Russian socio-political thought and action.

In the 1770s, when reaction to the 1760's 'thaw' had begun to be felt, Novikov remained a tireless and consistent advocate of liberation, eventually becoming a dissident – the best way of widely promoting political thought. Russian comedy, especially in the 1770s, against the recent background of agitation, naturally reacted vividly. Its heroes were simple people, always represented as positive figures.

The Herderian notion of song as a medium revealing a people's soul closely suited the Russian fondness for singing, while the Rousseauistic patriarchal vision of village life as spiritual purity seemed to embody the Russian ideal of social balance and common prosperity. French and German rival influences on Russian culture were reconciled in the ideas of the Enlightenment. The folk song as a great spiritual symbol became a focus of socio-cultural attention as a primarily national treasure and 'the soul of the people', gaining an idealized image in the public consciousness. The figure of the singing peasant constituted an ideal, uniting the nation. It was a manifestation of the dream of freedom – if not social then at least spiritual: after all, birds do not sing in captivity. Seeing singing and dancing 'folk' was a reassuring experience for the Empress, who truly appreciated the old German proverb 'Wo Menschen singen lass dich rubig nieder: Denn bösse Menschen singen keine Lieder' [Where people are singing rest easy since bad people sing no songs].

When comedy and folk song met – both of which were recognized as signs of identity – Russian opera was born. In the same year of 1772 that Reverend Coxe had been amused by the omnipresence of singing in Russian life, the poet Mikhail Vasilyevich Popov (1742–90, a former actor at the Yaroslavl theatre), who himself collected about a thousand folk song texts, entered Russian musical history with the creation of the first Russian opera – *Anyuta*. It was a one-act versified comedy printed in his collection *Dosugi* [Leisures] and staged at the Court Theatre of the Imperial summer residence Tsarskoe selo on 26 August.

The score of the opera has not been preserved and its composer remains unknown. The only indication of music is the italics in the printed text (as in all eighteenth-century libretti). This opera has been traditionally considered as an opera *na golosa* – based on familiar tunes, or song-opera (Levasheva, 1985:8–9), being labelled so by analogy with another opera from the same year, the anonymous *Lyubovnik-koldun* [The Lover-magician] in which 14 of the 24 monologues were set to specifically indicated song tunes. The character of the italicized text fragments in *Anyuta* shows that only a few of them could have functioned as purely decorative folk songs, while various other fragments must have been in the usual operatic forms: arias, couplets, duet and finale, whose music was not necessarily based on folk tunes.

The only merit Soviet scholars have noted in *Anyta* is its anti-serfdom bent (Rabinovich, 1948:40–1; Keldysh, 1965:285; Berkov, 1977:182–88; Levasheva, 1985:27–8), which was exaggerated by them and seems to have been a response to official demands. The character Filat's verse '… peasants know how to stand up for themselves as well as do gentry'[6] was neither a secret nor a great revelation of the peasants' attitude to the landowners, considering the amount of open discussion that had taken place at the Legislative Commission meetings in 1767–8. The piece was a typical early eighteenth-century European story of pseudo-misalliance solved by the revelation of the truly noble origins of the peasant girl. Similar intrigues could be found in many salon stories and in the libretti of both *seria* and *buffa* operas, and must have been inspired by the repertories of the English, French and Italian troupes that appeared throughout Russia during 1770–71.

Between 1772 and 1776 the Muse of the newly-born Russian comic opera remained silent. The Russian peasant, whose image had just begun to gain a

---

6   '…такжо и крестьяне / Умеют за себя стоять, как и дворяне.'

respectable place on the Russian scene, joined Yemelian Pugachev, leader of the peasant war and pretender (calling himself Emperor Peter III). Now peasants played their own drama, farcifying plain comedy. Now it was the gentry who had to stand up for themselves, and not on the stage but in real life.

When the crisis was over, entertainment was enthusiastically re-established and a proliferation of new Russian comic operas appeared every year. New theatres opened: the Maddox in Moscow, theatres in the provincial cities of Tula and Kaluga, following establishment of the earlier theatre in Yaroslavl – all in 1776; two years later the Free Theatre of Knipper opened in St Petersburg.

The peasant war did not change the attitude of the intellectuals to the folk. The new wave of operas still featured simple people as the protagonists, always superior to the gentry in their moral qualities. But topics varied, covering many aspects of current life. Chronologically, the first was *Rozana i Lyubim* (1776) with a libretto by the young N.P. Nikolev, presenting a version of Favart's *Annette et Lubin* (Berkov, 1977:190) – quite simple, though anti-feudal, with sentimental intrigue. Nikolev left detailed directions concerning the music, which was composed by one of the Kerzelli family, probably Joseph Kerzelli (Rabinovich, 1948:47).

Next was *Pererozhdenie* [Regeneration] (1777, libretto by M. Matinsky, music by D. Zorin). Its pastoral libretto had little intrinsic value and was used rather as a framework for actual allusions. The writer was obviously concerned about musical matters. For example, he played up a song sung by Milovida, filling the following dialogue with special references:

> Likomir: Well, to tell the truth, the song is good. And the voice is even better! I recently heard some famous singer in the city, who, they say arrived from overseas; truly, he sings no better than Milovida, but the salary they give him is higher than any of our generals. Why waste the money? Milovida's voice is better than his, besides she will agree to sing for a cheaper reward.

> Milovida: No, I sing for myself and for my sweetheart...[7]

The main allusion in Likomir's words must have been to a particular event that had taken place the same year, and which became a famous anecdote. When the Italian world star Caterina Gabrielli demanded 10,500 roubles as an annual salary for her new contract,[8] the indignant Empress had exclaimed: 'But only my field-marshals

---

7   'Ликомир: Ну, сказать истину, хороша песня. А голос еще лучше того! Я ономедни слышал в городе какого-то славного певца, который, говорят, из-за моря приехал: право, он не лучше поет Миловиды, а ему, слышно, дают жалованья больше, нежели нашему какому генералу. На что бы деньги тратить? Ведь у Миловиды голос лучше его голоса, да она же дешевле петь подрядится. / Миловида: Нет, я пою для себя и для милого мне человека...' (quoted from Ginzburg, 1941:40–1).

8   This sum included a salary for her sister, the singer Francesca Gabrielli (who earned six times less money).

have such a salary!' 'Then let them sing!' answered the prima donna, and left Russia for England where she had been promised the desired sum.[9]

The commonsense of the middle-class audiences resisted comprehension of such a budget while the overwhelming majority of the population was suffering from poverty. They did not realize, however, that Italian architecture and music, especially opera, constituted a standard court attribute for any large European State and that no star would come to Russia for a salary lower than that paid in other countries.

Another reference in *Pererozhdenie* was to the fashionable repertory of new romance-like songs (according to the lyrics of Milovida's song it belonged to the new erotic poetry) and that of private music-making as an elegant and dignified pastime, an acculturated life style that had began to spread from the aristocratic salons to wider circles.

Another pastoral staged in the same year 1777 (Moscow), but this time heavily moralistic, was *Derevenskiy prazdnik ili Uvenchannaya dobrodetel'* [The Village Holiday or Virtue Rewarded], libretto by V.I. Maikov and music by Kerzelli,[10] which depicted the idyllic relations between a landlord and his subjects. A peasant choir sings about their happy life and moral purity as against urban corruption, while the landlord presents his credo:

> This is the idea of our household organization, that peasants won't be abused. They too are human beings: their obligation is to obey us and to serve by executing the fixed quitrent according to their ability; while ours is to defend them from any abuse and even, serving the sovereign and fatherland, to fight for them in war and die for their peace. This is our mutual duty.[11]

The year 1778 saw two premières: *Prikashchik* [The Clerk] (libretto by N. Nikolev, music by the young Frenchman, Grétri's student F.G. Darsi, killed shortly after in a duel); and the intermezzo *Derevensky vorojeya* [The Village Fortune-teller] (libretto author unknown, apparently a version of Rousseau's *Le devin du village*, music by J. Kerzelli). The next year, 1779, was the climax to 1770s opera development. Its most popular and beloved piece was *Melnik-koldun, obmanshchik i svat* [The Miller-magician, Deceiver and Matchmaker], libretto by A.O. Ablesimov, music by M. Sokolovsky), a folk vaudeville (as Belinsky called it as late as 1834) which

---

9   Yelagin, who as the director of theatres managed the negotiations, wrote in his report to the Empress: 'Since there is a sum of 14,500 roubles for all the Italian Company, it is neither possible to pay her alone such a terrible sum nor to keep other opera staff on the remaining sum of 4,000' (quoted by Khodorkovskaya, MPES, I:213).

10   Who exactly from the Kerzelli family composed music to *Derevensky prazdnik* remains unknown. Various sources mention both Joseph (Johann) and Mikhail Franzevich Kerzelli.

11   'Да в том-то и состоит прямое домостроительство, чтоб крестьяне не разорены были. Ведь они такие же люди: их долг – нам повиноваться и служить исполнением положенного на них оброка, соразмерного силам их; а наш – защищать их от всяких обид и даже, служа государю и отечеству, за них на войне сражаться и умирать за их спокойствие. Вот такая наша с ними обязанность' (quoted from Ginzburg, 1941:43).

was staged more times than all the other Russian operas together and received polemically: criticized for its vernacularisms on the one hand and praised for its natural simplicity on the other (Rabinovich, 1948:50–1; Levasheva, 1985:34).

Folk song was in focus from the opening scene. The Miller, first humming only a tune, without words or accompaniment, then asks himself: 'What song could it be? Well: "Once at night, from midnight"'.[12] The Miller begins to sing the words to this tune, continuing his work (see Example 7.1). The public's attention was obviously drawn to the song itself, which appeared to be a ballad about Stepan Razin from Chulkov's collection. The Miller sings only the first few lines of the ballad, but the reference to this particular song was interpreted as an anti-serfdom subtext (Berkov, 1977:200–01).

While this may indeed have been so, it is not obvious that this allusion would have been fully perceived by the public, whose awareness of the story of Stepan Razin (*c.* 1630–71) was about less than that of mid-twentieth-century Soviet society (whose authorities did care about people knowing its revolutionary past). Stepan Razin was a mid-seventeenth-century Cossack ataman who controlled the lands south of Muscovy and used to carry out raids on Turks, Crimean Tatars and Persians. In 1670 Razin led a major peasant uprising but was betrayed by a lieutenant-colonel in the Cossack troops, handed over to the Tsar's government and executed in 1671. The ballads on this folk hero must have appeared during his lifetime or soon after and, of course, contain an anti-serfdom significance since the meaning of Cossack itself is anti-serfdom. The word *Cossack*, from the Turkish *Kazak*, means freeman. Serf peasants fled from their masters to the unpopulated lands (of the former Khazar Empire), where they formed their own communities. They developed a rich folklore and of course songs on such a charismatic and talented leader had an honourable place in it. After a century of the existence of these songs, however, they became of epic nature and gradually lost their connections with the circumstances of their origin. Russian history as understood in the twentieth and even in the nineteenth century, was not only mostly unknown to the public but there were also no common educational institutions to teach it. Who among the public, therefore, could truly have understood this allusion? As for the author Alexander Ablesimov (1742–83), a talented writer, once patronized by Sumarokov, by that time he was a retired captain residing in Moscow. Bored by his service as an executor in the Chancellery of the Deanery and starting to write comedies, it is unlikely that he had intended such a hidden message in this particular piece.

Whatever the reasons for this opera's special attractiveness for the Russian public, there is one message in this comedy that seems to have passed unnoticed by researchers. The social status of the protagonist Filimon is that of odnodvorets (literally one-house farmer) – a free peasant or villager possessing some privileges of the gentry, including land with its occupants. The status of both peasant and

---

12 'Какая бишь это песня?.. Да: "Как вечор у нас со полуночи"' (quoted from Ginzburg, 1941:66).

Example 7.1   Sokolovsky: Miller's song from the opera *The Miller-magician, Deceiver and Matchmaker*, **act I, scene 1**

landlord in one person is specially played up. The localities of the action are named Khleborodnoe, which means abundant in grain crops, and derevnya Dobroi pozhni – a village of good harvest. All the semantics thus convey the (still inaccessible) ideal of the time of common wealth and the dream of a productive harvest. The topic was very much on the agenda. As early as 1765, in order to improve the economic situation and to maximize agriculture by more sophisticated methods than further forced exploitation of the serfs, the Free Economic Society was founded (by the Counts G. Orlov, R. Vorontsov and others). It regularly published proceedings on economics, agronomy and various fields of agriculture and stock-raising. The longing for a satisfied, well-stocked and rationally organized Russia had always been (and still is) so strong that even a good-humoured, eclectic and merry tale with folksongs and artless music could arouse a positive response in the Russian public, tired of self-reproach. Ablesimov, who had worked in 1767–8 in the Legislative Commission and was perfectly familiar with Russia's socio-economic problems, may indeed have been influenced by the idea of Odnodvortsy.

The successful *The Miller* was followed by *Neschastie ot karety* [The Misfortune of Having a Carriage], a piece by Ya. Knyazhnin, music by V. Pashkevich, which was a satire on the Francophilia and self-hatred of the Russian gentry. Next came *Dobrye soldaty* [The Good Soldiers], a sentimental comedy by M. Kheraskov, set to music by H. Raupach, and *Sankt-Peterburgskii Gostinyi dvor* [The St Petersburg Bazaar], libretto and music by M. Matinsky, which is interesting not so much for its plot as for the burning topics of the day referred to in numerous couplets. These included bribe-taking, so widespread that there were many Imperial edicts against it (which naturally did not work); the growing practice of usury, with anti-Semitic hints; the struggle of the merchants for a commercial monopoly; the 1775 reform of provinces and provincial towns, establishing the power of the governor and the city magistrate, where people arrested for non-payment of debts were kept in jail; rising capitalism and its reflection in Russian society, which opposed cynical mercantilism and called for a display of conscience.

The 'musicalization' of comedy developed intensively, gradually enriching it with recitatives accompaniato and final ensembles until the entire text was eventually professionally set to music. As their style developed, folk songs gave place to the common European comic-opera mode with more or less successful attempts at organically incorporating the Russian folk idiom. In general, however, the musical stuff of the new comic opera was also greatly influenced by the French style and, to a lesser extent, the Italian, as might be expected. The emergence of Russian comic opera followed two decades of performing Italian, French, English and German comedies and operas buffa. It is hardly surprising that both the dramaturgy and the music of Russian works were based on an integrated European style as the Russians understood it, selecting those elements that were the most enjoyable and suitable for their mentality and patterns of hearing.

This stylistic process was new in opera since the national opera itself was new and it organically continued the direction of the 1750s in the genre of the Russian popular song. Teplov's 1750's songs were themselves a product of interaction with these other cultures. By the 1770s songs from Teplov's collection had gained an anonymous existence, constituting the best evidence for their wide popularity and integration within Russian urban folklore. The initial borrowing of Teplov's songs took place in Moscow, 1774, where they appeared in the first Russian musical journal, *Muzykal'nye uveseleniya* [Musical entertainments]. The journal remained in publication for only two years, but it deserves special consideration.

The editor and bookseller Christian Ludvig Vever worked from the Moscow University Press and was associated with Novikov. His publishing activity had a clear educational character. The university, oriented toward the humanities, was inaugurated in 1755 at the initiative of Mikhail Vasilievich Lomonosov (1711–65), a Renaissance-like Russian cultural hero and founder of many scientific fields in Russia. The staff of the university, 'Germanized' like the St Petersburg Academy of Science, constituted a stronghold of Russian German-influenced Freemasonry and formed the core of Rosicrucian, the so-called 'Moscow mystic', masonry. In 1772, Novikov, then a young graduate, joined the lodge and was appointed sole manager of the University Press, where he initiated educational publishing on an unprecedented scale.

Vever purchased music-print from Breitkopf in Leipzig, and began his music publishing enterprise with a prominent announcement in a Moscow newspaper supplement (1772). He declared his intention to meet the evident public demand for publication of easily accessible, moderately priced music for all tastes. Vever worked in close cooperation with Joseph (Johann) Kerzelli. The latter, a *Kapellmeister* (supposedly of Czech origin, settling in Moscow), belonged to a family that greatly contributed to the repertories and musical education in Moscow in the eighteenth and nineteenth centuries.[13] Together, Vever and Kerzelli reflected the growth of national enlightenment in music. In 1773 Kerzelli founded the Moscow Musical College. At the same time Vever published two books on musical instruction, translated from the French into Russian: *Methodical Experiment*, on musical theory by a non-indicated French author and *Clavier-Schulee* by Georg Simon Löhlein. He also advertised (though never published) an instructive book on violin playing, probably *Versuch einer gründlichen Violinschule* by Leopold Mozart (Volman, 1959:55), and *Anleitung zur Singe Kunst* (*Opinioni de'cantori antichi e moderni* by Pier Francesco Tosi, 1723) translated into German by Johann Friedrich Agricola in 1757. Considering that the same year had witnessed the opening of vocal and instrumental music classes at the Kharkov Collegium (known as Kharkov State school or Latin School) – one can see that the publisher was ready for the new market. Kharkov and Moscow had had strong cultural connections since the founding of this 'Russian' town in the Ukraine

---

13 Another well-known Kerzelli from this family with unclear and branching genealogy was Franz Kerzelli. Cellist, composer, kapellmeister and teacher, he was in service to Count Kirill Razumovsky as follows from the register of passports issued by the Vienna office of Count D.M. Golitsyn from 29 June/10 July 1765, where he is mentioned as going to Moscow with a wife, two sons, their teachers and two servants (AVPRI, *Vnutrennie kollezhskie dela 1762–1776*, op 2/6, no 3638, L 14). He is also known to have lived in Vienna until the mid-1770s, where he became Haydn's associate and proponent of his music.

at the end of the seventeenth century, and the Collegium founded in 1726 was the authoritative Ukrainian educational institution.

The collection from *Muzykal'nye uveselenia* presents a remarkably wide range of genres. Its contents begin with the official ode-like *kant* on the conclusion of the peace agreement with the Ottoman Porta on 10 June 1774, and contain vocal and choral pieces, both secular and spiritual, including *Abendslied* by Carl Phillip Emanuel Bach and one 'philosophical' (probably Freemason) song based on the text of 'M.Kh.' (Mikhail Kheraskov, Russian poet, Rector of Moscow University and head of the Moscow Rosicrucian lodge). Also included were popular European dances (among them an Ukrainian one), airs and songs (some of which were Russian and Ukrainian), and works for cembalo and various ensembles. Most of the compositions were written by Kerzelli himself, and some by the composer Friedrich Gottlob Fleischer. This was the context in which three songs from Teplov's collection appeared anonymously.

Listing the contents, the editor termed some Russian romance-like urban songs as *Rossiyskie pesni* [Russian songs]. He probably did not mean to invent a new generic definition, but had no other choice as to how to define songs with Russian texts, set to tunes by Russian musicians and addressed to Russian singers and listeners. Naming popular dances according to their countries of origin had been the practice in Europe since at least the seventeenth century, but Anglaise, Polonaise or Allemande (Tedeska) were applied to *foreign* and not native dances, marking their acculturation in a particular national culture. Giving national definition to Russian songs as *Rossiyskaya pesnya*, Vever and Kerzelli thus both mapped them in the context of European music and nationalized them in the Russian context. A generation earlier, in St Petersburg, Teplov had attracted his customers with the foreign words 'minuet' and 'siciliana', but what was more important to the audience of the mid-1770s in Moscow was the label *Rossiyskaya pesnya*, coined there forever.

Both *Rossiyskaya pesnya* and *Russkaya* or *Ruskaya* (with one 's') *pesnya* mean 'Russian song'. These terms are not simply variants of the same but are two definitions referring to two different genres and, moreover, to two types of Russian national identity.[14] While *Rossiyskaya pesnya* refers to the romance-like urban popular and westernized style relating to the new Petrine Imperial State of Russia, *Russkaya pesnya* indicates the vernacular and authentic, pure Russian, old and peasant folk songs, recalling a historical image of Ancient Rus'.

The definition *Ruskaya pesnya* consequently appeared two years later in *Sobranie ruskikh prostykh pesen c notami* [A Collection of Simple Russian Songs with Music] published by the court *Kammerguslist* Vasily Fedorovich Trutovsky (1740? – before 1816). The edition appeared in four volumes over two decades, in 1776, 1778, 1779 and 1795. (Remarkably, the first volume appeared in 1776, earlier than Johann Gottfrid Herder's *Volkslieder nebst untermischten Stücken...* 1778–9.)

---

14 See O.N. Trubachev, '*Russkiy – rossiyskiy*: istoria dvukh atributov natsii', in *E.R. Dashkova i rossiyskoe obshchestvo XVIII stoletia*. Eds. L.V. Tychinina and I.V. Makarova, Moscow: Moskovskiy Gumanitarniy institut imeni E.R. Dashkovoy, 2001: 13–21.

Volume I was twice reprinted, in 1782 and 1796, for subscribers only. Based on Chulkov's collection, Trutovsky selected about one tenth of its texts[15] and offered the simplest two-voice piano arrangement that was greatly in demand due to the widespread fondness for Russian songs (see Example 7.2). This is unquestionably the first example of national musical ethnography.

Example 7.2   Russian folk song *Ivushka, ivushka, zelenaya moya* **from V. Trutovsky's collection**

Trutovsky (*c*. 1740–*c*. 1810) was in court service, close to the Empress. For decades he had been fixated by the desire to have the title of Polish *shlyachetstvo* restored, lost in an earlier generation. For this reason he never agreed to be registered as a chamber musician and was recorded instead as 'quartermaster'. His applications for a restored title were never approved. What is interesting, however, is that, as Lobanov noted, such applications always followed the publication of his volumes or other successful undertakings (MPES, III:172). This may suggest that the approval of such activity from Her Imperial Majesty constituted a strong element of his motivation and it indicates a certain link with the campaign of official nationalism – the Empress's brilliant invention, and one that has continued to work until the present day. Her own style of dress *à la russe* and writing of edifying libretti and *proverby*, as well as encouraging nationalistic activity – were all important facets of her policy. Trutovsky's collection, no matter what his intentions, matched the tone most desired by Catherine II.

The song collections of the 1770s thus presented three different types reflecting three facets of Russian identity: one was an ideologically neutral anthology of the current repertoire (Chulkov), another gave an idea of the contemporaneous commercially westernized trend (Vever-Kerzelli), and the third one presented

---

15 Lobanov noted an interesting proportion between 200 songs in each of the four volumes of Chulkov's collection and only 20 in Trutovsky's (MPES, III:174–81).

the officially-ethnographical approach and established the term *russkaya pesnya* (Trutovsky). Each had its continuation and development in the following two decades of the century.

Chapter 8

Bortniansky and the 1780s

The 1780s offered a decade of stability before the Russian monarchy was to be shaken once again, this time by the reverberation of the French Revolution from without and the revolutionary wing of the Russian Enlightenment from within. Meanwhile, Enlightenment was becoming a dominant drive in Russian cultural life, resulting in a great demand for education and the arts. It was also a time when the cultural seeds sown much earlier began a lively germination and fruition on a wide scale. From the social point of view, whereas the main audiences for the arts had previously consisted almost solely of the nobility, they now also embraced some of the lower strata of Russian society, including the middle class and the expanding mixed-cast intelligentsia. The rapid growth of an audience for the new music in turn stimulated the wide-ranging development of various musical institutions. Music became the most prestigious pastime in public and in private and – accordingly – an indispensable element of the general educational curriculum. Every professional musician, foreign and national, then available on the Russian map, was provided with opportunities to work in composition, arrangement, teaching and performance. In parallel, there was a proportional development in music publishing, production of instruments, civic opera spectacles and concert enterprises.

While the extreme poles of Russian society – the court and the peasantry – maintained the traditional forms of their musical life intact, there was also an area of lively interaction. This was affected by the two middle social spheres – the estate and the urban. Both were developing apace, becoming the arena where the new Russian musical language was formed. Not constrained by such extra-musical factors as ideology, censure or class conventions, they spontaneously selected and adopted whatever spoke to the people's hearts, and the most enjoyable was European, which was how they saw themselves.

In the 1780s, the arts in Russia crystallized into what would later be considered as the main style of the eighteenth century, reflecting the spirit of stability, grandeur and glorification. As the consumption of fine arts increased and diversified, the artistic forms and genres broadened their range. The arts became increasingly flexible, with a blurring of the distinctions between royal and democratic values, and the gap between the court and the wider public culture became significantly reduced. This generated new and more viable forms of expression, until by the 1780s they were fully compatible.

On the aristocratic estates thousands of trained serf musicians reproduced the culture of the capital city, adjusting it to their own tastes and enabling a musical environment even far from the cultural centres. In the cities urban folklore was effectively absorbing Ukrainian, Polish, German, Italian and French influences. Many native composers began to work side by side with the foreigners, together creating a totally new sound.

Bortniansky's Return to Russia

This new sound was especially notable in the sphere of choral music, which had remained somewhat neglected in the late 1770s while Paisiello was occupied with musical theatre, chamber music-making and instruction. The Court Choir remained outside his sphere of activity, unlike the times of Galuppi and Traetta, who had contributed to its repertoire. Berezovsky, whose knowledge of choral works had been so appropriate for the 1760s, but who had not survived the musical hard times of the mid-1770s, had to be replaced. This might have been what Yelagin had in mind when he wrote to recall Bortniansky to Russia.

Bortniansky indeed received the nice (at least initially) position of 'director of ecclesiastical music' at the court. It was a new position that released the chief kapellmeister from obligations regarding the repertoire of the Court Capella. Bortniansky's appointment was confirmed between December 1779 and January 1780 and his annual salary of 1000 roubles was authorized on 18 January 1780. This salary, relatively high for a Russian musician (Berezovsky was paid 500 rubles), was equivalent to that of a lieutenant-colonel (or Court Counsellor) and of a 'cabinet virtuoso of Her Imperial Majesty', a position that Johann Gottfried Wilhelm Palschau enjoyed for a short period at about this time. In addition, Bortniansky received 500 roubles for firewood and carriage. Shortly after Bortniansky's arrival in St Petersburg, Galuppi received 1000 zecchins for 'his efforts to teach the court singer Dmitry Bortniansky, who had been sent for this purpose.'[1] Bortniansky's Italian chapter was closed.

Few details are known about the first years following his return, or indeed about the rest of his life. In addition to his obligations with the Court Choir, there are indirect data relating to his participation as choirmaster in spectacles presented by Knipper's Free Russian Theatre (Keldysh, 1965:116), although these have failed to be confirmed by a recent revision (Khodorkovskaya, MPES, II:59–63). Three of his pieces appeared in print in the early 1780s. Two of them were spiritual: *Kheruvimskaya* [Cherubic Hymn] (1782) and *Da ispravitsya molitva moya* [Let my prayer be set forth 1783] – and they could be written as early as 1780.[2] The third was a French romance *Dans le verger de Cythère* [1784], previously considered as lost but recently found by N. Ogarkova (MPES, I:191).

---

1 A.Ya. Bezborodko to A.V. Olsuf'ev, 17 January 1780. RNB, f 874, op 2, no 182.

2 There are manuscripts of both pieces dated to 1780 (Howard Gotlieb Archival Research Center at US Boston University, U.C. Robbins London Collection, Bos 5, Folder 5).

Figure 8.1   Bortniansky, portrait by unknown artist

The original editions of both spiritual works remain unknown and these compositions are probably those that reached us in Bortniansky's later revised publication of his works in the 1810s, though not definitely identified as such. Bortniansky then published seven *Kheruvimskie* and three *Da ispravitsya molitva moya* but it is impossible to determine which of them (if any) had been published in the early 1780s. There are, however, versions of both pieces found among late eighteenth-century manuscripts and they correspond to numbers 1 of both *Kheruvimskie* and *Da ispravitsya molitva moya* in Bortniansky's later edition. If we assume that the composer kept a chronological order and the numbers 1 of both series were the earliest to be written, we can deduce that those were the pieces with which Bortniansky first appeared publicly in the 1780s. *Kheruvimskaya* in *E flat major* and *Da ispravitsya molitva moya* in *F Major* – the supposed pieces in question – are frankly popular and light in style. They reveal Bortniansky's exceptional melodic gift that gained him such outstanding popularity among the contemporary Russian public as well as in the years to follow.

Everything was new about all three published pieces. They were the first in the composer's biography; they were the first (and the only at the time) Russian publications in these genres – contemporary spiritual music and French romance; and they were modern in style. *Kheruvimskaya* in *E flat major* was indeed very close to the *Rossiyskaya pesnya* 'Lyutoy rok opredelyaet' [Ferocious fate determines],published in the late 1790s in the huge Song collection by I.D. Gertstenberg and F.A. Dittmas (Examples 8.1a, b).

Example 8.1 (a) Bortniansky: *Cherubic Hymn*

Example 8.1 (b) Rossiyskaya pesnya *Lutoy rok opredelyayet*

The intriguing phraseology of the *Sankt-Peterburgskie vedomosti* announcement is worth noting: 'On Lugovaya Millionnaya 61, the bookseller Miller has on sale the Kheruvimskaya song, composed by Mr Bortniansky, printed by a music lover with the permission of the composer himself; the price on Alexandrian paper is 40 kopeks.'[3]

Music in Russia was usually printed at the expense of either the publisher or the composer. Mention of a third party hinted at a certain patronage, although on the other hand it could have been one of the first projects of Bernhard Breitkopf, who opened a print shop in St Petersburg in 1781 (together with J.K. Schnoor) and during the early years concealed his name, keeping to the conventions of the upper class, since he was married to A.I. Paris, director of the Ekaterininsky Institute for noble maidens (Kartsovnik MPES, I:155, Volman, 1957:94–5). In any event, such announcements created a fashionable aura and, considering that there were at least three portraits of the young (and handsome) Bortniansky done in the 1780s, and that there are no definitive portraits of other Russian composers of the time, one can conclude that Bortniansky was indeed in fashion.

Whether it was due to Bortniansky's attractive personality or to the Russian love of choral/ensemble singing, or to both, the genre of choral spiritual music, to which Bortniansky had contributed in the course of his court service, also became highly fashionable. There may too have been an interconnection between the intensive development of estate musical culture and the increasing number of serf choirs, which both consumed and stimulated new choral repertoires.

This flourishing of choral music in the 1780s, with Bortniansky as a central figure, has not always been obvious in Russian historiography, which has traditionally associated the creation of Bortniansky's choral work with a much later period, when he became director of the Imperial Court Cappella, that is from 1796 to 1825. However, the hand-written catalogue of choral music (KPN), compiled by an anonymous music lover in 1793 (discussed in detail later), included not only most of Bortniansky's choral compositions, but many works by his contemporaries too. Existing musical manuscripts also contain many of Bortniansky's pieces, often varying in score details, frequently appearing as anonymous or, on the contrary, in fact being the works of other musicians but ascribed to him. All these features reflect a lively praxis, demonstrate the great popularity of this genre in the 1780s and indicate Bortniansky as its style-setting leader. A later published corpus of his oeuvre contains ten double-choir and thirty-five four-voice concertos (some of them had double-choir versions), fourteen Te Deum compositions (four of them for four voices and ten double-choir) and various liturgical works. However it is hardly possible to assert the exact number of his choral compositions. At least five additional four-voice concertos ascribed to Bortniansky: *Gotovo serdtse moe* [My heart is fixed], *Nadeyushchisya na Gospoda* [They that trust in the Lord], *Blazhen muzh izhe ne eide* [Blessed is the man that walketh not in the counsel of the ungodly], *Na Tya Gospodi, upovakh* [In thee, O Lord, do I put my trust], *Bozhe, sud Tvoy tsarevi dazhd'* [Judge

---

3   'В Луговой Миллионной под № 61 у книгопродавца Миллера продается Херувимская песнь, сочинения г. Бортнянского, напечатанная с одобрением самого автора некоторым любителем музыки; Цена на александрийской бумаге 40 копеек' (*Sankt-Peterburgskie vedomosti*, 1782; ns 59, 83).

me, O God, and plead my cause] – can be found in the collection of the beginning of the nineteenth century (see Rytsareva, 1973: Supplement);[4] one, the concerto *Dnes' Khristos* [Today Christ], in another collection;[5] one six-voice concerto Bogootets ubo David [David, the divine forefather] was published in part at the beginning of the twentieth century; and many of his unknown compositions are mentioned in catalogues and exist in separate parts in different hand-written sources.

Bortniansky's Concertos of the 1780s

The choral concerto was a lively genre and it vividly reacted to changes in the musical environment that, in turn, endowed it with great popularity. Each decade marked choral spiritual music with new stylistic features, as illustrated in the oeuvre of Bortniansky himself. His works of the 1780s, most of which were choral concertos and *Te Deum* compositions, unmistakably convey the spirit of the time. They are emphatically superficial in style, as well as shorter and lighter than the 1760's baroquesque work of Berezovsky and Galuppi, obviously also due to the same general curtailing of spectacles and ceremonies that had influenced Paisiello's operas.

Bortniansky's concertos are little developed in harmony and texture, always written in major mode and standardized in structure. They usually have three or four contrasting sections such as march-like and *gallant* characters. Overall they have a ceremonial, somewhat decorative, function. Their popularity could probably be explained by the novelty of their style, sharply contrasting that of the previous era, and by the suitability of their format to the general atmosphere of the court. Nevertheless, their *gallant* minuet-like lyrical middle sections and, sometimes, slow introductions, must have captivated the audiences of the time with the charm of their French-style pastoral elegance and sentimental sincerity.

Although the general techniques, originating in the musical rhetoric of the eighteenth century, represented a common background for Berezovsky, Galuppi and Bortniansky, certain notable points distinguish the latter's choral style (the 1780s) from the earlier one of Berezovsky and Galuppi (the 1760s–70s).

To begin with generic sources, to which their themes referred, it can be seen that while Berezovsky and Galuppi used quite strict baroque polyphonic themes, including some motives characteristic of *partes*-singing or that could be interpreted as belonging to the Russian *protyazhnaya* folk song (Berezovsky), Bortniansky, while basing his works on the same sources, also incorporated many elements of other genres that were widespread in the Russian capital in the 1780s. These included fanfares, marches, *kanty* (both *vivat* type and lyrical ones), *Rossiyskaya pesnya* and the entire sphere of *style gallant*, as well as traits of orchestral and operatic music. Bortniansky yearned for the music of the city, that of the capital, of the larger world, a music in which genres and national traditions interacted in a natural, flexible and fruitful way.

---

4   GMMK, f 283, ns 4, 48, 51.
5   GMMK, f 283, no 125, Ll. 3–4.

Bortniansky's comprehensive choral style ensured his popularity not only within various social strata but also among various age groups. If the youth preferred the *Rossiyskaya pesnya* to the *kanty*, the older generation cherished the latter. Both genres had much in common. They were three-voiced (two high voices in a third or sixth and a bass part) and Bortniansky's compositions give equal weight to both these genres and at various composition levels, at times amounting to exact quotations from these sources. This can be seen from comparison of the second section from the concerto no 1 *Vospoyte Gospodevi pesn' novu* [Praise ye the Lord. Sing unto the Lord a new song] with *kant* 'Na konchinu Petra i vosshestvie na prestol Ekateriny I' [On the occasion of Peter's death and Catherine I ascending the throne] (Examples 8.2a, b) and

Example 8.2 (a) Bortniansky: *Concerto Vospoyte Gospodevi pesn' novu*, **section 3**

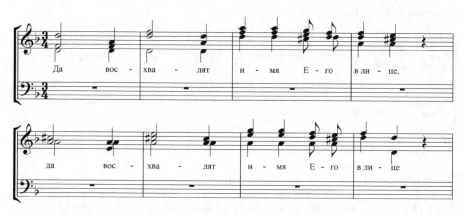

Example 8.2 (b) Kant on the occasion of Peter's death and Catherine I ascending the throne

Kheruvimskaya [Cherubic Hymn] from three-voice Liturgy with *kant* 'Shedshie tri tsari' [Three tsars were going] (Examples 8.3a, b).

Example 8.3 (a) Bortniansky: *Cherubic hymn*

Example 8.3 (b) Kant *Shedshie tri tsari*

Example 8.4   Bortniansky: Concerto *Voskliknite Gospodevi vsya zemlya*, **finale**

A prominent component in Bortniansky's concertos was that of the genre of the march, contributing energy and imperial glitter. In the earlier concertos march elements could be found mainly in the final sections of the cycle. The double metre, the slightly abrupt rhythm, the precise periodicity, and the simplified harmonic texture confer on them a lightness reminiscent of Bortniansky's secular compositions: the March in Act I of his Italian opera *Quinto Fabio* (1778), the Finale in Act II of *Le Fils Rival* (1787), and finally the *Gatchinskiy marsh* [Gatchina march] itself (1787). (Example 8.4) Sometimes he managed to merge the march with dance rhythms, especially in cadences (Example 8.5). Despite all this lightness and energy, however, Bortniansky's choral style also possesses a definite hymnal quality, softening the march connotations (Asafiev, 1971:286) and recalling its ecclesiastical background. On the one hand, the sound of an *a cappella* choir will endow this quality upon any music, thereby explaining its use as the prime means of church music in the Christian tradition. On the other hand, here and there Bortniansky has obviously used elements of cantillations from *znamenny* chant, especially in cadenzas (Skrebkov, 1980:191) (Example 8.6).

Example 8.5   Bortniansky: Concerto *Gospod' prosveshchenie moe*, **finale**

No less a role in the individuality of Bortniansky's choral style is played by the lyrical minuet, whose rhythm is definitely heard in the slow sections (Example 8.7). The minuet rhythm had been frequently used earlier, in *partes*-singing concerto, where, hidden under heavy notation in 3/2 proportions (Kholopova, 1983:126) it was actually characteristic of *kanty*. It was thus only natural for Bortniansky to use minuet, especially because it also continued to be the basic rhythm for *Rossiyskaya pesnya*. Of course Bortniansky's minuet was different – operatically gallant and implying the grace of polite society. The question arises, however, as to why Berezovsky and Galuppi did not use this rhythm too, if it had already been adopted by the *partes*-singing concerto? Did it abuse their idea of high spiritual art? Was the genre of concerto devalued in this sense by Bortniansky, or perhaps by the era itself? It might partly be related to the undulating waves of

Example 8.6 Bortniansky: Concerto *Vospoyte Gospodevi pesn' novu*, **closing measures of the finale**

Крот - ки - я во спа - се - - ни - е.

fashion for the minuet in Russia. After its rise in Petrine and post-Petrine decades the minuet was then replaced by the polonaise during Elizabeth's epoch, only to be restored in the early 1760s as a pan-European fashion (Voznesensky, MPES, II:203–4). In 1764 the Christmas ball at the Winter Palace was opened with a minuet. Could this, two decades prior to Bortniansky, have been a too functionally defined rhythm at the time to be used in ecclesiastic music?

This contrast between two generations of composers regarding the thematic material naturally led to differences in texture and harmony. Berezovsky's music was stressed and intensified by rhythmically concentrated harmonic development, and Galuppi's by detailed polyphonic elaboration. In contrast, Bortniansky's music tended to homophonic texture, détente harmony and more spacious and well-rounded melodic phrases. Bortniansky minimized the use of polyphony, and at an early stage even rejected the traditional fugue in the *finale* of the cycle (to return to it later).

The young composer, however, compensated for Berezovsky's melodic and harmonic abundance, and Galuppi's polyphonic virtuosity, with a remarkably diverse textural development. He made extensive use of alternating various soloist ensembles and *tutti* phrases. This, along with the use of antiphony in various combinations and pedals, served to form an attractive play of timbres (Khivrich, 1971:211). The textural makeup continuously changes, even within small-scale constructions such as a period or a single phrase. Only the *finali* of his concertos usually present a consistently denser *tutti* texture. The Court Cappella included able young soloists and these were exploited through the composer's extensive use of trios for the soloists with an alto in the top voice, and of fanfare-like 'angelic' duets for boy *descant* and *alto*. Such devices as their juxtaposition with *tutti* passages performed *pianissimo* probably made a specifically enjoyable effect. In these combinations the composer revealed fantasy somewhat comparable to the diversity of architectural designs.

Example 8.7 Bortniansky: Concerto *Blago est' ispovedatisya Gospodevi,*
section 2

In many cases not only were single phrases given to soloist ensembles but also
entire sections, particularly the slow ones. Such sections usually introduce a new
verse from the text. Sometimes they separate a faster *tutti* section and at times they
open the entire composition: this suggests that the composer gave them a special
aesthetic significance, drawing closer to the western cantata or mass. Having these
soloist ensembles perform in the most notable sections of the composition gave the
concerto greater liveliness and intimacy, and was an unmistakable attraction for both

performers and audience. Perhaps this development in the concerto style offered some compensation for the lack of instruments that became more obvious along with secularization and westernization of the genre. This technique, initiated by Bortniansky, was later developed and widely used by his younger contemporaries.

Correspondingly, the principles of composition differ. While Berezovsky kept motet-like alternations of short polyphonic structures and chorale summations, Bortniansky (also mastering this principle) tended to classicist periodical organization. He liked to link homophonic structures and avoided harmonic resolutions, which resulted in a spiralling, unfolding effect. This type of structure is quite typical for the baroque sonata with its binary principle aa^1bb^1 where b is a development of a, incorporating some of its elements.

The similarities and differences between the styles of Galuppi–Bortniansky and Berezovsky–Bortniansky can be best depicted in a comparative analysis of their concertos based on the same text.

In comparing the two concertos entitled *Gotovo serdtse moe* [My heart is fixed] by Galuppi and Bortniansky, it becomes evident that Galuppi's composition has more substance and weight than Bortniansky's elegant and laconic piece.[6] There is little apparent similarity between these pieces beyond the text, the key of *D major*, and the identical rhythmic outline of the introductory themes. It is obvious that the two compositions targeted audiences of different generations: Bortniansky's was lighter and more appropriate to the new faster pace of life (Examples 8.8a, b).

Example 8.8 (a) Galuppi: Concerto *Gotovo serdtse moe*, **section 1**

---

6   Bortniansky's concerto was not published. There are two copies of it, one in *Sbornik khorovykh dukhovnykh kontsertov* (GMMK, f 283, ns 4, 48, 51) and the other in *Sbornik dukhovnykh kontsertov XVIII–nachala XIX veka* (RNB, f 1021, op 3 (1), no 2) where the concerto is attributed to Galuppi.

Example 8.8 (b) Bortniansky: Concerto *Gotovo serdtse moe*, **section 1**

A better example for comparison of styles is found in the concertos *Da voskresnet Bog* [Let God arise] (Psalm 68), by Berezovsky and Bortniansky. Berezovsky used most of the verses in the psalm and, in addition to the panegyric, introduced the verse *Da smiatutsya ot litsa ego otsa sirykh i sudii vdovits* [So let the wicked perish at the presence of God], which enabled him to create strong and dramatic qualities in the spirit of *Sturm und Drang*. He wrote an extensive six-part

Table 8.1   Textual structures of Berezovsky's and Bortniansky's concertos
        Da voskresnet Bog

BEREZOVSKY	Psalm 68	BORTNIANSKY
1. *Da voskresnet Bog* F major	Let God arise	1. *Da voskresnet Bog* F major
2. *A pravednitsy da vozveselyatsya* C major – A minor	But let the righteous be glad	2. *A pravednitsy da vozveselyatsya* B major – A minor
3. *Da smyatutsya ot litsa ego* D minor	So let the wicked perish at the presence of God	
4. *Bozhe vsegda iskhodite* Es major	O God, when thou wentest forth	
5. *Zemlya potryasesya* Es minor	The earth shook	
6. *Diven Bog vo svyatykh* F major	O God, *thou art terrible out of thy holy places*	3. *Diven Bog vo svyatykh* F major

composition with contrasting sections and a multitude of affects. Bortniansky, in contrast, used only the first four and the last two verses of the psalm, similar in mood. He composed a compact three-section cycle of a generally festive ceremonial character with a moderately contrasting lyrical hymn-like middle part. Table 8.1 presents the textual structures of the concertos. Both concertos coincide in the key *F major* and have so much else in common that Bortniansky's composition looks like a version of Berezovsky's. Parts 1, 2 and 6 of Berezovsky's concerto and 1, 2 and 3 of Bortniansky's generally coincide in text and musical character. Moreover, their opening sections and *finali* have virtually an identical number of bars: the former having 42 bars each and the latter having 36 measures of 4/4 (Berezovsky) against 66 measures of 2/4 (Bortniansky). The initial themes of these sections are also quite similar (Examples 8.9a, b) as are their internal developments. In both cases we have a sequence of short structural units, each corresponding to a verse of the psalm. The middle section of Bortniansky's concerto, textually coinciding with the second section of Berezovsky's, also resembles it in its lyrical character and use of soloist ensembles. In spite of beginning in different keys (Berezovsky's in *C major* and Bortniansky's in *B major*) they both end in *A minor*, although Berezovsky proceeds in *D minor*, while Bortniansky returns to the main key.

A distinction between the choral textures of these two compositions is, however, evident. In Berezovsky's concerto the imitative technique is strict, forceful and consistent, demonstrating that his compositional style was still strongly indebted to the motet. In contrast, Bortniansky's imitations, whose rhythmic features are dictated by the text rather than musical considerations, are freely used. They rather serve as a pretext for the antiphonic dialogue between the choral groups, which plays a role in the overall textural strategy of the concerto.

Example 8.9 (a) Berezovsky: Concerto *Da voskresnet Bog*, section 1

Example 8.9 (b) Bortniansky: Concerto *Da voskresnet Bog,* **section 1**

A comparison of the final fugues is also telling. Berezovsky's brilliant fugue has two themes with consistent counter-themes and was composed in accordance with the rules of free counterpoint. It is technically perfect, compact, contains vivid material and represents a worthy model of choral polyphony within the Russian repertoire. The polyphonic development of Bortniansky's finale is relatively free, conforming to the fugue form only in its outward contour. The overall texture is homophonic, and imitations are used only to intensify the texture toward the completion of the cyclic composition. Berezovsky's monumental composition, rich in the contrast and density of polyphonic texture (the third section also being a well-formulated *fugato* in D *minor*), reveals him as a master of the baroque era. Bortniansky's lighter and shorter version demonstrates a true classical work, whose polyphony is not a logical mechanism, but rather an element of textural development. Bortniansky's concerto *Da voskresnet Bog* is thus not a reworking of Berezovsky's composition, although it was strongly influenced by it. Bortniansky had apparently heard Berezovsky's concerto on many occasions and might have even performed it with the Court Choir in the 1760s. He thus grew up in this tradition and his following and developing it was only natural. What was pioneering for Berezovsky as representative of the transition from baroque to classicism, became routine for Bortniansky who, at ease with classical expression, could exploit Berezovsky's models.

An apocryphal biography of Bortniansky suggests that he was highly in demand and mentions his writing his scores in great haste, sometimes even in his carriage. Where was he hurrying to?

Bortniansky and the Young Court

With Paisiello's departure, the Grand Duchess Maria Fedorovna remained without a piano instructor and Bortniansky had the good fortune to be appointed to this position in addition to his obligations at the Capella.

Grand Duke Pavel Petrovich, an educated and refined young man, although already mature enough to ascend the throne, had no chance of doing so while the Empress was at the height of her activity. Moreover, subscribing to his father's Prussian orientation, and supported by Masonic circles, he maintained a hidden opposition to his mother's policy. The Empress kept a keen watch over him and held him at a safe distance from all State and political affairs. He would have many years ahead to prepare himself for his eventual role, indeed too many, which eventually spoiled his character and made him unrealistic, impatient and, finally, an unsuccessful ruler.

His second wife, Maria Fedorovna, the Prussian Princess of Württemberg, was a pleasant and well-educated woman. Relieved of most of her maternal duties by her mother-in-law, who took over the education of Alexander and Constantine, the Grand Duchess kept herself busy with drawing, wood and bone sculpture, mathematics, physics and music, although these pastimes were interrupted by annual childbirth, changes of residence and the resulting renovations, and so on.

Bortniansky joined the Young court at the right moment, when the atmosphere was one of constant demand for entertainment, naturally with music. Grand Duke Pavel Petrovich and his wife, just recently back from their European tour, travelling incognito under the names of Count and Countess Severnye [Northerns], during which they had visited major musical centres, returned with great impressions and having become acquainted with many musical celebrities, including Haydn (from whom the Grand Duchess took piano lessons) and Mozart. The Grand Duke himself played piano.

Example 8.10   Bortniansky: Sonata *F major*, first movement

Example 8.11   Bortniansky: Sonata *C major*, second movement

Evidence of Bortniansky's work as instructor to the Grand Duchess is found in the collection of pieces for keyboard instruments (piano, harpsichord and clavichord) solo or in various ensembles, and somewhat continuing Paisiello's album, dedicated to Maria Fedorovna. The collection appears to have been lost, and the last to see it was N. Findeizen, who presented the content, incipits and general description of the style in a supplement to his *Ocherki po istorii muzyki v Rossii* (Findeizen, 1929, II:268–73). Three sonatas survived and were published in Soviet times[7] (Examples 8.10, 8.11).

The collection as seen by Findeizen was already incomplete, but still had 96 folios and, according to the scholar's impression, was the original draft of the composer, although mostly appearing in clean copy. Five of the seventeen works have dedications to the Grand Duchess, including the one opening the collection. Three of the first ten compositions were dated to 1784, though Findeizen believed the collection to have been initiated earlier, in 1783, probably reflecting Bortniansky's contacts with Maria Fedorovna before his official appointment. Interestingly, the collection begins with eight sonatas for harpsichord, presumably owing to Maria Fedorovna's passion for sonatas. An anecdote recounts a dispute that she had had with Paisiello over such compositions. At the conclusion of his employment, Maria Fedorovna promised him a pension. Deeply touched, the maestro promised in return to dedicate some new sonatas to her. However, as is often the case, they both soon forgot their promises. Thus, when Paisiello complained to the Grand Duchess about the non-existent pension, the pretext was ready: no sonatas had been written.[8] Other sources, however, state that Paisiello did receive a pension from Maria Fedorovna of 900 roubles annually.(Hunt, 1975:34).

---

7   There are vague rumours that the album exists in private ownership somewhere in South America.

8   See A. Weydemeyer, *Dvor i zamechatel'nye lyudi v Rossii vo vtoroy polovine XVIII stoletia*. Parts I and II. St Petersburg, 1846.

Figure 8.2   Pavlovsk palace, Chamber of the Grand Duchess Maria
Fedorovna

Bortniansky's keyboard works reveal his pedagogic intentions as well as the high level of proficiency achieved by his pupil. For ensemble playing, Bortniansky wrote three accompanied violin sonatas (*obligato* violin in the fifth and sixth sonatas and *ad libitum* in the eighth). Additional works included a piano quartet in *C major* (of unknown instrumentation), a fortepiano *organizé*[9] quintet in *A minor* including harp, violin, viola da gamba, and cello, followed by the Concerto di Cembalo in *C major*, written to demonstrate the Grand Duchess's mastery. There was at least one more Concerto, *D major*, also dedicated to the Grand Duchess but not included in this collection; it had been found in the Paris National Library and edited by M. Stepanenko.[10]

The collection also contained four smaller pieces (*Larghetto cantabile*, *Capriccio di Cembalo*, *Rondo* and *Allegro*) and three piano arrangements of Bortniansky's own choral spiritual compositions, two of which coincide in title with his advertised editions of 1782 and 1783: *Kheruvimskaya* and *Da ispravitsya molitva moya*.

N. Findeizen, the only person to have fully studied the collection in its entirety, noted the complete correspondence of Bortniansky's style to European standards of the time, appreciating it as melodically more attractive than those of Clementi, Pleyel or Dušek and approaching those of Haydn and Mozart. He emphasized the melodic grace and charm and the presence of Russian and Ukrainian gestures and structural peculiarities in certain themes.

Besides the music lessons given to the Grand Duchess, Bortniansky's main musical duties at the Young court were related to summer entertainment. The Pavlovsk and Gatchina Palaces were places of rare beauty, surrounded by parks, elegantly harmonizing with the architecture and stimulating pastimes in *plein air*. The ducal couple and their entourage were very inventive when it came to recreation, which played an integral part in their day-to-day activities. Music was an essential diversion. On sunny days musicians performed outdoors, in pavilions or on natural terraces, on small boats on rivers or lakes, and of course at the banquets.

The concerts were an indispensable part of the daily routine. Their programmes incorporated the wide repertoire circulating in Europe at the time, mostly oriented on the Viennese and Parisian styles, as can be seen from the archives of the Pavlovsk Palace Museum. Other entertainments included pantomime performances, quasi-improvised sketches with ensemble singing, couplet songs, dances, games, skits, swings and blind-man's-bluff, and many others, in the evening accompanied by music in the park. The performers included both professional and amateur musicians (Dolgoruky, 1916:86). One constant element was that of military music provided for the Grand Duke's regiment exercising in Prussian style. Bortniansky's *Gatchinsky march* written for this purpose can be equated with Sousa's modern classic marches (Example 8.12).

---

9   Fortepiano organizé, a combination of piano and organ, known also as Claviorganum.

10   The concerto was edited by M. Stepanenko and published as a score for two pianos in Kiev: Muzychna Ukraina, 1985.

Example 8.12   Bortniansky: *Gatchina March,* **piano score**

Enamoured with the French theatre since his teens, Pavel Petrovich established it as the primary form of entertainment at the Pavlovsk Palace. Both the Pavlovsk and Gatchina palaces had theatre halls where enthusiastic courtiers staged amateur shows reasonably well. They were trained in the performing arts, which were an indispensable element in the curriculum of educational institutions for noble youth. Several of the ladies-in-waiting were graduates of the eminent Smolny Institute for Noble Maidens, and many of the cavaliers were alumni of the prestigious *Suhoputny shliakhetskiy korpus* [Cadet Corps]. Most of these smart young courtiers had knowledge and taste in music.

The court also included men of letters and drama such as Count G.I. Chernyshev, A.A. Musin-Pushkin, A.F. Violier and F.H. Lafermiére. The latter was initially Pavel's tutor (instead of D'Alembert who had declined Catherine's offer of this position) and afterwards his librarian and companion, a role similar to Stählin's at his father's side. A Frenchman born in Switzerland, graduate of Strasbourg University, litterateur and acquaintance of 'encyclopaedists', a jovial and expansive man, Lafermiére played a central role in this social circle including everything related to the Pavlovsk-Gatchina theatre.

The palace repertory contained comedies, pastoral *intermezzi,* dramas, tragic parodies, and often incorporated musical pieces. 'Le goût des spectacles est dans toute sa force ici, ce ne sont que répétitions et représentations...' – wrote Prince Alexey Kurakin to his brother Alexander from Gatchina on 15 September 1786 (Rozanov, 1975:694). The success of these performances stimulated the notion of fully-fledged musical productions at the court, which naturally involved Lafermiére's libretti and Bortniansky's music. These amateur productions were among the most convivial and rewarding events of 1786–7. The operas were written and immediately performed. The lively and creative atmosphere has been entertainingly described in the memoirs of one of the regular participants, Prince Ivan Mikhaylovich Dolgoruky. A keen observer and man of talent, he wrote reliable, brief, light and non-pretentious characterizations of the events and their *dramatis personae*, recording the most vivid traits of Bortniansky's personality.

Prince Dolgoruky, a remarkable amateur actor, began his 'career' with minor comic roles but advanced to the role of a serious character in Bortniansky's last opera, alongside Evgenia Sergeevna Smirnaya, whom he would soon marry and who was known for her intense dramatic characterizations. (Pavel Petrovich appreciated their enthusiasm so greatly that for their wedding he spent an enormous sum from his own funds, eliciting his mother's anger.) Main tenor parts were routinely awarded to Pavel's chamberlain F.F. Vadkovsky (whose father, Colonel Vadkovsky, was the proprietor of the foremost horn-band in St Petersburg). The lady-in-waiting Ekaterina Ivanovna Nelidova was a highly spirited interpreter of female comic parts. Although plain in appearance, she was intelligent, renowned and charming, and played a key role at Pavel Petrovich's court (to the extent of making Maria Fedorovna jealous).

The Princes F.N. Golitsyn and P.M. Volkonsky were also members of the opera troupe, as was Count A.A. Musin-Pushkin, a scientist who did research in chemistry and mineralogy; A.F. Violier, Maria Fedorovna's secretary; the translator S.I. Pleshcheev, the ladies-in-waiting V.N. Schatz and N.S. Hoven, and others.

While for most of the courtiers their work amounted to entertainment, Bortniansky's role involved considerable effort and responsibility. Within eighteen months he had written three operas, in addition to instrumental and choral music. His duties also included rehearsing with the amateur singers, who, despite their relatively good musical and dramatic skills, and the enthusiasm that they brought to their work, were not always fluent in sight-reading. Dolgoruky noted:

> I was taught how to sing by Mr. Bortniansky, who produced our operas, and the mention of his name brings back the great pleasure of our many rehearsals... He was an easy-going, pleasant, affable artist and his tutelage soon transformed me into a good opera performer. Without any previous musical training or knowledge, I was memorizing my part and singing quite complicated scenes, in pace with the orchestra and my colleagues.[11]

In his other book Prince Dolgoruky recollects that the Grand Duchess couldn't believe her ears when she heard about this, and came to one of the rehearsals to see for herself.

> Bortniansky was sitting at his piano and we all, including myself, had scores in our hands. Each sang his part and when my turn came I sang my verse looking at the music. 'How come?' – exclaimed the Grand Duchess, – 'that you, messieurs, told me he doesn't know how to read music, and yet he sings according to the score.' 'If you don't mind, Your Highness, order Prince Dolgoruky to indicate which passage he has just performed,'

---

11 'Я обучался петь у г. Бортнянского, он руководствовал нашими операми, и при имени его я с удовольствием воображаю многие репетиции наши... Он был артист снисходительный, добрый, любезный, попечения его сделали из меня в короткое время хорошего оперного лицедея, и не зная вовсе музыки, не учась ей никогда, я памятью одной вытверживал и певал в театре довольно мудрые сцены, не разбиваясь ни с оркестром, ни с товарищами' (Dolgoruky, 1890:230).

answered Bortniansky. The Duchess approached me and to her surprise discovered not only that I was holding the wrong score... but it was also upside down...[12]

Under such circumstances the composer had to exercise much patience and restraint, imagination and pedagogic tact, in order to achieve a good quality production and on schedule.

The Pavlovsk court was updated in contemporary operatic repertory and thoroughly familiar with the latest works by A. Grétry, A. Dezède and other French composers. Bortniansky, therefore, was expected to reproduce the French *opera-comique* style, for which he proved himself to be fully equipped. He did not, however, merely copy it but smoothly hybridized the French and Italian traditions (Asafiev, 1927:18; Rabinovich, 46:118; Keldysh, 1985:179), which allowed him to express a generous spectrum of lyrical emotions – be they aggressive frivolity, sentimental tenderness or mature passion borrowed from the *opera seria* mode. With all this, he never failed to produce work with temperament, melodic beauty and orchestral elegance.

Bortniansky's first opera at the Young court was *La Fête du Seigneur*. Since the libretto was anonymous, this indicates it having involved aristocratic writers, probably Count G.I. Chernyshev and A.A. Musin-Pushkin (who often wrote together) and A.F. Violier, who specialized in lyrics for ariettas and couplets (Rozanov, 1970:21). This opera, referred to as 'a comedy with accompanying arias and ballets' and written according to the traditional court pastoral, alluded to devotion to the *seigneur* – the Grand Duke Pavel Petrovich. There were also references to the *seigneur*'s ideal marriage (not entirely: Catherine II maliciously noted that they lived like cat and dog)[13] and praise for his predilection for war games. The opera was scheduled to première on Pavel Petrovich's name-day at the end of June 1786.

The score does not strike one with originality and seems to have been written by a fast hand and with consideration for the limited operatic possibilities of the amateur troupe. The overture is an adaptation of one written for *Quinto Fabio*. The musical make-up of the characters lacks overall development and the result is an elegant 'musical garland'. The short musical numbers are all in French song style, simple and narrow in range, except for a few more complex ones for the female voices of Mademoiselles Nelidova, Smirnaya and Mme Hoven, who had performed in operas by Philidor and Monsigny while training at the Smolny Institute. A certain

---

12 'Бортнянский сидел за своим фортепиано, у нас у всех, в том числе и у меня, ноты были в руках, всякой пел свою партию; дошла до меня очередь, и я, глядя на ноту, очень исправно пропел свой куплет. – Как же, – вскричала Великая Княгиня, – государи мои, вы сказали, что он музыки не знает, да он поет по ноте. – Извольте, Ваше Высочество, приказать Князю Долгорукому показать Вам место на бумаге, которое он теперь протвердил, – ответствовал Бортнянский. Государыня подошла ко мне ближе, и каково было ее удивление, когда она изволила увидеть, что не только я схватил совсем не ту партию... но даже бумагу держал вверх ногами...' (Dolgoruky, 1916:89–90).

13 *Ekaterina II i G.A. Potemkin, Lichnaya perepiska 1769–91*. V.S. Lopatin, ed. Moscow: Akademia Nauk, 1997:154.

Example 8.13 Bortniansky: Prophêtie du corcier Gripouille from the opera *La Fête du Seigneur*, **act II**

piquancy to the score would have been provided by the musical description of the wizard Gripouille, parodying the 'infernal powers' of Gluck's *Orpheus* (Example 8.13). The first measures of his aria indeed resemble the Dance of the Furies, using the same *D minor* key and some of its rhythmic patterns. The successful endeavour encouraged the Young court to continue their operatic games. The next opera, *Le Faucon*, premièring the same year on October 11, was already the genuine thing. Its libretto, this time written by Lafermiére, was unrelated to the court life, and its score was significantly more complex than that of *La Fête du Seigneur*. According to I.M. Dolgoruky:

> ... Their Highnesses liked it very much: it was intriguing and conformed with fashion, (that is to say very romantic)... The remarkable music was composed by Mr. Bortniansky and their Highnesses were keen to see it performed.... It was read by the author himself in front of us all, one afternoon in the Grand Duke's study. The roles were distributed on the spot and we were ordered to study the opera.[14]

---

14 '...понравилась Их Высочествам, и действительно была затейлива, вся в тогдашнем вкусе, то есть очень романическая... Музыку сочинил для нее г. Бортнянский превосходную. Их Высочествам угодно было, чтобы мы ее разыграли... Читана она автором самим публично при всех при нас в одно пополуденное время, в кабинете Великого Князя. Тут же розданы роли и назначено ее учить' (Dolgoruky, 1916:88).

Lafermiére chose for this opera a traditional subject that had originated in ancient Hindu legends and became disseminated throughout Europe through G. Boccaccio's *Decameron* (Day 5, Story 9) – the story of Federigo delli Alberighi and his falcon. Appearing widely in literature and drama, this theme was also exploited by M. Sedaine in his libretto for an opera by P. Monsigny, which became the prototype for Lafermiére's libretto. Of all three operas written by Bortniansky for the Pavlovsk-Gatchina theatre, *Le Faucon* was the only one also to be produced outside of the Young court. Copies of the score were found at the estates of Count Stepan Apraxin, Shuvalov and Orlov-Davydov. There are five known copies including the original score. The full text of the libretto was found only recently by M. Pryashnikova in the library of Count Vorontsov, Lafermiére's associate. Until then only the first half of the libretto had been found – by A. Rozanov, who reconstructed the rest according to Sedaine's plot, for further editing and publishing of the full score (Rozanov, 1975). This has eventually enabled the staging of the opera in modern times.

The overall tone of the score resembles that of a pastoral, and is written mostly in major mode, the minor keys being reserved for genuinely comic numbers: the trio of the two doctors and Marina, and the famous *G minor* romance of Jeannette, *Le beau Tirsis* (Example 8.14). However, unlike the *soubrette* pastoral *La Fête du Seigneur*, *Le Faucon* score is more developed. Two pairs of lovers – one noble and the other plebeian (the servants) – furnished the composer with an opportunity to depict them in styles of *seria* and *buffa* respectively, creating thereby the *demi–seria* type rather than the genuinely *buffa* genre (Rozanov, 1975:693). The parts of the main characters are based mostly on the Italian cantilena, while those of the *buffa* characters have mostly French sources.

The score is full of action and has no extraneous moments; the text and the music are well coordinated. The arias of the two lovers (Federico in Act I and Elvira in Act II) contain similar motivic material, which appears later in their 'duet of reconciliation', and in the final sextet. The action proceeds as a succession of short numbers, giving way to a more flexible and organic development towards the finale. The tonal dramaturgy, similar to Bortniansky's Italian scores, is well constructed. The arias of Elvira and Federico are similar not only thematically, but also in their keys: *D* and *B major*. All three acts of the opera end in *B major*.

The music of *Le Faucon* remained a favourite in Pavlovsk, and a suite of selections from the opera arranged for wind sextet (pairs of clarinets, horns and bassoons) could also be heard beyond the walls of the palace, in the open air.

Bortniansky's last opera, *Le Fils Rival* (or *La Moderne Stratonice*), which was also the last production in the series of the Young court spectacles, premièred exactly one year later, on 11 October 1787. This work is properly regarded as Bortniansky's best French opera. By this time, the composer was assured of the skills and enthusiasm of his performers and wrote freely and with unrestrained creativity, stimulated by the successful libretto. This time, Lafermiére combined two plots. The first was the story recounted by Appianus, Lucianus and Plutarch about Antioch, the son of the Syrian King Seleucus-Nicator (formerly one of Alexander the Great's commanders), who was

Example 8.14   Bortniansky: Jeannette's romance from the opera *Le Faucon,*
act II

in love with his father's second wife Stratonice, the daughter of the Macedonian
king (Rozanov, 1976:23–4). The second source was F. Schiller's tragedy *Don
Carlos*, recounting Don Carlos's love for his step-mother, Elizabeth of France,
the second wife of King Philip II of Spain. I.M. Dolgoruky recalls that the opera

had been prepared with extraordinary splendour. Bortniansky's music was even better and more touching than that of the previous opera; the new sets were designed by a great painter and the Court had ordered Spanish costumes for all the actors. The production of *Don Carlos* must have cost the palace some four thousand roubles... (Dolgoruky, 1916:129). *Don Carlos* seems to have been a working title for *Le Fils Rival ou La Moderne Stratonice*, which Dolgoruky remembered and mentioned in his memoirs. Mooser interpreted it as a title for the fourth opera by Bortniansky in this Pavlovsk-Gatchina series and the mistake has been repeated by others.

The librettist set the action in a nobleman's castle in eighteenth-century Spain, and softened the situation, making the female protagonist Eleonora the fiancée of the widowed Spanish nobleman Don Pedro. The love triangle is at the centre of the plot and each of the lovers is tormented individually by the tragic situation, finally solved by the doctor who acts as their advocate (or Helper and Dispatcher in Propp's terminology). The protagonists are joined by another noble pair as well as a triangle of servant lovers, presenting the traditional comedy of errors. The libretto is well developed and based on conflict of duty versus emotions, conforming to the traditional *opera seria*. Seizing this opportunity, Bortniansky bestowed upon the three main protagonists equal measures of spiritual beauty and magnanimity and depicted them by means of material similar to his Italian operas. He used accompanied recitative (Don Carlos at the beginning of Act II) and clarinet solo dialoguing with the protagonist in his central aria, among other techniques of *opera seria* (Example 8.15). Forming a contrast, the musical strategy of the pastoral-comic stratum of the opera differs sharply from the serious tone of the dramatic sphere. Here the music is based on dance themes with typical *buffa* parlance. The opera was thus another example of the *demi-seria* genre. This was a timely phenomenon in 1787 and, had it been performed outside of Russia, it would undoubtedly have enjoyed a European popularity no less than, for example, Piccini's operas.

The year 1788 in the Young court was somewhat of a musical lacuna. In 1789, although the musical activity renewed, the atmosphere had changed for the worse due to the deteriorating relationship between Pavel and the Empress. The enthusiastic pursuit of entertainment among the courtiers had become exhausted. Four years later, in 1793, Bortniansky published his collection of French romances, some of which were from his operas. They included the romance *Paul and Virginia*, which differed greatly from his other romances and resembled an operatic scene in style and structure. Since the novella by Bernardin de Saint-Pierre *Paul and Virginia* (1788) was in fashion at the time, O. Levasheva has suggested that this might have been meant for the unrealized project of the next opera at the Young court (1984:214–15). Bortniansky's opera career came to an end at the very peak of his creative activity. Nevertheless, although opera productions ceased, other musical events still continued. For these Bortniansky wrote at least two compositions: *Quintet* for piano, harp, cello, viola da gamba and violin, 1787; and *Synfonie Concertante* for seven instruments – fortepiano *organisé*, two violins, harp, viola da gamba, bassoon, and cello, 1790. Both works are written for non-standard ensembles, including similar sets of instruments that suggest some permanent participants, most probably from the same circle of courtiers for

Example 8.15 **Bortniansky: Don Carlos's aria from the opera** *Le Fils Rival,*
 act II

whom this music-making was a continuation of their operatic doings. The music of these
compositions seems to be depicting characters and situations from theatrical spectacles.
For example, Part II of the *Quintet* bears a striking resemblance to the final 'happy' trio of
Don Carlos, Eleonora and Don Pedro from *Le Fils Rival*. The entire form of the *Quintet*
is free and defined by a lively and engaging dialogue between piano and violin.
The music is rich in thematic material and texture, imparting typical theatrical images.
Bortniansky, as in his choral compositions, avoids the repetition of melodic material,
always offering his audiences new thematic configurations.

The same resemblance to operatic action is found in his *Synfonie Concertante*,
actually a septet, which in addition to the same turbulent energy and richness of musical
events also displays an exceptional quality in his use of the fortepiano *organizé*, which
must have combined with the harp in a highly contrasting and interesting way (Example
8.16). The score suggests virtuoso performers and it is intriguing as to whom they might
have been. No indication has been found to date, and one can only surmise that the usual
combination of professional musicians and skilled amateurs comprised this ensemble.
The overall sound of this composition has a remarkably festive elegance. It is probably
with this in mind that A. Rabinovich compared Bortniansky's music with Levitsky's
portraits, Kozlovsky's statues, Bogdanovich's poems and the edifices built by Rinaldi,
Kazakov and particularly Cameron, who had designed the impeccably elegant yet intimate
Pavlovsky Palace, seeing in all these arts the self-confidence, hedonism and ostentation of
the Catherinian era (1948:118).

Example 8.16   Bortniansky: *Synfonie concertante*, **second movement**

Chapter 9

The Late Eighteenth-Century Russian Salon

An exhibition of splendid eighteenth-century keyboard instruments is now housed at the St Petersburg State Museum of Music and Theatre Arts, where it occupies several halls of Count Sheremetev's former palace. With a little contextual imagination, this can serve us as impressive evidence of the extent to which musical entertainment at home and in the salons had spread in Russia by the 1780s, and of its luxuriant nature. Behind a single, generously embellished harpsichord or piano, would stand the entire household, with its enlightened master, his prettily playing daughters, their instructors, a circle of amateur musician friends, perhaps a foreign musician enjoying patronage and several dozen serf performers. No less important would have been the financial ability of the aristocratic music lover to invite external professional performers to play at these concerts. The entire entourage would have been installed in a magnificent residence at the heart of which lay a spatial hall of refined beauty. Polite society was both wealthy and widespread and looked upon music as a highly prestigious pastime.

The tradition of musical evenings was established in the 1740s, but gained momentum in the 1760s when other wealthy music lovers began to follow the lead of Prince Michael Kazimir Ogiński (1728–1800). Ogiński was the Grand Hetman of Lithuania and the Polish ambassador to St Petersburg; a poet and serious musician known for his skilful violin playing (he was a pupil of Viotti), clarinet and harp (he wrote an article on the latter for Diderot's Encyclopédie and improved its pedal system, an invention adopted by Erard in 1762). Among the grand houses that hosted such concerts were those of S.P. Yaguzhinsky, Papanelopulo ('grand Italian and French concerts'), Kizel, Count Lev Naryshkin, Count P.A. Zubov, Count I.I. Shuvalov (known also as the residence of Prince I.S. Baryatinsky), Prince G.A. Potemkin, A.L. Shcherbachev, Prince A.Ya. Bezborodko, Count A.S. Stroganov, Count M.I. Vorontsov and others (Petrovskaya, 1998:102–5).

The era of virtuosi and amateur performers had begun. One of its most remarkable manifestations was the *New Musical Society* or *New Musical Club* that emerged in St Petersburg in 1778 and was active till the early 1790s (following the less well organized *Musical Club* that had functioned from 1772–7). Its membership (all male) ran to six hundred during the first two years, and included not only a wide variety of musicians but also music lovers from both the artistic milieu and a broad social circle. (Its doings are discussed in Chapter 11.) The musical life of the country in general was vivid and full of action. The number of musical instrument workshops and music publishers grew intensively, and new initiatives were welcomed. Not only St Petersburg but Moscow too became a great consumer of music, and musicians began to share their time between the two capitals. All this activity promised them a good market and often stimulated them to combine the functions of virtuoso, composer and entrepreneur.

Foreign Virtuosi

Many musicians from other countries tried their fortunes in Russia, some of them already of international repute. Their mediators (who were often their sponsors too) were usually Russian diplomats, who enjoyed their status as art patrons and whose salons became notable music centres, like those of Prince Dmitry Mikhaylovich Golitsyn and Count Andrey Kirillovich Razumovsky in Vienna; Prince A.M. Beloselsky-Belozersky in Dresden; Prince Filosofoff in Copenhagen; Dmitry Alexeevich Golitsyn in Paris; Count Simon Romanovich Vorontsov in London; and earlier, in the 1760s – Count Alexey Grigorievich Orlov in Pisa. Haydn, Mozart and Beethoven were some of the most notable recipients of such patronage. The patrons often provided musicians seeking a position in Russia with information on the realities of Russian life and letters of recommendation to other key musical patrons in St Petersburg and Moscow.

Just as they had done in earlier periods, musicians still had to be fairly closely connected with the court service that provided the basis for their livelihood. Competition, however, was fierce and they seldom became wealthy. Many of them nonetheless enjoyed their Russian experience; indeed, several of them left the country for a few years only to return to live out their lives there. The following few brief sketches of several of the most notable virtuosi and composers provide a general idea of their contribution to Russian musical affairs.

Antonio Lolli

Antonio Lolli (1725–1802), renowned Italian violin virtuoso and a composer of the older generation, worked in St Petersburg from 1774–7 (under the special patronage of Empress Catherine II and Prince Potemkin); and again from 1780–4, following an interval in Paris. He held the position of 'concertmaster' (in this particular case meaning court virtuoso responsible for concerts at the court), with an annual salary of 3,300–4000 roubles. Lolli organized many concerts, mostly at the Potemkin palace. Like most virtuosi, he played first and foremost his own compositions, and also spent much time composing and teaching. Eventually, however, his employers became dissatisfied with his activities and in 1781, when Giovanni Viotti was visiting St Petersburg with his teacher G. Pugnani, he was offered Lolli's position. However, this did not suit the young virtuoso's plans and he turned down the offer.

Louis Henri Paisible

Having established his reputation in Europe during his concert tour of 1776–8, the French violinist Louis Henri Paisible (*c.* 1745–82) arrived in Russia at a point in time when Lolli was absent from court. Paisible may well have hoped to exploit the situation and obtain Lolli's position. Seeing an opportunity to perform some major oratorical works, and applying his Parisian experience in organizing *Concerts Spirituels*, he prepared an extraordinary programme for Lent in February 1779. He showered the Russian public with a series of performances, including *Te Deum* by K. Graun, *Salve Regina* by J. Hasse, *La Passione di nostro Signor Giesù Cristo* by N. Jomelli and fragments from operas by Gluck, Sacchini and Grétri. He even announced his own oratorio, but failed to finish it in time (it finally premièred in December of that year). The full Imperial Court Choir was utilized (it was probably this that prompted Yelagin to realize the necessity to bring Bortniansky back from Italy). Major oratorical works were alternated with instrumental concertos played by Paisible himself, the harpsichordist Palschau and other virtuosi. This unprecedented grandiose and ambitious endeavour, however, could not be sustained, and Paisible himself gained little financial benefit from it.

Shortly after Paisible's programme had finished Lolli returned and picked up the initiative. Organizing the *Concerts Spirituels* for the following season, in 1780, he discarded such a highly varied repertoire in favour of a more simple programme. Paisible left for Moscow in search of work, but soon returned to St Petersburg and began announcing his as yet unwritten symphonies. He might have been aware of the negotiations of the court with Viotti in 1781 over Lolli's position, and in March 1782 he announced his own concerts. These never transpired, however; Paisible shot himself on the night before the first concert was due to take place.

Paisible's initiative had nonetheless made a profound impact upon Russian musical life and endeared the Russian public to the oratorical genre. The influence of the potential of the oratorio on Paisiello, for example, might explain his composition *Passione di Gesù Cristo*, with Metastasio's text, as well as his cantata *Efraim* in 1783. Later, in 1785, Sarti's effective entrance upon the musical scene with an oratorio, and his continued predilection for this genre, might also be traced to this same influence.

Giovanni Giornovichi

While Paisible's tragic example reveals the difficulties encountered by freelance musicians trying to survive on Russian soil, another European celebrity, Giovanni Giornovichi (Jarnovič, Jiornovichi, *c.* 1740–1804), was invited by the Russian court to replace Lolli, with whom he probably overlapped for one season. He was appointed to the position of a chamber musician with an annual salary of 3,000 roubles and spent his first period in Russia from 1783–6, often performing in St Petersburg and Moscow and spicing the artistic atmosphere with his flashes of temperament. Following three years in Vienna and other European centres, Giornovichi returned to St Petersburg from 1789–91. He spent the following three years, until 1794, working as part of Johann Salomon's Hanover Square enterprise in London and then in the series of Professional Concerts. In 1796 he settled in Hamburg (where he was to be known as a billiard player rather than a violinist) until 1802, when he made a welcome return to St Petersburg, to receive a position in the First Court Orchestra, albeit for a short period. His sudden death in 1804 caused much grief among a highly appreciative public.

Anton Ferdinand Tietz

Anton Ferdinand Tietz (Ditz, 1742–1810), German violinist and composer, was enticed away by the Russian Director of Theatres from the Vienna Court Opera orchestra, where he had worked as concertmaster (recommended by Gluck). Tietz was invited to Russia in 1771 and with the exception of two periods in the early 1780s and late 1790s when he visited Vienna and worked in Germany and Bohemia, the musician lived in St Petersburg. His particular contribution to Russian musical life was to inculcate in the Russian public a taste for ensemble music-making and the Viennese repertoire, particularly Haydn. He is also considered to have been the founder of Russian quartet literature. Playing both violin and viola d'amour, he participated in various ensembles with professional colleagues (mainly G. Giornovichi, the Bohemian clarinettist J. Beer, the clavichordist E. Wanzhura and the Italian cellist A. Delfino) and talented amateurs like Count Platon Zubov and Grand Duke Alexander Pavlovich. The latter (the future Emperor Alexander I) was his student, to whom Tietz dedicated his *Three quartets*, published in Leipzig in 1803. He was also close to Gregory Teplov's family, known for the musicality of all its members, and he wrote *Three quartets* for A. Teplov. As a composer he was quite well-known for having been in his youth a pupil of Haydn, to whom he dedicated *Three duets* for violins and *Six quartets*.

In addition to providing chamber music for the elite circles, Tietz was also part of the popular song and poetry milieu and his sentimental songs gained much popularity among early nineteenth-century Russian society. In 1797 the musician began to suffer from some kind of psychic disorder, which resulted in his losing his ability to speak and establishing the legend of his insanity.[1] His sociable artistry, however, helped him to continue his professional activities and retain recognition, and despite his communicative difficulties he was never isolated.

Johann Wilhelm Hässler

Johann Wilhelm Hässler (1747–1822), a German organist, clavierist and composer was already a mature musician when he arrived in Russia. While his

---

1   The reasons behind Tietz's disease are unknown, although he had been prone to attacks of melancholy from a young age. The year 1797, when he   lost his ability to speak, was one of stress for society as a whole, with the beginning of Paul I's reforms and severe edicts.

accomplishments in Germany and London (March 1792, Haydn's series) are well known, the motivation behind his decision to seek his fortune in Russia is unclear. (One can only surmise that the Russian ambassador to England, Chancellor Roman Illarionovich Vorontsov, a distinguished Freemason functionary who was in close contact with Haydn at the time, may have suggested the plan and assisted Hässler through recommendations and connections.) As early as September 1792, Hässler was in Riga, performing – following the necessary dose of publicity – his eloquently entitled cantata *Catarina, die Mutter ihres Volkes*. By November he was already in St Petersburg, opening the season of the *Musical Club* with a widely announced concert in which he played a concerto of his own composition as well as one of Haydn's recently written symphonies – both works probably replicating the London spring programme.

Having arrived in Russia, Hässler, somewhat a counterpart of Tietz, gained special popularity based on his association with Haydn. He not only popularized Haydn, developing his cult in Russia, but also himself as Haydn's devotee. While Tietz was violin teacher to Grand Duke Alexander Pavlovich, Hässler was his piano teacher; and the splendid volume of his piano works was dedicated and presented to the Grand Duke. Another link between Hässler and Tietz was the Russian song 'Stonet sizy golubochek' [The little blue-grey pigeon is moaning], with lyrics by Ivan Dmitriev: Tietz composed one of its versions, and Hässler wrote 32 variations on one of its tunes (whether it was the same tune composed by Tietz or not remains to be clarified). The poet Dmitriev dedicated poems to both musicians.

Shortly after his arrival in St Petersburg, Hässler became active in music publishing. He had been involved in this field earlier in Germany, where his wife had remained and continued to maintain the business. Hässler found a partner, Johann-Dietrich Gerstenberg, whom he convinced to start a music publishing enterprise in St Petersburg. In 1796 Hässler settled in Moscow (for reasons no clearer than his settling in Russia at all). He left the publishing business but continued to advise Gerstenberg on the repertory of European composers and to send him his own work, mostly variations on Russian songs and pedagogical pieces. Hässler spent the rest of his life as a highly regarded piano teacher and a deeply respected embodiment of the German tradition of musical education in general, which is still cultivated in Russia today. His own legacy of works was almost entirely destroyed by two fires. The first was in Moscow during Napoleon's invasion in 1812; following this, the remainder of Hässler's work was moved to Hamburg, but this was also destroyed in a fire after the composer's death (Volman, 1957:158).

Johann Palschau

Johann Gotfrid Wilhelm Palschau (1742/5–1813), German pianist and composer, gained a European reputation as a *wunderkind* (as a composer he was believed to have been the student of Johann Gottfried Müthel, J.S. Bach's pupil, who was a kapellmeister to Russian Privy Counsellor O.H. von Vietinghoff in Riga). He was already on the St Petersburg scene by 1777. His attachment to the court service as a Cabinet virtuoso was somewhat problematic: his salary of 1000 roubles was allotted concomitantly with Bortniansky's in 1780, but later, in 1785, the Governor of the Board of St Petersburg refused to recognize his employment during the course of some legal proceedings (Porfirieva, MPES, II:336). Palschau's life in Russia was mostly that of a freelancer, including concert performances on the harpsichord, piano and fortepiano *organisé* in St Petersburg and Moscow, sometimes in duet with the violinist L.P. Yershov. In the newspaper advertisements for these concerts, Palschau was invariably described as the 'famous virtuoso' and several of his piano variations on 'Chanson russe', familiar from publications in the 1790s, appear to have been a success.

Ernest Wanzhura

Our next figure, the clavichordist and composer Baron Ernest Wanzhura (or Wančura, Wanžura, *c*. 1750–1802) from Bohemia, was a colourful personality. He began his career as an infantry officer in the Austrian army and then, encouraged by the success of his dance pieces, he switched to music. From 1779 he worked as a harpsichordist (liking to amuse his audience with such fashionable tricks as playing with palms up) and as opera and ballet producer at the court of General Semen Gavriilovich Zorich in Shklov (Byelorussia), which presented a wide repertoire consisting of Paisiello's, Galuppi's, Sarti's and Dalayrac's operas (Dadiomova, 2002:167–9). In 1780, when the Empress visited Shklov to meet with the Austrian Emperor Joseph, she obtained a very pleasant impression of both young men, Zorich and Wanzhura. The former eventually became her favourite, while the latter was invited to work in St Petersburg.

Caught between the desire to retain his title – a somewhat doubtful title according to his contemporaries – and so signing his works as 'amateur', and his wish to make his living from music, which implied striving to obtain appointments, Wanzhura managed to leave a definite mark in more than one field of Russian culture. Beginning with civic theatre, he first participated in the reconstruction of the Bolshoy (Kameny) Theatre in St Petersburg. Then, shrewdly evaluating the general situation, he realized that there was a shortage of musically trained actors for the provinces. Wanzhura suggested establishing a studio at the Moscow Home for Foundlings and was put in charge of the project there. He also worked at the Petrovsky theatre as a producer, but when he tried to set up his own opera company in Moscow he failed to break the theatrical monopoly held by the entrepreneur M. Maddox. Upon his return to St Petersburg he concentrated mostly on composition, publishing and concert management. He is known for example as having organized twice weekly masquerades and balls in the garden of Count Alexander Naryshkin from 1793 (Petrovskaya 1998; Georgi, 1794:625–7). His living was provided by a somewhat vague musical position on the Board of Imperial Theatres, with a salary of 1800 roubles, and the rank of Court Counsellor (equivalent to lieutenant-colonel).

Wanzhura's early three symphonies on Slavic themes noted as op 1, although published only in 1798 as orchestra parts by Sprewitz in St Petersburg (*Trois sinfonies nationales à grand orchestre arrangées de plusieurs chansons russes, ukrainiennes et polonaises composées par Mr. Baron de Wanzhura. Oeuv. 1*), were probably the cornerstone of his career. Pryashnikova, who published the score and researched its folklore sources, pointed out that Wanzhura's idea of what was Russian and what was Ukrainian among those songs mostly differed from the classification of modern scholars: Wanzhura's 'Russian symphony' contains Ukrainian songs and vice versa.[2] That the confusion was not considered as such at the time follows from a subtitle *Sinfonie russe, composée d'airs ukrainiens* that Wanczura gave to the piano score published in his *Journal de musique*. An example of his work with the folk tune can be seen from a comparison between the score (second theme of the first part) and the song 'Oy gay, gay, zelenen'kiy' (as transcribed and arranged later in the Lvov-Prach *Collection of Russian Folk Songs*) (Examples 9.1 and 9.2).

Example 9.1   Ukrainian folk song *Oy gay gay zelenen'ky* **from the Lvov-Prach Collection of Russian folk songs**

Having developed a Russified style, he joined the circle of nationalist operatic composers like Pashkevich and Martín y Soler, employed by Empress Catherine II to write music for her moralistic libretti. He composed *Khrabroi i smeloy vityaz'*

---

2   Wanzhura, E. *Tri simfonii na slavyanskie temy*. Score. Ed. and Introduction by M. Pryashnikova. Kiev: Muzychna Ukraina, 1983:9.

Example 9.2   Wanzhura: Symphony No.1 (*Ukrainian*), first movement, second theme.

Example 9.2, *continued*

Akhrideich or *Ivan-tsarevich*, [The Brave and Bold Knight Akhrideich] which had been played at the Hermitage Theatre in 1787, as well as several other comic operas, of which only a few individual numbers remain. These he published in his Musical Journal for Ladies, whose 1785–94 announcements read as follows: (with the titles in French as the language of the Russian elite classes, and which became traditional for music publications, until Soviet times):

Journal de musique pour le clavecin ou piano-forte, dédié aux dames par B. W., amateur. Ce journal contiendra douze numéros, dont il paroitre un chaque mois. Dans ces douze numéros on donnera successivement les pièces suivantes, nouvellement composées et arrangées pour le clavecin seul, savoir: 6 ouvertures; 2 symphonies russes; 12 airs tirés de deux opéras comiques, savoir *L'Officier bien-faisant* et *Le Touteur trompé*; 12 chansons françoises; 24 diverses pièces tirées de quelques ballets et pantomimes; 72 diverses danses, polonaises, contredanses, cosaques etc. Chez I.I. Weitbrecht, libraire de la cour à St.-Pétersbourg.

Example 9.2, *continued*

Anton Bullant

Another contemporary figure worthy of mention is that of Anton (Jean) Bullant, (?–1821), virtuoso bassoonist and composer, whose origins and nationality are unclear (Bohemian or French). His decision to settle in Russia was probably linked to his acquaintance with Count Alexander Sergeevich Stroganov, to whom he dedicated the *Four Symphonies* for a large orchestra, published in Paris in 1773. He arrived in Russia in 1780 and it took him more than four years to obtain a position with the First Court Orchestra, due to some strong resistance from the Board of the Imperial Theatres (for unknown reasons, see Porfirieva, MPES, I:159–60). In the interim he wrote the comic opera *Sbitenshchik* (The Hot-Mead Vendor, 1783/4). Ya. Knyazhnin's libretto for this opera parodied Paisiello's *Il Barbiere di Siviglia* and the music skilfully displayed the Russian style. The opera became

Example 9.2, *continued*

a long-running success and the composer was honoured with a commission from the Empress to write a massive prologue with ballets and choruses, *Schastlivaya Rossia ili dvadtsatipyatiletniy yubiley* [Happy Russia or Twenty-fifth Anniversary] (of Catherine the Great's rule, 1787, libretto by M. Kheraskov, Moscow). Bullant seemed to have known how to combine art and business successfully: he was a seller of keyboard instruments and owned a house on Nevsky Prospekt which he rented out to *The New Musical Club*.

Example 9.2, *continued*

Jean Batiste Cardon

Another of the foreign virtuosi was Jean Batiste Cardon (1760–1803), a famous
French court harpist and composer whose reasons for settling in Russia are unclear.
The earliest known mention of him refers to 1789 when he was employed by Count
Nikolai Sheremetev. The date suggests that Cardon may have joined the wave of
French immigration to Russia at this time. In 1790 he was offered a three-year
contract to work at the Imperial court and his first offering was an imitation of the

ancient Greek lyre in *The Early Reign of Oleg* – one of the crowd-pleasers at the climax of a splendid spectacle (discussed below). Cardon had many pupils, mostly female (the silhouette of a woman harpist was considered especially attractive within the aesthetic context of the late classicism and Empire styles). They included Grand Duchess Elizaveta Alexeevna and Grand Duchess Elena Pavlovna – both very advanced players, judging by his dedication to them of three-sonata cycles (op. 10 and op. 11 respectively). Some evidence of the popularity of both Cardon and the harp is reflected in his *Journal d'ariettes italiennes et autres avec accompagnement de la Harpe Par J.B. Cardon*, published in 1797. The edition contained a wide repertoire including his own arrangements and compositions, some of which expertly developed the Russian idiom (Porfirieva, MPES, II:49).

The list of musicians of similar stature could be continued and at least doubled without difficulty. Many features of their lives and activities unite them, including posthumous neglect on the part of the society that had once hosted them, a ubiquitous phenomenon that seems almost inevitable among immigrant artists. Although the contribution of these musicians was crucial to Russian music, the nationalist attitude that developed in the writing of Russian music history has tended to diminish their achievements, a priori depriving these composers of their 'right' to musical ingenuity, which is considered to be the sole prerogative of native-born musicians. But nationalism is not a specifically Russian attribute; it is characteristic of any society to a greater or lesser degree. The further one is from the cultural centre – the more apparent it becomes. Indeed, the situation seems to have been very similar in England during the same epoch. Peter Holman refers to those who

> spent most of their working lives in these islands, and contributed a good deal to musical life. Yet they have suffered from a Catch-22 situation in modern times: English musicologists and performers tend to ignore them because they were foreigners, while they are of little interest in their countries of origin because they left home at an early age, never to return. It is certainly difficult to make sense of some English genres without including the contribution of immigrants… England has always been a nation of immigrants, and it makes no sense to restrict an account of its culture to the work of natives or, more accurately, to the work of the descendants of less recent immigrants.
>
> What is often forgotten is that immigrant composers, anxious to be accepted in England, adapted their own idioms to conform to English taste. Although the basic language of English eighteenth-century music came mostly from abroad, it has a highly distinctive accent, which can often be found as strongly in the work of immigrants as that of native composers. (Holman, 2002:5)

Ivan Khandoshkin and the Rus'ian Idiom

While these other composers' contribution is prejudicially perceived in Russian historiography as merely *à la russe*, the privilege of being an ingenious *Rus'ian* was unequivocally granted to Ivan Khandoshkin (1747–1804), a Russian virtuoso-violinist and composer of the same calibre as the immigrant musicians described above. Khandoshkin was obviously no less a brilliant violinist than Lolli, Paisible or Giornovici, and he was also hardly more 'authentically' a Russian composer in his variations on Russian tunes (widely applying Tartini's devices) and sonatas than Wanzhura, Hässler, Palschau, Giornovici, Cardon and others. But he was a native. Consequently his biography has been given greater attention and his legacy has received careful examination and research. While the immigrant musicians have been fated to receive little more than a passing mention in encyclopaedias, Khandoshkin, as a source of national pride, has been the subject of whole chapters and even books (Yampolsky, 1951; Keldysh, 1965; Raaben, 1967; Fesechko, 1972; Dobrokhotov, 1983; for English readers, see Mishchakoff, 1983).

Khandoshkin's record was perfect for the developing image of a nationalist composer. His origins were humble enough: his father Evstafy Khandoshkin, a waldhornist at the court of Count Peter Borisovich Sheremetev, was a second generation liberated serf. Ivan Khandoshkin himself had never left Russia, although his teacher was Italian – Tito Porta, a violinist from the Italian Company. He came from a similar background to Berezovsky – apprenticeship at the court of Grand Duke Peter Fedorovich, followed by affiliation to the Italian Company. Khandoshkin was highly regarded for his outstanding virtuosity and held the position of kapellmeister with standard salary and obligations, mostly associated with the ball-music orchestra. He also performed a great deal at both public and private concerts and developed certain attributes that particularly distinguished him from his foreign colleagues, to the constant delight of his audience. First was his use of scordatura, which, having passed the peak of fashion in the seventeenth century, was rarely used by the end of the eighteenth. Khandoshkin, however, applied it widely, sometimes for an entire programme (specially announced!). Another distinguishing feature was his brilliant improvisations on Russian tunes, which is partly reflected in what remains of his collection of compositions, mostly published during his lifetime. And then there was his playing on his home-made balalaika. The instrument possessed a unique 'silver' timbre due to the powdered crystal glued to the inner surface of the pumpkin shell that comprised its body.

Khandoshkin's musicality and style appealed to the taste of Prince Potemkin, who in the 1770s and early 1780s wanted him close at hand and promised him a directorship of the planned Musical Academy at the 'University of Ekaterinoslav' in the south. When, at the beginning of 1785, the project seemed to be taking shape, the Prince arranged for Khandoshkin's retirement from the Imperial court with a pension amounting to half of his salary. Shortly afterwards Khandoshkin addressed the *Committee of Management of Spectacles and Music* with a request regarding his salary for the promised directorship (Berezovchuk, MPES, III:214). He then started his journey southward but had to stop in Moscow due to a cholera outbreak in the southern regions (Fesechko, 1972:33).

While the overall situation at the Academy still remained uncertain, Khandoshkin stayed in Moscow. Meanwhile, another unpredictable sequence of events occurred in St Petersburg. The prima donna Luisa da Todi succeeded in undermining the court's opinion of the first *Kapellmeister*, Giuseppe Sarti, and his contract was not renewed. Prince Potemkin consequently offered Sarti his patronage, which implied accompanying the Prince to the south and included directorship of the famous Academy. Khandoshkin was thus sidelined; evidently realizing this, he returned to St Petersburg in 1787, when the court was already on its historic journey to Kherson. Khandoshkin thus lost both his position, which had given him his basic income, and the expected directorship of the Academy, which was given to Sarti. As the Academy position turned out to be more of a fiction than a reality, this was no great blow for Khandoshkin. However the loss of his position at the court and the modest pension constituted a serious hardship and left him virtually a freelance musician. He eventually began to obtain occasional patronage, as can be seen from his dedication of a sonata to Peter Veliaminov, a connoisseur of the fine arts. Like most of his colleagues, Khandoshkin made his living from a combination of performance, teaching, publications and trade in instruments.

The fashion for salon virtuosity, which had peaked in the 1780s, was virtually over by the end of the century. Khandoshkin died suddenly in 1804, in the same year as Giornovichi, but in quite an impecunious state and with low social status. The nineteenth-century romantic-nationalist portrayal of Khandoshkin, assembled and written down by Prince Odoevsky, hinted at his abuse of alcohol and presented Sarti as his adversary, somehow combining Khandoshkin's and Berezovsky's images into that of a victim of the foreign (Italian) musicians' predominance and the neglect of the native musicians by those in power.

Besides about ten sonatas, most of Khandoshkin's compositional legacy consists of variation cycles (more than fifty), all of which are on Russian tunes. This was characteristic not only of this composer but also of other musicians in Russia at the time, indicating the appeal of Russian folk and *Rossiyskie* songs along with popular operatic arias (to a lesser extent) for those who attended the Russian salons. The pioneer of this movement was Vasily Trutovsky. In 1780, his *Variations on Russian songs for harpsichord or piano* were published in St Petersburg, opening the way for similar editions, which proliferated toward the very end of the century and became a kind of artistic norm. Trutovsky did not continue along this path, however, instead concentrating on his collecting activity. Khandoshkin, on the other hand, carried on with his sets of variations and, judging by the number of editions (1783, 1786, 1794, 1796, each including several cycles), there was a ready market for them among lovers of Russian music.

Khandoshkin named his first collection of six songs with variations (1783) *Shest' starinnykh ruskikh pesen, s prilozhennymi k onym variatsyiami dlya odnoi skripki i alto-violy* [Six ancient Rus'ian songs with variations attached for violin and viola].[3] This noteworthy combination of the words 'ancient' and 'Rus'ian' was a first in Russian music (discussed in Mischakoff, 1983:21–2) and the sign of a new wave in the development of a national consciousness. In the newspaper announcement of the

---

3   The date 1786 appears on the title of the unique copy of the edition from the collection of the Russian National Library in St Petersburg, but Volman has asserted that the date is hand-written and that the edition appeared in 1783 as the newspaper *Sanktpeterburgskie vedomosti* announced it in 1783, no 94 (Volman, 1957:74).

collection the title was followed by the words: 'composed for the benefit of music lovers of this taste by Court chamber musician Ivan Khandoshkin'.[4]

The number of 'music lovers of this taste' appears to have been quite large. In the same year, 1783, the important institution *Rossiyskaya Academia* [The Russian Academy] was founded at the initiative of Empress Catherine II, who managed to persuade Princess Ekaterina Romanovna Dashkova to head it. Considering their complicated relationship, the Princess had long avoided being too close to the court. However, the goal of 'exalting Russian letters, and putting in order the grammar, stylistic, and pronunciation norms of the Russian language' was a noble one and suited her predilection for the ideals of Enlightenment, as well as her competence, energy and organizational talent (Teplova, SRP, 1988:246). The Academy's most significant achievement (among many) was the publication of *Slovar' Akademii Rossiyskoy* [The Lexicon of the Russian Academy] in 1789–94, with an annotated text on concepts of morals, politics and State structure. Such noted intellectuals as Prince M. Shcherbatov, I. Boltin and Count A.I. Musin-Pushkin were closely associated with the work of the Academy, publishing such monuments of ancient Russian literature as *Russkaya pravda* [Russian Truth] (1792) and the *Dukhovnaya* [Testament] (1793). The crowning glory of their achievements was Musin-Pushkin's publication in 1795[5] of *The Lay of Igor's Host* (whose authenticity is no less problematic than that of Macpherson's *Ossian*).[6]

The year 1783 was indeed a landmark in the increasing public interest in national antiquity, and Khandoshkin's appeal to 'lovers of this taste' was well justified. Enthusiasm in this field inevitably lead to 'macphersonism' – the unquestioning desire to ascribe to the national past as many of the present cultural values as possible. (Along these lines, it is worth noting that some three decades later, the German folk fairy tales collected and published by the Grimm brothers were also neither all German nor all folk.)[7]

Khandoshkin's mere reference to 'ancient' and 'Rus'ian' was considered in itself as sufficient proof of the 'authenticity' of the songs and of their roots in vernacular sources. In reality, however, one of these 'ancient Rus'ian songs' was actually a Ukrainian song of rather late origin *Raz polosyn'ku ya zhala* [Once I reaped] (Volman, 1957:76–7, 264); but nobody cared. It is impossible to tell whether the idea behind this definition of the songs was that of Khandoshkin himself or of his

---

4   'Сочиненные в пользу любящих играть сего вкуса музыку придворным камер-музыкантом Иваном Хандошкиным.'

5   A detailed description and historical analysis of this collecting-publishing activity is given by Hans Rogger (1960, 2nd edn 1969) in the chapter 'The Discovery of the Folk'.

6   There are two centuries of polemics over the origins of *The Lay of Igor's Host*, which forms a special part of the historiography-mythography relations in Russian cultural history. The latest hypothesis on its attribution to Feofan Prokopovič is that by Tatiana Fefer, 'Did the "Heretic" Feofan Prokopovič write the *Slovo o Polku Igoreve*?' in *Russian Literature* XLIV, 1998:41–115.

7   See Jack Zipes, *The Brothers Grimm: From Enchanted Forests to the Modern World*. New York: Routledge, 1988:75.

publisher Friedrich Meyer or of some other adviser. The important thing was that it worked, attracting lovers of national music. From this time on, variations on Russian songs became one of the most popular genres in late-eighteenth-century Russian music and the Russian idiom in general became its aesthetic norm.

At the Lvov House or the Temple of Rus'ian Idiom

Khandoshkin's accomplishments signified that the cult of *russkaya narodnaya pesnya* (Rus'ian folk song) as a basis for national art music had been established. Its temple was another Russian 'Academy', albeit an unofficial one – the salon of Nikolai Alexandrovich Lvov (1751–1803), a Russian nobleman, gifted and active in many fields, including architecture, engraving and poetry, whose role in eighteenth-century Russian music was followed by Vladimir Vasilievich Stasov in the nineteenth century. Known as *Kruzhok L'vova* [Lvov's Circle], his salon attracted the cream of the nationalistic Enlightenment-oriented intelligentsia. The salon began its gatherings in 1779 and initially united men of letters like Lvov, V.V. Kapnist and G.R. Derzhavin (1743–1816) – three brothers-in-law, married to the three Diakov sisters (Derzhavin, through his second marriage much later); as well as I.I. Khemnitser, I.I. Dmitriev and others. In 1783, Lvov and Derzhavin were among the first members of Dashkova's Russian Academy.

Among the frequent visitors to Lvov's salon were the finest Russian painters of the time, V.D. Borovikovsky and D.G. Levitsky; and possibly also the engraver I.Ch. Nabholtz and the publishers I.D. Gerstenberg and J.K. Schnoor (Rapatskaya, 1995: 127). Among the musicians who joined the circle were F.M. Dubyansky, E.I. Fomin, N.P. Yakhontov (an amateur, Lvov's relative), I. Prach, and possibly also V.F. Trutovsky, J.A. Kozlovsky and A.F. Tietz. Khandoshkin and Bortniansky too are considered to have been among them, although there is little evidence of this. Gradually, music and musicians became the main focus of the circle, resulting in two key developments toward the end of the 1780s.

The first of these was associated with the opera *Yamshchiki na podstave* [Post-Drivers] by the young composer Evstigney Fomin (1761–1800), who had recently (autumn 1786) returned from Italy. Although one officially-Russian opera had been commissioned from him by the court (*Novgorodskiy bogatyr' Boeslavich* [Boeslavich, the Novgorod Bogatyr] to a libretto by Catherine II) it had been supervised by the more experienced Martín y Soler and Wanzhura. Lvov is traditionally considered to have been the one to recognize Fomin's potential as a national opera composer and he indeed actively participated in the opera's development. In 1787, an opportunity arose.

In March 1786, Gavrila Romanovich Derzhavin, Lvov's close friend, had been appointed governor of the new town of Tambov after his unsuccessful (due to conflict with the corrupt local deputies) attempt to govern the northern town of Olonetsk. The planned journey of the Empress in the south was to include a stop in Tambov. It is clear that an elegantly organized reception for the Empress was Derzhavin's

Figure 9.1   Nikolai Lvov (1751–1803), portrait by D. Levitsky

prime concern. Lvov, with his innate talent for theatrical effects, was obviously the best producer. His plan was to arrange the Empress's entrance into the town as the high point of the spectacle, the finale, when the conflict of the plot would be solved by Her Majesty herself personally appearing on the stage.

The idea brilliantly combined the Empress's inclination to playful behaviour and readiness to cooperate with a chance to help Derzhavin and young Fomin, both of whom needed to restore themselves to her favour. Lvov's project of the opera *Post-Drivers* was original from a musical aspect too, highlighting the participation of 'folklore ensemble' (in today's terminology) directed by the Court Counsellor S.M. Mitrofanov. The latter was an equally talented balalaika performer and choirmaster of a folk choir of boat-rowers who specialized in singing *protyazhnaya* songs (Keldysh, 1978, 134–9). Their most popular number was the polyphonic *Vysoko sokol letaet*, a gem known from Fomin's score and from Lvov's folksong *Collection*, and which became a kind of musical emblem among Lvov's circle.

The itinerary of the Empress's grand tour was changed, however, and the project never transpired. Although there are indirect sources provoking speculation concerning the opera's later staging in St Petersburg, it is clear that the participation of the Empress in the spectacle had been intended to make it a one-time event. The score nonetheless survived, making this opera an important landmark in Russian opera history and attracting devoted research (Keldysh, 1978; Vetlitsyna, 1987; Taruskin, 1997: the chapter 'Lvov and the Folk').

The second significant development to arise from that enthusiastic and productive decade was Lvov's own great endeavour – the famous *Sobranie narodnykh russkikh pesen* [Collection of Folk Russian Songs], published in 1790, an accomplishment comparable to the literary publications of the Russian Academy. Although Lvov's name is absent from the *Collection*, it was posited later by Pal'chikov (based on Lvov's nephew Fedor Lvov's evidence) and in general has been accepted by Soviet scholars. The only name appearing in the title is that of the arranger Ivan Prach (*c.* 1750–1818) – the Russified Bohemian musician, permanently attached to Lvov as a kind of 'house composer'. The second, expanded edition, of 1806, was entitled *Sobranie russkikh narodnykh pesen* [A Collection of Russian Folk Songs] – interchanging 'folk' and 'Russian' against the first edition – and reprinted in 1815.[8]

The *Collection* has been thoroughly researched by modern scholars and the reader is well rewarded by the highly commendable sixth edition, which is a facsimile of the second edition, accompanied by Margarita Mazo's studies combining ethnomusicological and historiographical approaches and supplying very valuable references (Mazo, 1987).

The *Collection* in fact reflects the academic perspective of the Enlightenment era. It presents about one hundred (in the second edition, one hundred and fifty) Russian folk songs, organized according to their generic classification, and contains a Preface that can be considered as a scholarly introduction. While the songs themselves comprise artistic documentation of a folk music legacy, the Preface is

---

8   The full title reads: A Collection of Russian Folk Songs with their tunes, arranged by Ivan Prach, newly edited with the addition of the second part. In St Petersburg, printed in the press of Schnoor, 1806.

a documentation of aesthetics and national consciousness, a kind of programmatic manifesto of Lvov's circle or, in other words, of a sector of the Russian intellectual elite, characterized by a conspicuous nationalist bent. In the context of eighteenth-century Russian life in general and of the Russian Academy trend in particular, this nationalism is not surprising. As an element of the Enlightenment, it was pluralistically compatible with the admiration for Western civilization. However, nationalism displayed from different social standpoints significantly differed in its essence. While official nationalism (that of Empress Catherine II) strove to neutralize social contradictions and – at least in its theatrical forms – to represent the people as happy, dancing, singing and glorifying their ruler, democratic (later even called revolutionary) nationalism was more realistic, as reflected in Radishchev's *The Journey from St Petersburg to Moscow*. It related to the people's suffering, poverty and lack of rights, thereby demonstrating sympathy with them, highlighting their spiritual beauty and creativity and – consequently – recognizing their right to freedom, which was the final point qualifying Radishchev as a revolutionary.

There is, however, a strong element in common between these two kinds of nationalism – idealization and flattery of the folk. This particular point – to show their spiritual beauty and dignity – was Lvov's goal too. Lvov concludes his ideological part of the Preface, otherwise emphatically loyal, with the words:

> ...present-day philosophers will perceive from the content of the folk songs the love of Russians for glory, their commitment to courageous deeds, glorification of bravery and military valor, sacred fealty in all ways to their sovereigns, affection and respect for their parents, close family ties among brothers and sisters, and the inconsolable grief of a woman over the loss of her beloved. The conclusions of the philosophers will be quite favourable for the Russian people, and the testimony of history will support the validity of their opinion. (trans. by Mazo, 1987:82)[9]

Despite the seeming universality of the *Collection*, it was not a strictly scientific cross-section of living folklore, but a selective anthology. Although Lvov did choose several genres of songs, presenting many facets of Russian folklore (including the old lyrical protracted, ritual and dance, Ukrainian and Gypsy songs), all these genres belonged to one repertoire only. Any repertoire will tend to encompass the identity of one particular social group, and, indeed, the entire corpus of the *Collection* belonged to a particular contemporary repertoire of domestic urban music-making (Asafiev, 1968:55–6). Lvov did not include in it any songs that were vulgar or subverted the existing social order. His selection was as polished as its piano arrangements.

---

9   '...нынешние Философы увидят из содержания народных песен любовь Россиян ко славе, решимость их на отважные подвиги, прославление храбрости и воинских доблестей, везде священное подобострастие к Государям, привязанность и почтение к родителям, тесный союз родства между братьями и сестрами, неутешную горесть любовницы о потере милого друга. Заключение Философов будет весьма выгодное для Русского народа; а свидетельство Истории подтвердит справедливость их мнения' (Lvov, 1806, 6th 1987:xiv, facsimile 12).

Figure 9.2   Title-page of the Lvov-Prach Collection of Russian Folk Songs, 1790

To be fair, one cannot demand from an eighteenth-century collection the methodology of contemporary ethnomusicology, which also leaves something to be desired. Nonetheless, what Lvov did was a real achievement for its time. In no way attempting to diminish the value of the *Collection*, whose historical, aesthetic and scientific significance has been proven by history and canonized by its status as a source for many pieces of art music, including Beethoven's Razumovsky quartets, I simply note that this work presents a particular – and quite limited – dimension of Russian folk music, and one which reflects Lvov's own attitude to the concept of Russian national identity. Lvov, with all his creative energy, constructed a loyal national musical identity as he best saw it. 'Sacred fealty in all ways to their sovereigns,' he stated, as if there had not been any great peasant uprising in 1772–4.

Lvov indeed contributed greatly to construction of the Russian national identity for both his contemporaries and future generations. One of the main features promoting the *Collection*'s popularity and influence was its popular and utilitarian style (despite such academic elements as the Preface and generic classification). It accommodated the existing tradition and included many songs previously published by Trutovsky and Chulkov (the latter without music). The appearance in the title of the name of the musician, Ivan Prach, who was known for his fondness for writing variations on Russian songs, indicated that one aim of the edition was to provide material for salon music-making. Like other popular editions, it interacted with the ongoing practice in a give-and-take process, not only reflecting what people were singing but also giving them a formal repertoire for its continued existence in oral form (Mazo, 1987:76). The 'utilitarian' genre of the edition endowed the Lvov-Prach Collection with additional authenticity for future generations, serving as an authoritative source of Russian folklore. Its songs were broadly used as symbols of Russian authenticity throughout the entire nineteenth century, in its turn contributing to the construction of a Russian national identity in classical music (see Mazo, 1987: Appendix C 'LPC Songs Used by Composers before 1917'). Both the contemporaneous and the later success of the *Collection* thus established it as an important cultural foundation.

Interestingly, in the same year, 1790, another song collection appeared (with a continuation in 1791), although without music, *Novy rossiyskiy pesennik ili Sobranie lyubovnykh, khorovodnykh, pastush'ikh, plyasovykh, teatral'nykh, Tsyganskikh, Malorossiyskikh prostonarodnykh pesen, i v nastoyashchuyu voinu na porazhenie nepriateley i na raznye drugie sluchai sochinennykh, izdannoe izhdiveniem I.K. Sch. i T.P.* [New Russian Songbook or the Collection of Love, *khorovodnye* (round dance), shepherd, dance, theatrical, Gypsy, Ukrainian simple folk songs, as well as of victory songs composed during the ongoing war and on various other occasions, sponsored by I.K. Sch. and T.P.]. This collection is little known today but at the time it was popular and more than a third of its songs were published with music by Gerstenberg and Dittmar in 1797–8 (Rapatskaya, 1975:202–3).

Behind the initials I.K. Sch. and T.P. were Johann (Ivan) Karl Schnoor and Fedor Polezhaev. The later was a Muscovite bookseller whose name is well known to historians as having been taken to court in connection with Novikov's arrest in 1792–6; and to musicologists in connection with another collection with a similarly beginning title (*Novy rossiyskiy pesennik*), 1792, with music, including reprints of some of Teplov's songs as well as the addition of Russian folk songs (Volman, 1957:152–5).

It is obvious that Lvov's *Collection* had undergone a lengthy period of preparation and it could have been mere coincidence that both Lvov's and Schnoor-Polezhaev's collections were published in the same year that *The Journey from St Petersburg to Moscow* by Radishchev came out (in spring 1790). It could also, however, have been something more than coincidence. Lvov's *Collection*, with his phrase 'sacred fealty in all ways to their sovereigns', relating to the Russian folk, could have been Lvov's special message to express his own loyalty and/or to publicize it as a pro-monarchy and anti-dissident action. The bill for printing the *Collection* has been dated to 1791 or 1792, which suggests the preparation of the edition later in 1790, that is after the appearance of Radishchev's book.

Keldysh has shrewdly noted that Lvov edited the lyrics of the songs, amplifying and emphasizing 'sentimental happiness or faithful patriotism' (Keldysh, 1984, IRM:250). The same propagandist motive could be suggested for the Schnoor-Polezhaev songbook. Both were involved in Radishchev's case: Schnoor supplied the writer with typographical fonts and Polezhaev was one of the distributors of the book.[10] They could well have been in need of some more innocent action, such as propagating a folk song collection, as a genre encouraged by Catherine II. Their inclusion of an air from Pashkevich's opera *Fevey* with Catherine's libretto as well as 'victory songs composed during the ongoing war' could be interpreted as a gesture of reverence toward the Empress.

Both Lvov's and Schnoor-Polezhaev's editions had their titles embellished with a remarkably similar engraving, depicting the same idealized image of a satisfied and well-dressed peasant sitting at leisure under a tree. Use of the same engraving, probably created by I.Ch. Nabholtz (Rapatskaya, 1975:202), in addition to the same date of publication, indicates a certain link between Lvov and Schnoor, which was to become more obvious much later, in 1806, when Schnoor published the second edition of Lvov's *Collection* after the latter's death.

E. Vasilieva and V. Lapin have drown our attention to the fact that the quality, style and context of Lvov's edition are quite similar to those of the operas written for Catherine II's libretti, which were deliberately intended to construct a national identity. The *Collection* was published by the College of Mines Press, where, during that same short period (1789–91), four special musical publications had been prepared: the comic operas *Fevey* (Pashkevich), *Gorebogatyr' Kosometovich* [Kosometovich, the Woeful Knight] (Martín y Soler; both editions appeared in 1789), *Pesnolyubie* [Melomania] (Martín y Soler, 1790) and the 'historical spectacle' *The Early Reign of Oleg* (Cannobio, Pashkevich, Sarti, 1791) (Vasilieva and Lapin, MPES, II:153). All of the operas in their piano reductions were published immediately after their premières. Three of the librettos were written by Catherine II herself and arranged by her secretary, Khrapovitsky, who was the author of the fourth libretto. Scholars have detected additional links: the gorgeous engravings in *The Early Reign of Oleg* were

---

10 See D.S. Babkin, *Process A. N. Radishcheva*. Moscow-Leningrad, 1956:28, 36, 151.

produced by Lvov, who was a friend of both Khrapovitsky and A.I. Musin-Pushkin. The latter, besides being an active member of the *Rossiyskaya Academia* was also director of the publishing house. In this context, the absence of Lvov's name on the edition, and instead the name of the composer Prach as arranger, strikingly parallels the editorial style of these four operas. The author of the librettos is not mentioned – everyone who was supposed to know knew – only the names of the composers were printed. Finally, Prach himself was common to both publications; not only was he Lvov's associate but he was also a member of the circle of those who served Catherine's own operatic projects and who immediately created the piano reductions of the operas.

It should be noted that music engraving in Russia at that time was very expensive. While piano reductions of the above-mentioned operas must have been sponsored by the court, the same holds true for Lvov's *Collection*, whose publication had a similar national significance as that of the *Rossiyskaya Academia* monuments. The LPC was published at the expense of the Cabinet of Her Imperial Majesty (Rozanov, forthcoming; Lapin, 2003).[11]

It is impossible to define precisely Lvov's socio-political attitude. On the one hand he was 'an active loyalist', faithful to and patronized by both Catherine II and Paul I (Mazo, 1987:26–7). On the other hand it was he who had tried (sadly in vain) to prevent Radishchev's trial. In both public and in private, Lvov fell somewhere between Catherine II and Radishchev. This is less paradoxical than it may seem. Radishchev could hardly have predicted that he would be sentenced to exile in Siberia, although he must have realized the serious risk he was taking. The entire case might have gone better had not the French revolution brought Catherine's cautious move toward liberalism to an end. The Russian members of the Enlightenment had misjudged the situation, which changed after July 1789. Radishchev himself was a close friend (and fellow member of the St Petersburg Rosicrucian Masonic lodge 'Urania') of Count Alexander Romanovich Vorontsov, Princess Dashkova's brother, and worked in the State service under his supervision. Various shades of Russian Enlightenment intermingled within the wide circle of the nobility. Obsessed with achieving a bright future for the Russian people, they differed in their views about what should come first: liberation (Radishchev) or enlightenment (Dashkova, who nevertheless came under the Empress's suspicion as a possible Radishchev supporter).

The Eighteenth-Century Russian Idiom: Policy, Perception, Proofs

Lvov presented his vision of folklore as an inspirational source for art–music composers in his article 'O russkom narodnom penii' [On Russian folk singing] serving as a Preface to the first edition in 1790.

---

11 The bill from the director of the College of Mines Press I.T. Tretiakovsky, for printing Lvov's Collection was found by A.S. Rozanov, who wrote a manuscript on his finding; the MS was later found among the bequest of M.S. Pekelis in GMMK. M.P. Pryashnikova, who found it in the archive, sent the article to A.B. Nikitina, who is currently preparing the collection of papers presented at the conference dedicated to the 250th anniversary of Lvov's birth (Lapin, 2003:52).

One would hope that this collection will serve as a rich source for the musically gifted and for opera composers, who, making use not only of the motives but also of the strangeness itself of certain Russian songs, will afford by means of their gracious art new pleasures to the ear and new delights to music lovers... (trans. by Mazo, 1987:82)[12]

In the second edition (1806, posthumous) a list of composers was added to the above:

...examples of which have already been provided with great success by Messrs. Sarti, Martini [Vicente Martín y Soler], Paskevich, Tietz, Jarnoviki [Giornovichi], Palschau, Karaulov (an amateur), and others. (trans. by Mazo, 1987:82)[13]

The list of composers mentioned here is in many ways puzzling. First of all, it more befits the situation in 1790 than the early 1800s, when, if we accept the common theory, Lvov would have been preparing the second edition, not long before his death in 1803. By this time, however, both Sarti and Pashkevich had been dismissed and were already dead. Martín y Soler's (extant) music in which he utilized the Russian idiom must have been effectively forgotten, and by the 1790s he was popular mostly for his operas, ballets and *canzonette*. Only Tietz, Palschau, Karauloff and, less probably, Giarnovichi were still relatively active in this field. In contrast, it is surprising that such a prominent figure of the 1790s as Hässler was not included in the list.

These puzzling aspects of the Preface, together with its anonymity and the need to remember that we are dealing with the 'historiographical' rather than the historical figure of Lvov, suggests that the list of exemplary composers may indeed have originally related to 1790, but for some reason was omitted from the printed version of the first edition and included in the second one by an (again) anonymous compiler. What follows is based on the premise that this list of composers was originally intended for inclusion in the 1790 edition.

The first three musicians, Sarti, Martini [Martín y Soler] and Pashkevich, had certain things in common, such as four operas composed to accompany libretti written by the Empress herself or written for her special projects: Vasily Paskevich wrote the music to *Fevey* (1786), Vicente Martín y Soler composed *Gorebogatyr' Kosometovich* (1789) and *Pesnolyubie* (1790), and Giuseppe Sarti together with Pashkevich and Carlo Canobbio (not mentioned by Lvov) wrote *The Early Reign of Oleg* (1790).

The contributions of the three men to development of the Russian idiom were uneven at best. Pashkevich, continuing his successful work with the Russian folk style,

---

12 '...Должно надеяться, что сие Собрание послужит богатым источником для музыкальных талантов и для сочинителей опер, которые воспользуясь не только мотивами, но и самою странностию некоторых Русских песен, посредством изящного своего искусства доставят слуху новые приятности, и любителям музыки новыя наслаждения...' (Lvov, 1806, 6th edn 1987:xiv, facsimile 12).

13 '...чему уже с большим успехом подали пример господа: Сарти, Мартини, Паскевич, Тиц, Жарновики, Пальшау, Караулов (amateur) и другие' (ibid.).

wrote a brilliant score, which members of the nineteenth-century *The Mighty Five* could justifiably envy for its natural elegance in dealing with ancient Russian folklore. Vicente Martín y Soler (Martini) (1754–1806), the Italian kapellmeister of Spanish origin, who had arrived in Russia only in 1788, displayed a very limited command of the Russian style. His opera *Pesnolyubie* was a parody on S. Champeine's *La mélomanie* (1790) and bore no relation to the Russian style. His opera *Gorebogatyr' Kosometovich* was a satire on the Swedish king Gustav III, Catherine's cousin, who, despite the latter's long and assiduous diplomatic efforts to keep the peace, declared war on Russia in 1788. The opera was written on the occasion of the first successful military operations and, for reasons of political prudence, was played only a few times and only for a narrow circle of courtiers. Martín's score was worthy of this famous composer and contains some 'graceful incrustations of Russian folk songs, sometimes producing a sudden humoristic effect' (Porfirieva, Butir, MPES, II:180), but little more than that.

The appearance of Sarti at the head of Lvov's list is more difficult to explain. *The Early Reign of Oleg* was quite a unique piece, whose genre was defined as an 'imitation of Shakespeare without observing the usual theatrical rules', and was in fact a 'theatralized political chronicle' (Rabinovich, 1948:81–2) retelling events of the close of the ninth century. Sarti wrote only two series of numbers for it, all for the final scene. The first series comprised four solemn choruses on the texts of Lomonosov's odes, glorifying the might of Ancient Rus'. The second series comprised melodrama and choruses presenting a fragment of Euripides' *Alceste* – 'theatre-within-a-theatre', imitating a spectacle that Prince Oleg had attended together with the Emperor of Byzantium at the hippodrome during his visit to Constantinople. The latter series, as a stylized representation of ancient Greek music, was the artistic point of the entire show, about which Sarti wrote his learned Explanation (translated by Lvov and printed in the libretto book), with the newcomer and Parisian star-harpist Jean Batiste Cardon being recruited to perform, as a reference to the Apollonian harp of Greek mythology. The rest of the music for the spectacle was composed by Pashkevich (music for ancient Rus'ian wedding songs), and Carlo Canobbio, who was responsible for the ballets and created pleasing arrangements of Russian folk songs, among them a humouristic polyphonic combination of the famous 'Kamarinskaya' and a minuet.

In Sarti's other known scores, despite their including such contemporaneous Russian realities as horn orchestra and cannonade, no typical Russian elements have yet been identified. His most Russian works are his sacred *a cappella* choral compositions – concertos and liturgies (see Chapter 10). However, it is doubtful that Lvov had these in mind. Oriented toward pagan folklore in his musical ideology, Lvov barely referred to spiritual compositions. Had he done so he would probably have mentioned Berezovsky or Bortniansky in his list.

Three possibilities thus remain. Either Sarti did write some composition/s (unknown today) in which he luminously elaborated upon Russian folklore, or he succeeded somehow in creating a public impression at the time that his work did indeed include reference to folklore; or, perhaps such references do exist in his known works today but have yet to be discovered by Russian-Soviet scholars. Just as the highbrow public accepted the authenticity of his Greek style (based on Pindar's ode from Kircher's *Musurgia*), so too might it have believed in the 'Russian' realism of his settings of Lomonosov's odes. The world still believes in the true Russian epic spirit of Borodin's *Prince Igor*, despite its contemporaneous nineteenth-century style, including the polonaise rhythm, as revealed by Taruskin (1997:284). Sarti's success here was due to his intuitive understanding of the syncretic possibilities of the concepts of 'national' and 'old'. The 'old' *nationalized* the ninth-century Varangian Prince Oleg, making him Russian (or more correctly Rus'ian) which was extremely important for the Empress, herself of German origin.

Sarti was invited to Russia as a first-rate Italian maestro, to represent the Italian standard. In doing so, however, he displayed a remarkable openness and interest in the local culture and its musical idioms. With time, he inscribed himself naturally into Russian music. When he arrived in Russia in 1784, Sarti must have noted that the nationalistic trend in Russian culture was enjoying great support from the Empress. Having probably learned from his Danish experience regarding the importance of nationalism for those countries on the European periphery, Sarti would have paid keen attention to this trend. He had already learned the art of acculturation in Copenhagen, while participating in such national opera projects as Bredal's *Gram og Signe* 1755–6 (remarkably paralleling Sumarokov-Araja's Russian opera *Tsefal i Prokris*) and later *Tronfølgen i Sidon*, 1771.

There is an oft-cited episode concerning Sarti from the memoirs of Vasily Kapnist, probably referring to the mid-1780s.

It happened once that relatives and friends, gathering at the house of my friend Nikolai Alexandrovich Lvov, sang the folk song 'Vysoko sokol letel'. At the same moment Sarti, famous for his excellent musical compositions, enters. He stops and attentively listens. Noticing him, the singers stop singing. He inquires about the name of the composer and receives the answer that this is a Russian folk song. Amused, he asks them to repeat it. Greatly praising this piece, he is much surprised by the art of singing such a difficult chorus. The singers reply that it is easy and the common folk sing it with the same accuracy. Sarti refuses to believe this. One hour later he is invited to come into the spacious court where a dozen rowers, hired by the late Count Bezborodko, sing the same chorus. Astounded, the venerable Sarti runs from one singer to another, listening, and by the end of the song he confesses that he has witnessed the unbelievable: it appeared impossible to him that ordinarily coarse voices could assume such a perfection in performance, the more so that the singers did not observe any strict tune but often improvised without upsetting the general consonance in the choir...[14]

---

14 'Случилось так, что у друга моего, покойного Николая Александровича Львова, собравшиеся родственницы и приятели пели простонародную песню "Высоко сокол летел"; в то же самое время входит известный превосходными музыкальными сочинениями Сарти; он останавливается, слушает со вниманием, наконец примечают его и перестают петь. – Он осведомляется о имени сочинителя и получает в ответ, что это простонародная русская песня. Удивленный, просит он о повторении оной. – Превознося похвалами отменного музыкального рода сочинение сие, удивляется

The aforementioned episode describing Sarti's admiration for Russian folk polyphony indeed suggest that it was Sarti's interest in the Russian idiom that led him to attempts of such kind in his own creative work. Moreover, the entire episode coincides with the one described by Lvov himself about a famous Italian maestro who refused to believe in the authenticity of such an elaborated style. The only drawback to this tale is that in Lvov's Preface to both editions of the *Collection* (in the first in detail and in the second only as a brief mention) he talks about another Italian maestro in a similar situation, namely Paisiello. To whose slip of memory should we relate this? Probably to Kapnist's, since he wrote much later and it is hard to imagine Lvov in 1790 being mistaken or consciously deceiving the public in connection with Sarti. In any event, Sarti's new wave of popularity upon his return to the capital (being specially called for by the Empress) could have played a role in Lvov's 'politically correct' considerations in placing him first on the list.

Returning to Lvov's list, the aforementioned triad of opera composers is followed by Tietz and Giornovichi. In the late 1780s both were well established court musicians, often performing together in ensembles and competing in developing a Russified instrumental style, each in his preferred genre: quartet and sonata (Tietz) and violin concerto (Giornovichi). They were both popular and skilful and served Lvov as good examples indeed.

The third and last group in Lvov's list comprises Palschau and Karauloff (an amateur). Their use of the folk idiom was to create variations on Russian songs. Palschau, who published such works in the mid and late 1790s (competing with Hässler who shared the same publisher, Gerstenberg), might also have sold his music in handwritten copies, as was common in Russia in the 1780s. He probably performed these variations in his concerts and was a familiar figure to the public of St Petersburg. Karauloff was a talented amateur musician, whose name is only known today through the 1787 edition of *Trois airs russes variés pour le clavecin ou forte-piano par m-r. de Karaoulof suivis d'une sonate composée par I. Pratch*, and the appearance of his name on the list of subscribers for the 1806 edition of LPC. Karauloff's association with Prach, whose sonatas also exploited Russian tunes, indicates his proximity to the Lvov circle.

Any answer to the question of who were the 'others', whom Lvov did not name, is of course speculative. Among the musicians to whom Lvov might have been referring are Fomin, the 'baby' of the circle, Khandoshkin, whose Russianness

---

искусству поющих столь, по мнению его, трудный хор. – Ему отвечают, что нет ничего легче и что простонародные певцы поют оный с такою же точностью. – Сему ученый музыкант никак верить не хочет. – Спустя час, просят его выйти на широкий двор, где 12 гребцов, нанятых покойным графом Безбородком, пели сей хор. – В изумлении почтенный Сарти перебегал от одного певца к другому, вслушивался и по окончании песни признался, что был свидетелем делу неимоверному; что по грубости голосов невозможно было предположить такой точности в исполнении; тем более, что певцы, каждый особенно, не наблюдали в напеве своем определенных каждому голосу нот; но часто переменяли оные без нарушения общего стройногласия в хоре...' (Kapnist, *Sobranie sochineniy v 2-kh tomakh*, 1960, II:184–5).

needs no comment, and Wanzhura, who shared the same stylistic trend as Tietz and Giornovichi and appeared in concerts with them. Clearly many more names should or could have appeared in such a list, but it is obvious that Lvov could not include them all. (This may have been a sensible reason for omitting the entire list from the first edition.) It is interesting that apart from Pashkevich, who besides his indisputable contribution to the creation of a Russian style was also especially close to the Empress, and thus definitely deserved mention, there is only one other Russian on the list – Vasily Semenovich Karauloff. All the others were foreign musicians of international repute who had settled in Russia. Like Prach himself, they were considered Russian and seemed to have no problem with their national-cultural identity among the local audience.

Whereas nineteenth-century Russian historiography formed a nationalistic attitude of neglect towards immigrant musicians, which twentieth-century Russian–Soviet historiography has been in no hurry to revise, there was an attempt by A. Rabinovich in the early twentieth century, albeit empirical, to determine the objective criteria of a national style in eighteenth-century Russia:

> If not the most important problem at this stage [of eighteenth–century Russian studies], the problem of forming a national musical language is nonetheless an issue. In opera, as in other spheres of Russian art music at the time, there were two approaches.
>
> The first was initiated mainly by the composer of *Melnik* [The Miller-magician, Deceiver and Matchmaker], although the music to the opera *Lyubovnik-koldun* [The Lover who was a Wizard] (1772)[15] had already presented song tunes. The most important steps in this direction, however, can be found in the work of more distinguished masters – *Yamshchiki* [The Post-drivers] by Fomin and the second act of *Gostinny dvor* (The St Petersburg Bazaar) by Pashkevich. This approach drew melodic material from the native folklore and elaborated upon it with techniques from classical music. [The author's footnote: 'In total there are eight operas among the preserved material, in which a significant part of the music is based on folk tunes: *Melnik, Yamshchiki, Gostinny dvor, Fevey, Bogatyr' Boeslaevich, Oleg, Vityaz' Akhrideich* and *Starinnye svyatki*.] In fact this combined several approaches, reflecting a variety of methods and forms. The composers' problem of choosing the best approach in this highly important musical historical process has remained vital throughout the entire history of Russian music…
>
> The second approach can be traced through the examples of Zorin, Raupach and Sarti; in its most consistent form in the French operas by Bortniansky; and to some extent in the works of the leading masters of the period – Pashkevich and Fomin. The musicians taking this approach modified the classical procedure, bringing it closer to the tastes and artistic demands of Russian society. This was a complex and long-term process of selection and creative blending and innovation. Thus, new, already nationalistically-coloured stylistic formations gradually originated from the classical elements …
>
> Anyone familiar with the typically eloquent music scores of eighteenth-century Russian operas, and impartially listening to them attentively, while also acquainted with

---

15 The mention is erroneous. *Lyubovnik Koldun* was composed in 1777, while in 1772 *Anyuta*, the first Russian opera 'on tunes', was staged. According to the context this is probably what the author meant.

West-European music of the epoch, will undoubtedly sense in them an already complete Russian musical style whose signs cannot be reduced to national folklore but are clearly associated with eighteenth-century classical music.[16]

Formed within Asafiev's school of thought in the 1920s–30s, Rabinovich's conception, including the characteristics of particular individual styles, still remains widely in use. Its only vulnerability is in giving too much credit to the ear. While within the school itself this was sufficient, as time passed and audiences widened, such notions began to demand analytic theoretical proofs if they were not to remain susceptible to accusations of nationalist tendencies. Two generations later, a scholar who could hardly be suspected of Russian nationalism produced such valuable research. Evangeline Vassiliades (in her unpublished Ph.D. dissertation 'Overture and Symphony in Eighteenth-Century Russia'; New York University, 1977) applied Jan LaRue's method of morphological analysis (1970) to both Russian orchestral works and Russian folk songs, as written by Lvov and Prach. This pioneering approach and multi-dimensional analysis allowed her, among other results, to define the syntactical idiom of Russian song on the structural level. Vassiliades traced its presence in those compositions in whose style the twentieth-century ear

---

16 'Едва ли не важнейшей проблемой этой стадии является проблема формирования национального музыкального языка. В опере, как и в других областях российского музыкального творчества, в это время существуют два пути. Первый путь начат в основном автором "Мельника", хотя уже в опере "Любовник-колдун" (1772) музыка состояла из песенных "голосов". У более крупных мастеров важнейшие шаги в этом направлении – "Ямщики" Фомина и второй акт "Гостиного двора". Художник, идущий по этому пути, черпает мелодический материал из отечественного фольклора, и обрабатывает его приемами классической музыкальной техники. [the author's footnote: Всего среди дошедшего до нас нотного материала имеется восемь опер, в коих значительная часть музыки основана на народных мелодиях: "Мельник", "Ямщики", "Гостиный двор", "Февей", "Богатырь Боеславеич", "Олег", "Витязь Ахридеич" и "Старинные святки".] Это, собственно, не путь, а несколько путей, до того разнообразны формы и методы, возможные в этой плоскости. Проблема выбора наиболее правильного пути в этом важнейшем музыкальном историческом процессе оставалась актуальной на всем протяжении истории русской музыки... Второй путь можно проследить на примерах Зорина, Раупаха, Сарти; в наиболее последовательной форме – во французских операх Бортнянского и в известной мере и у ведущих мастеров этого периода – Пашкевича и Фомина. Художник, идущий этим путем, модифицирует формообразующий материал классики, приближая его к вкусам и художественным запросам русского общества. Это сложный и длительный процесс отбора и творческого претворения. Так в известной мере из классических элементов постепенно возникают новые, уже национально–окрашенные стилистические образования... Тот, кто ознакомится с наиболее показательными музыкальными страницами русских опер XVIII века и беспристрастно вслушается в них, будучи одновременно знаком с западноевропейской музыкой той эпохи, несомненно, ощутит в них уже определенно сложившийся русский музыкальный стиль, признаки которого отнюдь не исчерпываются национальным фольклором, а связаны с классикой XVIII века' (Rabinovich, 1948:31–5).

can hardly distinguish anything more than common eighteenth-century musical writing. In relation to elaborating upon the Russian idiom, Vassiliades noted five distinctly Russian thematic styles (the fourth and fifth belong to the next generation of composers and are thus not dealt with here):

> First, the composer may quote an entire folksong or fragments of a folksong. Occurring in the works of Pashkevich, Fomin and Wanzhura, these themes contain reminiscences of specific folksongs and establish quickened local interest and a resulting sense of movement. Other themes in overtures by Pashkevich and Wanzhura may not derive from folksong, but offer such obvious folk-like characteristics that we may assign them to this first style.
>
> A second approach combines folksong with Western traits, producing a Russian Classical style. A theme in this style may seem only remotely folk-like, because the composer utilizes isolated processes from folksong, such as juxtapositions of major and relative minor, a small melodic range, and stamping motives. Western aspects may include a central melodic peak, a variety of surface rhythms, and the use of sequential motives. This combined style occurs occasionally in the works of the first-generation composers (Bortniansky, Tietz, and Blyma) but more frequently in the works by second-generation composers (Titov, Davydov, Pleshcheev, Cavos).
>
> A third style merges folksong and Western procedures so thoroughly that an entirely new blended idiom results. Whereas the Russian Classical style employs rather free combinations of folksong and Western traits, the blended approach reflects more consistent treatment from theme to theme, for example typically associating wave-form contours and small-scale repetition from folksong with a variety of surface activity and developmental treatment of motives from Western styles. These features commonly interact to produce themes marked by cumulative textural and rhythmic activity, undulating lines, and prolonged repetition of rhythmic patterns. Further research seems likely to establish links between the blended styles of Bortniansky, Skokov, Wanzhura, Biulandt, and Titov and the propulsive, cumulative motion in the music of Musorgsky, Borodin, and other nineteenth-century composers. (273–4)

A comparison of Lvov's, Rabinovich's and Vassiliades' lists is interesting, although two circumstances should be kept in mind: all three deal with different genres, but with opera (or operatic overture) in common, and all three lists are incomplete and overgeneralize their authors' opinions. While Lvov simply added 'and others' to his list, Rabinovich and Vassiliades both relate to many more composers than those mentioned in the particular above-quoted generalizations. Interestingly, in contrast to the 1950–90 Soviet official-nationalist musicology, Lvov, Rabinovich and Vassiliades all gave lists of composers who had mastered the organic style of opera, free from nationalist prejudices and equalizing Russian and foreign musicians.

Vassiliades' conclusions on stylistic classification are generally compatible with those of Rabinovich, although the names vary. For comparison, while Lvov mentions Sarti, Pashkevich and Martín y Soler, Rabinovich evaluates Bortniansky, Zorin, Raupach, Sarti, Pashkevich and Fomin, and Vassiliades' theoretical analysis raises the names of Bortniansky, Skokov, Wanzhura, Bullant, Titov, Tietz and Blyma. (The names in both Rabinovich's and Vassiliades' lists are given here in the order of most to least organic style composers.)

To summarize, while Sarti and Pashkevich coincide in Lvov's and Rabinovich's lists, Lvov names Pashkevich among the first and ignores Fomin, whereas Rabinovich mentions Pashkevich and Fomin among the last, and Vassiliades excludes them entirely from the blended-style category. Notably, both Rabinovich and Vassiliades emphasize Bortniansky as an example of the most organic Russian style of the time, while both Tietz and Blyma stand up well to Vassiliades' test. Two surprising entries are those of Peter Skokov (1758–1817), composer and architect, who studied in Italy and is now known only through his Italian opera *Rinaldo*, and the flexible Ernest Wanzhura.

The use of folk song as inspiration/source for instrumental compositions was neither specifically Russian nor an entirely new phenomenon. The first attempts in this direction made by the German Reinhardt Keiser and the Italians Domenico Dall'Oglio and Luigi Madonis in the 1730s (mentioned in Chapter 3), paralleled Telemann's Polish partite, concertos and trio sonatas, mentioned in the latter's autobiography (1739). These were probably known to Jacob von Stählin, who was the central figure in Russian musical life of the 1730s–60s and, having been educated in Germany, was in fact a representative of German culture in Russia. Later, Haydn worked with Czech folklore and set Scottish songs to music (in the 1790s). But while these composers discovered the Other (note, non-German/Austrian Other), the Russians seemed to be especially concerned, or even obsessed, with their own Slavic Self. The richer the agrarian population – the richer its authentic folklore. In an era of approaching sentimentalism, this Russian social structure, greatly differing from the Western urbanization, constituted both its socio-economic drama and its cultural advantage at one and the same time.

Elsewhere in the European periphery too, the issue of national music accompanied local Enlightenment movements. Each country had its own interrelationships with other cultures and its own social structures and problems, but the idea of a national language in letters and music symbolized its particular identity and displayed itself in a strikingly similar way. It was here that the interests of the enlightened aristocracy, the middle classes and the monarchy encountered one another, uniting all these secular forces. In Russia, the main tendencies in this direction – folksong collections and comic opera – initiated in the 1770s, strengthened and broadened in the 1780s with the development of a national instrumental music, transforming in the process from an exotic phenomenon to the cultural norm.

Chapter 10

Sarti in Russia

Of all the eighteenth-century 'Russian Italians', Giuseppe Sarti (1729–1802) is privileged with the greatest number of mentions in contemporary memoirs, documents and other reminiscences. This was partly due to objective reasons. By the last two decades of the eighteenth century, life among the upper echelons of Russian society had reached a remarkable intellectual level. Epistles and other written sources became an indispensable element of culture, as indeed they still are. The significance of the political events that were celebrated with Sarti's music also contributed to promoting his name in the late 1780s. Finally, Sarti's great contribution to Russian music, his extravert nature, public displays of temperament and talent, all stimulated intense Russian interest in his activities.

It was Paisiello's departure from Russia in 1784 that determined Sarti's good fortune. Despite occupying the respectable position of kapellmeister of St Mark's Cathedral in Venice, Sarti was probably experiencing nostalgia for the intensive musical activity then taking place across the Alps, which were so familiar to him from his youth in Copenhagen. He would also have fondly remembered the patronage of the Russian ambassador to Denmark, Prince Filosofoff (Thrane, 1901, 2:535–8). Sarti was fortunate to join the Russian scene in a period so greatly favourable to music.

The slightly less than two decades of Sarti's life and work in Russia – from 1784–1802 – somewhat similarly reflected the slightly more than two decades he had spent in Copenhagen – 1753–68 and 1770–75. Creative and industrious, gifted in many fields, he probably possessed a charismatic and charming personality. Surprisingly, he managed to remain in favour with all the many rival factions at court, who had a tendency to somewhat abruptly replace the people in their service. Sarti, however, remained both at Queen Juliane Marie's court after Queen Karoline Mathilde in Denmark and at the court of Paul I after his service to Catherine II and Prince Potemkin in Russia. He was the only one among his Italian colleagues to receive the Russian rank of Collegial Counsellor, which was equal to the military rank of colonel, thus corresponding to his rank in Denmark. Despite his deftness in dealing with the various royal families, however, he nonetheless eventually became the victim of intrigues by various figures at both courts.

The St Petersburg public had begun to appreciate Sarti's music as early as 1779, when the Italian troupe of M. Mattei and A. Orecia presented his Venetian masterpiece *Fra i due litiganti il terzo gode*. It may have been Paisiello who recommended Sarti to the Russian court, although it is also possible that Grand Duke Pavel Petrovich, during his incognito travels and impressed by *Alessandro e Timoteo* (Parma, 1782), may have suggested his appointment to the Empress. The first contract with the composer was from 1 March 1784 until 1 January 1787. He was to be paid 3,000 roubles per year plus a one-time payment of 500 roubles for travel expenses, and to be given an apartment with firewood and permission to give an annual benefit concert. The librettist Ferdinando Moretti, with whom the composer had successfully collaborated at La Scala, was invited in the same year, probably in response to Sarti's request.

Sarti's first presentation in St Petersburg was the *buffa Gli Amanti consolati*, written shortly before his arrival and dedicated to Empress Catherine II. Staged in December 1784, the opera captivated its audience, bringing Sarti many influential admirers. One of these was Prince Gregory Potemkin, with whom the composer was to remain associated for the next six years, until the Prince's death in 1791. Potemkin's first commissions for Sarti were two oratorios with Russian texts (from the Psalms) *Gospodi, vozzvakh k Tebe* [I cried unto thee, O Lord] and *Pomiluy mya, Bozhe* [Have mercy upon me, O Lord] (Miserere) performed on 13 and 25 April 1785 respectively. 'Yesterday we attended at Prince Potemkin's an oratorio with Russian text, in which the music was singularly beautiful and very well received,' wrote Prince Nikolai Repnin to Prince Fedor Golitsyn on the day following the première.[1] Above and beyond the beauty and majesty of polyphonic music by such a master, the audience was especially delighted by the novelty that Sarti had introduced into this genre – a horn band.

At the peak of their popularity in Russia the horn bands had their own repertoire (arrangements of popular music), constituting a kind of singular genre that did not interact with any other genre, especially the traditional Western ones. Sarti was the first to legitimize and elevate this music to the level of a high genre. This was no mere eccentricity on his part but the serendipitous discovery that the haunting sound of the horns was similar to that of an organ. The composer gave the horns the low tones of the accords, using the standard device of organ application in oratorical music. In many further works of this kind Sarti used horn bands interchangeably, to the grateful delight of his listeners. After his highly successful debut at Prince Potemkin's Tavrichesky Palace, Sarti's oratories soon began to occupy a firm place in the repertoire of the 1780s–90s. He included them in the programmes of his benefit concerts, and they were sometimes even performed without the presence of the composer himself.

During the term of his contract Sarti staged his recently composed *seria Idalide* (Milan, 1783, première in St Petersburg in January 1785), and the buffas *Le gelosie villane* and *Fra i due litiganti*, as well as some opera pieces at his benefit concert (30 October 1785, Kamenny Theatre).[2] His popularity in Russia continued to grow. In

---

1   'Nous avons eu hier chez le P-ce Potemkin un oratoire avec paroles Russes dont la musique a été singulièrement belle et qui a très bien réussie' (Nikolai Repnin to Fedor Golitsyn, 14 April 1785. GIM, f 17, no 806a, L 53).

2   Various sources indicate three different operas, which may have been presented at this benefit concert: *I filosofi immaginari* or *I finti eredi* and/or *Amor notaio*, on this see Porfirieva,

November of the same year the Italian opera troupe also performed his operas *Fra i due litiganti il terzo gode* and *Le gelosie villane*.

With the beginning of Sarti's work in Russia two singing stars arrived in St Petersburg: Luisa da Todi (May 1784) and the male soprano Luigi Marchesi (mid-1785), for whom Sarti wrote the *seria Armida e Rinaldo* (16 February 1786, upon the opening of the Hermitage Theatre at the Winter Palace, to great acclaim and followed by many additional performances at various venues); the cantata *La scelta d'amore* (spring 1786); and the opera seria *Castore e Polluce* (23 June 1786).

All the works of that period were composed with the spectacular performance potential of the Court opera troupe in mind, such as the impressive quantity and quality of the orchestra players, and of course its brilliant soloists Todi and Marchesi. This idyllic collaboration, however, did not last long, although the exact reason for the crisis is unknown. Contemporary sources vaguely mention intrigues instigated by Todi, who had been against inviting Marchesi. Sarti, at the end of a century filled with scandals between prima donnas throughout Europe, and he himself married to the prima donna Camilla Pasi, should have known better than to invite the second star. Todi subsequently managed to damage the court's opinion of both Sarti and Marchesi. Both wise and calculating, the Empress consequently cut the Gordian knot. Her journey to the south of Russia for the meeting with Joseph II had to begin in early January 1787. Considering that for the moment this costly trio was not of prime necessity, she dismissed all three of them from the court. Marchesi left first, and by March 1787 he was already performing in Berlin. In April 1787, Todi too left Russia, offering a splendid farewell in the form of a theatralized musical fête in Moscow; and on 12 June 1787 Sarti was formally notified of the non-renewal of his contract, obviously after a contract with his successor had already been signed. Unlike the singers, however, Sarti did not leave Russia. He preferred to choose an unusual alternative, proposed by Prince Potemkin. Indeed, there was little that was 'usual' about the Prince.

Sarti and Prince Potemkin

Potemkin's more commonly known image, fixed in history by his successors, portrays him as the wily designer of the famous 'Potemkin's props'; as a man whose position as a favourite gave him unlimited possibilities to realize his adventurous ideas. This, however, is not the true essence of his nature. A more objective portrayal reveals him as a well-educated man with an extraordinary ability to accumulate knowledge and a great productive talent. With his creative nature and freedom to realize daring and large-scale projects, he was a highly energetic personality and ideally suited as a friend and political partner to H.I.M. As her right hand and faithful supporter, Potemkin played a leading part in fulfilling the Empress's major imperial strategy – to gain access to the Black Sea and thereby displace the Turkish forces. He not only achieved distinguished victories in war, but also developed the southern lands, stimulating population increase in the region, giving rise to improved economy, and building cities with their infrastructure and cultural institutions. A recent study, totally revising earlier depictions of Potemkin's personality, can be found in Sebag Montefiore's *Prince of Princes: the life of Potemkin* (2001).

The Prince was a refined music lover, never short of musical facilities, or indeed of any items of luxury, whether at home or on the battlefield. His court maintained a symphony orchestra, the best horn band (bought for 40,000 roubles from Kirill Razumovsky), a church choir, an organ, a military orchestra, a small Italian cappella and a ballet troupe – most of which were quite standard for the late-eighteenth-century Russian high-ranking aristocracy.

> He liked to begin the day with music, so he would order his ever present musicians and one of his collection of choirs to perform for him. They also played during dinner at 1 p.m. and had to be ready at 6 p.m. to play wherever the Prince appeared – and they traveled with him whether he was in the Crimea or at war. Music was intensely important to him – he wrote it himself and it soothed him. Potemkin had to have music wherever he went and he often sang to himself. (Montefiore, 2001:330)

Although the Russian sources do not mention Potemkin's musical literacy or even that he composed music at all (with the exception of his possibly being the composer of the song 'Na berezhku u stavka'), the French ambassador to Russia, Count de Ségur, mentioned that sometimes the Prince would interrupt his writings on politics or trade and instead work on a musical piece or poem.[3] Even more interesting details are provided by the famous eighteenth-century adventurer Francisco de Miranda, who was

> … Potemkin's cynical travelling guest and a just witness, [and] was impressed by his musical talents. He met Sarti in the south and watched Potemkin 'writing scores here and there, then gave them back to Sarti indicating the tone, rhythm and melody of the two points composition written on the spur of the moment, which gives some idea of his fecundity and great skill'. Sarti presumably then took Potemkin's ideas and arranged them for the orchestra. (Montefiore, 2001:331)

It is clear now that wherever Potemkin might have gone he would certainly have desired to have such a dynamic figure as Sarti nearby. He needed the latter for a wide range of music services: from providing his private musical background to producing the splendid sound of the grand ceremonies.

---

3   L.-F. Ségur. 'Zapiski o prebyvanii v Rossii v tsarstvovanie Ekateriny II', in *Rossiya XVIII v. glazami inostrantsev.* Ed. Yu. A. Limonov. Leningrad: Lenizdat, 1989:387. See also Ségur, Louis Philippe, Comte de, *Memoirs and Recollections of Count Ségur, ambassador from France to the Courts of Russia and Prussia etc., written by himself.* London, 1825–7; *Memoirs of the Comte de Ségur,* ed. Gerard Shelley, New York, 1925.

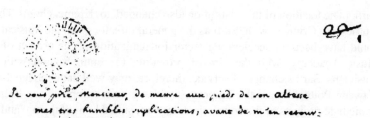

Je vous prie, Monsieur, de mettre aux pieds de son altesse
mes tres humbles suplications, avant de m'en retour-
ner à Kremenciouk.

1°. En faveur des Musiciens Italiens qui ont étés ce tems à Elisabeth,
pour leur obtenir quelque souvention en dedomagement de l'a-
chat de leur chaufage, et de la perte de l'agio sur l'echange
des assignations de banque.

2do. En faveur du Medecin schiassi qui est venu à Kremenciouk à ma
requisition (selon ce que son Altesse eut la bonté de m'aprouver à
Petersbourg) qui a guari tous les Chantres, et donne la santé à tous
les malades qu'on lui presente. Il est trop necessaire pour moi,
pour ma Famille, pour la jevarchie musicale, en: dans un Pays
ou l'on manque de Medecins.
Si son Altesse n'a pas la bonté de lui assigner les gages, et lui
faire rembourser l'argent de son voyage, je serai obligé de le lui
payer de ma poche, il sera contraint de s'en aller, et nous resterons
tous dans une miserable situation. Mais je met toute mon
esperance dans le Coeur de son Altesse qui est bon autant
qu'il est Grand.

Figure 10.1   Sarti's letter to V.S. Popov, secretary of Prince Potemkin, 1788

As a highly enlightened statesman, Potemkin must have realized that one of the contradictions of eighteenth-century Russia was that of the drastic disproportion between its grand size and the small number of cultural institutions, which were, moreover, mostly concentrated in St Petersburg and Moscow. The absence of trained musicians in other places made the production of court or other official ceremonies outside the capital very problematic. Probably prompted by the difficulties inherent in organizing a long sojourn of the court in Moscow in 1775, as early as the mid-1770s Potemkin was already playing with the idea of founding a Music Academy in the new city of Ekaterinoslav in the south of Russia. Initially having Berezovsky and then Khandoshkin in mind as its directors, the Prince finally settled on the candidature of

Sarti. (The location of this institution also changed to Kremenchug.) The Empress's journey to Crimea, with Sarti as the general director of all the musical productions, could have been an accelerating factor for realization of the project of the southern Music Academy, with the aim of providing the entire region with professional musicians. Sarti's change of service, therefore, may well have reflected an agreement between Potemkin and the Empress, and have been completely in keeping with the immediate projects of the court schedule. Sarti suited both of them – and the times.

Early in 1787, Sarti and his family embarked with the court upon the journey to the Crimea, passing through Byelorussia, the Ukraine and southern Russia. His music was played at every significant stop. During the sojourn of the court in Moscow he presented his new oratorio for choir, symphonic and horn orchestras (21 February, Petrovsky Theatre). In April, when the court reached Kremenchug, then the administrative centre of Potemkin's activity in the south, one of Sarti's cantatas was performed. In April–May the court visited Yassy, where the performance of his *Te Deum* is mentioned. The oratorio was repeated at the final stop – the place of the two Emperors' meeting – Kherson. For this special occasion Sarti wrote the beautiful and sophisticated *Fuga a otto voci reali (Kyrie eleison)*. It should be added that the entire journey not only featured a great many balls and receptions, but it was also constantly accompanied by music. The cruise taken by the court down the river Dnieper, from Kiev to Kherson, was on seventy beautiful and comfortable galleys, fitted out according to the highest contemporaneous standards. Each galley had its own music.

Potemkin and Sarti must have found in each other an understanding in their romantic vision of reality. According to one of Sarti's students, the composer Daniil Kashin, and reported later by the writer Sergei Glinka, 'Sarti was somewhat the same kind of romantic as Potemkin: they both thought that a soaring intellect acts beyond the rules, bonding human thinking.'[4] At any rate, the project of the Music Academy in an undeveloped region of Russia constituted a kind of very Russian Enlightened Utopia.

A complete picture of Sarti's directorship of the Music Academy is difficult to reconstruct. However, some documents found among Potemkin's papers show that the maestro took his obligations very seriously.[5] It is hard to judge how long it took him before he was able to come to terms with the pioneering spirit of his task: to implant a musical education in the middle of nowhere. On the one hand he lived in a new building at Potemkin's palace. On the other hand, the palace was built in the new city of Kremenchug (not far from Ekaterinoslav, the would-be modern capital of the flourishing, newly developed lands of New Russia). One has only to visualize the hundreds of miles of desolate Russian steppes around this new city (or rather its embryo) in order to imagine the measure of Sarti's despair when he wrote to Potemkin's secretary chancellor Vasily Stepanovich Popov about the

---

4   'В своем роде Сарти был такой же романтик, как и Потемкин: оба они думали, что ум парящий действует мимо правил, оцепляющих мысль человеческую' (S. Glinka, 1895:186, quoted by Porfirieva, MPES, III:83).

5   Potemkin's papers are located in RGADA, Moscow.

students' miserable existence, not receiving any money, lacking clothing and paper and ink for their studies, not to mention a doctor for Sarti's own family.[6] It would be interesting to know too how he coped with his new function as a landlord. In 1789, Potemkin granted Sarti a property from the state treasure, about 22,000 hectares of land, together with the village Sofia, Ekaterinoslav district, on the river Kamenka, with a stone house, 150 serfs, 800 sheep, a hundred cattle and so on, at a total cost of 10,000 roubles. However, later documents concerning land grants in 1797 indirectly suggest that Potemkin's land grant had not undergone the appropriate confirmation, and it is unclear whether this property was in fact ever legitimized.[7]

Documentation relating to the Academy indicates that its staff included F. Branca (Branchino), F. Dal'Occha, A. Delfino and other well-known Italian musicians. Among the twelve students were the above-mentioned musician Artemy Vedel (*c.* 1770–1808) and Ivan Turchaninov (1779–1856), both of whom later became church-music composers, as well as Daniil Kashin (1770–1841).

Along with the Academy, Sarti's other major occupation of that period was to arrange the musical part of those major events that occurred in the region in the late 1780s. His oratorios marked a series of festivities on the occasions of Potemkin's victories at war, celebrated in Yassy (*Te Deum* on the occasion of taking the fortress at Ochakov, 1789, written in Kremenchug and sent to St Petersburg, where it was performed at the Alexandro-Nevsky monastery, 30 August 1789), and Bendery (premières of Italian cantata *Giove, la gloria e morte* and *Te Deum* on the occasion of taking the fortress of Kelia, 1790). Within the euphoria of victory, Sarti was a matchless producer of ceremonial cantatas and oratorios, never failing to surprise his audience with some impressive invention. These performances numbered about three hundred participants and, in addition to orchestra, choir and horn band, also included a traditional component in eighteenth-century Russia – cannon firing, which must have provided a special delight. Music was of course a constant demand at the everyday entertainments of the military aristocracy. Thus, Sarti was kapellmeister for the group of Italian musicians at the camp too.

Although away from the capital and the Imperial court, Sarti was aware that the new kapellmeister, Domenico Cimarosa, had arrived in St Petersburg, and he must have known of his success. The greater must have been his surprise, therefore, to receive a special command (through the Empress's letter to Prince Potemkin, 3 December 1789 and accompanied by gifts valued at 3500 roubles) to compose choruses for a new Russian opera with the libretto written by the Empress herself.[8] He must also have been pleased to hear what she had written along with the command:

---

6   RGADA, f 17, op 1, no 285, Ll 98–9.

7   Karl Lau, *Kapellmeister* of horn music in service to Prince Potemkin, and to whom land in the same region was granted, was in a similar situation. Later (after Potemkin's death), in 1794, Lau addressed the Empress with a request about the legitimization of his property (RNB, f 878, op 2, no 113); however her decision is unknown.

8   Gifts to Sarti are mentioned in the papers of State Secretary Alexander Khrapovitsky. RGIA, f 468, 1789, op 43, no 279 (part 1), L 28.

'They, here, don't know how to compose so beautifully.' There must have been something a little less than perfect with Cimarosa.

Cimarosa's Russian Episode

Cimarosa had been invited to St Petersburg to replace Sarti at the advice of the Duke of Serra-Capriola, the Ambassador to Russia of the Kingdom of the Two Sicilies. Cimarosa's arrival was welcomed and prepared for by the public's recent acquaintance with his opera *L'amor costante* (Rome, 1782), which was staged by the Italian company in 1786. Appearing in the Russian capital in December 1787, the composer sailed through the standard admission procedure and met with a warm and enthusiastic reception. In addition to the usual obligations to the Italian Company, he was appointed to teach the children of Grand Duke Pavel Petrovich – the young Grand Dukes Alexander and Constantine. (Cimarosa probably enjoyed a special relationship with Pavel Petrovich, who was the godfather of Cimarosa's own son Paolo.) As a court kapellmeister Cimarosa wrote two serious operas, *La vergine del sole* (22 September 1788) and *La Cleopatra* (27 September 1789) and the dramatic cantata *Atene edificata* (6 and 29 June 1788). He also composed one cantata commissioned by Prince Potemkin, *La Serenata non preveduta* (28 April 1791?) and another ordered by Prince Bezborodko, *La sorpresa* (cantata pastorale a cinque voci con cori e balli, 1790 or 1791). Everything appeared normal, with one exception: instead of supporting each new *Kapellmeister* with new star singers (and/or librettists, decorators, ballet masters and so on) as had formerly occurred, this period saw the unequivocal decline of the Italian opera at the court. Positions that fell vacant when artists departed were not filled by new artists; the staff shrank and the troupe faded. Italian opera as a symbol of prestige and power of the Russian Imperial court ceased to exist.

The events of July 1789 in Paris dictated new values to the wily Russian monarch. Cimarosa had arrived in Russia at the wrong time. Furthermore, whether it was the indifference of the Empress to the Italian opera that affected her taste or the political tension that affected her sense of humour, Cimarosa was drastically mistreated: the composer with an outstanding talent for *buffa* was forced to compose *opere serie*. His failure to deduce Catherine's intentions concerning the style so important to her for her opera *The Early Reign of Oleg* (1790), probably determined his fate. He left Russia in June 1791 for Vienna, where fame awaited him. By February 1792 his *Il matrimonio segreto*, commissioned by Leopold II, was already being staged.

In addition to having been less than effective on the Russian court scene, Cimarosa was strangely boycotted in private written sources. As a personality, he lost out to Sarti in the art of communication – for many music aficionados this was a far more important criterion than that of music itself. As for the Russian public, it continued to applaud with delight at least six of his operas staged in St Petersburg throughout the 1790s.

Example 10.1 Sarti: Chorus from the opera *The Early Reign of Oleg*, **act III**

Sarti Returns to St Petersburg

In autumn 1790 Sarti probably returned to St Petersburg to participate in producing *The Early Reign of Oleg*, which premièred on 22 and 29 October, at the Hermitage and Kamenny theatres respectively. What was expected from him as the most suitable style for this pompous and politically important project for Catherine II, can be seen in one of his choruses on Lomonosov's ode (see Example 10.1).

There are no precise data concerning his status at the time. Both his previous positions had come to an end. The project with the Music Academy in Ekaterinoslav and Kremenchug and Sarti's need to be close to Potemkin in the south were over. On the other hand, the Court Italian company in St Petersburg had been disbanded and the epoch of prestigious court productions was also over. What remained was to continue with Potemkin's musical affairs at St Petersburg and some court obligations, probably mostly at the Young court of the Grand Duke Pavel Petrovich. Soon, however, Sarti's association with Prince Potemkin was also to come to an end. The Prince left for the south, where he shortly became ill and died on 5 October 1791 – two months earlier than Mozart, whom he had been going to invite for a visit in view of his possible service...[9] Sarti's last significant performance at Potemkin's palace in St Petersburg was a concert with the première of his new choruses (with the participation of a horn band), which took place on 30 March 1791 (repeated at a special event on 28 April, see Chapter 11).

Sheremetev and Sarti

During this uncertain period in the early 1790s, Sarti must have enjoyed the limited patronage of Count Sheremetev, although in the well-preserved Sheremetev archives there is no direct evidence that Sarti ever served at his court as a kapellmeister. One can only safely mention their association, reflected in occasional services on the part of Sarti and some protection on the part of the Count during the uncertain period in Sarti's life after Prince Potemkin's death. A cantata was composed by Sarti on the occasion of the Count's recovery from illness. It was also obviously due to Sheremetev that Sarti developed his connections with the Moscow nobility.

Moscow, as a former feudal capital, traditionally consisted of a large number of aristocratic estates. In the 1780s, when theatre and music were flourishing, serf troupes, choirs and horn bands proliferated. This probably furnished Sarti with the idea of his grandiose project there. On 8 February 1791, at the Moscow Petrovsky Theatre, the widely advertised concert of Sarti's oratorical works took place. Its uniqueness lay in the participation of four serf choirs: those of Count V.G. Orlov, Count N.P. Sheremetev, Prince P.M. Volkonsky, and G.I. Bibikov, as well as the horn band of N.F. Kolychev. The success of the concert is clear from its being repeated on 30 March, with the price of tickets rising from the original one or two roubles to five roubles.

In the 1790s, Sheremetev probably commissioned from Sarti *Il trionfo d'Atalanta* for his theatre in Kuskovo. There are a total of six Sarti opera scores in the preserved part of Sheremetev's library, including some written in the late 1790s indicating their performance at his theatres.

Two documents from Sheremetev's archives speak of Sarti's travel abroad at the end of 1791: the Count's application (20 September) to the court chancellery for a passport for Sarti;[10] and his order (28 September) to store Sarti's belongings

---

9　There is an oft-cited letter by Count Andrey Razumovsky to Prince Potemkin from 15 September 1791, revealing his role as intermediary in the Mozart–Potemkin negotiations. See Galkina, 1985:269.

10　The document is published in *Russian Archive*, 1896, VI, p 197.

(with all possible care) in his Moscow residence – fifteen trunks and boxes.[11] (It was indeed a problem for the traumatized Sarti to safeguard his belongings after their theft in St Petersburg, on 31 August, 1786; later partly returned by the thief).[12] These documents match the mention in the biography of Sheremetev's serf composer, Stepan Degtyarev, of his journey with Sarti to Italy.

Close to Lvov's circle, Sarti taught music to Lvov's young serf Alexander Shaposhnikov, whom Lvov had purchased from Countess Golovkina in order to develop his talent, give him a profession and liberate him. Sarti had never accepted payment for this but Lvov repaid him with paintings and various services (Fedorovskaya, 1977:21). Sarti also taught singing at the St Petersburg Theatre School, where, as Fedorovskaya believes, he trained the young Russian composer Stepan Davydov (1777–1825, see Fedorovskaya 1977:17).

Back to the Imperial Court

From 1792, Sarti's talents began again to be exploited at court. He was reappointed court kapellmeister from March 1793, where his duties were mostly as a composer of official ceremonial music, for which there were many occasions. The end of the Russian–Turkish war and the conclusion of a peace treaty in Yassy demanded two final laudations: the cantata *Slava v vyshnikh Bogu* [Glory to God in the Highest], and *Tzaritsa Severa, mat'russkogo naroda* [Ode per la pace]. In addition there were occasional cantatas written for ceremonies within the Imperial family. The Empress's solidarity with Louis XVI was commemorated with Sarti's cantata *Adieux de la reine de France à sa prison du Temple* (after 10 August 1792) and *Missa di Requiem* for Louis XVI (26 March 1793, St Petersburg Catholic Church).

Sarti also widely participated in the endless musical entertainments of the high-ranking courtiers, including the new favourite, Count Zubov. His teaching the children of the Grand Duke Pavel Petrovich and his association with Count Sheremetev, probably enabled Sarti to develop a special relationship with Pavel Petrovich when the latter became Emperor. Considering that Paul I had had Potemkin's palace turned into stables, Sarti was fortunate indeed.

Reorganizing the Cabinet, the new Emperor made use of several of those who had been under-exploited during the previous regime. Sarti was one of them. Paul I awarded him the respectable hereditary sixth-grade rank of Collegial Counsellor (28 February 1798) – the precondition for possessing lands[13] – and two villages with 218 serfs (19 February 1797, Stanovaya and Patkino in Sofino volost, the Bronitsky district, Moscow region).[14]

As a kapellmeister, Sarti had the usual obligations. He composed ceremonial music (probably beginning with the pre-coronation *Inno per il Natale*, 1796),

---

11 RGIA, f 1088, op 3, 1791, no 139, L 58v.
12 RGIA, f 1280, 1786, op 2, no 31, Ll 406–9.
13 RGIA, f 469, 1798, op 4, no 397, Ll 1, 36.
14 RGIA, f 1374, 1797, op 1, no 347, Ll 382–4.

then *Inno concertato con ripieni per l'incoronazione di S. M. Paolo I* and *Il genio della Russia*, a cantata upon the coronation of Paul I – both with text by F. Moretti and performed on 5 and 12 April 1797, Moscow; *Requiem* for the Grand Duke of Württemberg (16 January, St Petersburg, Catholic Church); and a cantata upon the wedding of Grand Duchess Alexandra Pavlovna, *La gloria d'Imineo, Epitalamio* (19 October 1799, Gatchina).

To Sarti's surprise – or perhaps not – the Emperor, remaining faithful to Vincenzo Manfredini, the teacher from his youth, decided to invite him back to Russia, regardless of the facts that during the past three decades the composer had failed to develop an international repute and that his name did not add any lustre to the Russian court. Arriving in St Petersburg in 1798, Manfredini was cordially welcomed and generously rewarded. Shortly after, however, he fell ill and died. At the request of Manfredini's son, the Emperor granted a pension of 3,000 roubles to the widow, increasing an initial sum of 2,000 suggested by the Cabinet. The only legacy that remains from Manfredini's sad return is his book *Regole armoniche, o sieno Precetti ragionati*, which appeared later in a Russian translation by Stepan Degtyarev (1805). Thus Manfredini's Russian chapter had an epilogue somewhat similar to that of Araja during Peter the Third's short rule. Faithful to the memory and ideas of his father, Paul I had also inherited the same codes of the unsuccessful reformer; and he too was murdered and discredited by his successor.

How Sarti's career might have or have not developed further if Manfredini had survived will never be known, but the fact is that the Emperor satisfied his nostalgia for old *opera seria* productions through Sarti, who wrote *Andromeda* (4 November 1798, Hermitage Theatre) and *Enea nel Lazio* with the grand ballet *Il sogno d'Enea* (15 October 1799, Gatchina) giving a final tribute to the genre and ending its epoch in Russia. Both had Angelo Testore in mind for the main role, the last *castrate* on the Russian scene.

Sarti also began to compose in genres that were new for him: the French opera *La famille indienne en Angleterre* (30 April 1799, at the Kamenny theatre, a benefit concert for Mme Chevalier) and the anacréontique ballet *Les amours de Flore et de Zéphire* (19 October, Gatchina). The latter two productions were associated with the Emperor's charismatic favourite, the French soprano M-me Chevalier, whose status exceeded even that of the prima donnas of Catherine's era, and who obtained the position of chief ballet master for her husband, Pierre Chevalier.

Sarti also continued to teach the Imperial children. In 1797 he was appointed musical instructor to Paul's daughters, for whom he wrote the cantata *Ommagio a S.M. Paolo I afferto e cantato dalle suo figlie* for five sopranos and chamber orchestra (1799, Gatchina).

His creativity displayed itself further in his invention of a tool for defining pitch and establishing the St Petersburg standard as $a^1=436$. Presenting it to the Academy of Sciences (the description on 12 May 1796 and the tool itself on 3 October of the same year), Sarti was accepted as a member.

He enjoyed great popularity among a broad circle of Russian music lovers. He arranged concerts with his oratorical compositions accompanied by a horn band, so adored by the public, presented organ recitals at St Petersburg Catholic Church, worked as a music instructor at the Theatre School, and wrote spiritual choral music with Orthodox texts, which became widespread among the aristocracy's serf choirs.

Russian Spiritual Compositions

In this quite solid corpus of choral works – about two dozen compositions are known to us today (from manuscripts, printed music and newspaper announcements) – Sarti displayed a highly successful flair for combining Russian tradition with his own polyphonic style.

According to KPN (1793), his works *Nyne sily nebesnyya* [Now the heavenly powers], *O Tebe raduetsya* [All creation rejoices in Thee] and *Dostoino est'* [It is truly meet], (the latter two are parts of a four-voice Liturgy) were already popular. His choral compositions include a double-choir Liturgy and concertos for six and eight voices. The works tend to a monumental, rich and colourful sound, as well as to extension of forms. His six-voice concerto *Otrygnu serdtse moe* [My heart is inditing a good matter], for example, is written in grand five-section rondo-like form. Along with the normal sized four-voice liturgical pieces he converted some traditionally short parts into grand concertos, such as the above *Nyne sily nebesnyya* [Now the heavenly powers] and the unique double-choir concerto on the text of *Veruyu* [The Creed], otherwise usually the modest psalmodic part.

Like the mutual influence of Galuppi and Berezovsky in the 1760s, there was obviously a similar interrelation between Sarti and Bortniansky in the 1780s–90s. The new music at the time was distinguished by its broad use of various generic sources, mostly from contemporary popular music. The most fundamental of these had remained the *kant*, which for the century of its existence in Russia had become a basic element of urban folklore. Probably realizing this, Sarti applied many *kant* elements: motives, specific and simple harmonic sequences, and a characteristic textural device – parallel thirds in pairs of upper voices. He often used three-beat rhythm for the opening sections of his concertos, full of festive fanfare motifs, obviously corresponding to *partes*-singing tradition.

Sarti's choral texture was mostly based on chorale setting, without any noticeable leaning to polyphony or homophony. In the most developed fragments it recalls the orchestral texture due to the distribution of pedalling and passage-producing lines. The composer made wide use of cantillations and melodic figurations, striving to achieve the baroquesque splendour of a multi-voice ensemble. In his development of the form too he differed from Bortniansky. While the latter linked quite protracted phrases united by the same melodic breathing into fluid and dynamic constructions, Sarti strung shorter phrases, achieving a highly energetic and dynamic procedure full of expressive contrasts in dynamics and texture. Although the listeners of the period were already used to the laconic pieces composed by Bortniansky, they appreciated (and probably expected) Sarti's monumentality, familiar to them from his oratorical works.

Some of Sarti's compositions have obvious prototypes in those by Bortniansky. For example, the opening theme of *Slava edinorodny* [Glory: O only-begotten Son] closely recalls Bortniansky's concerto no 6 *Slava vo vyshnikh Bogu* [Glory to God in the Highest] (Example 10.2), while Sarti's *Vkusite i vidite* [O taste and see that the Lord is good] (Example 10.3) seems to be imitating Bortniansky's settings of ancient chant (see Chapter 14). There is, however, one example of a reverse influence: Bortniansky's *Kheruvimskaya* in *D major*, no 7, seems to have had Sarti's piece as a prototype (Examples 10.4 a, b). Although such a feature as the asymmetrical extension of the second sentence is more characteristic of Bortniansky's themes than of Sarti's, there is unarguable evidence of Sarti's priority: Bortniansky composed his work ten years after Sarti's death, as revealed by the former's manuscript, which was presented to Emperor Alexander I on his birthday on 12 December 1811.[15]

Example 10.2   Sarti: *Slava edinorodny*

Example 10.3   Sarti: *Vkusite i vidite*

Example 10.4 (a) Sarti: *Cherubic hymn*

---

15   RIII, f 2, op 1, no 800.

Example 10.4 (b) Bortniansky: *Cherubic hymn*

There is clear evidence of the popularity of Sarti's choral compositions – the existence of the redaction of his concerto *Slava vo vyshnikh Bogu*. Two versions of the work are found in two sources relating to the same period of the late nineteenth – early twentieth century: a printed edition of the *Istoricheskaya khrestomatia*[16] and a manuscript collection (probably Muscovite).[17] Since the printed edition was based on the manuscripts stored at the Imperial Cappella, it must have been the closest to the original, thus making the version from the manuscript collection a redaction. Although the collection relates to the later epoch, the redaction seems to have been made much earlier – during the period when this repertoire was at its height. All the changes in the score touch upon different elements of composition, but they reflect overall the entire stylistic system of Russian choral music, oriented mainly back to the *partes*-singing tradition. The tendency traced in these changes indicates the influence of Russian folklore. A similar process took place in the adjustment of poetry, for example Lomonosov's, to the folk idiom. While his original lines have an iambic meter:

> Kto tam stuchitsya smelo? –
> So gnevom ya vskrichal.

The folk variant offers a metric transformation characteristic of Russian limericks:

> Ya so gnevom zakrichala:
> – Eshche kto eto takoi? (Novikova, 1982:17)

The changes in this variant of Sarti's concerto touch mainly upon harmony, melodic style and partly the musical material itself. (Such details as appoggiaturas, replacing dotted rhythm with an even one, changes in voice leading and so on are no more than the usual differences found between different manuscript versions and are not considered here as signs of redaction.)

---

16 *Istorichyeskaya khrestomatia tserkovnogo penia*, vol. 1, ed. by M.A. Lisitsyn, (Supplement to the journal *Muzyka i penie*, 1902).

17 Dukhovnye khorovye sochinenia russkikh kompozitorov kontsa XVIII–nachala XIX vekov. GMMK, f 283, no 127.

The harmonic procedures, although mostly preserved, have very few albeit telling changes, including those from the sphere of the dominant function: the seventh in inversed dominant seventh chords is reduced (mm. 30 and 33), or the entire dominant chord is even replaced by the subdominant one (mm. 43, 171=166);[18] the leading seventh chord is substituted by the subdominant six-four chord in order to protract the tonic organ point (mm. 119=118; 127=126) or repetitive authentic cadences is replaced by tonic chords (mm. 61=62). In the SDT cadence the tonic is substituted by extension of the dominant with appoggiatura (mm. 116–117=118). In other cases simplifications of a similar kind occur in the subdominant group; for example, the second six-five chord is replaced by the fourth chord (m. 68). Finally, the small elongation in *F sharp minor* within the *D major* episode has been entirely eliminated (m. 100). Thus, the entire intention of the changes was to soften the functionally strong progressions by means of the simpler ones, which Russian musicians were used to from *partes*-singing praxis.

In contrast to the harmonic sphere, which looked back to *partes*-singing, the melodic sphere looked both back and forward. The signs of a retro style can be traced in one case, where the melodic diapason has been shortened and stepwise melodic figuration of *znamenny chant* kind introduced (mm. 91–92=92–93); in other cases, however, the melodic phrases based on pure harmonic motives have been filled in with smooth melodic gestures (132=131; 142=141).

The most interesting alterations seem to be the melodic variants leading to changes in expression. The first example is a short dialogue between tenor and two altos (with harmonic support of the tenor) in mm. 49–53. The redaction changes both phrases in the prosody (Examples 10.5a, b). While the first phrase of the redaction corrects the wrong one in the original, the second – in contrast – spoils the correct one. This is inevitable because the prosaic text resists setting on a periodical (or tending to such) structure. It is worth noting, however, that while Sarti was usually careful about the prosody, the local Russian musicians ignored it in such key words as *pomiluy nas* [have mercy upon us]. For them, a text was no more than a formal guide for moods and images, while the musical expression came first and what they wanted of the phrasing was rather the old iambic rhythm of *kanty* than the more gracious slow siciliana of Sarti's music.

Example 10.5 (a) Sarti: Concerto *Slava vo vyshnikh Bogu*, **fragment of section 1**

взем - - ляй грех ми - ра по - ми - луй нас

---

18   The number of measures varies in both versions. When referring to similar fragments in both versions I note first the number of the measure in the printed edition, followed by the symbol = and the number of the similar measure in the manuscript redaction.

Example 10.5 (b) Sarti: Concerto *Slava vo vyshnikh Bogu* **(anonymous redaction), fragment of section 1**

Another soloist fragment was introduced into the composition for direct speech (oratio recta) *Az rek: Gospodi, pomiluy mya, istseli dushu moyu, yako sogreshikh Tebe* [I said, Lord, be merciful unto me: heal my soul; for I have sinned against thee] (Examples 10.6a,b). The redaction has four significant changes in comparison with the original: 1) placing the rest of the indirect speech (oratio oblique) – *Az rek:* [I said] – at the end of the choral section; 2) giving the first phrase of the solo to the alto instead of the bass; 3) transforming the entire solo section to *Adagio*; and 4) motivic modifications. In addition, such devices as harmonization of *Az rek:* by a dominant four-three chord 'hanging' on the fermata without resolution in place of Sarti's unison and emphasizing the leading tone in solo phrases, suggests all these changes as tending to more powerful lyrical expression. Its recitative style refers to the operatic tradition.

Example 10.6 (a) Sarti: Concerto *Slava vo vyshnikh Bogu*, **fragment of section 2**

Example 10.6 (b) Sarti: Concerto *Slava vo vyshnikh Bogu* **(anonymous redaction),
fragment of section 2**

The final section of the concerto presents the most dramatic changes. In the beginning, the redaction follows the original quite closely, but the last fraction sets the text to entirely new music, using the method of pasticcio. The latter was widespread in *partes*-singing concertos (Zabolotnaya, 1983:168–9).

The style of this composition by Sarti was no more Italian and no less Russian than that of Bortniansky, Degtyarev or Pashkevich and it required no further 'Russification'. The fact of its redaction thus speaks not only for the need having arisen to adjust it to someone else's taste, but also of its having been accepted into the popular repertoire and dealt with according to the laws of ongoing practice. The very fact of co-creation of the composition signifies its popularity, like many anonymous works, in accordance with the liberal system that applied to dealing with any musical text in eighteenth-century Europe.

Although greatly in demand during Paul's rule, Sarti became redundant to the court after the death of his patron on 12 March 1801. Since there are no documents relating to a continuation of his service, and Sarti was by then 72 years old, one can only guess whose decision this had been. Had it been his own decision to retire, he would probably have been awarded some gift or pension. It is more probable, however, that he was disliked by the young Emperor or his mother Maria Fedorovna, who had at least one reason for a strong personal antipathy to Sarti – his support for Paul the First's favourite M-me Chevalier, for whom and for her husband Sarti had written his last opera and ballet. The couple were exiled from Russia within twenty-four hours after the *coup d'état* (Khodorkovskaya, MPES, III:263–4). Having no appointed position Sarti had nothing left to do in Russia. It took some time for him to examine the situation and settle his affairs. He was probably not the healthiest of men by the time he embarked upon his final journey, to his daughter in Berlin, only to arrive mortally ill.

Sarti's process of acculturation had been a successful one. Looking through the many amateur albums from the end of the eighteenth and beginning of the nineteenth centuries, one often comes across his arias, offering the best evidence of his genuine popularity. The reminiscences from Sarti's most beloved *Miserere* can be heard in such popular early nineteenth-century Russian music as Alexander Verstovsky's *Askold's Grave*. He was recognized and remembered as 'ours' for his Empire style and his respect for and display of Russian nationalist sentiments.

Chapter 11

1790s: Muses and Cannons

The Polonaise: Polish Honour and Russian Empire

On 28 April 1791 there took place what was probably the most grandiose and splendid gala known in eighteenth-century Russia. Its host, chief designer and protagonist was Prince Potemkin. The location of the fête was his Tavrichesky palace, recently built (1783–89) by the Russian architect Ivan Starov. The immediate reason for the event was to celebrate the taking of the fortress of Ismail, but in fact it held a greater significance – the end of the Russian-Turkish war of 1787–91. This (following the victory over Sweden) signified the confirmation of Russian power in Europe, much to the disappointment of England and Prussia, which had supported the Turkish and Swedish pretensions.

His Highness Prince Potemkin-Tavrichesky,[1] who had coordinated the entire campaign, could be justly proud of his accomplishments in developing the Russian southern lands and he had every reason to celebrate this at his own place and in his own style. Spending most of his time in the south, he had had little time as yet to enjoy his new abode. Now was the occasion to truly celebrate – and in the place of his dreams. On the other hand, whether he may have sensed it or not, this was to be his *only* opportunity to do so. Indeed, he left the capital shortly after and died four months later in the southern steppes. The incredible commemoration gala was thus also his farewell to Her Majesty, to St Petersburg and to his entire life – his swansong to the world.

The externally simple appearance of Prince Potemkin's palace had, in contrast, a most luxurious interior. Its Oval Hall could hold five thousand people. Flowers and tropical plants decorated its walls. Crystal chandeliers hung from the ceiling centre and between the columns, while 140 white and coloured (icon)-lamps (shaped like lilies, roses and tulips) and twenty thousand candles shone from the walls. A complex system of reflectors and glass visors hidden in flowers created a panorama of the Garden of Eden, astounding all who entered the hall.

The event was organized as an immense para-theatrical act: the all-night programme was punctuated by a sumptuous dinner. The scenario is known from the *Description of the Festivity at Prince Potemkin's House on the Occasion of Taking*

---

1   The title, meaning 'the Prince of Taurida', was conferred upon Potemkin together with 'His Highness' in 1783, after annexation of the Crimean peninsula, traditionally called Taurida, together with the entire lands of the northern bank of the Black Sea and southern Ukraine.

Ismail, written by Gavrila Derzhavin, who also wrote the lyrics to the choral songs of praise. The ensemble of about three hundred musicians, including a horn band of course, entertained the guests. All the kapellmeisters, and primarily Sarti and Cimarosa, were involved.

The central ceremonial point of the event and its real beginning was the arrival of the Empress. Her entrance was accompanied by fanfares and when Her Majesty and her entourage took their seats, the ball began. The opening number was a magnificent quadrille, performed by twenty-four pairs of young people from the foremost noble families, including the pair comprising the Grand Duke Pavel Petrovich and the Grand Duchess Maria Fedorovna. Dressed in white satin (covered with diamonds worth several million roubles) they danced a polonaise. The dance, however, was not the usual ball music, but a polonaise with chorus, set to Derzhavin's panegyric: 'Thunder of victory, resound! Rejoice, brave Ross! Adorn yourself with the sonorous glory: you have shaken Mohammed.'[2] Several other choral polonaises (alternating with other dances and songs inside the palace and a folk choir and horn music outside) followed in the course of the festive night. All the polonaises had been composed by Joseph Kozlovsky. The man became the composer of the decade.

The opening polonaise not only greatly contributed to the huge success of the splendid event but it consequently also became Russia's first national anthem and defined one of the key semantic points in Russian music of the long nineteenth century. What was it that made the piece so popular and – eventually – so symbolically significant for Russia?

First and foremost, the song was indeed written with talent and taste (Example 11.1). It combined simplicity and individuality in such successful proportions that it was both easy to remember and interesting to sing and to listen to. Naturally, the piece had all the characteristic elements of a European anthem, such as a chordal base to the melody, dotted rhythm and a minimum of intra-syllabic cantillations. Its individuality lies in that despite the regular two-measure melodic module, both periods expand standard eight-measure structure: to ten measures in the couplet and to twelve in the refrain. Since these extensions are made through ascendable sequences and harmonic development, it confers upon them a sound filled with poignant tension and delight, making the climactic ending that follows even more rousing and affirmative. The entire melodic contour is well-balanced and the ascending movement clearly dominates over the descending one.

Following the standard of popular songs, the tune of the refrain surpasses that of the verses in beauty. The beginning of a refrain, where the masculine rhythms of the verses are replaced by cantilena, is usually a crucial point. It is here, where the panegyric to the Empress begins (*Slav'sya sim Yekaterina,.. Slav'sya nezhnaya k nam mat'*, [Be glorified by this, O Catherine, be glorified, thou tender mother of ours!] – the translation is borrowed from Taruskin, 1997:285), that Kozlovsky inserted the

---

2   'Гром победы, раздавайся / Веселися, храбрый росс! / Звучной славой украшайся: /Магомета ты потрёс.'

Example 11.1 Kozlovsky: Polonaise *Grom pobedy razdavaysya*

Example 11.1,   *continued*

sweetest Italian phrase, thrillingly ending on an unprepared seventh of the dominant seventh chord that indeed combined majesty with a feminine grace that suggested the image of that great Empress. One can only imagine how elegantly these melodic gestures would have been amplified by the choreography of the quadrille. Kozlovsky, Derzhavin (in these, alas, far from his best verses) and the cream of her subjects all combined to glorify the valour of the nation in the verses; and its 'Mother' – the Empress – in the refrain. This approach ideally suited the object of praise, Her Majesty; and the entire anthem demonstrated idyllic unity and harmony – directly illustrating the key notion in Lvov's Preface to his *Collection of Russian Folk Songs*, which had appeared just shortly before.

Setting aside its artistic merits and the exceptionally fitting tone of the song itself, the extraordinary historico-political context of the event would probably have elevated any choral panegyric to this same level, and bestowed upon it the imprint of a national anthem. Responding to this marvellous opportunity, however, Kozlovsky had presented more than just a pretty song: it was an entirely new genre hybridizing the Russian choral *vivat* (originating from the Polish *kanty*, the type of official Russian festival hymn of Petrine times) with the polonaise. Not that the polonaise or, as the Russians used to call it, the *Pol'sky* or *Pol'sky tanets* [Polish Dance] was unknown in Russia. On the contrary, it was already popular as early as in the pre-Petrine times and had secured its own place in Russian culture, including its traditional use at festive assemblies and aristocratic weddings. Having been replaced by the minuet in the 1760s, the polonaise then returned to become a main dance at balls and masquerades, having acquired the erotic overtones of the minuet and thus being especially attractive to the young people. There was a special type, the so-called

> … round polonaise that seemed to be invented for intrigues: it continued for several hours, with everybody making the appropriate figure according to their turn, standing in place and with every couple talking about something; of course, such conversations were not philosophical: it was the place where modest and noble love sought sensual and affectionate [expression].[3]

Kozlovsky's novelty was that he took the polonaise out to the masses, almost to the city square (his contemporaries indeed compared the enormous Oval Hall with a square) and created a song for the masses (who just happened also to be noble guests).[4] The pompous style that Sarti had developed in his cantatas was translated

---

3 '… круглый польский, который, кажется, был выдуман для интриг: он продолжался по нескольку часов, все в свою очередь, отделав по условию фигуру, стояли на своих местах, и каждая пара о чем-нибудь перебирала; разумеется, что разговоры такие были не философские: тут скромная и благородная любовь искала торжества чувствительного и нежного' (Dolgoruky, 1890:232, quoted by Voznesensky, MPES, II:380).

4 The palace Tavrichesky indeed acquired the status of a state-public hall: in 1906–17 it was used for the meetings of the State Duma and in the Soviet period for the meetings of the Communist Party elite.

by Kozlovsky into a more attractive, democratic, semantically appropriate and quite native format. Moreover, because Kozlovsky was also a young military officer, it was as if he had personally brought straight from the battle–field the masculine aura of a victor, expressing the euphoria of the Russian army.

The song appeared a year before the *Marseillaise*, but this kind of anthem had only just begun to come into fashion (after 1789). Music that was march-like in character was becoming increasingly attractive, although minuet or *kanty* rhythms, despite becoming old-fashioned, were still much loved. Against this background the polonaise, as a hybrid of three-beat dances (minuet, sarabanda), with its energetic dotted rhythmic patterns of a march, not only gained a firm hold on the Russian soil but also acquired the additional element of noble supremacy that even the march did not possess. A march usually has a weak dotted beat, making its tread heavy and straight, whereas a polonaise has a strong dotted beat with two following weak beats to accumulate energy for the next strong one, suggestive of the haughty prancing comportment of the eighteenth-century horseback statues of great men. The polonaise surpassed the march in both power and grandeur. As Taruskin noted in his analysis of the specific significance of the polonaise in nineteenth-century Russian music, 'it often replaced the march where a specific overtone of official pomp was wanted' (1997:284). Joseph Kozlovsky, who had invented this 'specific overtone', was the right man at the right moment and in the right place, fortuitously defining the imprint of the new Russian Empire style.

This Polish officer (1757–1831) who had served in the Russian army from 1786–91 and was noticed and retained by Prince Potemkin, came from noble Byelorussian stock and happened to be a nephew of Vasily Trutovsky (Dadiomova, 2001:120). Receiving his early musical training in Warsaw, during the mid-1770s to mid-1780s, he had acquired experience in various private Byelorussian cappellas, including that of Mikhail Kazimir Ogiński (1728–1800) in Slonim, the Polish ambassador in Russia, who had set the tone of St Petersburg musical life through initiating the tradition of house concerts. Having far-reaching connections in the European musical world, he was among those who inspired Haydn to compose *The Creation* (Ciechanowiecki, 1961). In Slonim, among other duties, Kozlovsky taught piano to Ogiński's nephew – Mikhail Kleofas Ogiński (1765–1833), a future top-ranking Polish political figure and composer.

In some ways Kozlovsky's path in Russian music was similar to that of Ernst Wanzhura. Both these noblemen had begun their careers in the military and then gone on to devote their lives to music, always signing their works 'Amateur'. Both appeared in St Petersburg among the entourage of their commanders-in-chief, the Empress Catherine's influential favourites. They were well educated, flexible and talented musicians who contributed to various genres and repertoires. Wanzhura was also Kozlovsky's first publisher (in his *Journal de misique*).

Kozlovsky was popular not only for his polonaises (of various kinds: choral, orchestral and piano), but also for his romances and *rossiyskie pesni*, his Requiem to the King of Poland Stanislas-Augustus, opera, choral concertos *a cappella*, and later – especially in the 1800s – music for numerous dramatic spectacles, full of delicate early romantic idioms. However, 'Kozlovsky's great specialty was polonaise writing;

indeed, he seemed to be able to turn anything he touched into polonaises, including themes from popular quintets by Pleyel, even Mozart arias' (Taruskin, 1997:282). Nor did he have any problem in creating polonaises out of various songs, even from those Russian protracted ones known for their specifically free rhythm. This 'polonaisical' thinking that Kozlovsky inculcated in Russian music at the climactic point of eighteenth-century Russian imperial power is worth briefly tracing in its historical perspective.

In the Tchaikovsky chapter of his book *Defining Russia Musically*, Taruskin paid special attention to the genre of the polonaise, showing how in Russian music – in its functional and semantic senses – it had served as a symbol of Russian imperialism. Referring mostly to Tchaikovsky, the grandeur of whose polonaises is only comparable with Chopin's, Taruskin also offered a revealing example: the Introduction from Borodin's *Prince Igor*, where the thirteenth-century Rus'ian Prince calls his men to arms for a predatory invasion campaign ('Brothers, let us sit upon our swift steed and behold the blue sea!'), was written as an heroic polonaise (1997:289). What is amazing here is not that Borodin did this, but that both contemporaneous and future listeners took it as natural, not at all disturbed by this historic-generic incongruity. There could hardly have been more eloquent evidence of music in all its spontaneity defining Russia.

The eighteenth-century Prince Potemkin had solved the geopolitical problem faced by all the ancient Rus'ian princes and gained access to the Black Sea (temporarily at least). It was not by chance that Catherine used Russian history for justification of her politics, and her opera *The Early Reign of Oleg* was an attempt to turn historical fact into a fact of national culture, which went hand in hand with the revelation of the Rus'ian chronicles in the late 1780s and shortly after, 'miraculously', also the 'finding' of the epic, *The Lay of Igor's Host*. (Had Catherine lived longer – the opera *Prince Igor* would probably have been composed somewhere in the late 1790s, by Kozlovsky.) Both the Rus'ian epic works and the polonaise were thus founded in the early 1790s as cornerstone symbols of a national artistic identity.

It is little wonder therefore, that Kozlovsky's triumphal polonaise was probably what had subconsciously prompted Borodin to use it for a Russian epic work and for his listeners to accept it as natural. Begun in 1869, his work on the opera *Prince Igor* gained momentum in 1875 and its best fragments were premièred in 1879, shortly after the end of the last Russian-Turkish war (1877–8). The war was the last indeed, the sixth in the series in the eighteenth to nineteenth centuries, very much like the series of anti-Byzantium campaigns led by Prince Oleg and Prince Igor (a different one) in the ninth-tenth centuries.

While the late nineteenth-century Russian polonaises fit Taruskin's conception perfectly, the question remains as to what it is about Chopin's polonaises that, as we usually know and understand them, condemn the Russian Empire rather than glorify it? Taruskin had answered this earlier, defining Chopin's music as being from the "other side" of the Russian Empire (Taruskin, 1984:331). This 'other side', however, had in fact already appeared much earlier than Chopin's self-exile from Poland.

Example 11.2   Oginsky: Polonaise *Les adieux*, **section 1**

As the French Revolution progressed, its danger to the European monarchies and to Catherine II became more obvious. In contrast to her Western counterparts, Catherine was only too familiar with what a Russian peasant uprising was like, having experienced one in the early 1770s. She became the initiator of an anti-revolutionary coalition, attempting to unite England, Sweden, Austria and Prussia. While Catherine's closest allies fell – the kings of Austria and Sweden (Leopold II was possibly poisoned and Gustav III was shot in March 1792), England and Prussia – the main Russian adversaries in the 1780s – remained difficult to enlist. One of the conditions set by Prussia for joining the coalition was a second division of Poland between Russia and Prussia. In January 1793 the alliance was signed. This reinforced the Polish movement for national liberation (which had grown intensively during the 1780s, after the first partition of Poland) and in spring 1794 the powerful Polish peasant uprising began, headed by Tadeush Kostyushko. Kozlovsky once again enlisted in the Russian army, this time participating in suppression of the rebellion. On the other side of the border, his student and friend Mikhail Kleofas Ogiński fought for the liberty of his nation (Dadiomova, 2001:120). Both Byelorussian officers, Kozlovsky and Ogiński, wrote polonaises (along with other pieces) but while the one glorified the Russian Empire, the other strove to elevate the spirits of the Polish insurgents while the revolt was underway (indeed much like Claude-Joseph Rouget de Lisle), and then mourned his conquered homeland when the revolt was suppressed. Following the defeat, Ogiński emigrated to Italy. Ironically, his *Les adieux* (Example 11.2), whose creation was

Example 11.3   Alexandrov: *Svyashchennaya voyna*

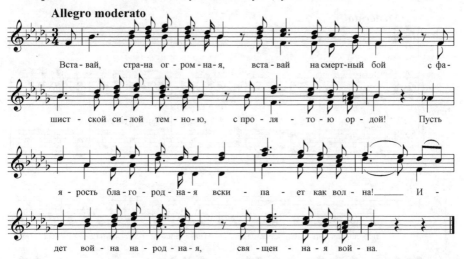

associated with his flight from Poland (similar to Chopin's 'Revolutionary' étude written in Stuttgart on his way to Paris), remained the most popular salon piece in Russian society until the middle of the twentieth century. Today it is the national anthem of Byelorussia, commemorating Mikhail Kleofas Ogiński as its national hero, although few people actually know who Ogiński was, or the circumstances that had inspired this piece. They simply love *polonez Oginskogo* for its ultimate nostalgia and dignity. Thus, Russian society, itself suffering from Russian imperialism, identified with its counterpart on the other side of the border.

In June 1941, exactly 150 years after Kozlovsky's composition, this ambiguity of the polonaise genre in its Russian context displayed itself once more, thus closing the long nineteenth century in Russian music. Two final Russian polonaises (to the best of my knowledge) and again as choral songs, were written within a month, at the beginning of Hitler's invasion of the Soviet Union. This appears to have been an unconscious use of the polonaise rhythm by both composers, who were writing patriotic songs for the masses. The first was 'Svyashchennaya voyna' [The Sacred War], composed by Alexander Vasilievich Alexandrov, chief choirmaster of the Red Army, and Vasily Lebedev-Kumach, the official Soviet poet. This song was traditionally considered by Russian scholars (probably influenced by the film *My zhdem vas s pobedoy* in which the soldiers' march is accompanied by this song) as a unique three-beat march[5] (Example 11.3). The polonaise that followed was Shostakovich's 'Klyatva Narodnomu Kommissaru' [Oath to the People's

---

5   See M.G. Rytsareva, 'Nepodvlastnost' somneniyu v pobede', in *Sovetskaya muzyka*, 1986, 5:4–6.

Example 11.4   Shostakovich: *Velikiy den' nastal* (*Klyatva*)

Commissar],[6] (Example 11.4) – a totally forced work, in contrast to Alexandrov's truly great song that became the unofficial anthem of the Great Patriotic War and has remained its emblem for at least two post-war generations. The problem is that if we are to accept Taruskin's point that the polonaise conveys the spirit of the Russian Empire, this song, with its particular pain and dignity, does not fit: both its socio-political meaning and its function relate to defending the country and not to

---

6   In the post-Stalin era the song was retitled 'Velikiy den' nastal' [Great day arrived], retaining only the word 'Klyatva' [Oath] as a subtitle.

aggression. It is here that the modern historical debates over the pre-war situation cast new light on the essence of the song.

The Molotov-Ribbentrop pact (23 August 1939) was one of the tactical traps designed by Hitler in Europe. Giving Stalin East Poland and the Baltic, he provoked the latter into using Poland as a bridge-head for an attack. Indeed, Stalin duly deconstructed his defensive fortifications along the previous border and transferred them to the west, making all the available weaponry directed toward attack and absolutely unready for defence. This allowed the Nazi forces to destroy the entire Russian army there within the first few hours of the war, thus leaving the Russian frontier unguarded. There is still fierce discussion today over Stalin's intent to attack, which was not documented but clearly expressed in action.[7]

The discussions focus on interpretation of these actions: the question of why, if Stalin was ready to attack, he did not do so – has as one possible answer the suggestion that he could not have begun his attack without first being sure of Churchill's support and of the situation in the Balkans. While he waited for clarification, Hitler outmanoeuvred him. It was not, thus, a matter of Stalin's high ideological principles: he had never shown hesitation in matters of invasion or usurpation – be it Finland, Eastern Poland, Bessarabia or the Baltic countries – in the name of 'liberation'. The inevitable war with Nazi Germany would thus be called a defensive and patriotic one no matter on whose territory (inside or outside the Soviet frontiers) it took place. Moving the state borders westward from 1939 to 1940 of course implied a war on foreign territory. From this perspective, the occupation of other countries was fully compatible with the concept of a defensive war.

Legend has it that the song was broadcasted throughout the country on the second day of the war, which broke out on 22 June 1941. Generations have believed this, considering the extraordinary emotional and psychological tension of the moment and that technically more complicated things were achieved within a single day or night in that era of dictatorship. Yury Biryukov, a researcher of patriotic Soviet songs, offers more precise dates: 24 June – publication of the lyrics by Lebedev-Kumach in the newspapers 'Krasnaya zvezda' and 'Izvestia'; 27 June – publication of the song with music by Matvey Blanter (composer of the legendary song 'Katyusha') and information in 'Pravda' about ongoing rehearsals of Alexandrov's song in the Central House of the Red Army; and 30 June – the song was authorized for publication in sheet format by Muzgiz (the State Publishing House for Music).[8]

Today, however, in the stream of total demythologization of many of Stalin's disinformation actions, the official legend of this song has lost its credibility. The anti-legend, based on two premises, has it that the song had been written before the war. The first premise is that the lyrics (slightly differing) were written in 1916 by Alexander Adolfovich Bode, a teacher of the Rybinsk gymnasium, who then

---

7   See Victor Suvorov, *Ledokol*. Moscow, 1990; Gabriel Gorodetsky, *Mif Ledokola*. Moscow, 1996.

8   See Yury Biryukov, *Pesni, opalennye voynoy*. Moscow: Voennoe izdatel'stvo, 1984: 195.

gave them to Lebedev-Kumach in 1937 (or 1941).[9] The second premise is that if (and most probably) the Soviet attack on Germany from Polish territory had been planned in advance, this would also have been supported by the official propaganda, of which the song *Svyashchennaya voyna* would have been a necessary element. At the present time, however, there are already too many speculations, although what seems to ring true is that the aggressive rhythm of a classic Russian polonaise as a morpheme of the Russian Empire style did not contradict the defensive spirit of the song in the perception of Soviet society.

Marseillaise and Russian Monarchs

Returning to the 1790s, Catherine II, though depicted by her contemporaries as a non-musical person, was highly sensitive when it came to the ideological role of music. Sergei Nikolaevich Glinka, who had translated the *Marseillaise* into Russian, recollected in his *Notes*:

> Having read in the newspaper about the miraculous effect that the Marseille march had produced on the young French militia, she ordered the piece played by the full orchestra at the Hermitage theatre; the more attentively she listened, the more her face changed; her eyes burned, she was beside herself and suddenly, waving her hand, she exclaimed: 'enough, enough'![10]

Although the writer does not date the event, his mention of a newspaper indicates that the above episode could have taken place relatively soon after the appearance of the song, in April 1792. It was eventually put on the list of banned works, which included those forbidden to import from abroad. This, however, did not prevent the illegal spread of the song in Russia, for which several members of Lvov's and Radishchev's circles were responsible. First and foremost were the publishers Johann Karl Schnoor and Johann Gerstenberg, whom Hässler had converted to musical publishing at about that time (both mentioned in Chapter 9). Despite the autonomous activities of these two publishers, they related similarly to the numerous works by Fedor Vasilievich Karzhavin (1745–1812), which they published under dozens of pseudonyms.[11]

---

9   The polemics regarding the attribution of the lyrics are presented on two Russian websites: http://www.aif.ru/online/longliver/27/2101 and http://www.litrossia.ru/litrossia/viewitem?item_id=1730.

10   Прочитав в ведомостях о чудесном действии Марсельского марша над молодым французским войском, она (Екатерина) приказала полному оркестру играть этот марш в Эрмитажном театре; чем больше вслушивалась в эти звуки, тем более изменялось ея лицо; глаза ея пылали, она была вне себя и вдруг, махнув рукою, вскричала: 'полно, полно! (Sergei Glinka, *Zapiski*. St Petersburg, 1895:60; quoted by Rapatskaya, 1975a:57).

11   Valery I. Rabinovich, *Revolyutsionny prosvetitel' F.V. Karzhavin*. Trudy GMPI im. Gnesinykh, vol. V, Moscow, 1966.

This fabled Russian personality was an Enlightenment writer and revolutionary, a fighter against slavery, a traveller, participant in the Revolutionary War and possibly also a participant in the storming of the Bastille, a theoretician of architecture, philology and ethnography, and an unusual graphic artist. His papers contain a manuscript copy of the *Marseillaise* alongside his own anti-monarchy epigram on the 'corrupted Nymph', whom his contemporaries obviously identified with the Empress.

Another channel that popularized the *Marseillaise* was through its circulation in Russian society in the innocent form of a piano piece. Thus, *Marche des Marseillois avec des Variations Arraggée par L.C. Charpentier Organiste de l'Eglise de Paris* could be found under the same cover as sonatas by I. Pleyel and polonaises and pieces like *Air tiré de l'opera Nina avec Variations pour le Clavecin ou Piano Forte* by the Russian amateur composer Prince Parfeny d'Engalitschew, as well as works by several contemporaneous European composers (Rapatskaya, 1975a:53–4).

Finally, it was even advertised in the newspaper, showing a Karzhavin-like impertinence and ingenuity in circumventing the censor. The second *Supplement du Catalogue de Livres de musique quise vendent chez I.D. Gerstenberg et Comp.* published in 1796 concomitantly with the supplement to the *Magazine for Universally Useful Knowledge and Inventions with the addition of a Journal of Mode, Colourful Drawings and Music* mentioned the following pieces:

Song by the grave of Marie Antoinette, by Schmidt for pianoforte – 1 r. 50 kop.
Drinking song in the finest style – 35 kop.
Parody on the Marseilles' March – 45 kop.

The publication apparently caused no problems, whether due to lack of vigilance on the part of the Empress at the very end of her reign (when she was being troubled by far more serious problems), or to the uncertainty in the air at the beginning of the rule of Paul I.

The tension that had surrounded the Russian establishment after the French revolution increased, reaching a climax when Paul I ascended the throne (7 November 1796) and began to terrorize society with his super-Prussian discipline. It would be hard to list all the drastic contrasts between the rules of the Mother and the Son. Highly critical of his mother's criteria and style, he had spent many years planning his own conception of what the Russian State should be. Oriented on the Prussian model of economy and discipline, he believed that the necessary reforms could put the Russian house in order and save the Empire from corruption and self-destruction. Having suffered from being long kept by his mother at a safe distance from all State affairs, he now attempted to implement his reforms more quickly than was feasible (if at all), and using highly radical methods. In contrast to Catherine II, however, he unfortunately underestimated the role of the gentry as the mainstay of the monarchy. Opposing this sector of society cost him his life after only four years of tragic reign.

One of the most characteristic and disastrous episodes took place in Moscow, where the new Music Academy (only recently established, 1800) was almost immediately closed by the order of Paul I. Its members were accused of Jacobinism in that they performed songs 'insulting [His] Majesty'. Three of its foreign members were sentenced to whipping and exile to Siberia for this political crime. Among them was the Italian, Becker, who claimed that 'he had been forced to copy some French song, and since his French was bad, somebody had dictated it to him and he did not remember its content'. All the Academy's papers and music were sealed up in three boxes and taken away by the Secret Service. Most of the Academy members were of the Moscow nobility. The board of directors included Myatlev, Prince Dolgorukov, Fedor Saltykov, Afrosimov and Karamzin, while the principal members were Yushkov, Bobarykin, Zholobov, Danilov, Zhuravlev, Yudin, Bakhmetev, Khitrov, Nelidov and Akulov (Rapatskaya, 1975a:64–5). At the inquiries, some of the members denied any performance of music at the Academy evenings, while others claimed that the only music performed was played by serf musicians belonging to the Moscow gentry. It seems, however, that the Emperor's suspicions were not ungrounded. He might have been aware of the mood of sympathy toward the French Revolution shared by some of the aristocratic intelligentsia; it eventually became known that Karamzin had wept when he heard about the execution of Robespierre. Prince Ivan Mikhaylovich Dolgoruky wrote later that: 'The French revolution was at the peak of its strength... I, as an enthusiast, was captured by the sophisms of monsignors philosophers and was not indifferent toward their successes.'[12]

While Catherine II had only used extreme measures of persecution and censorship in special cases, seeking to maintain the image of an enlightened monarch, she worked hard to ensure her people's obedience as an integral part of the national tradition and culture. Music and musicians played an important part in this, as can be seen from her operatic productions and encouragement of the Trutovsky-Lvov-Prach folkloristic path and of nationalist composers. Paul I did not waste his time on such propaganda, preferring rather more direct methods like the above-mentioned dismantling of the Music Academy or introducing censorship into church music (see Chapter 14).

In contrast, music composed purely for entertainment does not seem to have experienced any political pressure. We can trace the interesting path of such music through two kinds of song collections that had developed by the end of the century. The first, that of western-secular-urban oriented music, had begun with Teplov's *Rossiyskaya pesnya* and continued in Meyer's collections in the 1780s; its development progressed further with the relatively new genre of French romance in works by Bortniansky, Kozlovsky and such amateurs as Princess Natalie de Kurakin.[13]

---

12 'Революция французская была в самой пущей своей силе... я как энтузиаст, пленялся софизмами гг. философов и не равнодушен был к их успехам' (Dolgoruky, 1890:165).

13 There is one edition: *Huit romances, composées et arrangées puor le harpe, par la princesse Natalie de Kourakin.* A St.-Pétersbourg, de l'imprimerie de Breitkopf, en 1795.

The second kind was originally established by Chulkov's collection of song texts. Embracing various genres, this music reflected the naturally eclectic repertory of a wide stratum of Russian urban society. A development in this direction had already begun in the songbooks of Novikov and Popov and in the 1790–92 editions of the Schnoor-Polezaev collection. Finally, between 1797 and 1799 the three-volume *Pesennik, ili Polnoe sobranie starykh i novykh Rossiyskikh narodnykh i protchikh pesen dlya fortepiano, sobrannykh izdatelyami* [Songbook, or Complete Collection of Ancient and New Russian Folk and Other Songs for Piano, Collected by the Editors] appeared in print. The publishers Gerstenberg and Dittmar, partly using material from other collections (about thirty songs were taken unchanged from the Schnoor-Polezaev collection (1792), see Volman, 1957:152–5; Rapatskaya, 1975b:198–99) initiated a new editorial policy. Tracing the history of this collection, Lobanov marked the moment when the editors addressed the readers from the pages of their *Karmannaya kniga dlya lyubiteley muzyki na 1795 god* [Pocket Book for Music Lovers for 1795] with the request to send them 'original Russian musical compositions and the newest, *not yet published simple folk songs* for the purpose of their publication in their annual volume and afterwards in the separate edition' (quoted in Lobanov, MPES, II:239). The following year, they thanked those who had sent them material and announced that they were continuing the work.

The edition included the largest number of romance-like songs compared to previous publications, and many newly transcribed folk songs. In his analysis of the contents of the collection, Lobanov noted the amazing absence of official-patriotic songs and, in contrast, the presence of a folk song dedicated to Suvorov, who had continued to remain a folk hero despite his official disgrace and exile during the rule of Paul I.

Russian Freemasonry and Music

Russian Freemasonry, only vaguely rooted in Peter I's times (his own possible initiation may have taken place during his European voyages), was officially established by 1770. Later 'Russian Freemasonry gained European status when the Order of Royal York in Berlin, centre of rational English Freemasonry in Germany, granted Elagin a formal charter or patent for a Directorial or Grand Provincial Lodge to work in accordance with the Ancient English System'.[14] Consequently, it bore many traits of the English tradition. There were, however, numerous lodges and trends, representing different European connections and influences. As elsewhere, music played a fairly large role in their activities, both as an element of ritual (hymns, songs, glees, cantatas) and in public doings promoting the ideas of the Enlightenment. Although eighteenth-century Russian music and musical life in connection with the Freemasons still require much research, it is clear that the Freemasons' contribution

---

14 See Lauren G. Leighton, The Esoteric Tradition in Russian Romantic Literature: Decembrism and Freemasonry. The Pennsylvania State University Press, 1994: 26. According to other versions Russian Freemasonry had been established by the English general, the Provincial Grand Master James Keith in 1741.

to cultivating high-quality audiences with their own special reverence for music in the concert hall – a reverence still felt today – was crucial.

Since most of the Russian aristocracy and intellectuals (including Paul I) were both Freemasons and patrons of music, theatre, literature and the arts, it is clear that musical activities, as both a ritual part of Masonic meetings and of public concert life, were closely interlaced. It could not have been otherwise for the simple reason that on the whole they comprised the same milieu and were the same organizers and the same musicians; only the public arena differed somewhat in that female presence was encouraged. To give only one example of a leading Masonic functionary, Ivan Perfilievich Yelagin was also a key figure in the musical life of the court.

The Russian Freemasons seem to have maintained a general practice of having professional musicians as members of the lodges (on a lower hierarchical level) in order not to have to pay them for ritual performances. As early as 1756 the Lodge 'zum Verschweigenheit' [The Lodge of Modesty] was formed from the cream of the aristocracy, intellectuals and military officers, totalling thirty-five members among whom were Roman Vorontsov, Mikhail Dashkov, Mikhail Shcherbatov, the three Golitsyn brothers, Alexander Sumarokov and others, as well as several professional musicians. It is also known that later, in the 1780s, such court Italian singers as Gaetano di Pauli and Lorenzo Canobbio were initiated into the lodge 'Urania', whose protocols also feature the name of Vasily Pashkevich (Porfirieva, MPES, II:193). The general scenario thus seems to have been one of mutual interests: musicians performed gratis at the lodge meetings (even paying an annual membership fee) in exchange for favours by the upper Masonic echelon in the form of having private concerts obtained for them or using their connections to gain them employment, and so on. A similar set-up could be found during Soviet times, when those musicians who performed the works of the Composers' Union elite enjoyed its patronage in all other forms of their activity.

In this connection, one interesting endeavour is that of the St Petersburg New Musical Club (or Musical Society). This used to be interpreted – fairly truly – as simply a public enterprise, indicating the growing musical culture and the penetration of Enlightenment ideas into the wider circles of the capital's population. It is worth considering, however, its history, rules and membership from the Masonic angle, comparing them for example with the English tradition.[15] To begin with, the New Musical Club continued the activity of the previous Musical Club, which had existed from 1772–77 (coincidently founded in the same year that Yelagin had become the Provincial Grand Master of the English Grand Lodge in Russia). The Rules of the first club remain unknown, but those of the new one accord with the main Masonic principles:

1 THE SOLIDITY OF THE SOCIETY
having been established, thus unarguably demands that the selection of its members must be guided by the main object of the society, namely to eliminate as much as possible

---

15 See Simon McVeigh, 'Freemasonry and Musical Life in London in the Late Eighteenth Century', in *Music in Eighteenth-Century Britain*, ed. David Wyn Jones. Aldershot: Ashgate, 2000:72–100.

any inequality in wealth and difference in thoughts in order to prevent any kind of inconvenience that could be caused by such. Thus, based on this rule, our prime concern will be not to admit people whose behaviour or way of life would be reprehensible to our society.

2 DECENCY DEMANDS

that one observes order and respectable behaviour. One should avoid drunkenness, expressing nonrespectable and caustic comments and mockery, noise and guffaw, which constitute a source for quarrels and upsets. If, nevertheless, some of the members contravene this, then the senior associates present should reprimand them and fine them to give to the poor upon a first offence and to warn them that they will be excluded from the Society should they repeat it. Those who express profanities or even come to blows will be excluded immediately.

3 MUSIC COMPRISES THE MAIN OBJECT

of our Society, for which the large hall is allotted. Concerts will be played twice a week, i.e. on Wednesdays and Saturdays and will begin at 6 p.m. and end at 9 p.m. On this occasion each member is allowed once a week to bring one female member of his family.

4 IN WINTERTIME THE SOCIETY WILL

give masquerades or balls once a month. However, it is not prohibited for the members to gather every day and to entertain themselves until midnight playing billiards, cards and other games, excluding those banned. Those who do not leave the place at the proper time will pay a fine to the treasurer to be given to the poor, for each additional quarter of an hour overstayed.[16]

---

16 1: твердость учреждаемого общества не отменно требует того, чтоб при выборе членов, долженствующих оное составлять, иметь главным предметом, удалять елико возможно неравенство состояний и разнообразие мыслей, для предупреждения всем могущим от того возродиться неустройствам. И так основываясь на сем правиле, первый при выборе сочленов наших предмет да будет тот, чтоб не принимать таковых, которых поведение и образ жизни могли бы быть предосудительны обществу нашему. 2: благопристойность требует того, чтоб в собраниях соблюдать хороший порядок и добропорядочное поведение: И так надлежит убегать в оных пьянства, произношения неблагопристойных и язвительных речей и насмешек, шума и хохотания, яко единых источников всякого роду ссор и неустройств. Если паче чаяния кто из членов в противность сего поступит, то старшины, кои при том будут, должны, учиня ему за то выговор, наложить в первый раз денежную пень для казны убогих, извещая его при том, что если в другой раз равному подвергнется преступлению, то из Общества выключен быть имеет. Кто из сочленов произнесет бранные слова или дойдет даже до драки, имеет быть тотчас выключен из Общества. 3: музыка составляет главный предмет Общества нашего: большая зала назначена для оной. Концерт будут играть два раза в неделю, т.е. по средам и по субботам, и начнется в 6 по полудни, а кончится в 9 часов. К сему случаю позволяется каждому члену приводить раз в неделю одну даму из фамилии своей. 4: в зимнее время общество станет давать маскерады или балы раз в месяц. Впрочем не возбраняется членам собираться ежедневно и забавляться до первого часа по полуночи играм в биллиард, в карты и прочими, исключая запрещенных игр. Кто же напротив того

The Rules of the Society indicate that it was rather a Musical *Club* than a *Musical* Club and that the principles it preached could be reasonably related to the Freemasons movement. The opening statement 'to eliminate as much as possible any inequality in wealth and difference in thoughts' points to a fraternity that was one of the cornerstones of Freemasonry. The second paragraph, imposing a 'fine to be given to the poor', implies charity as one of the organizers' vital concerns.

The third paragraph contains two crucial Masonic features. One is music ('Music comprises the main object of our Society'), which constituted the main medium of spiritual interaction both among the members themselves, between them and the sublime and between them and outside society. The special permission to bring a female relation – 'On this occasion each member is allowed once a week to bring one female member of his family' – refers to the Masonic codes, which did not admit women, to the latter's regret. It is clear from this that only male addressees existed for the Masonic organizers. If concerts were to be held twice a week and a female family member could attend only once a week, this suggests that the average ratio was two male attendees to one female. The limited admission of women to the Club concerts only (and not to any of the other forms of activity) also shows that despite the partly open character of the Society, its organizers were still mainly oriented toward the basic principles of the Masonic lodges.

The easiest way to trace any direct links between the Musical Club and St Petersburg Masonry would be through a comparison of their membership lists, but this must remain for future research. However, the assuredly famous names of such members as Count Alexander Stroganov, the kapellmeister Dmitry Bortniansky and the actor Ivan Dmitrevsky, who are known to have been associated with Masonic activities, also suggest a certain Masonic orientation of the Society. On the other hand, by the end of the century so many people had become involved in Freemasonry and, in parallel, musical culture had developed so greatly, that the two streams became virtually inseparable and overlap between them were inevitable. The cult of Haydn should also be related to the same Masonic trend. His works were sent to Russia from Vienna by Prince Dmitry Mikhaylovich Golitsyn immediately upon their composition. Haydn's *The Creation* also became the focus of special attention by Russian Freemasons from its very conception, for which its connections to Alexander Radishchev, and possibly also Chancellor Roman Vorontsov, deserve examination (Klimovitsky, MPES, I:214–26; Shteinpress, 1970); as does the translation of its text by Nikolai Karamzin for its Russian edition and première in 1802. The latter commemorated the inauguration of the St Petersburg Philharmonic Society, maintained by the same people (primarily Baron Alexander Alexandrovich Rall) who had previously been behind the Musical Club.

The musical repertoire of the lodge meetings, whose collections have recently been studied by Porfirieva, reveal quite an extensive stock of songs, hymns and glees, sometimes in the typically Russian style of panegyric *kanty* – especially the earlier

из сочленов не выедет в означенный час, тот да заплатит в казну убогих предписанный штраф за каждый лишний четверть часа (quoted by Findeizen 1928, II:162–3).

ones. The texts often refer to current events in the lodges, associated with the absence or return of some of its members or news concerning interaction between the lodges or branches of the same lodge and so on. There were also lodges whose membership comprised people of different nationalities or of specific communities like German, French or English. These also printed their own musical collections, especially the Germans (Porfirieva, MPES, II:192–4).

Three pieces that were widely known as Masonic hymns belong to Bortniansky: *Kol' slaven nash Gospod' v Sione* on the Moscow Rosicrucian Lodge member Mikhail Kheraskov's text, *Predvechny i Neobkhodimy*, setting Yuriy Neledinsky-Meletsky's lyrics; and *Gimn spasitelyu* on Dmitry Ivanovich Khvostov's verses. The first is a sweet and elegant, almost waltz-like, three-beat song (not without reference to *kanty*). It had numerous contrafactums in the eighteenth century, enjoyed the greatest possible popularity in nineteenth-century Russian society and was curiously revived in a twentieth-century hymn-like song *Rodina slyshit* by Shostakovich (Examples 11.5a, b). The second and the third were probably written in the early nineteenth century. They are less interesting, serious, march-like hymns, whose elements precisely reflect the norms of the genre, but they lack the specific charm of some of Bortniansky's other popular tunes.

Example. 11.5 (a) Bortniansky: *Kol' slaven nash Gospod' v Sione*

Example 11.5 (b) Shostakovich: *Rodina slyshit*

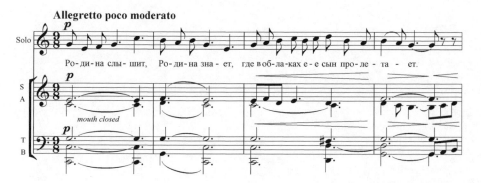

The question of whether Bortniansky belonged to the St Petersburg Freemasonry is unclear. Despite his obvious involvement or contribution to the Masonic movement and his constant direct contacts and connections with its most notable members, his own membership has as yet to be confirmed by documents. At least in the post-Napoleonic war years, when the secret societies were banned, those documents confirming the loyalty of various state officials do not contain any mention of Bortniansky as belonging to them.[17]

17　*Delo o dostavlenii A.A. Arakcheevu svedeniy o sluzhbe direktora Pridvornoy pevcheskoy kapelly D.S. Bortnianskogo*. RGIA, f 319, op 1, 1817.

Chapter 12

Master and Serf

The style and atmosphere of late eighteenth-century Russian musical life cannot be understood without including the role of serf musicians. The following exemplary announcements from the newspaper *Moskovskie vedomosti* provide some idea of their importance:

On sale is a very good musician who plays the viola in instrumental music and the bassoon in brass music; he is also a good footman, of a good height, twenty years old; price 1200 roubles.

On sale 12 or 13 musicians, constituting vocal and instrumental ensembles, playing [Russian] horns.

Looking for the position of *Kapellmeister* of wind and instrumental music, skilful chef and gardener... can come [to the address]...

The house of His Excellency major-general Zagryazhsky requires a singer, third or second bassist possessing a good vocal octave ...[1]

A runaway: the musician Vasily, son of Osip Baboshin, 20 years old. Distinguishing signs: height 2 arshins 5 vershoks, face clean, brown eyes, light-brown hair, slight moustache and beard ... He possess a flûte traversière made of black wood with the trade-mark of master Klein.

For those who would like to take four boys singers... three of whom are altos and one – descant, twenty roubles annually for each of them...

On sale a musician playing violin and singing bass, he is also a good doctor's assistant; with his wife, who is suitable for any job. Both are young people.[2]

---

1   'A good octave' probably meant possessing the lowest octave within his range, or so-called 'basso-octavist' (profundo) with the range (A_1) B_1 – a (c^1) typical for old Russian choirs.

2   Продается очень хороший музыкант и певчий, который в инструментальной музыке играет на альте, а в духовой на фаготе, он же и хороший лакей, немалого росту, от роду ему 20 лет, цена 1200 руб... (MV 1791, no 56:857). Продается музыкантов 12 или 13 человек составляющих вокальную и инструментальную музыку, играющих на рогах (MV 1794 no 3:53). Желающие приняться капельмейстер для содержания духовой и инструментальной музыки, искусный повар и садовник... могут явиться [по адресу]... (MV 1794, no 3:64). Потребен в дом Его Превосходительства генерал-

At the Court of Count Sheremetev

The legendary wealth of the eighteenth-century Russian aristocracy was accumulated mainly from the results of serf labour. The latter provided not only the income for the luxurious lifestyle of the former, including their consumption of the arts, but often also the arts themselves. Serf participation in and contribution to Russian musical culture was immense, and was associated first and foremost with horn and symphony orchestras, choirs and theatrical troupes. A vast number of high quality serf musicians was particularly to be found in the domains of Count Nikolai Petrovich Sheremetev (1751–1809),[3] who built up an entire 'industry', investing in it means that no State body could have managed.

The descendent of an ancient boyar family, the Count was the richest landowner in Russia and his property, including over 200,000 serfs, was even larger than that of the Emperor himself. Emulating the Imperial court, he developed all the facets of contemporary music-performing institutions, with the only difference being that it was mostly serfs who were in his service, rather than the free men who were employed by the Imperial court. Echoing the style of the Imperial court in the estate culture (the so-called *usadebnaya kul'tura*) Count Sheremetev and other wealthy aristocrats (albeit usually more modestly) adapted this style into more domestic and democratic forms and disseminated it throughout Russia, with Moscow remaining its principle centre.

Among the numerous residences owned by the Count the most well known are those in the Moscow suburbs of Ostankino and Kuskovo, as well as the Fountain House in St Petersburg. Both of the Moscow palaces were designed in the tradition of so-called 'Russian classicism'. Their architecture, interiors and external design are definitely recognizable as European, but doubly acculturated, through both the Petersburgian court culture and its adaptation by the Muscovite serf artisans. Upon returning from his studies abroad (in 1773), the young Count started to manage his father's theatre, originally built as a nod to fashion, and swiftly developed it into a grand institution, following both the increasing public fondness for theatre and his own predilection. The two hundred or so actors together with all the other

---

майора Загряжского певчий бассист третий или вторый, имеющий хорошую октаву своего голоса... (MV 1794, no 7:171). Бежал музыкант Василий Осипов сын Бабошин, от роду ему 20 лет. Приметы оного: росту 2 аршина 5 вершков, лицем чист, глаза карие, волосы темно–русые, ус и борода пробиваются... При нем флейт-траверс черного дерева с клеймом мастера Клейна (MV 1794, no 41:928). Желающие взять 4-х мальчиков певчих... из коих 3 альта и дишкант, с заплатою господину их за каждого по 20 рублей в год... (MV 1794, no 98:1894). Продается музыкант , который играет на скрипке и поет баса, он же хороший подлекарь, с женою, которая способна ко всяким должностям. Оба люди молодые (MV 1795, no 3:57).

    3   There are two variants of the name: Sheremetev and Sheremet'yev (with the Russian 'ь'). According to tradition, the former variant relates to the Count's family and the latter to their serfs.

Figure 12.1 The Ostankino palace of Count Nikolai Petrovich Sheremetev, Italian hall

theatrical staff reached a total of one thousand people. The Kuskovo residence had several theatre houses: the old 'closed' one; the new one; and a third theatre in the open air, grassed over and constituting part of the garden. He also had two theatres in Moscow (one on Nikol'skaya Street and another – purchased from Talyzins – on Vozdvizhenka Street) as well as one at his hunting dacha in Markovo. Finally, at the climax of this theatremania, the splendid Palace-Theatre was built in Ostankino in 1792–7 (designed by the serf architect Pavel Argunov). After the revolution this was turned into the Museum of Serf Arts. (Today a Moscow television tower has been built in Ostankino, not far from the palace, while the name *Sheremetevo* is an internationally familiar name for Moscow Airport.) There were also two unrealized projects: a grandiose theatre in the Palace of the Arts in Moscow and a portable stage in the Egyptian pavilion of the Ostankino complex.

The Count was a passionate and ambitious music lover. A man of European education, he had refined taste and extensive knowledge of the arts. He was an accomplished professional musician, played the cello (which he had studied in Paris) and enjoyed orchestral performance and conducting. Sheremetev's desire was to have the entire range of entertainment combined with unlimited material resources at his disposal. Aristocrats usually had one, two or a maximum of three performing bodies: a choir and horn orchestra or a choir and symphony orchestra (a combination enabling the production of operas). The incomparable Sheremetev, however, did everything on a grand scale: a theatre including opera and ballet groups and equipped with the most sophisticated machinery, a symphony orchestra, a brass orchestra, a horn orchestra, and a choir – all staffed by every kind of artisan, including designers of musical instruments. Paralleling the Imperial structure of music-making, Sheremetev chose his own particular repertoire, in which contrasting features of the old and the new, the native and the borrowed, the aristocratic and the popular, were brought together in an unprecedented way. It is thus no wonder that Sheremetev could offer positions to first-rate musicians. Jean Batiste Cardon began his Russian career from the Count's house. Within his musical domain there would also certainly have been a place for such a figure as Sarti.

The oldest of all the forms presented in Ostankino was the serf choir, inherited by the Count from his father, Peter Borisovich Sheremetev. The choir kept its audience well into the nineteenth century and was the only ensemble to survive the disbanding of the entire performing structure after Sheremetev's death in 1809. This choir continued its activity throughout the nineteenth century and became the famous Cappella of Count Dmitry Nikolayevich Sheremetev (the son of Nikolai Petrovich), managed by Gavriil Lomakin. The thread was picked up by his grandson, Count Alexander Dmitrievich Sheremetev (1859–1931) – statesman and musician, who both conducted and composed. The latter, inheriting an enormous sum, reconstructed the choir, founded the orchestra and subsidized concert enterprises in St Petersburg, including free concerts for the public at the beginning of the twentieth century. He was active in organizing the Society for Music History and so on, until the revolution when he was forced to emigrate.

Sheremetev's musicians represented all three main national elements of eighteenth-century Russian culture – Russian, Ukrainian and Western. Most of them were recruited at an early age from the Kursk and Belgorod districts belonging to the so-called *Slobodskaya Ukraina*, which was formed in the seventeenth and eighteenth centuries in the south-western part of Russia and consisted of the Ukrainian population, both kazaks and peasants, who had fled from Polish oppression. The combination of their Italian training and the broad European and native repertoire that South Russian musicians practised at Sheremetev's court, moulded their mentality into that particular quality that is called 'Russian'.

The Count's serf musicians were trained exclusively by foreign teachers or by Russians who had themselves been previously trained by foreign tutors. One such example was the singer Elizaveta Semenovna Sandunova, the first teacher of some of Sheremetev's singers, and herself a pupil of Martín y Soler, Sarti and Paisiello. The repertoire reflected a developed variety of preferences in the Russian secular culture of the second half of the eighteenth century: Italian, French and Russian operas, instrumental music by contemporary European composers, and choral music (mostly Russian spiritual concertos and occasionally some Italian pieces).

Even the Count's father, Peter Borisovich Sheremetev, had given instructions in the late 1770s and early 1780s that a newly discovered tenor with an excellent voice, who could also act, was to be taught singing and acting from the Italians; as well as bowing, proper hand gesticulations, instruction in stage and society manners – from the Russians (Lepskaya, 1980:47–8). As was usual for the time, Sheremetev's theatre troupe originated from within the choir and both employed the same singers. Just as Berezovsky and Bortniansky had begun their performing careers on the court stage, Degtyarev too performed solo parts in opera productions at the Sheremetev estate.

The singers were trained exclusively according to the principles of the Italian school and worked on their operatic and choral repertoires in parallel. An extract from the singer Volkov's report (February 1797) offers some idea of the miscellaneous repertoire at work. It includes rehearsals of the studied concertos with all the singers, the parts from *La colonie* (A. Sacchini), *Paul and Virginia*, (R. Kreutzer) and from *La finta amante* (G. Paisiello) with soloists, Italian duet, solfeggio with junior singers, choruses from *Azemia* (N. Dalayrac), *kheruvimskie* with all the singers, scales with juniors, the concerto *Bozhe moy* (full choir), scales and solfeggio with girls and so on (Elizarova, 1944:274–5).

Sheremetev's approach to his serfs was neither liberal nor sadistic, just rigidly exploitative. It was well known that he did not grant freedom from his service to those who requested it, although such a practice already existed to a certain extent among the enlightened Russian nobility. The exception – and absolute precedent – is found in the history of Ostankino, which contains a most romantic and tragic story: the romance between Sheremetev and his serf actress and singer of rare talent, beauty and personality, Praskovia Kovaleva-Zhemchugova (1768–1803), who first appeared

**Figure 12.2   Praskovia Ivanovna Kovaleva-Zhemchugova in the role of Eliana
in an opera by Grétry,** *Les Mariages Samnites*

on the stage at the age of about ten, in 1779.[4] Discovering her extraordinary talent, Sheremetev gave her the best education and training that money could buy. Her governess was the Count's relative, the widow Princess Marfa Mikhaylovna Dolgorukaya, and she later studied acting (1790–96) with Maria Sinyavskaya, a leading Moscow actress known for her roles as noble female protagonists. Praskovia possessed a rich coloratura soprano and played the harpsichord, guitar and harp (studying with Jean Batiste Cardon). She was a true star and core of the theatre, and must have inspired the Count in the development of his projects. She was his mistress for two decades, from the age of thirteen until their marriage in 1801. Her ambiguous and stressful position, especially in the late 1790s, when their relations were no longer a secret, appears to have stimulated tuberculosis, which became full-blown when they had to move to St Petersburg because of the Count's appointment as Chief Marshal of the Imperial court. This took place at the end of 1797, when Catherine II died and Paul I ascended the throne.

An entirely new way of life – *regime* would better characterize the years of Paul's rule – sent Sheremetev's theatres into decline. Moreover, the sick Praskovia could no longer act on the stage. In 1800 the troupe was disbanded. Seeking a solution to their relationship, the Count signed her liberation in 1798. After March 1801, following the assassination of Paul I and the ascent of Alexander I to the throne, the atmosphere of relief allowed Sheremetev to think about marriage. Meanwhile Praskovia's illness progressed and her condition seemed hopeless. Conscious of his being the cause of her troubles, Sheremetev decided to marry her in the hope of achieving a miraculous cure. The miracle appeared to happen and the young woman recovered. The archivists of his court forged Kovaleva's origins as being from the Polish *szlachta* (gentry) and in November 1801 they secretly married. Nonetheless, the Countess died two years later, from galloping consumption, having given birth to only one heir, Count Dmitry Sheremetev.

This misalliance brought together the social poles of eighteenth-century Russian society, reflecting the Enlightenment and the *fin de siècle* sentimentalist ideas of human value regardless of class. Wishing to justify his marriage, the Count collected a solid list of historical precedents, but Russian aristocratic society of the time was still unsympathetically opposed to Sheremetev's marriage, looking upon it as posing a drastic challenge to the existing system of values, and almost ostracizing the couple. True romantic aristocracy of spirit had not yet arisen.

Sheremetev's theatre was thus a theatre of one generation, flourishing in the 1780s–1790s and attracting the passionate enthusiasm of the nobility and gentry. The Ostankino Palace-Theatre Museum still has its machinery preserved, as well as the sets, the props, numerous sketches and costumes, and documentation relevant to the construction of the theatre itself (it is still beautifully kept today and equipped with an electronic guide). The designers included the Italian painters Valezini and Antony Claudo, as well as the set designers Giuseppe and Carlo Bibiena and Francesco

---

4   The Russian word *zhemchug* means pearl. Sheremetev gave his serf actors pseudonyms such as the names of gems.

Gradizzi (the latter also worked for the Imperial court). There were also the German painters Keller and Friedrich Hilverding, and the Russian painters Ivan Volokhov, Gregory Mukhin and others. The library contains scores of performed operas by Grétry, Dalayrac, Piccini, Monsigny, and the Russian composers Kozlovsky, Pashkevich and many others, as well as printed librettos and Russian eighteenth-century editions of translated plays by Corneille, Racine, Voltaire, Molière and others (many translated by Sheremetev's serf writer Vasily Grigorievich Voroblevsky).

Based mostly in the Moscow area, Sheremetev's court divided its time between Moscow and St Petersburg. Thus his theatre entertained both the Moscow public, always known for its devotion to theatre, and the courtiers in the capital. It was not always easy however for everyone who so desired to gain access to the theatre spectacles, as can be seen from the following letter by Princess Dolgorukaya to the Count (3 July 1790):

> My Dear Sir Nikolai Petrovich! Many ladies among my friends would like to enjoy the spectacle given yesterday, therefore I ask Y.E. to kindly reserve for me the middle lodge for next Sunday if it has not been given or promised to someone else. I would be very obliged to you for your kindness. I remain honourably yours,
>
> Pr. Dolgorukaya.[5]

A perfect administrator, the Count not only managed his business pedantically but also strove for professionalism and perfection in every sphere. He personally attended the dress rehearsals, intent on achieving well-coordinated spectacles. In training his actors, he invited the best actors to teach them the various acting styles and manners, bought them subscriptions to the Petrovsky Theatre in order to provide them with more experience, and corresponded with leading specialists, seeking their advice, and so on. He not only possessed a beautiful collection of musical instruments, but also had some of them specially manufactured for him.

The outstanding serf artisan Ivan Andreevich Batov (1767–1841) made string instruments and guitars and restored all kinds of antiquarian instruments including cembalos and clavichords. In 1822 he was freed together with his family by the young Count Dmitry Nikolaevich Sheremetev as a reward for making an outstanding cello for the Count himself. In 1829 he was awarded the Grand Silver Medal for making the violin and cello that were displayed in the first public exhibition of products manufactured in Russia. Batov's instruments were known for their delicate and unique timbre. His cellos were similar in design to those of Stradivarius but his technique was adopted from the French masters. His guitars too were beautifully made and distinguished by their high quality of sound.

---

5   Милостивый государь мой Николай Петрович! Многие дамы из моих знакомых желают иметь удовольствие видеть вчерашний Ваш спектакль, и потому покорнейше прошу в. с. одолжить меня среднею ложею для будущего воскресенья, если она никому не отдана и не обещана. Вы чувствительно одолжите пребывающую с почтением кн. Долгорукую' (Elizarova, 1944:171).

The large archive contains many documents that reveal the true conditions of the serf staff's everyday life. Among them are an instruction concerning training singers in the Italian style, financial accounts, many of Count Sheremetev's routine directions for the preparation and performance of productions, and an order to reduce the salary of the above-mentioned serf writer due to his selling some of his works, etc. The absolutely prison-like existence of serf actresses is documented in the Count's following letter of instruction:

> To the House Mother of the female members of the ballet company Arina Antonova: Move to the upper story of the building where the girls have their quarters and record the daily events in your diary, that is: to observe every girl's activities without exception, and not to allow anyone to go anywhere except to church, precisely the church of Mironositsy, and especially to watch each girl as she walks there. If there is any disorderly behaviour, bring this to the attention of Michayla Smirnov, and watch him as well. Tell the girls that they are to strictly obey you and not to do anything without your approval.[6]

Another document gives an idea of the repertoire and schedule for ballet performances in May 1796:

May 1 – a.m.:	three ballets from *Armida*, p.m.: *The American* and *Azemia*.	
" 2 – a.m.:	lessons for men and women	
" 3 – p.m.:	*Deserter*	
" 4 – a.m.:	*Turkish* and *Medea & Jason*	
" 5 – a.m.:	*Lebedyansky Fair* and *Vanyushin*	
p.m.:	*Two Sylphs* and *Venice Fair*	
" 6 – a.m.:	lessons for men and women	
p.m.:	*Medea & Jason* and *Cupidon s Girliandoi* [Cupid With Garland]	
" 7 – p.m.:	*Tirsis* and *Cupidon s Verevochkoi* [Cupid With a String]	
" 8 – p.m.:	*Deserter*	
"10 - a.m.:	*Deserter* and *Turkish*	
p.m.:	lessons for men and women	
"12 – a.m.:	lessons for men and *Medea & Jason*, and *Azemia*,	
p.m.:	trip to the *banya* [bath–house]	

and so on (Elizarova, 1944:289–90).

Although their work schedule was intensive the serf artists did have some free time, but even this was strictly controlled by the great number of supervisors employed

---

6 'Объявить живущей при девушках кастелянше Арине Антоновой, чтоб из нижних покоев перешли жить в верхние покои, где живут девушки, кому ж в которой комнате поместиться прилагается реестр и приказать ей Антоновой, чтобы за всеми смотрела, не выключая ни одной и никуда б не пущала, опричь того, как только в церковь, да и то к Мироносицам, в чем иметь ей неослабное смотрение. Если же какие будут выходить беспорядки, относиться к Михайле Смирнову, которому так же иметь смотрение. Девушкам же приказать не выключая ни одной, чтоб все были у нее в послушании и без ее воли ничего б сами собою не делали.' *Nauchny Arkhiv* [Counts Sheremetevs' archive], no 1051, *Povelenie* no 99, April 27, 1800. Quoted by Elizarova, 1944:325.

by the Count. The male performers were under no less strict surveillance, being forbidden even 'to drink and act freely'. The supervisors were instructed not to allow them to leave the house without permission, nor to teach pupils, to hold teaching jobs in other households, or to sing in churches. Sheremetev took a great deal of care to prevent his singers and musicians from using their skills outside his theatre (Lepskaya, 1980:50).

Stepan Anikeevich Degtyarev

The life and works of the serf musician Stepan Anikeevich Degtyarev (sometimes Dekhtyarev or Degtyarevsky, 1766–1813) constitute a unique phenomenon in world culture. Despite the large number of serf musicians in Russia, including composers, most of them remained unknown outside the courts to which they belonged. One of the few exceptions was Count Nikolai Sheremetev's serf Degtyarev, whose works and reputation were known far beyond his owner's estate, owing to his exceptional gift and the popularity of the genre in which he worked. He stood out among the other serf composers in much the same way that Sheremetev did among the other aristocrats.

Degtyarev was recruited into the Count's troupe at the age of seven, among the first such group of children, together with Praskovia Kovaleva, Tatiana Shlykova (later Granatova) and Kuz'ma Serdolikov. Like all of Sheremetev's serf artists and artisans he studied with Italian teachers. During the period that his voice was breaking he attended courses on Russian letters and the Italian language at Moscow University (Yazovitskaya 1956:155). First training and then performing as an opera singer in the early 1780s, Degtyarev was soon promoted to the positions of conductor and vocal coach (1789, *uchitel' kontsertov*). He may also have studied theory with Sheremetev's kapellmeister and cellist-virtuoso J.G. Facius (Levashev, 1986:188), and then composition with Bortniansky, Antonio Sapienza Sr. and Giuseppe Sarti (Elizarova, 1944:337–8), whom he probably accompanied to Italy for a short period around 1790.[7] In the 1790s he also became kapellmeister of the orchestra and his duties included adapting operatic scores for the performers.[8]

The Count not only paid Degtyarev a very low annual salary (as late as 1802 it was only 63 roubles 50 kopecks plus apartment, meal and a servant), but also kept strict watch that he did not earn money elsewhere. In 1793, having discovered that Degtyarev was doing so nonetheless, the Count built a network of informers and

---

7   Degtyarev's trip to Italy has no documental confirmation and the suggestion circulated by word of mouth for many years until it was recorded by A.V. Nikitenko's *Zapiski i dnevnik* (St Petersburg, 1904, vol. 1), as Nadezhda Alekseeva Elizarova explained to me in a interview (summer 1984).

8   Elizarova mentioned Boris Dobrokhotov's research (regretfully unpublished) on the score of the leading role of Eliana in *Les Mariages Samnites* by Grétry, with notes by Degtyarev and Kovaleva-Zhemchugova on her part (1969:26).

issued special orders to one of his managers.[9] That the musician continued to disobey can be understood from the Count's oft-quoted order No. 128 of 8 June 1794: 'To reduce the salary of the concerto teacher Stepan Degtyarev by 5 roubles for giving *kontserts* to other people and to grant this sum to the singer Chapov for revealing the information.'[10] Since the Russian word *kontsert* means both 'concert' and 'concerto', the combination *davanie kontsertov* can be translated as either 'giving (the scores of) concertos' or 'performance'. The latter interpretation, offered by Elizarova and Yazovitskaya (1956:156), seems to be less probable. A performance at another house would have demanded the musician's absence for some time, considering the necessity for rehearsals, and would probably have been too difficult to conceal. To give somebody a score, however, would have been a much easier operation, and this was what the composer probably did, although, as we see, a witness-informer was on the alert even for this. Considering that the dealers' price for copies of concertos was then about 2 roubles 50 kopecks (of which Degtyarev would have received only part) it would have been an important supplement to his meagre less than five roubles per month.

At the time of this episode Degtyarev was already well known and self-confident. He probably knew he could have made a good living as a freelancer. It is thus little wonder that he begged for emancipation, which the Count for some reason never granted him, although Sheremetev did sometimes permit his actors to perform in other theatres. Not all serf musicians shared the same cruel fate. Generalissimo Alexander Suvorov, for example, known for his liberalism in the army, allowed his singers to perform and earn in other Moscow houses (Kots, 1926:94). On the other hand, that Count Sheremetev never permitted Degtyarev to do so might not necessarily have been a reflection of cruelty: he had invested too much in educating the composer – and other artists – and would have wanted to keep his lead as the first and the best among his class. He was also known for his exceptional stinginess (which was one reason why Paul I wanted him as Super Marshall of the Imperial court when he introduced his regime of strict economy following Catherine's squanderings), and he may have wanted to keep for himself all the revenue that Degtyarev would have brought in. It will not be too surprising if it is some day revealed that the capitalistic Count had considered Degtyarev's music to be his own personal property – and sold it. There is one circumstance that encourages hypothesis in this direction.

Degtyarev's Pseudonyms

Numerous announcements in the newspaper *Moskovskie vedomosti* in the 1790s–1800s mention the name Stepan Nikeev as a composer of choral concertos. He was so popular that Mr. Kessler, the German correspondent to *Allgemeine musikalische*

---

9 RGADA, f 1287, op 1 no 4819, L 27, 1793 (quoted by Levashev 1986:189–90).

10 'У учителя концертов Степана Дегтярева за давание им посторонним людям концертов вычесть из жалования 5 рублей и отдать певчему Чапову за объявление об оном' (quoted by Elizarova, 1944:339).

Zeitung, mentioned him alongside Bortniansky in his letters on Russian music ('Briefe über den Musikzustand von Russland und besonders von Moskow') in 1801 (Gourevich, 2003a). Since no other known source refers to this musician, the scholars Elizarova and Natanson tentatively suggested (in oral discussions in the mid-twentieth century) that this may have been the pseudonym of Stepan Degtyarev. Their arguments are convincing. Russian family names often originate from patronymics, and in the eighteenth century, among the serfs, the process of establishing family names was ongoing. Since the surname 'Nikeev' resembles his patronymic 'Anikeevich', theoretically at least it seems likely that Degtyarev could have used it.

In the course of a thorough examination of sources related to Russian choral concertos of the second half of the eighteenth century, I came across abundant overlaps between concertos by Degtyarev and Nikeev that strongly support the Elizarova-Natanson hypothesis. Moreover, the additional (and previously unnoticed) name of 'Anikeev', which is even closer to his patronymic name, together with the westernized 'Stefan' rather than the Russian 'Stepan', fits the story of Degtyarev's possible pseudonyms.

About 120 compositions (found in various printed and manuscript collections as well as mentioned in catalogues) can be attributed to Degtyarev today and about 100 of them are concertos, mostly for four voices (the other pieces are liturgical).[11] The HLAs, printed in supplements to the MV for 1794, 1796, 1800, 1804 and 1806, list 84 concertos by Stepan Nikeev.[12] Forty of the titles among these concertos coincide with those by Stepan Degtyarev. Moreover, the listings of the works by Degtyarev and Nikeev share some rare titles, not presented among the works of other composers, such as: *Gryadi ot Livana nevesto* [Come with me from Lebanon, my spouse], *Ne revnuy lukavnuyushchim* [Fret not thyself because of evil-doers], *Da vozraduetsya dusha* [And my soul shall be joyful in the Lord], *Dnes' nebes i zemli Tvorets prikhodit* [Today the Creator of the heavens and the earth arriveth], *Krepost' moya i penie* [The Lord is my strength and song], *Preslavnaya dnes'* [All glorious things today], *Priidite novago vinograda* [Come ye, of the new vine], *Ty moya krepost'* [For thou art the God of my strength], *Slyshi, Bozhe, molenie* [Give ear to my prayer, O God].[13]

The surname 'Anikeev' appears only three times on scores, and is not listed in any catalogues of music dealers. Coincidentally, or not, it appears only on scores stored in the St Petersburg archives, whereas 'Nikeev' is also found in the Moscow and Yaroslavl archives.

---

11 To establish the precise number of choral concertos written by Degtyarev is impossible, just as it is regarding other eighteenth-century Russian composers, because of their dissemination through many archival sources and complications with attribution.

12 Haehne, the only music dealer to advertise Nikeev, was probably Degtyarev's confidant. Numbers 64–70 from his catalogue have not been found to date in any announcements.

13 Degtyarev's use of titles unique in Russian choral literature has been noted by Levashev (1986:199).

Finally, there are a number of concertos whose copies are attributed in some cases to Stepan Degtyarev and in others to Stepan Nikeev or Stefan Anikeev. Although the number of incorrect attributions was not unusual for the time, such a high rate of error can nonetheless not be ignored. For example, the concerto *Blagoslavlyu Gospoda* [I will bless the Lord] from the St Petersburg archive[14] has been copied under the name of Anikeev, while in the Yaroslavl collection it is listed as Degtyarev's,[15] as it is in the collection of Degtyarev's concertos from the Ostankino Palace-Museum.[16] (The same concerto is erroneously attributed to Artemy Vedel in the printed *Collection of spiritual concertos by Vedel and Degtyarev* of the early twentieth century). The concerto *Poyte Gospodevi* (Praise ye the Lord) in the Muscovite collection has been copied as Nikeev's,[17] while in the St Petersburg collection it is attributed to Degtyarev[18] (as it is in the Ostankino volume). The concerto *Dnes' vsyakaya tvar'* [Today all creation] was known as Nikeev's in Yaroslavl,[19] while having been published as Degtyarev's in the Historical Ontology of Church Singing *Istoricheskaya khrestomatia tserkovnogo penia* (1902). The concerto *Khvalite Boga vo svyatykh* [Praise God in his sanctuary] was copied as Anikeev's in St Petersburg and included in the Ostankino volume as Degtyarev's work. The concerto *Bozhe, Bozhe moy, k Tebe utrennyuyu* [From the rising of the sun] is noted in the Moscow sources in 1793 as Nikeev's and in an early nineteenth-century collection as Degtyarev's.[20] Finally, there is an interesting copy of the concerto *Izmi mya ot vrag moikh* [Deliver me from the workers of iniquity] in St Petersburg, on which the name Nikeev appears in the title; while below – which is a note in nineteenth-century handwriting – is added 'and Degtyarev's'.[21] Various catalogues of spiritual music frequently also mention compositions by both – Degtyarev and Nikeev – as if they are two different composers.

Against the background of the common practice of repeating the same titles with different music and disseminating the music in part books and not in scores, not to mention the usual muddle of attribution and legitimacy of plagiarism in that epoch, nobody ran to compare between Degtyarev's and Nikeev's concertos. Dealers and their clients might not even have been aware that these two composers could have been the same person. The uncovering of similarities between works composed under

---

14 *Sbornik khorovykh dukhovnykh kontsertov.* Score, RGIA, f 1119, op 1, 1825, no 58.

15 *Sbornik khorovykh dukhovnykh kontsertov Yaroslavskogo Kazanskogo zhenskogo monastyrya.* Part books 'абвг'. GMMK, f 283, ns 918–21.

16 Degtyarev, *Sbornik khorovykh kontsertov.* Score. Ostankino Muzey tvorchestva krepostnykh, Department of written sources, no 567.

17 *Sbornik khorovykh dukhovnykh kontsertov.* Parts of descant, tenor and bass. GMMK, f 283, ns. 4, 48, 51.

18 *Sbornik khorovykh dukhovnykh kontsertov.* Score, RGIA, f 1119, op 1, 1825, no 58.

19 *Sbornik khorovykh dukhovnykh kontsertov* (parts of descant, alto and bass). Gosudarstvenny Istoricheskiy Arkhiv Yaroslavskoy oblasti, f Yaroslavskoy gubernskoy uchenoy arkhivnoy komissii, not numbered.

20 *Sbornik khorovykh dukhovnykh kontsertov.* Parts of descant, tenor and bass. GMMK, f 283, ns 4, 48, 51.

21 Score, RGIA, f 1119, no 56.

these different names was most likely a gradual, spontaneous process. Degtyarev may also have had additional pseudonyms. Thus in the Yaroslavl collection, his concertos were copied as Elizarov's or as Elizar Matveev's (*Prikloni, Gospodi, ukho Tvoe* [Bow down thine ear, O Lord]).[22] This, however, can be related to piracy by some enterprising provincial musician who was fishing in the murky waters of popular production.

Since Degtyarev could not sell his works under his own name, it could only have been his owner who had done so. If the composer himself had thus been selling his music under a pseudonym(s) – some of the music would have been the same that the Count had sold and some new.

This is where we must address the issue of the anonymity of Degtyarev's concertos. A great number of his concertos appeared as anonymous and, according to Gerasimova-Persidskaya's knowledge of existing *partes*-singing concertos, this is directly proportional to their prolificacy and popularity: the mediocre works were not copied, did not acquire anonymous status, were not widely circulated, and were of local importance only (1983:129). However, along with Degtyarev's popularity, the necessity to conceal his true identity could also have contributed to the abundance of the composer's anonymous works. This is especially noticeable in the St Petersburg collections. For example, the well-known volume of the Russian spiritual concertos in the RNB contains 27 concertos.[23] In the table of contents, 21 of them are attributed and six are anonymous, five of which coincide with Degtyarev's scores, but his name is not mentioned anywhere in the volume. Another collection, in IRLI,[24] is completely anonymous and has 29 concertos, 18 of which are Degtyarev's, two are Bortniansky's and nine are unknown. In contrast, some later St Petersburg collections compiled in the 1820s, notably after Degtyarev's death, do attribute concertos to him (and to Anikeev).[25]

The catalogue of spiritual music from Sheremetev's own library, containing 79 titles of Degtyarev's concertos, as well as other composers' works, including those not known to me from any other source, mentions neither Nikeev nor Anikeev.[26] This seems to offer another argument on behalf of the pseudonym hypothesis: in the Count's house nobody was supposed to know about the existence of these 'other' composers.

Serf-Freelancer

The HLA of 1806 seems to have been the last to have advertised compositions by Nikeev. At about that time, the other dealers' announcements of Degtyarev's

---

22 *Sbornik khorovykh dukhovnykh kontsertov Yaroslavskogo Kazanskogo zhenskogo monastyrya*. Part books 'абвг'. GMMK, f 283, ns 918–21.

23 RNB, f 1021, op 3 (I), no 2.

24 *Sbornik dukhovnykh kontsertov*, part of bass. IRLI, Drevlekhranilishche, Collection of M.V. Brazhnikov, no 24.

25 *Sbornik khorovykh dukhovnykh kontsertov*. Score, RGIA, f 1119, op 1, 1825, no 58; *Sbornik dukhovnykh kontsertov*. Score, RGIA, f 1009, op 1, no 181.

26 *Reestr dukhovnym p'esam, nakhodyashchimsya v pevcheskom otdelenii biblioteki Sheremetevykh*. RGIA, f 1088, op 3, no 1732, L 39.

compositions began to appear. His works were not listed in special catalogues but rather as individual compositions, with additional descriptive advertisements. For example, the music dealer Nazar Nikolaev advertised in MV on 25 November 1805 a few of Degtyarev's concertos among the 250 Italian vocal concertos, both new and old:

> ...there is also a special concerto for six voices: *Uslyshi Bozhe molenie moe* [Give ear to my prayer, O God], a new one worthy of mention, composed by Mr. Degtyarev, in *dis* tone; recently received from St Petersburg, all in variations, especially Adagio, with two cadences; the price 10 r...[27]

The texts of such announcements cast some light on the composer's whereabouts during this period. (Like all the members of the Count's entourage, he was either at one of the Moscow residences or in St Petersburg. For instance, there is a brief mention that after 1802 he taught at the Ostankino School for serf children, see Kurmacheva, 1983:96.)

Whereas in 1805–06 Degtyarev's concertos were noted as being received from St Petersburg, in 1808 the capital was not indicated. An announcement on 3 June by the merchant Pavel Molchanov (whose trading shop was located on Lenivka, opposite Kamenny bridge), mentioned fifteen Degtyarev concertos for sale, among which were not only Degtyarev's new concertos but also some from the 1790s, including several pieces noted in HLA as Nikeev's.

A few years before the Count's death in 1809, when only the choir still remained of all Sheremetev's former musical complex, Degtyarev in all probability moved to Moscow where he would have been relatively free. The pseudonyms were no longer needed and the reverse process began – that of reconstructing the composer's real name. In 1808 (upon Sheremetev's order) he married Agrafena Kokhanovsky, the daughter of one of Sheremetev's former actors.

Although the Count had promised that his will would also contain Degtyarev's emancipation, such a document was not found. The Board of Guardians for the infant heir, Count Dmitry Nikolaevich, considered Degtyarev's case and forwarded it to the Senate. Meanwhile the composer received a temporary passport, allowing him to live and work independently, with an annual pension of 150 roubles.[28]

Degtyarev finally established himself in Moscow where, due to the number of aristocratic courts and serf choirs, he had hoped to find a higher demand for his work. In search of work, he published personal advertisements, which were a rare phenomenon at the time (as were freelancers in general). The previously mentioned newspaper, following Degtyarev's announcement also gave a long list of other works for sale. Among them were twenty-five 'huge [concertos] for two choirs', thirty-one concertos, 'the best' concertos for four voices, thirty-five 'annual and for sacred

27 'Особенной из них концерт на 6 голосов: Услыши Боже моление мое, новой, замечания достойной, сочинения Г. Дегтярева, дисного тону; получен недавно из Петербурга, весь в вариациях, а особливо адажио, с двумя кодансами; цена за оной 10 р...'

28 RGIA, f 1088, op 3, 1816–20, no 1615, L 39.

holidays' (*godovykh i Svyatitel'nym prazdnikam*) concertos, 'twenty-five full Italian liturgies, all of different chants (*vsekh raznogo napeva*)' and so on. The composer of all this informed the public that he had diligently covered every possible aspect and that there was no prayer or trope that could not be set to music This was followed by lists of a large number of other compositions – vocal, instrumental, oratorical, with horn music etc. Although this entire record is anonymous, it could be related to Degtyarev's legacy, considering his experience with a variety of tasks over his three decades of working as the *Kapellmeister* of Sheremetev's musical complex, as well as the remaining odd fragments of his compositions for different ensembles (mentioned by Levashev, 1986:188–9).

MV of 11 August 1809 read:

> I have the honour to announce to the venerable music lovers that I wish to take up a position as a house musician who can direct a choir and teach singers, specializing in both a cappella singing and instrumental music; for the pleasure of those who will entrust me with such a position I shall also compose new pieces for his singers and musicians.[29]

This, however, does not seem to have overwhelmed him with work. For example, one such advertisement published on 14 December 1810 reads:

> Several new vocal concertos as well as a new full liturgy of my own composition are on sale. Gentlemen desiring to have these works that nobody else possesses are kindly welcomed to send for them to my place in Sheremetev Hospital, near Sukhareva tower. I can also visit houses by arrangement, for instruction or improvement of choristers a cappella or with instrumental music. I am also honoured to inform the revered Public that in the coming February, I shall premier my new grand musical oratorio entitled *Liberation of Moscow*. This first national oratorio has music composed by me and text by Nikolai Gorchakov.
>
> Stepan Dekhtyarev[30]

The conditions for the composer became increasingly unfavourable, possibly a reflection of the general cultural changes resulting from the Napoleonic wars, which had contributed to a decline in aristocratic wealth and in its culture. Serf choirs, horn bands and other performing bodies were attracting less attention and money

---

29 'Честь имею объявить почтеннейшим любителям музыки, что я имею намерение взять на себя должность у кого–либо из господ управлять хором певчих и обучать оных особенно или с музыкою инструментальною; а для удовольствия того, кому угодно будет поручить мне сию должность, буду сочинять для певчих его и музыкантов новые пьесы.'

30 Продаются моего сочинения несколько новых певческих концертов и новая же полная обедня. Господа, желающие иметь сии сочинения, которых ни у кого еще нет, благоволят присылать ко мне в Шереметевскую больницу, что у Сухаревой башни. Я могу ездить и в домы по билетам для обучения и поправления певчих одних; или с музыкою инструментальною. При сем имею честь известить почтенную Публику, что в будущем феврале месяце дана мною будет новая большая музыкальная Оратория, называемая Освобождение Москвы. В сей первой еще отечественной Оратории музыка моего сочинения, а слова Николая Горчакова. / Степан Дехтерев. MV, 1810, no 100:3282–3.

from their owners. Stylistic development of the repertoire ground to a halt. Nothing remained to surprise the lovers of the choral concerto, and Degtyarev switched to oratorio – a genre addressed to a broader public, referring to the great deeds recounted in the national history (based on the struggle of the national irregular soldiers against the Polish invasion of 1612) and appealing to the patriotic mood of the time.

His oratorio, finally titled *Minin and Pozharsky, or Liberation of Moscow*, appeared at the climax of the growing interest in the topic, as an allusion to the threat of Napoleonic invasion. Recalled by Peter Zakhar'in in his twelve-verse poem *Pozharsky*,[31] the theme was developed further by Gavrila Gerakov. The latter's book *Tverdost' dukha nekotorykh rossiyan* [The Russian firmness of spirit] inspired the sculptor Ivan Martos, who in 1803 created a model of the monument to Minin and Pozharsky. Gavrila Derzhavin picked up the thread and, partially obsessed with this analogy, wrote an ode *To the Insidiousness of the French Uprising and in Honour of Prince Pozharsky*, an unfinished poem *Pozharsky* and an heroic spectacle in four acts with choruses and recitatives *Pozharsky or the Liberation of Moscow* (1806). *The Laud to Pozharsky and Minin* by Pavel Lvov had been read at Derzhavin's house, and this had been followed by Kryukovsky's tragedy *Pozharsky, or the Liberated Moscow* (1807), Prince Shakhmatov's poem *Pozharsky, Minin and Germogen* and others (Yazovitskaya, 1956:158–9).

The closer to Moscow that Napoleon's army came, the louder the subject sounded. The composer of the music to Derzhavin's spectacle is unknown (it may have been Bortniansky, Kozlovsky or somebody else), but it was created and performed in St Petersburg. There was certainly also a place for such a composition as Gorchakov's-Degtyarev's oratorio in the increasingly endangered Moscow, where the monument to Minin and Pozharsky by the sculptor Ivan Martos had been founded in 1811. Public enthusiasm and the authority of Degtyarev's name, however, this time outstripped the quality of his music, whose diluted Empire style had not survived the times (like most compositions of the period throughout Europe).

Having escaped the French invasion on a Kursk landowner's estate where he had found a short-term position, Degtyarev then returned to Moscow, where he died on 23 April 1813, leaving behind a widow and three children. Two years later, the Senate finally issued his emancipation; a catastrophe for his widow who was eventually to be deprived of even that minimal pension that serf status had given her. The tale of Agrafena's efforts to restore her serf status is one of the saddest and most paradoxical episodes of Degtyarev's story in particular and of Russian reality in general.

Upon receiving the letter of enfranchisement from the Senate, the widow refused to accept it and appealed both to the Board of Guardians for the infant heir and personally to the thirteen-year-old Count Dmitry Nikolaevich himself, begging him to rescind the letter. In a similar petition, she referred to Degtyarev's forty years of devoted service to Sheremetev's family, and to herself having been left with three

---

31 The precise date of the poem (tentatively suggested as the end of the eighteenth century) as well as of the author's death: 1798, 1800 or 1810 – remain unknown (Rak, SRP, 1988:331–4).

small children (born in 1809, 1812 and 1813), the eldest of whom was a cripple, and her complete inability to support the family unless through charity. Considering the general policy of the Board of Guardians to get rid of unproductive serf personnel, the situation did not bode well for her. However, the young Count Dmitry Nikolaevich not only insisted on granting her petition, but also demanded from the Board of Guardians that they provide her with an average living. The decision of the Board, noted on the back of Agrafena Degtyarev's petition, was positive. Degtyareva and her children were to be granted an annual subsistence pension of three hundreds roubles from the Count's income, to be paid retrospectively from the moment of termination of the previous pension until her marriage; and for the children, until their majority. She could, if she so wished, continue to live at her former residence in Kuskovo, on the same basis as before receiving the letter of enfranchisement.[32]

Degtyarev's Choral Music: Aesthetics and Style

Degtyarev probably began composing his concertos in the late 1780s, that is during the first peak of public enthusiasm for the genre, with Bortniansky as a key figure. Serf choirs rapidly proliferated and so did their repertoire, based on Bortniansky's works and initially imitating his style. The owners of these choirs avidly sought new concertos and liturgical pieces, competing among themselves in the quality of their choirs and breadth of their repertoires. The post of serf choirmaster gained increasing stature.

Count Sheremetev naturally paid much attention to his choir and was greatly interested in Degtyarev's development as a composer. Choral repertoire offered a good market. He possibly viewed Degtyarev as his own private 'petit Bortniansky'. Indeed, already in 1793 the KPN lists eighteen titles common to both Degtyarev and Bortniansky. Eight of these are attributed to Degtyarev, seven to both Degtyarev and Nikeev, and three to Nikeev.[33] These works by Degtyarev were exceedingly popular and are found in other sources too.

Degtyarev of course not only used texts of the same Psalms that Bortniansky used, but also Bortniansky's and Sarti's models, just as Bortniansky had used Berezovsky's and Galuppi's models. Moreover, he simplified Bortniansky's mode, reducing the polyphonic devices, exactly as Bortniansky had done with Berezovsky. The difference was that while Bortniansky had done so twenty years after Berezovsky, when baroquesque writing was already *passé*, Degtyarev carried out his adaptations closely following Bortniansky in time, but for other reasons. One was that he simply lacked technique: although Bortniansky, Sapienza and Sarti are mentioned as his

---

32 RGIA, f 1088, op 3, 1816–20, no 1615, L 32v.

33 These numbers should be considered as approximate, since the precise total number of choral concertos written by either Degtyarev or Bortniansky (or any other eighteenth-century Russian composer) is impossible to establish because of their dissemination through many archival sources and complications with attribution. The ratio of Degtyarev to Bortniansky appears to be 2:1.

teachers, he had hardly received any systematic training in counterpoint. Another reason was that Degtyarev was much younger than Bortniansky and belonged to the next generation. He must have keenly sensed that the modern audience placed significantly less value on the skill of counterpoint and significantly more on expressions of a new kind.

The genre of choral concerto also notably changed in both function and audience. It emanated from the Winter Palace and St Petersburg select residences and spread to greater Moscow and the provincial gentry's estates. Its new audience wanted music that was more nostalgic, more sentimental and more Italian. Despite the firm presence of the German tradition, the intensive advance of the French style and the strong development of the Russian native musical school, Italian music continued to expand in significance and influence, penetrating more and more genres and social sectors and reaching an almost hysterical 'Italomania' by the beginning of the nineteenth century. At its peak, the expression "Italian taste" became a synonym for beauty and served as a trademark in the process of commercialization of music and painting.

Not that Degtyarev was any more Italian in style than Berezovsky or Bortniansky, or the Russified works of Galuppi and Sarti. Rather the original Italian idiom had already been nationalized, every era had bestowed a new sense upon the term 'Italian', and indeed the very word itself continued to suggest the 'new'. When music dealers advertised the scores of 'Italian Masses' (*Italianskie obedni*), they did not mean masses written by Italian composers, but rather indigenous liturgies composed in a modern style. In an announcement in *Sankt–Peterburgskie vedomosti* in 1794 one could read 'New Russian song with the refrain in Italian taste, arranged for piano, as well as for harpsichord. It can equally be performed with violin, *gusli* and other instruments'. This use of 'Italian' did not only apply to musical compositions. As late as 1814, MV issued an advertisement for the sale of serf singers 'knowing *partes*-singing in the Italian manner';[34] and a Moscow merchant produced an iconostasis for the church of Serpukhov's dragoon regiment 'of the very best Italian painting'.[35] All 'Italian' works cost more. Count Vladimir Grigorievich Orlov wrote to his son Alexander in a letter dated 15 October 1787:

> There is much praise for an Italian who arrived here last winter and teaches singing. I think his name is Minarelli, he is employed by Bibikov where he teaches two boys and is paid 200 [roubles] a month. This is an insane sum, and it is surprising that such a stingy man should be so generous when it comes to music.[36]

---

34 'петь по партесу на итальянский манер', quoted by Vertkov, 1948:43.

35 'самой лучшей итальянской живописи' (BRAN, Manuscript Department, Collection of Kartavov, file 22, cart. 533).

36 Хвалят очень итальянца, которой учит петь, он приехал сюда прошедшую зиму. Помнится имя ему Минарелли, учит у Бибикова 2 мальчиков, получает по 200 на месяц, цена бешеная, удивительно, что такой скупец столячлив на музыку.' Vladimir Grigorievich Orlov to Alexander Vladimirovich Orlov, 15 October 1787. RGB, Manuscript Department, f 219, cart. 8, no 8, L 28v.

Italianization was the general direction upon which Degtyarev's style developed. When he began to advertise his music in the late 1800s, both 'Italian' and 'new' were key words in his announcements, as well as 'sensitive' (*chuvstvitel'ny*), 'empathetic in tone' (*zhalostlivogo tonu*) , 'with cadences', and so on. The word that was not mentioned was 'operatic', but this was actually what his listeners were hoping for from the new choral concerto. 'Italian' served as a noble euphemism for secularized and operaized expression.

There is hardly any kind of spiritual music in the European tradition that has not been directly or indirectly influenced by opera, be it Christian oratorio, cantata, passions, liturgy or Jewish khazanut. The same holds true for the Russian concerto, which started its mutation from *partes*-singing only after opera had been introduced into Russia. Its style changed and developed in parallel with the operatic styles. When the sentimental mood took over the theatrical stage, young Degtyarev swiftly perceived this and expressed it in his music.

Early Concertos

The KPN (1793) lists several of Degtyarev's concertos. Three of these are under his own name: *Khvalite imya Gospodne* [Praise ye the name of the Lord] (in Catalog no 85), *Uslyshi, Gospodi, molitvu moyu* [Give ear, O Lord, unto my prayer] (no 111) and *Gryadi ot Livana, nevesto* [Come with me from Lebanon, my spouse] (no 113); two are anonymous: *Posobivy Gospodi* [Help us, O God of our salvation] (no 78) and *Miloserdia dveri otverzi nam* [O prepare mercy and truth] (no 80); and four are under the pseudonym Nikeev: *Poyte Gospodevi* [Praise ye the Lord] (no 83), *Bozhe, Bozhe moy, k Tebe utrennyuyu* [From the rising of the sun] (no 84), *Zlatokovannuyu trubu* [The trumpet of beaten gold] (no 90) and *Svyatiteley udobrenie* [Adorment of hole hierarchs] (no 91). Two years later, in 1795, MV announced two Nikeev concertos: *Da vozraduetsya dusha* [And my soul shall be joyful in the Lord] and *Priidite novago vinograda* [Come ye, of new vine]. This list of compositions reveals Degtyarev's prolific and professional writing, and suggests that a significantly larger number of works may have been composed by this time.

The concertos were mainly oriented on the highly useful musical clichés invented by Bortniansky (and Sarti), for example: *Gryadi ot Livana, nevesto, Priidite novago vinograda* as well as *Dnes' vsyakaya tvar' veselitsya, Preslavnaya dnes', Sey narechenny* and some others. All these concertos are standardized and written in *C major* as a three-section cycle: 4/4 Allegro, 3/4 slow middle piece in *F major* and 2/4 final Allegro (in *Dnes' vsyakaya tvar' veselitsya* – 6/8). The difference between Bortniansky's original and Degtyarev's imitative style is that what had served for Bortniansky only as the basis upon which to superimpose his own individual refined style, Degtyarev turned into his final product, thus stereotyping and diluting Bortniansky's idiom.

Degtyarev imitated Bortniansky not only in the latter's plain festive style but also in more profound elements that referred to *opera seria* too, in such concertos as *Uslyshi, Gospodi, molitvu moyu* or *Poyte Gospodevi*. For example, the opening theme of the latter concerto is close in character and motifs to Bortniansky's *Otrygnu serdse moe* (Examples 12.1a, b).

Example 12.1 (a) Degtyarev: Concerto *Poyte Gospodevi*, **section 1**

Example 12.1 (b) Bortniansky: Concerto *Otrygnu serdtse moe*, **section 1**

The opening themes of Degtyarev's concertos (and sections within them) are based on material typical for lyrical concertos of the time. Mutually analogous within the work, (Examples 12.2a, b) they are also similar to many of Degtyarev's other

Example 12.2 (a) Degtyarev: Concerto *Bozhe, Bozhe moy, k Tebe utrennyuyu*, **section 1**

Example 12.2 (b) Degtyarev: Concerto *Bozhe, Bozhe moy, k Tebe utrennyuyu,*
section 2

themes, as well as those by Bortniansky and in anonymous works. Similar themes can be found too in Degtyarev's *Uslyshi, Gospodi, molitvu moyu* and *Uslyshi, Gospodi, glas molenia moego*; in Bortniansky's *Uslyshi, Gospodi, molitvu moyu*; and in the anonymous *Uslyshi, Bozhe, glas moy,*[37] *Uslyshi, Gospodi, glas moleniya moego*[38] and *Gospodi, uslyshi, molitvu moyu.*[39] It is obvious that motivic similarity (six-four chord as a base) is directly connected with textual similarity ('Give ear, O Lord', 'Hear my prayer, O Lord' and so on – an appeal to the Almighty to listen) thereby producing a rhetoric specific to the time and place, probably rooted in the *kanty* idiom. (See the *kant* on Peter's death and Catherine I's ascent to the throne, Example 8.2b.) Since opening themes traditionally constitute a kind of emotional emblem of a concerto, their significance remains great even if they do not receive further development within the composition.

Like Bortniansky, Degtyarev too wrote a relatively small number of minor-mode concertos. By 1793, he had composed only two, and Bortniansky – only three. In total Degtyarev composed about fifteen such concertos but, again like Bortniansky, they were and still are the most popular. One such concerto is *Miloserdia dveri otverzi nam* (before 1793), probably one of his earliest. Besides its quite unusual tonal plan (Section 1 – *F minor – E flat major*; 2 – *E flat major*, 3 – *B major* and 4 – *A flat major*) the concert is also characterized by a strange voice-leading, abundant with obvious parallelisms. In general its music is reserved and melancholic, resembling Bortniansky's *F minor* concerto *Zhivy v pomoshchi vyshnyago*, and does not contain any specific embellishment.

Some of Degtyarev's minor-mode concertos are characterized by their semantic clash between the mode and the laudatory text (like *Da vozraduetsya dusha* in *C minor* (before 1795) and *Khvalite imya Gospodne*, also in *C minor*), though examples can be found in Western and Russian liturgies. Indeed, he probably wrote the first one with the Western mass in mind: its first section contains vocalizations characteristic of large fugues for a choir and orchestra ensemble.

Besides the above peculiarities, Degtyarev's early concertos have several common features, typical for his choral oeuvre in general. One of them is a tendency to expand the composition, in which he clearly followed Sarti. Consequently, the inner structure is more extensive, constructed from larger compositional units. Unlike Bortniansky, in whose music the minuet played a very important role, Degtyarev had no tendency

---

37 *Sbornik khorovykh dukhovnykh kontsertov Yaroslavskogo Kazanskogo zhenskogo monastyrya.* Part books 'абвг'. GMMK, f 283, ns 918–21, no 35.

38 *Sbornik khorovykh dukhovnykh kontsertov Yaroslavskogo Kazanskogo zhenskogo monastyrya.* Part books 'абвг'. GMMK, f 283, ns 918–21, no 55.

39 KPN, entry 71.

to the periodicity characteristic of dance genres, but cared more about wide melodic movement. He was fond of incorporating in his concertos the rhetorical figures of sigh motifs and others, by that time applied by others mostly only to operatic music (Example 12.3). Also closer to Sarti than to Bortniansky, Degtyarev made broad use of 3/4 meter in the opening sections of the concertos. Accordingly, his middle sections usually featured 4/4 meter. He thus rejected the vocalized minuet and *kanty* as a generic source for lyrical middle sections for the sake of the more energetic *kanty* rhythms in the opening sections of his concertos.

Initial motifs of Degtyarev's concertos are often clichés of declamatory intonations, followed by a melodic development based on chordal figuration and filled in by scaled or melismatic movement. Sentimentally melancholic gestures bordering upon heart-rending exclamations often break through the flow of his music, revealing Degtyarev as a Russian musician of the pre-Romantic era. This is always accompanied by a certain abuse of the dominant seventh chord, quite typical for early nineteenth-century music.

Degtyarev had a command of polyphony of course, but made only limited use of it, as was the custom of the time. His fugues are rare and simple. Like Bortniansky, he was usually satisfied with a brief hint of fugato at the beginning of a final section. Unlike Bortniansky, however, he made little use of imitations as a means of development, thus depriving the texture of a greater possible richness and intensity.

Example 12.3 Degtyarev: Concerto *Gospodi, vozlyubi blagolepie,* **fragment from
section 1**

Late Concertos

The second half of Degtyarev's creative path, including the first decade of the 1800s, was characterized by the development and eventual domination of an operatic, arioso-like style in his choral concertos. Although at the beginning this was manifested in somewhat reserved individual attempts, by the end it had developed into a self-contained style. This new manner, obviously highly appealing to the composer himself, gradually obtained – if not originality – a certain individuality. Finding his own sphere and free from Bortniansky's influence, Degtyarev increasingly tended to theatricalized expression. His creative self-liberation coincided with the decline of Sheremetev's theatres. The less that opera was heard on the stage (Kovaleva-Zhemchugova stopped performing in 1797 and the theatres were disbanded in 1803, after her death) – the more it found expression in his choral style. From the mid-1800s, the choral chapel was the only performing body that remained of the once musical splendour of Ostankino and Kuskovo.

At the same time, the intensive development and democratization of all forms of musical life in Russia also influenced the style of its spiritual music, which underwent modernization and was aimed at the new generation. The operatic style in spiritual music had already established itself in the Neapolitan school as early as the end of the seventeenth century, in the music of Francesco Durante or Leonardo Leo, and was not only criticized but also acclaimed.[40] Degtyarev, while translating Manfredini's *Regole armoniche, o sieno Precetti ragionati*, despite the author's hypocritical grumbling about the invasion of the operatic style into spiritual music,[41] nonetheless when advertising his own concertos generously emphasized their operatic traits. The phrases he used included 'with pleasant solos', 'in new taste, with variations, in touching tone', 'all the descant, up to the end, set in variations', 'with a cadence', 'enormous and with a cadence', 'in pitiful tone', 'in affecting tone', 'with manners', 'incomparable to the ear', 'the most moving', 'of rare harmony' '*s princhipaloyu* [the solo part of upper voice]', 'with manners and cadences' and so on. All these

---

40 The German theoretician Andreas Werkmeister offered an example of advocacy of the operatic style in spiritual music in his *Der ellen Musik-Kunst Wilrde, Gebrauch und Missbrauch* (1691).

41 One of Manfrefini's passages says: 'The spoiling of this style has increased to such an extent, to the great dismay of anyone with common sense, that indecent musical fancies touch even sacred compositions, in which some musicians present the church style as theatricalized and even improper. That is why it is necessary to remove from the churches all theatrical sinfonie and instruments, trumpets, timpani, horns and so on, whose sound seems to be more appropriate for taking a fortress than to inspiring sacred feelings through the expression of divine words. It would seem also, that all the long ritornellos, motets with arias and theatrical recitatives that are like arias and rondos written in two different tempos, in Adagio and in Allegro – must be forbidden too. Impermissible too are all the cadencies, used too often and inappropriately; while endless repetition of music and words is considered highly erroneous not only in church music but in the theatres also'.(translated from Degtyarev's translation into Russian of Manfredini's work: *Pravila garmonicheskie i melodicheskie dlya obuchenia vsey muzyki...*, 1805:157–8).

indicate the development of operatic melodic figurations, which was characteristic not only of Degtyarev but of the musical style of the early nineteenth century in general. Along with Degtyarev's advertisements one could also find announcements of popular songs for sale:

> Seven Russian folk songs with solos and cadence, with music [accompaniment] and voices [music transcriptions], each on 20 sheets, all for 15 r... Gypsy [songs] with variations, *Malorossiyskie* [Ukrainian] and love [songs], heart-rending passion of love; new speeches [new style of lyrics?] and new expressive [music set in high register] all for 20 r.[42]

Several of Degtyarev's concertos, dated by newspaper announcements to between 1805 and 1808, as well as a few undated concertos stylistically relating to Degtyarev's later manner, allow us to draw some conclusions. Similar to his earlier works, here too the composer does not seem to have attempted to unify in any way the form and type of his musical material. Their structures vary, although he generally kept a four-section cycle with a slow opening section or a three-section cycle: quick-slow-quick. The main and in fact the only sphere of innovation in his musical language lies in melody. It is filled with all kinds of adornments: appoggiaturas, sequences of whirling figures, scale-wise passages, gruppettos etc. Melisms are mainly used for upper voice/s, though the low parts sometimes also display them (in duos). In the manuscripts the upper voice is often marked as *soprano*, revealing that the tradition of women participating in church choirs instead of boys had already become established.

The melodic lines, in addition to being embellished by melismatic figures, also acquired wide intervallic leaps. The combinations of triples, dotted rhythm, sometimes Lombardic rhythm, sigh and exclamatory motifs and use of the wide diapason (until d^3), all indicate Degtyarev's mastery of the contemporary Italian operatic style and unimpeded transfer of it into the genre of choral concerto. The abundant use of melisms, so called 'variations', led to the wide application of alteration, especially in the subsidiary tones, giving the style *gallant* nuances.

The total liberation of Degtyarev's melody from the conventions of the choral genre promoted the appearance of new romance intonations, mostly based on sixes (ascending from the tonic to the sixth and from the fifth to the third or descending from the fifth to the leading tone). Just as he had done earlier, Degtyarev remained faithful to the piquancy provided by the dominant seventh chord: notable sentimental stops on either the leading tone or the seventh of this chord.

In Degtyarev's later concertos the solo segments were to have different functions. Like Bortniansky's concertos, they sometimes open the composition, setting a tone of intimacy (*Gospodi, vozlyubikh blagolepie, Uslyshi, Gospodi, glas molenia moego* and *Terpya poterpekh*). Unlike Bortniansky, however, Degtyarev often extended them and embellished the solo segments with melisms within the fast-movement

---

42 'Русских простонародных с солами и с кодансом, с музыкою и голосами, 7 песен, каждая на 20 листах, за все 15 р. ... Цыганския с вариациями, Малороссийския и любовныя, изъявляющия любви сострадание; новыя речи и новая выразительная нота высокого положения, за все 20 р' (MV, 25 November 1805).

sections traditionally characterized by massive choral sound, making them resemble the Finales of *semi-seria* operas. This development of operatic vocalization appears to have been important for both Degtyarev and his audience, as evident from the appearance of his own redactions of several of his earlier concertos.

Redactions

To date, I have found four pairs of redactions by Degtyarev. However, according to the various newspaper announcements and catalogues there must have been additional ones. Only the most popular concertos were redacted. The new versions were advertised, presenting the features of the new expression. For example, one of the most well-liked and indeed the best concerto, *Izmi mya ot vrag moikh, Bozhe* [Deliver me from the workers of iniquity], was promoted in the following announcement in MV 2 March 1807: 'Lenten concerto, composed by Mr. Degtyarev: *Izmi mya Gospodi*; set to new music and [having] speeches [recitative] in Adagio; 'Bozhe uvest' serdtse moe, izpytay mya I vizhd' bezzakonia vo mne, nastavi mya na put' pravdy Tvoeya' [Search me, O God, and know my heart: try me, and know my thoughts: And see if there be any wicked way in me, and lead me in the way

Example 12.4 (a) Degtyarev: Concerto *Izmi mya ot vrag moikh, Bozhe*, section 3, first version

everlasting], of high register, f minor, 3 r.'[43] It was also characterized by the definition *zhalostlivogo tonu* [of pitiful tone] in an advertisement on 3 June 1808.[44]

Indeed, the third section of the concerto, Largo, whose text was cited in the advertisement, featured highly dramatic alterations that reflected the trend of the new style. The initial emblematic motif had also been modified: instead of a

---

43 'великопостный концерт, сочинения Г. Дехтерева: Изми мя Господи; и новаго напева, а речи в адажио; Боже увесть сердце мое, испытай мя и виждь беззакония во мне, настави мя на путь правды Твоея, высокаго положения, эф моль, 3 р.'

44 Both versions of the concerto can be found in the printed editions. The first one – in *Sbornik dukhovnykh kontsertov Vedelya i Degtyareva* (St Petersburg, 1913) and the other in vol. III of *Istoricheskaya khrestomatia* ed. by M. Lisitsyn (St Petersburg, 1903).

Example 12.4 (b)   Degtyarev: Concerto *Izmi mya ot vrag moikh, Bozhe,* **section 3, second version**

trio of soloists it was given to a duo of upper voices on *pianissimo*, with added ornamentation. The key was changed from *E minor* to *F minor* – a more 'vocal' key. Accordingly, the Largo received the melancholic *B minor* instead of *A minor*. Appoggiaturas, melisms, chromatic gestures and fragmentary dotted rhythm were also added of course, and the harmony in the new version was slightly softened (Examples 12.4a, b).

The characteristic rhythm and melodic gestures appear to indicate the funeral march as its generic source, as confirmed by the further development of the material – its variation in smaller values and in the relative major. The first mention of this concerto occurred in 1800 in the catalogue of Nikeev's concertos (HLA, no 55). It was thus probably written between 1795, when the earlier section of Nikeev's catalogue had been published, and 1800.

Use of the *march funèbre* style in choral concertos was not widespread. In addition to a brief fragment in Bortniansky's concerto no 29, composed in all probability between 1793–6, and individual elements in concertos by Vedel, it can be found in the popular (and indeed very impressive) concerto *Plachu i rydayu* [I weep and wail when I think upon death], whose attribution is arguable, but for which Joseph Kozlovsky remains the most probable composer.[45] While in this latter concerto

---

45 All the known sources give various attribution of this concerto. Its copy in *Sbornik dukhovnykh kontsertov XVIII–nachala XIX veka.* RNB, f 1021, op 3 (I), no 2 ascribes the concerto to Sarti and a copy in the manuscript collection of the Nizhny Novgorod Regional Universal Academic Library, P/362, attributes it to Vedel. On the other hand, the most reliable source, the catalogue of the book-seller Haehne (1804), as well as the printed edition of 1913 (*Sbornik dukhovno-muzykal'nykh sochineniy*) give the name of Kozlovsky, although without the initials. The problem is that there was another Kozlovsky, Peter Timofeevich, who, apparently affiliated to the Court Choir, wrote concertos in quite a timid 'pre-Bortniansky' style. On the other hand, Joseph Kozlovsky is known for his monumental compositions in

use of this rhythm matches the text (*Plachu i rydayu, egda pomyshlyayu smert' i vizhdu vo grobakh lezhashchuyu po obrazu Bozhiyu sozdannuyu nashu krasotu, bezobraznu, besslavnu, neimushchuyu vida*), in Bortniansky's, Degtyarev's and Vedel's compositions textual phrases set to music with a *march funèbre* rhythm had no specifically funereal semantic references. This rhythm, disseminated in Europe after the French revolution, thus attracted composers by the newness of its expression rather than by its semantic meaning.

Another auto-redaction by Degtyarev was made according to the same principle of the above concerto: *Khvalite Boga vo svyatykh* [Praise God in his sanctuary]. The latter is mentioned in Nikeev's catalogue (HLA, no 63) in MV 1800. Copies of the initial version can be found in the St Petersburg collection (1825) as attributed to Anikeev[46] and in the Yaroslavl collection as anonymous.[47] An obviously later version is copied in the Ostankino collection, in which the initial theme-emblem has been changed and the second section Andante embroidered with melismatic 'variations'.

The third example of auto-redaction is the concerto *K Tebe, Gospodi, vozdvigokh* (Unto Thee, O Lord, have I lifted up). How long a period separated between the versions is unknown, as well as which version was advertised in the newspaper (12 December 1804) as 'a touching new concerto' among 'the newest excellent music'. It was probably the redaction, since this had certain emotive gestures and several fragments of 'variations' that were absent in the other version, in which the sections for soloists were quite modest and contrasted little with the choral sections, remaining on the whole close to the style of the 1780–90s.[48]

The differences between the versions can be seen in the various levels of composition. The final sections are almost identical (in the second version the finale is slightly shorter, fifty bars against the original sixty, due to condensation of some fragments). In contrast, their opening Adagio sections notably diverge: the redaction appears to have freely retold the original music (Examples 12.5a, b).

The two middle sections – the second and third – are completely different in the two versions; not only the musical material, including different keys and metres, but the text too. Whereas the second section in the original is *Yako utverzhdenie moe*

oratorical style and this concerto suits him more. The latter seems to be the more probable, although the absence of any other works by him in this genre seems strange in this context. It should also be mentioned that the huge Sheremetev's collection of Russian eighteenth-century spiritual music contained few copies of this concerto (both double-choir and four-voice versions), attributed to Kozlovsky. (See *Reesry svetskikh i dukhovnykh muzykal'nykh proizvedeniy, ispolnyavshikhsya v kontsertakh...*, RGIA, f 1088, op 3 no 1732.)

46 *Sbornik khorovykh dukhovnykh kontsertov*. Score. RGIA, f 1119, op 1, 1825, no 58.

47 *Sbornik khorovykh dukhovnykh kontsertov Yaroslavskogo Kazanskogo zhenskogo monastyrya*. Part books 'абвг'. GMMK, f 283, ns 918–21.

48 The supposed first version of the concerto was printed in *Sbornik dukhovnykh kontsertov Vedelya i Degtyareva* (1913), while the manuscript of the later one was found in *Sbornik dukhovnykh kontsertov XVIII–nachala XIX veka*. RNB, f 1021, op 3 (I), no 2, concerto no 14.

(Allegro, 3/4, *B major*, 49 bars), in the redaction it is *Vonmi glasu molenia* (3/4, *Es major*, 81 bars); and the third section is *Ne ostavi mene, Gospodi* (Largo, 3/4, *Es major*, 26 bars) in the original and *As zhe na milost' Tvoyu upovakh* (Adagio, *C minor*, 4/4, 22 bars) in the redaction. Within the conventions of this genre's existence, the epithets 'new' or 'newest' thus appear to have been applied not only to those compositions written on new texts, but also to revised or rewritten works, often in a pastiche manner.

Even greater differences can be seen between two concertos similarly entitled *Gospodi, vozlyubi blagolepie* [O Lord, I love the magnificence]. They share no musical material at all except for the opening exclamations (Examples 12.6a, b). The copy of the concerto in *B major* is in the St Petersburg collection[49] while the concerto in *D major* is in the Ostankino collection. The newspaper announcement

Example 12.5 (a) Degtyarev: Concerto *K Tebe, Gospodi, vozdvigokh*, **first version**

Example 12.5 (b) Degtyarev: Concerto *K Tebe, Gospodi, vozdvigokh*, **second version**

of 3 June 1808 advertised *Gospodi, vozlyubikh, ogromnoy i s kodansom*. This is puzzling because *ogromnoy* [huge] applies to the former and *s kodansom* [with cadence] to the latter. The concerto from the St Petersburg collection has an unusually large number of sections (Adagio, *B major*, 3/4; Adagio, *G minor*, 4/4; Larghetto, *G minor*, 3/8; Adagio, *G minor*, 4/4; Adagio moderato, *B major*, 2/4; 'Largo minor', *G minor*, 2/4 and 'Allegro moderato da capo', *B major*, 4/4), but almost no melismatic material. The concerto from Ostankino, in contrast, has only three sections (Allegro, *D major*, 4/4; Largo, *G major*, ¾ and Allegro moderato, *D major*, 4/4), but is huge

---

49 *Sbornik khorovykh dukhovnykh kontsertov.* Score. RGIA, f 1119, op 1, 1825, no 58.

indeed, its melodic material is abundantly embellished and the score has marked cadencies.

Degtyarev's late style, despite its natural closeness to his previous styles, was nonetheless a distinctive and novel one, combining all the elements adopted by the Russian concerto from Berezovsky's times with the new ones. The unevenness of his style is characteristic of transitional periods and can be compared to Berezovsky's and his contemporaries' search for a new style in the 1760s. The concertos contain much high quality music and Degtyarev's popularity flatters his audience's understanding rather than denigrates the composer for his populism in the purist view. The socio-cultural value of his style is confirmed to some extent by the existence of at least one follower. There are two concertos by the composer Derzhavin, probably a serf from a Moscow estate, but of whom no other details are known. (The poet Gavrila Romanovich Derzhavin is unlikely to have been responsible for this music, for there is no evidence of his actually having practised composition.) These concertos – *Vozvestit v Sione* [To declare the name of the Lord in Zion], dated to by 1811, and the undated *Pomolikhsya litsu Tvoemu* [I besought Thy countenance] – both from the Moscow collection,[50] are written professionally, in a style very similar to Degtyarev and equalling him in taste and expression.

Nonetheless, Degtyarev's overuse of roulades and strongly sentimental-syrupy Italianate style, as well as his inability to achieve harmonious fullness or general organic balance, were duly noted and criticized even by his contemporaries, some of whom justified it as resulting from his emotional sincerity.[51] Such a conglomeration of modes, whose various components resist blending, much like oil and water, was typical for the majority of eighteenth-century Russian arts and literature. For example, the epigones of Nikolai Karamzin (Bortniansky's counterpart in literature) were criticized for their lack of the natural elegancy and simplicity in combining the Russian and French lexicons that Karamzin had succeeded in achieving. The same occurred with serf architects, whose characteristics are equally applicable to Degtyarev: 'Not having enough training for deep absorption of the style, these masters were led mostly by their own taste and it was they who introduced into estate Classicism and Empire that naïve charm that distinguishes provincial buildings'.[52]

---

50 *Sbornik khorovykh dukhovnykh kontsertov*, parts of descant, tenor and bass. GMMK, f 283, ns 4, 48, 51.

51 For a critique of Degtyarev see Levashev, 1986:202 referring to Gorchakov, 1808:29; Elizarova, 1944:340, (quotation without reference).

52 'Не имевшие достаточной подготовки для глубокого усвоения стиля, эти мастера руководствовались главным образом собственным вкусом, и они-то и внесли в усадебный классицизм и ампир ту наивную прелесть, которой отличаются провинциальные постройки'. S.V. Bezsonov, *Krepostnye arkhitektory*. Moscow: Vsesoyuznaya Akademia arkhitektury, 1938:44.

Example 12.6 (a) Degtyarev: Concerto *Gospodi, vozlyubikh blagolepie,* **first version**

Example 12.6 (b) Degtyarev: Concerto *Gospodi, vozlyubikh blagolepie,* **second version**

This criticism did not, however, appear to upset his audience, who were compensated, like Degtyarev's admirer Gorchakov, by the moving spontaneity and artlessness of his melodic expression. His public in all likelihood perceived his frank 'Italianisms' as a special chic, which made him a highly influential musical figure. This type of diluted style was characteristic of many concertos by other serf (or hired) estate choirmasters of the time, as well as of anonymous works. It seemed to appeal to the pre-war Moscow audience more than the more skilled but somewhat *passé* compositions of Bortniansky or Sarti. Bortniansky's style too – in the 1780s, had been significantly more Italian than reflected in his redaction of the 1810s, which later critics kept in mind as an example for comparison.

Whereas in the 1780s–90s the creative paths of Degtyarev and Bortniansky had interlaced, in the 1800s they drifted apart. Bortniansky, who surpassed Degtyarev in proficiency, talent and universality, could in fact clearly have developed toward a new style both earlier and better. Speculating on why did he not do so, the only certain indication concerns the Imperial court policy, which had tended to canonize the church-music style of the 1780s and to obstruct any changes resulting from stylistic fusions. It was Bortniansky himself, as the director of the Imperial Court Cappella, who was responsible for censoring Russian church music from 1796 to 1825.

Degtyarev, in contrast, being at the opposite end of the social pole – a serf musician – was free to write what his audience liked. To have reproached him for having expanded the operatic (read secular) traits would have been anti-historical, since this was a natural ongoing process, for which Bortniansky himself had been no less responsible in his own younger years. Degtyarev was criticized, rather, not for introducing a new operatic style into the church choir, but for doing so unfiltered and thereby leading Russian nationalists to accuse his early nineteenth-century concertos of 'Italianshchina'.[53] The irony, however, lies in that Degtyarev's concertos were seldom performed during the nineteenth century (safely resting in landlords' collections) and consequently his reputation in the eyes of the nineteenth-century musicians did not suffer; whereas Bortniansky, whose oeuvre was continuously published and performed, paid for his 'Italianshchina' merely through being a representative of Catherine's era of wigs and minuets and the general westernized style of the period. In the nationalist view the dramatic difference in the social status of the two composers was to Degtyarev's advantage: what was forgivable for the serf (Degtyarev), was reprehensible for the Italian-trained court functionary (Bortniansky).

The problem of a national style existed nonetheless, irrespective of who approached it: nationalist or not. This was a problem, however, that probably existed more for historians than for Bortniansky or Degtyarev themselves, who hardly seem to have given thought to it. The historian's problem lies in that the nineteenth-century nationalists tied together the concepts of *national* and *sacred* versus another antinomian pair – *Italian* (Western) and *secularized* – exactly in the spirit of the medieval Rus'ian Orthodox decision-makers.

Setting aside this entirely European and totally anti-historical polemics, and looking at the problem historically, the process reveals itself as following. When Bortniansky employed elements borrowed from European secular genres for his choral music, he did so indirectly, through the filter of previously Russified popular genres that had already done their work of selection and adaptation of borrowed elements and made them 'ours'. In addition to relying on this process, Bortniansky's own irreproachable taste and way of musical thinking prevented him from any non-organic use of those elements still not adopted by popular genres.

The musical backgrounds of Russia of the 1780s and the 1790s nonetheless significantly differed. At the beginning of the 1780s *Rossiyskaya pesnya* (already developed, mature and deeply enrooted in the national repertoire) served as a standard for musical tastes and as a foundation for Bortniansky's style. In the 1790s, however, with the development of music printing in Russia and of international contacts, the stream of French and Italian popular music entering the country made the environment much more Westernized, which public music thinking failed to

---

53 The phenomenon of 'Italianshchina' in Russian music is considered in Taruskin, 1997:214–23, 234–5.

fully digest and make its own. It was thus not to Degtyarev's discredit that urban popular music (whether the older genres or the new ones) could not help him in the problem of creating an organic national style. Such a process was one that required a certain period of time, dooming the composers of Degtyarev's generation to living in a transitional period: between classicism and romanticism (according to our traditional categorization); but also with nuances of late classicism and pre- or early romanticism (if a label is absolutely necessary), in which Degtyarev represented the *Empire* style. The latter is distinguished by its extensive forms, tedious plethora of adornments and overuse of dominant seventh chords; all of which concealed the lack of truly lively idiom, as reflected in the works of many second-rate composers of this generation.

Chapter 13

The Choral Concerto in the 1790s

Another among the music lovers of the Moscow nobility who had the means to support an estate serf choir was Count Vladimir Grigorievich Orlov – the youngest of five brothers of this famous family. At the peak of the 1780's vogue for contemporaneous spiritual music he established his own serf choir and developed a repertoire. One can only guess at how he and others like him may have acquired the scores. Since music publishing in Russia was in its infancy, editions of choral concertos were very expensive and this kind of music was distributed in handwritten copies produced by the cheap labour of serf copyists. The music sellers made copies upon commission and from the early 1790s, when the trade in scores and serf singers intensified, they began to advertise entire catalogues in the newspapers. A typical copy has been preserved of the double-choir concerto *Na Bozhestvenney strazhe* [On divine watch] with the stamp of the bookseller Shchokh.[1] Its composer was Lev Gurilev (1770–1844), Count Orlov's serf, who was permitted by his owner to sell his music, in contrast to the Sheremetev–Degtyarev relations.[2] Such compositions often became disseminated as anonymous or were inaccurately attributed.

The vagueness of attribution among both the old *partes*-singing and the new concertos had accompanied the spiritual concerto throughout its entire existence. It reached a climax in the 1780s, when Bortniansky's works began to be increasingly widespread and many new names appeared too, while the same texts from the Psalms were also being set by different composers. The muddle in ascription troubled some choir owners, who often attempted to put their libraries in order and attribute anonymous compositions through hearsay, especially when far from St Petersburg.

In 1787, already possessing several scores, Count Vladimir Orlov addressed Bortniansky through his correspondent in St Petersburg, Ivan Fursov, requesting a full list of the latter's choral compositions with the intention of purchasing all the scores. The Count also asked Bortniansky about the attribution of two anonymous scores that he held: 'Inquire of D.S. [Bortniansky] and let me know who composed *Nyne sily nebesnyya* [Now the heavenly powers] and the concerto *Ne otverzhi mene*

---

1 GMMK, f 283, no 14.

2 Lev Stepanovich Gurilev was also a kapellmeister of Count Orlov's orchestra and composer of piano music, including variations on Russian songs, Sonata (1794) and a cycle of 24 Preludes in different keys (1810). He was emancipated after his owner's death. He is known to have been Sarti's pupil (among other teachers). His son, Alexander Gurilev (1803–58), was a famous Muscovite composer, violinist and pianist (having studied with his father and John Field), especially popular for his songs and romances.

[Cast me not off in the time of old age]. He has written to me that these compositions are not his'.[3] The problem with attribution was indeed a very real one, because late-eighteenth-century concertos, in continuation of the *partes*-singing tradition, were normally mentioned by title only, without the name of the composer (similar to songs and *kanty* performances). However, the reputation of live contemporaneous composers in the late eighteenth century, and first and foremost Bortniansky, had contributed to interest in authorship, and the last third of the century was characterized by parallel processes of the anonymous circulation of repertoires and attempts to ascertain their attribution.

Bortniansky's answer concerning the attribution of the works in the Count's possession did not appear to satisfy the latter. Bortniansky, however, who knew this anonymous performance praxis only too well, could not have reasonably attributed any work without first seeing the score and his reply was perfectly correct. *Nyne sily nebesnyya*, for example, had been set to music by Berezovsky, Biordi, Sarti and Degtyarev, and by Bortniansky himself twice (although at the time of Orlov's inquiry Bortniansky might not yet have composed his second version). As for the concerto on the text *Ne otverzhi mene*, although rarely set to music, it nevertheless had some record in the *partes*-singing repertoire and Berezovsky himself probably composed two versions: the famous one in *D minor* and another (noted in a not entirely reliable source) for two choirs;[4] not to mention the possibility that some grassroots serf composer may have also decided to compete with Berezovsky.

That the title of a work alone was not enough for its attribution soon became obvious to music lovers and those who really cared about the correct ascription began to use musical incipits. Mentioned in above chapters *Katalog pevcheskoy note, pisanny 1793 goda Genvarya 16 dnya* [Catalogue for Vocal Music written on 16 January 1793] (KPN) appears to be a highly useful document that was probably compiled by the librarian of an owner of a serf choir. KPN offers an excellent reflection of estate choir repertoires and is a priceless source of information, though – inevitably – not error free. Its current location in a Moscow museum suggests that it came from the collection of a local estate and it accords with the Moscow public's special fondness for this kind of music at the time.

Each entry of KPN includes an incipit of the composition including text (instead of only a title), number of voices and the name of the composer. While the two first columns have been filled in completely, the third one (composer's name) is often blank. Only about forty entries out of a total of one hundred and fourteen have all the columns filled in, and more than half of these have Bortniansky's name. Because the damaged edge of the manuscript makes it difficult – in some cases impossible – to read the contents, most of the collection listed must thus remain anonymous.

The collections of concertos themselves offer a similar case, with often only some of the pieces having the name of the composer indicated. What makes it worse is that the attribution of many compositions varies from one collection to another. For

---

3   'Наведайтесь у Д. С. [Бортнянского] и уведомьте меня, кто сочинил "Ныне силы небесныя" и концерт "Не отвержи мене". Он ко мне писал, что сии сочинения не его' (Orlov-Davydov, 1878, I:325).

4   The existence of this concerto is mentioned in Askochensky, 1856:277.

example, the concerto *Gotovo serdtse moe* [My heart is fixed] by Bortniansky is listed as a concerto by B. Galuppi in the Collection of Spiritual Concertos of RNB;[5] the concerto *Plachu i rydayu* [I weep and wail] by J. Kozlovsky is noted as a composition by G. Sarti in the same collection and as a work by A. Vedel in the Collection of the Nizhny Novgorod Regional Universal Academic Library.[6] The muddle over Degtyarev's works, aggravated by his possible pseudonyms, was described in the previous chapter. In addition, concertos by Bortniansky and Degtyarev, like those of other popular composers, were often written anonymously. The owners of anonymous manuscripts thus appear either not to have listed the composers' names at all, or to have based their attributions on not always authoritative consultations, often naively associating popular compositions with the names of popular composers who were known to have written concertos with identical titles.

The KPN contains several such mistakes. For example, the concerto *Gospod'votsarisya* [The Lord reigneth] listed as the work of T. Traetta (no 82) also appears as a concerto by Berezovsky in the *Istoricheskaya khrestomatia tserkovnogo penia*, [Historical Reader of Church Singing], edited by M. Lisitsyn in 1902, who evidently had had a different manuscript as a source. The piece *Angel vopiashe* [The angel cried] (no 66) mentioned as (Joseph?) Kerzelli's is actually a part from the Liturgy by Vasily Pashkevich found in the Yaroslavl collection.[7] The same Pashkevich's Liturgy was misattributed to Nikeev in the KPN (no 89).

Another unclear case among the entries is no 102: it notes Cherubic Hymn by Berezovsky. Berezovsky wrote at least three such pieces, as the incomplete register of his works in HLA shows. However, somewhere between 1810 and 1820 Bortniansky published his own composition *Nyne sily nebesnya I*, whose gracious theme coincides (with a minor motivic variation in the first beat of the third bar) with the above-mentioned work by Berezovsky in the KPN. It was obviously popular in the early 1780 since a clavicembalo arrangement is found in Bortniansky's Album for Grand Duchess Maria Fedorovna (Example 13.1).[8]

Example 13.1   Bortniansky: *Nyne sily nebesnyya I*, **piano arrangement**

---

5   *Sbornik dukhovnykh kontsertov XVIII–nachala XIX veka*, RNB, Department of Manuscripts, f 1021, op 3 (1), no 2, Ll 56–62.

6   *Sbornik dukhovnykh pesnopeniy*, The Nizhny Novgorod Regional Universal Academic Library, Department of Manuscripts, R/362.

7   *Sbornik khorovykh dukhovnykh kontsertov Yaroslavskogo Kazanskogo zhenskogo monastyrya*. Part books 'дежз'. GMMK, f 283, ns 903–6.

8   The ms of the Album has not been found but the incipits of its pieces were published by N.F. Findeizen (1928, II, Supplement: CXVI).

The same piece appears anonymously in handwritten and printed collections in various keys, mostly as Cherubic Hymn (Example 13.2). Curiously, in the collection from the Archive of Vologda region it is listed as an 'ancient court' piece.[9]

A similar occurrence happened with another, equally popular, melody by Bortniansky known as the three voice *Da ispravitsya molitva moya I* [Let my prayer be set forth] no 3, in *F major*. In Bortniansky's corpus of works it is known in two variants: the familiar version in Jurgenson's edition (Example 13.3) and the composer's own arrangement for clavicembalo in the same album of Maria Fedorovna (Example 13.4). There is also a variant of this piece in the 1780's music album from Prince Yusupoff's collection,[10] in *G major*, (Example 13.5) where,

Example 13.2 Anonymous Cherubic hymn (the tenor part is lost)

Example 13.3 Bortniansky: Da ispravitsya molitva moya (I), (edited by P. Tchaikovsky)

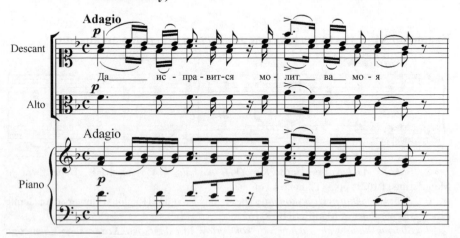

---

9   *Sbornik dukhovnykh pesnopeniy*, score, Gosudarstvenny Arkhiv Vologodskoy oblasti, without inventory number.

10   RNB, Department of Manuscripts, Collection of Yusupoff (f 891), no 31.

Example 13.4 **Bortniansky:** *Da ispravitsya molitva moya (I)*, **piano arrangement**

placed among popular operatic arias and embellished by vocalization (even more than in Degtyarev's latest concertos!) the source is hardly recognizable. It is not surprising, therefore, that there are also such contrafactums as an anonymous concerto titled *Na bezsmertnoe Tvoe uspenie* [To thy deathless Dormition] (Example 13.6) whose initial four measures resemble Bortniansky's choral version of the piece in *F major* published by the composer in the 1810s (Example 13.7) and a charming *rossiyskaya pesnya* 'Zhit' vo shchastie bez pomekhi' [To live happily without hindrance] (Example 13.8). These contrafactums, along with redactions and diversifications of the same compositions, were typical features of live choral music praxis and quite standard attributes of any popular vocal genre's development.

The above and following examples show how unreliable the old manuscripts could be. If today, in modern times, we find the misattribution of a piece in a manuscript or even in printed music from the end of the nineteenth or beginning of the twentieth century, when many eighteenth-century compositions were published, we should blame their compilers not for inaccuracy or arbitrariness, but for their credulity in blindly accepting the old sources, as if their very age automatically endowed them with trustworthiness. Even today, if there is only one source, whether it is an old or a later manuscript or edition, one has little choice but to trust it. One modern advantage over nineteenth-century musicians, however, is that we can critically, though tentatively, revise doubtful attributions, basing our hypotheses on different individual styles within the half-century period of this new concerto's existence.

In total, among the entire extant corpus of choral concertos of the period, there are about one hundred anonymous compositions *vis-à-vis* about two hundred attributed works whose existence is known about only from their mention in newspaper advertisements and other listings. Both groups include a number of titles in common, not found in any other source. While it is tempting to match up the anonymous works with titles of compositions that cannot be found today, it is safer to carefully apply stylistic analysis rather than repeat the mistakes of the owners of the serf choirs.

Example 13.5   Bortniansky: Da ispravitsya molitva moya (I), from an eighteenth–century handwritten album (Prince Yusupoff's collection)

Example 13.6 **Anonymous concerto** *Na bezsmertnoe Tvoe uspenie*

Example 13.7 **Bortniansky:** *Da ispravitsya molitva moya (I)*, **(1810s edition)**

Example 13.8 Rossiyskaya pesnya *Zhit' vo shchast'ye bez pomekhi*

Figure 13.1　Young singers. Unknown painter, late eighteenth – early nineteenth century

There was also the praxis of translating popular *partes*-singing works into the Italian notation. (One of such concertos was considered in Chapter 5 and a few are mentioned in the KPN.) In another case, an obvious *partes* concerto was attributed to Bortniansky.[11] Such pieces, though not belonging to the corpus of newly written concerto works, still belonged to the repertoire of the time and were performed in a secular milieu alongside the new music. This alone makes them sufficiently important to be considered in relation to the epoch.

It can be deduced from the sources of the late 1780s–90s that the repertory of the serf choirs, as well as their quality, became a subject of pride and prestige among the nobility, especially in Moscow. The entertainment of guests would often incorporate a mass at the estate's private church, as well as premières of new compositions of spiritual music (Krasnobaev, 1983:103). Count Orlov described one such event to his son:

> Monday, October 1: yesterday at mass we had chief chamberlain Golitsyn, Godin, I.M. Evreinov and Ammosov. Everyone enjoyed the singing very much. The concerto

---

11　*Sbornik khorovykh dukhovnykh kontsertov*, parts books, Yaroslavl, the 1780s. GMMK, f 283, ns 486, 487, 490.

performed was *Blagosloven Gospod'* [Blessed be the Lord]. The more Weinheimer listens to Bortniansky's concertos the more he loves them... Now they are performing the concerto *Da voskresnet Bog* [Let God arise], and it is very good. In ensembles of soloists Katin'ka sings the first part. We are leaving for mass in an hour.[12]

Bortniansky's popularity increased together with that of the choral concerto genre. The more concertos Bortniansky produced, the more the appetite of the audience was stimulated. It is not surprising that he was faced with serious competition from both professional composers, particularly Sarti, and home-grown serf musicians such as Stepan Degtyarev. Whether Bortniansky knew it or not, the peak of his popularity at the end of the 1780s was shortly to be followed by a fast approaching crisis, and the new musical idiom must already have been on the agenda.

The early 1790s brought about natural changes in preferences for particular genres by particular audiences, influencing the approach to musical life. Styles produced or preferred by the court began to play a lesser role in setting the tone in the arts. The serious opera – that baroque legacy that had been steadfastly maintained at the Imperial court – went into decline. The sentimental and comic operas, in contrast, continued to be welcome as usual and civic musical entertainment became established in many new cities. Serf culture with its horn music, choirs and theatres, reached a peak. Choral music continued to develop intensively and instrumental music-making became widespread. Popular music enjoyed a special boom. New romance firmly stood beside popular song, which also continued to proliferate. Generally, musical life took on contemporary European forms and progressed according to its own laws. As these forms became more natural with the broadening of the audience, a more organic and intimate style of musical expression evolved.

The eighteenth-century sentimentalist mood, to which the Russians were truly sensitive, had begun developing in literature since the 1760s in works by Fedor Emin (1735–70), Mikhail Popov (1742–c. 1790) and Mikhail Chulkov (1740–93). In the 1790s they were dramatically amplified by Nikolai Karamzin in his stories *Bednaya Liza*, *Frol Silin* and *Natalia – boyarskaya doch'*, which set the tone for well over the next decade. Music, too, played a considerable part in all this. In all the composers' works, whether those of the elder-generation Sarti, Tietz or Khandoshkin, the somewhat younger Kozlovsky and Bortniansky, or the youngest Fomin, Degtyarev, Vedel, Kashin and (later) Davydov, the new expression found its way into the genres and styles. The choral spiritual concerto of the 1790s particularly reflected the new mood.

By that time, westernized Russian society appears to have been experiencing a nostalgia for genres like the *Passion play*, *Stabat Mater* or *requiem*, which the

---

12 'Понедельник 1 октября. У обедни у нас были вчерась обер-камергер Голицын, Годен, И.М. Евреинов и Аммосов. Пение всем очень понравилось, пели концерт Благословен Господь. Вейнгамер чем чаще слышит концерты Бортнянского, тем более влюбляется в них... Сейчас пели концерт Да воскреснет Бог, шел хорошо, в выходных поет первой голос Катинька, через час пойдем к обедни...' (V.G. Orlov to A.V. Orlov, 27 October 1787. RGB, f 219, carton 8, no 8. L 35).

Greek Orthodox tradition did not develop, despite their having the function of a mourning liturgy for repose of the soul. What did exist was a melancholic kind of *partes* concerto – *repentant* concerto – as Gerasimova–Persidskaya has called it elsewhere, that functioned as a medium for compassion and catharsis. However, by the 1790s the baroquesque *repentant* concerto had fallen out of favour in the capitals because of its outdated style and Berezovsky's renewal had only just begun. It may have been felt that there was a certain lack of *repentant* concertos in the new style, especially after Russian society had begun to savour this experience through such works as Pergolesi's *Stabat Mater*, which was widely performed in the court repertoire and at Sheremetev's house; or oratorical compositions such as requiems that were composed only on such occasions as the death of Empress Elizabeth (Manfredini, 1762) or of Catherine's allies (Sarti and Kozlovsky in the 1790s); or Paisiello's *Passione di Gesù Cristo*. The time was ripe for Russia to begin creating her own music of this kind and, indeed, the genre of *repentant concerto* in the new style produced the most original works, and has remained a truly beloved part of the national eighteenth-century repertoire.

With the exception of Degtyarev, whose work was discussed in the previous chapter, the main practitioners of this new concerto were Bortniansky and Artemy Lukich Vedel (1767–1808), the latter of whom belonged to Degtyarev's generation. The choral music of all three composers written in the 1790s–1800s had important traits in common, first and foremost – predominant moods of melancholy, repentance and mourning. This is the main difference between these decades and that of the 1780s, when the major mode seemed to be the only one in which composers addressed their audience. Otherwise, however, the paths of these composers diverged. Compared to Degtyarev and Bortniansky, Vedel was closer to Degtyarev in the openness-to-exultation of his expression, but he achieved it from different sources to those employed by Degtyarev. While Degtyarev tended to the Italian operatic idiom, Vedel was more influenced by Ukrainian traditional music.

Artemy Vedel

A Ukrainian and a deeply religious man, Vedel graduated from the Kiev Ecclesiastic Academy already known for his expressive spiritual music. His first biographical mention relates to the end of January 1787, when he and Peter Ivanovich Turchaninov arrived with Sarti in Kremenchug from Kiev as students of Potemkin's Musical Academy. In 1788 he was called to Moscow by the governor-general, P.D. Eropkin, to manage his choir and orchestra. From 1792–6 Vedel lived in Kiev and from 1796–8 he worked in Kharkov as a director of vocal music and choirmaster at the State School (sometimes called the Latin School, or Kharkov Collegium). Vedel's whereabouts in 1798–1800 are unclear, but in 1800, as Kuck ascertained (1971), the musician was sentenced to life imprisonment for 'political crimes', and he died in 1808.

Differing from those who had grown up and worked in the capital cities of St Petersburg and Moscow, where the *partes*-singing repertoire had been almost completely replaced by the new style since the early 1760s, Vedel grew up in a stronghold of *partes*-singing tradition. The latter was characterized by the large number of *repentance* concertos, conveying a broad emotional spectrum including the 'profound grief, insurmountable "tearful" softness… emotional charge, ecstatic repentance and dissolution of the soul in tears' that led to the certain achievement of catharsis (Gerasimova-Persidskaya, 1994:111–12). Free of court officialism, Vedel naturally continued the *partes*-singing tradition, and primarily in the genre of *repentant* concertos.

One of the links that connected Vedel with this tradition was that of composer Maxim Prokhorovich Kontsevich, who was appointed a court musician in 1772. The date suggests that he belonged to the generation of Berezovsky and Bortniansky and was probably appointed to fill the lacuna formed by both talented men being away in Italy at the time. In 1773, when Berezovsky was already on his way back to Russia, Kontsevich was transferred from St Petersburg to the Kharkov Latin School, to institute musical classes. From this time on the school became a centre for preparing singers for the Imperial Court Cappella (Chudinova, MPES, II: 462). Kontsevich held this position until 1796 when he was replaced by Vedel.

One of the singers who graduated from the school was Pavel Balabin, who was Kontsevich's assistant and was taken to the Court Cappella in 1787. The event took place during the Empress's visit to Kharkov[13] after a performance of Kontsevich's welcoming cantata (Findeizen, 1929, II:n. XXVIII), and it may have been through Balabin that Kontsevich's concerto *Na Tya, Gospodi, upovakh* [In thee, O Lord, do I put my trust] reached the St Petersburg collection (Example 13.9).[14]

There is no indication of the date that this concerto was composed, but its stylistic features indicate the 1770s–80s, resembling the works of Tietz (who also composed choral pieces) and Peter Kozlovsky. The concerto continues the line of the *repentance* genre: from *partes*-singing – through Berezovsky. It presents a neat and simple classic style (without any *gallant* attributes) while avoiding *partes* heterophony on the one hand and the baroquesque serious polyphony of Berezovsky on the other. Kontsevich took the simplest elements from each of these established styles and blended them in a natural way. He succeeded in achieving the organic result that his fellow composers had tried to reach *before* Berezovsky, but which was only actually possible *after* Berezovsky.

This style, which can be interpreted as a new Ukrainian idiom, was the point of departure for Vedel. Picking up the unbroken line of *repentant partes* concertos that had been translated by Kontsevich into a contemporaneous classic idiom, Vedel, as a musician of the new generation, developed it further into a very specific style

---

13 Personal record of Pavel Balabin, RGIA, f 1349, op 4, 1805, no 1.

14 *Sbornik khorovykh sochineniy*. Score. RGIA, f 1119, no 60. Ed. by M. Rytsareva and published in *Ukrains'ka muzychna spadshchina: Statti, materiali, dokumenty*. Vyp. 1. Ed. M. M. Gordiychuk. Kiev: Muzychna Ukraina, 1989:137–50.

that resists any definition within the context of the two Russian capitals' culture. Although not all his scores bear this explicitly Vedel imprint, there are several concertos without which eighteenth-century Russian music would have been much the poorer. There are about sixty choral works known as Vedel's, one third of which are concertos and the others liturgical pieces. Most of his concertos are very long, sometimes expanding into a kind of choral fantasy poem. There is little contrast among the sections, much like among the concertos themselves. They display a typical succession of slow minor-mode sections in Vedel's common moods, from melancholia and the pathetic to the heart-rending. The overwhelming majority of his music is written in the minor mode. Major-mode fragments are rare and brief, usually contained within a few bars.

Example 13.9   Kontsevich: Concerto *Na Tya, Gospodi, upovakh,* **section 1**

Vedel's development of musical material is reflected mostly in melody, and only partly in texture. His melody is usually vivid and expressive, blending a multitude of idioms among which *znamenny* and *Kiev* chants, *kanty* and *psalmy* as well as Ukrainian songs can be recognized (Borovik, 1971:139–41). Motifs referring to the ancient chant are found mostly in cadences and Vedel usually gives them to the choral *tutti*, similar to Bortniansky. Such elements as syncope, dotted rhythm and wide use of the leading tone were also quite common in Degtyarev's and Bortniansky's later works (see below). Vedel's more individual style is manifested in ascending leaps to the tonic (with eventual filling) and energetic fourth leaps from the second to the fifth (harmonized as fifths of the dominant and tonic chords). Minor-mode motifs with leaps and dotted rhythm, though often put in three-beat metre, unequivocally associate the music with the *march funèbre*, which serves to reinforce the gravity of his music's temper. Examples of this can be found in the Adagio from *Poyu Bogu moemu* [I will sing unto the Lord] (Example 13.10), the slow section of *V molitvakh neusypayushchuyu* [Neither the tomb nor death had power over the Theotokos] (1794–95) and the Adagio from *Dokole, Gospodi* [How long wilt thou forget me, O Lord?]. The latter is interesting as an example of a long vocalization given to the tenor solo (sometimes in duos parallel in thirds).

Example 13.10   Vedel: Concerto *Poyu Bogu moemu*, **section 2**

Known as a tenor soloist himself, Vedel tended to bestow this part with special expression, generously filling it with melismatic cantillations, scale-like passages with augmented seconds and chromatic motives. Its painful melancholy and almost ecstatic effusions have no analogues in either earlier or later Russian-Ukrainian spiritual concertos, but it does refer to two other sources. One is the *dumy* (epic songs) of Ukrainian *kobzari* (blind wandering singers accompanying themselves on the *kobza*, a lute-like instrument, sometimes referred to as *bandura* and widespread in Moldova, Romania and Hungary). The second is the East-European Jewish *khazanut*, which has never previously been noted as a source but which is quite obviously apparent in the music and awaits confirmation by future research. Both *dumy* and *khazanut* only seem to be alien genres. First, their interconnectedness has already been ascertained, as well as that between Ukrainian and Jewish secular folklore.[15]

---

15 See Moisey Beregovsky, [Mutual Influences Between Ukrainian and Jewish Music (in Yiddish)], in *Visnshaft un revolutsye*, 6 (1935, no 2:79–101); in Ukrainian, in *Radjanska muzyka* 1936, no 5:30–50; Z. Skuditsky, [On Ukrainian Influences on Yiddish Folklore Song (in Yiddish)], in *Visnshaft un revolutsye*, 6 (1935, no 2:103–54); Moshe Hoch, [The Jewish

Second, both most probably are descended from Khazarian culture (Yasser, 1948; see also Introduction). Unlike *dumy* and *khazanut*, which have an augmented second between the third and the fourth, Vedel simply used the one between the sixth and the seventh of the harmonic minor mode compatible with the conventional European eighteenth-century idiom (Example 13.11).

Example 13.11   Vedel: Concerto *Dokole, Gospodi*, **section 2**

Paying all his attention to the melody, Vedel, similar to Degtyarev, neglected harmonic development, which creates an extraordinary event out of even a subdominant chord or tonic-dominant cadenzas in relative key. The texture is more interesting, since besides a flexible mastering of various kinds of choral sound, Vedel also widely applied an organum-like movement in parallel thirds (also favoured by Bortniansky and Sarti) typical for *partes*-singing. Regarding imitational polyphony, he, similar to Bortniansky, wrote fugato in finales, but unlike him (and like Degtyarev) he made little use of imitational technique within the sections as a means of development of form.

Avoiding the traditional devices of choral polyphony (again like Degtyarev), Vedel nevertheless sought to use the colourful and descriptive potential of choral texture. In his concerto *Na rekakh vavilonskikh* [By the rivers of Babylon] he divided the choir into two groups. The first group consisted of middle voices and second bass and formed a protracted pedal, with the second group – descants and first basses – imitating the undulating flow of the river (Example 13.12). The performance of such a fragment *pianissimo* by *tutti* must have produced an extraordinary sound, not known elsewhere in the eighteenth-century Russian choral repertoire.

Vedel's tragic biography on the one hand, and his belonging to the peripheral rather than to the mainstream culture of both capitals on the other, prevented his work from being known in the capitals at the beginning of the nineteenth century, when the culture of the choral spiritual concerto still existed. This probably explains why

Folksong and the Ukrainian Folksong: A Delineation of Musical Communication in Folklore] (in Hebrew, MA Thesis, Tel-Aviv University, 1977).

neither newspaper advertisements nor estate collections of choral music mention or contain his compositions. The only collection from St Petersburg known to me that includes his two concertos was compiled at the very end of the choral concerto's existence, in 1825.[16]

A completely different destiny for Vedel's works awaited him in the Ukraine and in the Russian provinces, where he was known and much loved. Economic and cultural connections between the Ukraine and Russia served to promote his compositions in Central Russia and the Volga-bank towns. Merchant lovers of choral music who visited Kharkov, where Vedel would have been popular, acquired the scores and thus broadened the repertoires of the amateur choirs that they themselves often established.[17]

Example 13.12 Vedel: Concerto *Na rekakh vavilonskikh*, fragment from section 5

---

16   *Sbornik khorovykh dukhovnykh kontsertov*. Score. RGIA, f 1119, op 1, 1825, no 58.
17   See I. Dryakhlov, Istoria razvitia khorovogo penia v sele Pavlovo Nizhegorodskoy gubernii. Pavlovo, 1914.

Bortniansky's 1790s Concertos

The question of who had set the new tone in the early 1790s is not as simple as it was in relation to the 1780s, when Bortniansky was the sole trend-setter. Any of the three – Bortniansky, Degtyarev or Vedel, may have been the pioneer. Bortniansky most probably began to produce *repentant* minor-mode concertos at the beginning of the 1790s, though alongside those in his earlier style (known as ns 5, 26, 29, 31). According to the KPN, by 1793 he had already written the concertos *Zhivy v pomoshchi Vyshnyago* [He Who dwelleth in the help of the Most High] (later known as no 21), *Glasom moim* [I cried unto the Lord with my voice] (no 27) and *Uslyshi, Bozhe, glas moy* [Hear my voice, O God] (no 30) in an eight-voice version. Newspaper advertisements from 1793 – 1796 add *Vozvedokh ochi moi v gory* [I will lift up mine eyes unto the hills] (no 24) and *Ne umolchim nikogda* [We, though unworthy, will never refrain from speaking of thy power] (no 25). The last information to be found on Bortniansky's compositions during his lifetime is in HLA (1804). Advertised for sale there were his twelve double-choir concertos, ten of which the composer later published, and fourteen four-voice concertos, which have never been printed and mostly remain unknown. Finally, Bortniansky's two best *repentant* concertos – *Skazhi mi, Gospodi, konchinu moyu* [Lord, make me to know mine end] and *Vskuyu priskorbna esi dushe moya* [O my God, my soul is cast down within me], have neither been mentioned in sales lists nor included in the collections, which suggests their having been written toward the end of the composer's life, in the late 1810s, coinciding with the end of the choral concerto era and the Russian long eighteenth century in general.

The seven *repentant* concertos written in the 1790s–1810s presented a new Bortniansky, dramatically differing from the earlier one as well as from his younger contemporaries – Degtyarev and Vedel. These concertos exhibit the most internalized, reserved and noble manner, combining a simple lyricism with slightly sentimental natural intimacy (somewhat limited by the choral genre) coloured by elegiac or melancholic tones. Their middle movements, written in the major mode, are strict and confident, totally lacking his earlier pastoral gallantry. They preserve features of the earlier hymnal and *kanty* genres, and avoid any references to minuet. Their melodic material, which acquired and organically fused a Russian-Ukrainian folksy-speech manner, clearly refers to *partes* repentant concertos and the style of Berezovsky.

The references to Berezovsky in Bortniansky's music suggest that the most serious competition to the latter came not from his younger contemporaries Degtyarev and Vedel but from the past – Berezovsky. In the late 1780s Bortniansky may already have realized that the present vogue for the choral concerto, for which he himself was responsible, had also led to Berezovsky's masterpiece *Ne otverzhi mene* [Cast me not off in the time of old age] coming into fashion.[18] In this connection, a certain

---

18 This follows not only from the evidence from Count Orlov's circle but also from the existence of a handwritten copy of the concerto with the stamp of the 1790's music dealer Shchokh, deposited in the British Museum.

nuance in the earlier-mentioned correspondence between Count Vladimir Orlov and Bortniansky in 1787, is worth consideration. As can be deduced from Orlov's words, Bortniansky had merely replied formally to him that the queried compositions (*Nyne sily nebesnyya* [Now the heavenly powers] and *Ne otverzhi mene*) were not his, without bothering to explain that there could be various attributions, or perhaps even offer the more polite suggestion that Orlov send him the musical incipits for identification. While *Nyne sily nebesnyya* had indeed been given multiple settings, the concerto in question in all probability was a popular *D minor* one by Berezovsky; but something appears to have prevented Bortniansky from mentioning Berezovsky's name. One way or another, Count Orlov shortly determined that the composer was indeed Berezovsky, and on 24 September 1787 he wrote to his son: 'Not long ago we learned Berezovsky's *Ne otverzhi mene*, a concerto of different taste than Bortniansky's, yet not bad at all.'[19] A month later he continued updating his son about the development of his choir. His letter of 27 October 1787 reads:

> Weinheimer has begun to fulfil his position (as a *Kapellmeister*). Three concertos have been performed in his presence: *Ne otverzhi mene* [Cast me not off in the time of old age], *Kol' vozlyublenna* [How amiable are thy tabernacles, O Lord of hosts!] and *Sei den' ego zhe* [This is the day which the Lord hath made]. Enjoying the first so much, he said: "I haven't heard anything like that before". After hearing the last two, he couldn't tell which he enjoyed most, liking both very much. I am sure that, upon hearing the others, he will like them no less; with the exception of *Ne otverzhi mene* by Berezovsky, all the other nine are composed by Bortniansky.[20]

Another attestation to Berezovsky's pre-eminence over Bortniansky, albeit in the opinion of a later generation, came from Pushkin's circle: 'Not at all, Berezovsky was even more original than Bortniansky' – answered the young A.O. Smirnova (Rosset) in the 1830s in her reply to A.S. Pushkin, who had thought that all the sacred music performed in churches was either composed by Bortniansky, or consisted of ancient chants.[21]

A comparison between Berezovsky and the new Bortniansky style reveals a new correlation, based more on similarity than on contrast. Bortniansky's choral writing

---

19 'Выучили недавно концерт: Не отверже мене сочинения Березовского, он другого вкусу как Бортнянского; однако же не дурен' (V.G. Orlov to A.V. Orlov, 24 September 1787. RGB, f 219, carton 8, no 8, L 25).

20 'Вейнгамер [капельмейстер] послупил в должность. Пели при нем три концерта: Не отверже мене, Коль возлюбленна и Сей день его же. Первой ему так полюбился, что говорит: подобного не слыхал, а прослушав два последние, не знал которому отдать преимущество, которотко сказать, все очень полюбились. Я уверен, что когда и другие услышит, что и те ему не меньше понравятся, кроме концерта Не отверже мене, который сочинения Березовского, все другие 9 сочинены Бортнянским' (V.G. Orlov to A.V. Orlov, 27 October 1787. RGB, f 219, carton 8, no 8, L 35).

21 'Ничуть, и даже Березовский отличался большей оригинальностью, чем Бортнянский' (А.O. Smirnova-Rosset, *Iz zapisnykh knizhek 1826–1845*. St Petersburg, 1895:326).

had become more polyphonic. While in the 1780s he had used the fugato form in one of the middle sections in four-section cycles, later, beginning with concerto no 19, he also used it in finale sections. The originality of the fugato forms in Bortniansky's concertos gained frequent mention (for example Khivrich, 1971; Mikhailenko, 1985; Protopopov, 1987). He played with these forms in an artistically free and informal style, utilizing their apparent 'irregularity' and avoiding traditional techniques. Sometimes his imitations were merely scattered symbolically, paying tribute to the conventionalism of the genre. He often chose to present the entire opening themes of his *repentant* concertos as motet-like imitative introductions, as if intentionally disciplining the formulation of the musical idea by referring to 'retro' associations.

Bortniansky was highly inventive in incorporating polyphonic devices into various kinds of texture. For example, in his concertos 21 and 30 he blended the technique of imitation with that of subsidiary voices (Examples 13.13a, b); in concerto 24 he distributed imitations between the bass and two upper voices in parallel sixth, similar to the solo introduction to a Russian protracted choral song (Example 13.14); in concerto 25 he made the introduction of the second voice similar to the *kanty* tradition (Example 13.15); and in concerto 27 he presented imitation as an antiphon between the upper and the lower voices – a device broadly

Example 13.13 (a)   Bortniansky: Concerto *Zhivy v pomoshchi Vyshnyago*

Example 13.13 (b)   Bortniansky: Concerto *Uslyshi, Bozhe, glas moy*

Example 13.14 Bortniansky: Concerto *Vozvedokh ochi moi*, **section 1**

Example 13.15 Bortniansky: Concerto *Ne umolchim nikogda*, **section 1**

used in his choral texture (Example 13.16). Sometimes his use of imitation was only in strict rhythm, leaving the melodic structure and intervals of introduction free (Example 13.17). The structure of his thematic material is full of folk song elements, like the restrained, strict stepwise motivic motion characteristic of Russian protracted songs, and the ornamental gestures surrounding the harmonic tones of the melody typical for Ukrainian songs. Another new feature for Bortniansky, albeit not new in itself, was the song-like repetition of themes within relatively short time spans in the introductory sections. This was one of the distinctive attributes of concertos in the 1760s, typical to Berezovsky and his contemporaries.

Example 13.16 Bortniansky: Concerto *Glasom moim ko Gospodu vozzvakh,*
                    section 1

Example 13.17   Bortniansky: Concerto *Vskuyu priskorbna esi*, **section 1**

Also reminiscent of Berezovsky in Bortniansky's works are such expressive elements as frequent tritons, dotted rhythms and most of all the *Sturm und Drang* repetitive 'knocking' (lately mostly associated with Beethoven's *The Fifth*) rhythmical formula, used by Bortniansky, similarly to Berezovsky, mainly in the finale sections (Example 13.18). In Bortniansky's music, however, all these elements are softened and smoothed, more sentimental and romantic, a foretaste of the early nineteenth-century popular style of Russian romance music by Alyabyev, Verstovsky and Varlamov.

Example 13.18   Bortniansky: Concerto *Glasom moim ko Gospodu vozzvakh*,
          fragment of Finale

Alongside the novelties in Bortniansky's later style, he remained faithful to march and *kanty* rhythms, as in his early major mode concertos. He seems to have achieved a special mastery of hybridization, probably thanks to the new (for him) element of the polonaise, as can be seen in his three-beat middle section from the concerto no 24 (Example 13.19).

Example 13.19   Bortniansky: Concerto *Vozvedokh ochi moi,* **section 2**

The march itself underwent change in his music within the context of *repentant* expression, much as it did with other composers in the 1790s. Bortniansky began to apply the march rhythm to the main – opening – material in the slow sections (Example 13.20). Accommodating this new taste, the composer also related to the *march funèbre,* as for example in concerto no 29 (Example 13.21).

Concertos no 32 *Skazhy mi, Gospodi, konchinu moyu* [Lord, make me to know mine end] and no 33, *Vskuyu priskorbna esi, dushe moya* [O my God, my soul is cast down within me], deserve special comment in being both the best and most complimented by historical reputation during the nineteenth century. The former enjoyed a special popularity to which Tchaikovsky's well publicized appraisal contributed: 'I consider this concerto to be the best among all thirty-five. P. Tch.'[22] The second concerto, according to the legend of Bortniansky's biography, was performed by court singers called to the composer's death bed.

Both compositions are of a mourning character and in a wider general aesthetic sense can be regarded as Russian requiems *a cappella.* They continue, develop and epitomize the Russian-Ukrainian 'repentant path' and each in its own way refers to Berezovsky's *Ne otverzhi mene vo vremya starosti* [Cast me not off in the time of old age], as if memorializing that unsurpassed masterpiece and paying tribute to the great master.

---

22 'Концерт этот я считаю лучшим из всех тридцати пяти. П. Ч.' Tchaikovsky edited the complete collection of Bortniansky's works, commissioned by P. Jurgenson: Bortniansky, *Dukhovno-muzykal'nye sochineniya na polny khor,* ed. by Tchaikovsky. St Petersburg: Yurgenson, 1881–2. For more details see Chapter 14.

Example 13.20   Bortniansky: Concerto *Gospod' prosveshchenie moe*, **fragment of section 3**

Example 13.21   Bortniansky: Concerto *Voskhvalyu imya Boga moego s pesniyu*, **fragment of section 3**

To begin with the opening themes, that of no 32 is constructed on the same tonic third as *Ne otverzhi*, while in no 33 the opening theme simulates its tonality, motifs and rising introductory theme. In addition, the themes of the first movement and of the finale are actually fragments from the main theme of *Ne otverzhi mene* (see Example 5.14). Many other reminiscences of Berezovsky's *Ne otverzhi* are scattered throughout both concertos, such as the energetic *B major* section of the *Allegro moderato* and a virile and impelling movement of the final fugue from no 33. Remarkably, no 32 is the only concerto that lacks Bortniansky's usual references to the *kanty* idiom.

   This concerto, no 32, has a unique place among Bortniansky's works. Distancing himself from his traditional sentimental popular idiom, the composer adopted here the elevated style of some of Beethoven's *Largo*, linking him with Gluck and, more distantly, with the styles of early eighteenth-century oratorio and *opera seria*. The ratio between choral and solo segments is unique in this concerto. No other

Example 13.22 Bortniansky: Concerto *Skazhi mi, Gospodi, konchinu moyu,* **section 2**

Bortniansky concerto has half of its duration dedicated to solo fragments, which reinforces its association with *opera seria* and the Catholic mourning mass. The material of the solo fragments, which comprise either a Neapolitan sixth chord in the cadence or declamatory and sigh motifs, link the concerto to the old style.

In this concerto, references to baroquesque *opera seria* continue to offer a sharp contrast between the two eight-bar periods, expressing the two *affekts* of humility and protest that constitute the *Largo*. The first – the *tutti* 'Otstavi ot mene rany Tvoya' [Remove thy stroke away from me] in *A flat major* and the second, 'Uslyshi molitvu moyu, Gospodi, i molenie moe vnushi, slez moikh ne premolchi' [Hear my prayer, O Lord, and give ear unto my cry; hold not thy peace at my tears], sung by a quartet of soloists in *F minor*, comprise a most impressive dialogue of emotions struggling in the mourning soul (Example 13.22).

Remarkably, this concerto is the only one among Bortniansky's works in which the finale fugue is indeed a real one, without any resemblance to the ironically formal finale fugues of his other concertos. The extensive, loquacious, deliberately monotonous but captivating fugue is seemingly meant to twirl, divert, distract and dissolve the thoughts of the mourner, to impart existential wisdom, to convey the unity of life and death.

Both ns 32 and 33 have a notable harmonic detail. Never before had Bortniansky used in his concertos such modal proceedings as I – VII natural – III. Highly typical for the eighteenth-century Ukrainian settings of the ancient chant and *partes*-singing, they then seem to have been deliberately avoided in the new concerto idiom for several decades. Consequently, they appear even more unexpected and significant in these later compositions. Bortniansky placed this chordal succession at the dramaturgically crucial point, approaching the finale, where it could not pass unnoticed. Their obvious semantic association with the ancient chant served as a symbol of eternity – already in accord with the new moods of the nineteenth century. The composer thus anticipated the use of this morpheme by the late nineteenth-century Russian composers. Making this *chef-d'œuvre* emphatically old-fashioned in comparison to the transient and superficially fashionable taste of his young semi-educated rivals, he probably rightly identified himself with Berezovsky and thereby aptly and with dignity closed the circle.

Chapter 14

Bortniansky in the Nineteenth Century

There is astonishingly little information available about Bortniansky's life in the early 1790s other than the mention of a small number of compositions. The noted works include the *Première livraison* of his French romances in 1793[1] (which was not, however, followed by a second volume), and the new choral concertos listed in music dealers' advertisements in 1793, 1795 and 1797. Derzhavin's text to Bortniansky's cantata *Lyubitelyu khudozhestv* [To the connoisseur of the arts] is also known, being written for the inauguration of Count Stroganov's house, rebuilt after a fire in 1791. And finally, there is the score of his hymn *Pesnoslovie* for male choir (1797) composed in honour of the new Emperor Paul I.

Bortniansky does not seem to have been greatly in demand at the (already not so young) Young court, although at the Imperial court he continued his work as director of vocal music, which he had begun in the early 1780s. The death in April 1795 of Mark Fedorovich Poltoratsky, director of the Imperial Court Cappella, did not result in Bortniansky's immediate promotion. The Empress clearly did not consider him a suitable replacement, despite Bortniansky's superior education and three decades of experience with the Cappella choir. It is hard to say how long this institution would have been able to continue to exist without a director had Catherine II lived longer, but Paul I settled the matter immediately upon his ascent to the throne (6 November 1796), appointing Bortniansky to the position (11 November). From then on, and for the next twenty-nine years, Bortniansky was its director, remembered in history as the person who so dramatically elevated its status.

Since Bortniansky's social rank did not correspond to the requirements of the new position he received simultaneous promotion to the VI grade, as Collegial Counsellor, equal to a Colonel. Half a year later (28 April 1797) he received promotion to the next rank, that of State Counsellor (Brigadier), and his last promotion, nine years later on 18 November 1806, was to the rank of Active State Counsellor (Major-General).[2] However, whatever Bortniansky may originally have thought would be

---

1   The full title of the edition is *Recueil de romances et chansons, composée pour Son Altesse Impérial Madame la Grand-Duchesse de Russie, par D. Bortniansky, Maitre de Chapelle au service de S. M. I. Première livraison. A St Petersbourg, de l'imprimérie de Breitkopf, en 1793.* There is also mention of a new publication of several of Bortniansky's romances in   Gerstenberg's announcement in the January 1795 issue of *Magasin   dlya rasprostranenia obshchepoleznykh znaniy i izobreteniy s prisovokupleniem modnogo zhurnala, raskrashennykh risunkov i muzykal'nykh not.* (Rapatskaya, 1977:40).

2   *Delo o dostavlenii A.A. Arakcheyevu svedeniy o sluzhbe direktora Pridvornoy pevcheskoy kapelly D.S. Bortnyanskogo.* RGIA, f 519, op 1, 1817, no 229.

his role at the Cappella, the decisions were not his alone to take. The shower of edicts and orders issued by the new Emperor fell heavily upon every aspect of Russian society (for example, the ban on wearing round hats or laces in boots because of their association with the French revolution). The vast number of these petty dictates were later to overshadow the more serious, rational and progressive reforms that Paul I was determined to achieve.

As one of the measures to stabilize the economy Paul set in motion a campaign to reduce waste and luxury at the court. (Setting a personal example, he even demanded that his own family begin to eat from simple pewter ware.) In charge of all this was the appointed Marshall of the Imperial court, Count Sheremetev, Paul's close friend from childhood, the richest and stingiest man in the country. Music, as always in periods of budgetary restrictions, was the first to suffer. The military regimental orchestras, for example, were reduced to five players each. As for the Court Cappella, Count Sheremetev presented a plan for such drastic cuts in the number of singers that it was quite a challenge for Bortniansky to fight for his choir members. His reply to the Count's demand reads:

Your Excellency the Count,
Dear Sir!

Upon receiving from Your Excellency the confirmed list of members of the staff, I have selected from the present number of ninety-three court singers twenty-four (as stated) singers of outstanding skill, a list of whom is enclosed herewith together with the names of the rest.

As to Your Excellency's request for my opinion regarding whether this number is sufficient for performing sacred services, I must reply as follows.

When, according to church regulations, the singers will be divided into two choirs, their number will undoubtedly appear to be insufficient, particularly during special ceremonies. Your Excellency might also be aware that a certain number of singers are usually assigned to the small church and it could consequently transpire that additional divisions would be needed during the trips of the Highest Imperial family, and also in the presence of His Imperial Majesty. My opinion is that we would need twenty-four singers in each choir and twenty-four for the small church, for other unexpected occasions and as replacements, should anyone in the two choirs be unable to perform for health reasons.

These three choirs would require a total of seventy-two singers. To these I consider it necessary to add underage singers undergoing training as well as the currently employed vocal instructors Vasiliy Pashkevich and Fedor Makarov.

However, all this depends on the highest will of His Imperial Majesty and I am merely expressing my views as to a possible arrangement should the number of singers prove to be insufficient!

The Director of the Court Choir, Collegial Counsellor,
Dmitry Bortniansky.
January... 1797.[3]

---

3   'Сиятельнейший граф, / Милостивый государь! / По объявлении мне от Вашего Сиятельства Высочайше конфирмованного штата, выбрал я из числа ныне состоящего девяносто трех придворного хора певчих, предписанное число двадцать

Bortniansky inherited a choir not only in a hostile period, but also in the same desperate economic and organizational state of all the subsidized institutions at the end of Catherine's rule, characterized by corruption and inflation. The salary allotted in the past to the singers had long become insufficient, and in order to provide for their families they had to seek additional work. Deprived of such extra earnings when accompanying the court on its imperial journeys, they were often left without means of support. In April 1797, upon returning from the Emperor's journey to Moscow for his coronation, and finding themselves penniless, they had no choice but to collectively appeal to the Emperor for financial assistance.

At that time, Bortniansky was apparently not in a position to help. But later, during Alexander's rule, Bortniansky's actions were to include the separation of the *a cappella* choir from the opera chorus, an increase in salaries for singers, and the purchase and renovations of new living quarters for the choir, and so on. These later achievements probably became possible only through the support of Her Imperial Majesty the Empress Mother Maria Fedorovna, Bortniansky's old student, who was involved in extensive charitable activities. For his part, Bortniansky was always available to Maria Fedorovna as her advisor when purchasing paintings, in such matters as quality, prices, frames, arrangement on the walls and so on – using the profession he had acquired in his youth. He had even presented her with the gift of a picture, an act that attested to his high status in being permitted to do so. (It was traditional at that time for the royal family to partially refund gifts given to them. In this case Bortniansky was returned half of the 3,000 roubles he had paid for the picture; but even so, this was still a considerable expenditure for him, considering his annual salary of 2,785 roubles.) A characteristic detail illustrating their friendly relationship is that Maria Fedorovna herself used to provide Bortniansky with the

---

четыре отличного достоинства, о которых при сем прилагаю реэстр с показанием остальных. /А как Вашему Сиятельству угодно было при том требовать моего мнения, может ли быть достаточно сего числа в пении церковного обряду, то должен дать на то некоторое объяснение. / Когда сей хор по церковному чиноположению разделится на два клироса, то несомненно окажется не достаточен, а нарочито в торжественные дни. При том Вашему Сиятельству небезызвестно, что некоторое число певчих отделяется обыкновенно к службе в малую церковь, а может впредь во время походов должно будет делать еще большие отделения для Высочайшей Императорской фамилии, следственно в присутствии Его Императорского Величества. По мнению моему понадобится положить число певчих по двадцать четыре на каждой клирос, а двадцать четыре для отделения в малую церковь, для иных впредь непредвиденных случаев, так и в дополнение тех оной из числа двух хоров по причине болезни могут не в состоянии исправлять их должность. / Сии три хора составляют семидесяти двух человек, к которым за необходимо нужно почитаю прибавить для учения малолетних, так как и ныне находящихся в должности учителей пения, Василия Пашкевича и Федора Макарова. / В прочем все состоит в Высочайшей воле Его Императорского Величества и не инако представляю сие мое мнение, как примерное начертание, в таком только случае, когда бы по ответу оказалось положенное по штату число недостаточным! / Правящий хором придворных певчих Коллежский советник / Дмитрий Бортнянский. / Генваря ... дня 1797 г.'D.S. Bortniansky to N.P. Sheremetev. January 1797' (RGIA, f 1088, op 1 no 376).

ginger water he took for its curative properties. Bortniansky's correspondence with Maria Fedorovna's secretary Grigory Ivanovich Villamov reveals that she also often addressed Bortniansky regarding various musical matters at the other institutions (Filshtein, 1989).

The increment in the singers' salaries eventually obtained by Bortniansky nonetheless proved to be insufficient against the increasingly expensive life in St Petersburg, and the composer sought every possible way to improve their state. During the summers he would invite some of the singers to Pavlovsk, where they lived on his estate. His influence when endorsing financial petitions to Maria Fedorovna, including his personal evaluations of the singers, affected her decisions and additional funds were indeed often provided. As an unofficial patroness of the Cappella, Maria Fedorovna also sometimes acted as godmother at the baptism of children born to choir members. Bortniansky himself served as the first address in all the singers' personal matters (applications, claims, certifications and so on).[4]

Apart from his achievements in improving the financial and living conditions of the singers, Bortniansky took special care of those who were minors. He rescinded corporal punishment, created a generally congenial atmosphere and organized their education in literacy, languages and math so as to prepare them to find work should they lose their singing voice. When recruiting young boys for the choir, Bortniansky took into consideration not only their singing talents but also their general intelligence.

Not everything was under his control, however. A great scandal broke out in 1819 when Ilya Umanets, the seventeen-year-old singer, possessor of a beautiful voice and handsome appearance, who enjoyed special favours (like long paid vacations and new uniforms) and was a distant relation of Bortniansky from the west Ukraine gentry, was suddenly fired. This was at the order of Emperor Alexander I, following the so-called 'denunciation of the singer Alyakritsky over various circumstances in the singers' house' which had reached the Emperor via Alexander Naryshkin, Marshall of the Imperial court.[5] The real reason was not mentioned in the protocols of the court office, but indirectly, from the measures eventually undertaken, one can infer that homosexual experiences were prevalent among the Court Cappella staff,

---

4　The following certificate may serve as an example of Bortniansky's official activity: 'Команды моей придворный певчий коллежский регистратор Михайло Витковский желание имеет совокупиться законным браком с девицей Римско-католического исповедания Елисаветой Михайловной дочерью Вердерского, – в сем его желании от меня ему позволяется, и что действительно он еще холост в том сим за подписем моим с приложением герба моего печати и свидетельствую. Ноября ... дня 1808 года. / Действительный Статский Советник / Бортнянский' [Mikhaylo Vitkovsky, a court singer under my jurisdiction, is willing to legally marry a Roman-Catholic woman, Elizaveta Mikhaylovna, daughter of Verdersky. I have agreed to this marriage and certify hereby that he is indeed a bachelor and in this matter I am signing and adding my personal seal. November..., 1808. / Active State Counsellor / *Bortniansky*] (GMMK, f 363, no 31).

5　*Protokoly zasedania Pridvornoy kontory* 19 October 1819. RGIA, f 469, no 120: 171–3.

Figure 14.1   Dmitry Bortniansky (1751–1825), lithography by G. Gippius, 1822

including the underage singers. As a result, some singers were fired and conscripted into the military, while elderly NCOs were placed on duty in the minor' dormitories and discipline in the whole institution was tightened up. Far from being rooted out, however, the practice still continued to influence future generations of Cappella singers far into the twentieth century.

Bortniansky's main professional concern at the Court Cappella was that of vocal training. Generation after generation, the singers underwent the same method of vocal training. This uniformity of background ensured timbral stability and homogeneity among the choir singers, from bass to soprano. A special significance was always given to the so-called *tsepnoe dykhanie* (chain breathing) based on imperceptible (purely diaphragmal, without lifting the shoulders) individual breathtaking during the pedalized tones, which enabled endless protraction. All the teachers were former singers, such as Bortniansky himself (one of the best masters of the vocal method), and his old-time colleague Fedor Fedorovich Makarov (whom Bortniansky had managed to defend while Pashkevich was being fired by Paul I and died shortly after).[6] In 1810, the building housing the Cappella, and belonging to senator Neplyuev, was bought by the Court and renovated by the architect Rusko, and on 1 November 1810 it was inaugurated as the House of the Cappella.[7] Bortniansky introduced weekly Saturday matinee open concerts in the Cappella hall and carried on this tradition for many years, always conducting himself, to a hall filled to capacity (Gusin and Tkachev, 1957:27).[8] He also provided full cooperation of the Cappella choir with the St Petersburg Philharmonic Society, founded in 1802, of which he became an honorary member in 1815. The Philharmonic Society was famous for its high-profile contemporary repertory and all of its great events of the time were associated with the oratorical genre, starting from the inaugural concert with Haydn's *The Creation* and continuing with Haydn's *The Seasons*, Mozart's *Requiem*, Cherubini's *Requiem*, and Handel's *Messiah*. Beethoven's *Missa solemnis* was premièred there in 1824.

This quarter-of-a-century of activity was sufficient to establish a certain cult of the Bortniansky tradition, which despite periods of neglect of his memory and changes in attitude to style and repertoire, still exists. Its particular aim is to perform Bortniansky with the authenticity of style established by this choir. Thus, in the late 1840s, even though Bortniansky's admirers considered their own preferred traditional approach to his music to have been corrupted, both the performances and his music still stirred the imagination of music lovers. The opinion of such a respected visitor to Russia as Hector Berlioz, as attested to in his *Evenings with the Orchestra*, is worth an extensive quote:

---

6 Porfirieva considers Pashkevich's closeness to the late Empress as a possible reason for Paul I's special dislike him, (MPES, II:342–4) and mentions the documentary source: RGIA, f 469, op 4, no 2229.

7 See M. Taranovskaya, *Architektura teatrov Leningrada*, Leningrad: Stroyizdat, 1988:152–4.

8   In order to finance maintenance of the building Bortniansky kept a bar in the cellar.

The only thing to which I can compare the effect of the gigantic unison of the children at St Paul's is the beautiful religious harmonizations written by Bortniansky for the Imperial Russian Chapel, and given in St Petersburg by the singers of the court with a perfection of ensemble, a delicacy of shading, and a beauty of tone of which you cannot form any idea. But instead of being the power resulting from a mass of uncultivated voices, it is a product of uncommon art; it is the result of painstaking and unremitting practice by a body of picked choristers... They perform works in four, six, and eight real parts, some of a rather lively turn and complicated with all the artifices of the fugal style, others calm and seraphic in expression and taken in an extremely slow tempo which calls for unusual voice-control and practice in sustaining it... To compare the choral singing of the Sistine Chapel in Rome with that of these marvelous singers is to compare the wretched little troupe of fiddle-scrapers in a third-rate Italian theater with the orchestra of the Paris Conservatoire.

The effect of this Russian choir and its music on nervous temperaments is irresistible. Under the impact of these unheard-of expressive accents one is seized by almost painful spasmodic movements that are beyond one's control. I have on several occasions tried by a determined effort of will-power to remain calm, but without success.

Motionless, with downcast eyes, they all waited in profound silence for the time to begin, and at a sign doubtless made by one of the leading singers – imperceptible, however, to the spectator – and without anyone's having given the pitch or indicated the tempo, they intoned one of Bortniansky's biggest eight-part concertos. In this harmonic web there were complications of part-writing that seemed impossible, there were sighs, vague murmurs such as one sometimes hears in dreams, and from time to time accents that in their intensity resembled cries, gripping the heart unawares, oppressing the breast, and catching the breath. Then it all died away in an incommensurable, misty, celestial decrescendo; one would have said it was a choir of angels rising from the earth and gradually vanishing into the empyrean.

In all these works [by Bortniansky] true religious feeling obtains, which frequently becomes a kind of mysticism that plunges the hearer into a profound ecstasy. He shows rare skill in the grouping of vocal masses, a miraculous sense of nuance and resonant harmony, and – still more surprising – an incredible freedom in the handling of the parts, a sovereign contempt for the rules respected by both his predecessors and his contemporaries, especially by the Italians whose disciple he is supposed to be (Berlioz, 1956:238–40).

Galuppi's words 'Un si magnifico coro, mai non sentito in Italia!' exclaimed in 1765, vividly echo in Berlioz's impression of the choir. The Russian Imperial Court Cappella was indeed a focus of national pride.

Repertoire

Bortniansky's directorship of the Cappella in the early nineteenth century coincided with the beginning of a new period in history and style, which totally changed his approach to its repertoire. His former active composing was now mostly replaced by his work in censorship and canonization of the existing repertoire, and any new

Figure 14.2 Imperial Court Cappella, St Petersburg

writings of his conformed to the new policy. The Bortniansky of the nineteenth century was in many ways the antithesis of the eighteenth-century Bortniansky, reflecting that which was happening in culture in general.

It all began with the new Emperor's journey to Moscow, which opened his eyes to how different the provincial culture was from the metropolitan one and how deeply the dissipated morals of Catherine's epoch had penetrated society. One of the objects of his indignation was the use of non-canonical texts during church services, probably in those towns where the choirs were too small and weak to perform concertos by Bortniansky or other pieces from the court repertoire. His Edict of 10 May 1797 commanded:

> Finding during my journey that in some churches, at the communion, instead of a concerto they sing self-composed verses, I desire that the Synod order all the Eparchial Bishops not to use any newly composed verses in church singing, but, instead of a concerto to perform either an appropriate psalm or the ordinary canon.[9]

9   'Нашед в нынешнее мое путешествие, что в некоторых церквах во время причастия вместо концерта поют стихи, сочиненные по произволению, желаю, чтобы от Синода предписано было всем Епархиальным Архиереям, дабы никаких выдуманных стихов в церковном пении не употребляли, но вместо концерта пели бы или приличный псалом, или же обыкновенный каноник.' (*O penii v tserkvakh vmesto kontsertov, prilichnykh psalmov ili kanonikov, sochinennykh po proizvoleniyu stikhov otnyud' ne upotreblyat'* (Polnoe sobranie zakonov Rossiyskoy Imperii, 1830).

When in Moscow, the Emperor would have also seen that performances of spiritual concertos had become the main attraction at any event where they took place, and that they could turn even a church service into a concert. Two years later, in 1799, the diplomat Yakov Ivanovich Bulgakov, upon retiring and settling in Moscow, wrote to his son:

> The famed singers of Kazakov, that now belong to Beketov, sing at the Dmitry Solunsky Church in Moscow. Such gatherings happen there that the entire Tverskoy Boulevard is crammed with carriages. Recently, the congregants became so shameless that they cried *fora* [bravo, encore] in the church. Luckily, the chief singer had enough sense to lead them out, otherwise an even greater indecency could have occurred.[10]

Whereas Paul I had cared only about the texts but did not involve himself in the matter of style, an issue that had not yet become as 'critical' as it was to become by the 1810s, Alexander I went further. He maintained a policy of canonization of both the old liturgical tradition and Bortniansky, and thus encouraged the composer to develop a new, stricter style of church music. In 1804, in order to unify Russian plainsong, which existed in countless different local traditions, the Metropolitan of Novgorod and St Petersburg Amvrosy suggested that Bortniansky set to music the plainsong of the *Divine Liturgy of John the Chrysostom* as it was performed at the Court and was considered to be the original (Belonenko, 1983:180). From 1810 to 1816 Russia had one of the most reactionary ministers of education, Count Alexey Kirillovich Razumovsky, who broadened the network of primary schools and gymnasiums but introduced theology as a main discipline. In 1814, Bortniansky received an Imperial directive to publish the plainsong as an official state Liturgy in the form of *Prostoe penie, Bozhestvennoy liturgii Zlatoustogo, izdrevle po edinomu predaniu upotreblyaemoe pri Vysochayshem dvore* [Plainsong of the Divine Liturgy of John the Chrysostom, which according to official legend, had long been used at the High Court]. There are three editions of this Liturgy: the first, commissioned by Bortniansky from the St Petersburg music publisher Dalmas in August 1814 (138 copies) for presentation at Court; the second, printed in 3,600 copies in 1815 at the expense of the Court Cabinet and distributed in the Eparchies; and the third, an undated reprint made by Dalmas.[11]

The plainsong sung at the Court is considered to have been influenced by the Ukrainian tradition introduced by Ukrainian singers. Originally based on monody, it probably existed in polyphonic or heterophonic variants and the aim of the edition was to determine an euphonious harmonization, which Bortniansky wrote, possibly resembling that familiar from the Court. His score is actually a two-voice liturgical

---

10 'Славные певчие Казакова, которые принадлежат ныне Бекетову, поют в церкви Дмитрия Солунского в Москве. Съезд такой бывает, что весь Тверской бульвар заставлен каретами. Недавно молельщики до такого дошли бесстыдства, что в церкви кричали "фора" (т. е. браво, бис). По счастью хозяин певчих имел догадку вывести певчих вон, без чего дошли–бы до большей непристойности' (quoted by Preobrazhensky, 1924:71).

11 *Delo o sochinenii Bortnyanskim liturgii*, RGIA, f 797, op 2, 1814–15, no 53000–a.

work, where free recitative canticles alternate with more or less metric ones. Its *Kheruvimskaya*, the prettiest song-like piece of the liturgy, seems to have been quoted from folklore. The bass voice suggests a delicate harmonization, referring to the modal approach rather than the functional one, reminiscent overall of Bortniansky's four-voice arrangements of ancient melodies. The latter genre, once referred to as settings or 'harmonizations', as in Berlioz's above-quoted essay, presents an interesting aspect of Bortniansky's work.

Four-voice settings of ancient chant had existed as early as *partes*-singing. Chant was performed by the tenor voice, like *cantus firmus*. However, there was no trace of the Italian imitative polyphony, or the rhythmic development characteristic of German *Tenorlied*. In Russian polyphonic settings, the rest of the voices presented mono-rhythmic, often *organum*-like parallel movement, with limited linear freedom of voices; while the bass fulfilled a harmonic function and was only rarely figurative. The whole texture gave an harmonic – rather acoustic – interpretation to the tones of the chant, a kind of fusion of modal and functional elements, which one can find in Italian vocal music of a century earlier. Settings of this kind dissolved modality and submitted it to harmony, which basically was already functional. The process was European in essence and developed the harmonic style in a similar way to *kanty* and *psalmy*; that is, based mainly on tonic-dominant successions of relative keys, featuring the harmonic dominant in minor mode.

It is likely, however, that at the beginning of the nineteenth century the style of these settings, similar to plainsong, would have been perceived as demanding modernization and unification. Since they had always been a part of the Cappella repertoire, Bortniansky had arranged several such settings in his younger years, as suggested by the keyboard reduction of one such piece in Maria Fedorovna's album (1784) and by Bortniansky's autograph of *Nemetskaya obednya* [German liturgy] related to the same period, where some pieces are very alike those printed later as his settings of Russian chant: *Bekennen will ich* corresponds to *Pod Tvoyu milost'* [I will come into thy house in the multitude of thy mercy], *Wo ist ein Gott* – to *Slava Ottsu i Synu* [Glory be to the Father and to the Son and to the Holy Spirit] and *Ehre sei dem* – to *Priidite ublazhim* [Come, let us bless]. The sources of the settings were indicated by Bortniansky as Kievan and Greek chant, both popular in *partes*-singing.[12]

However, most of Bortniansky's settings appeared during the same Alexandrian epoch when he had become responsible for style policy in church music. None, at least, were ever mentioned in eighteenth-century newspaper advertisements or copied in music collections. The above-mentioned piece from Maria Fedorovna's album *Nyne sily I* [Now the heavenly powers], in *E-flat* major, was published only around 1815, while other settings appeared in the advertisements in *Sankt Peterburgskie Vedomosti* as late as 1822. Later still, Victor Askochensky noted that Bortniansky's death had cut short this aspect of his career, suggesting that the latter's interest in this type of work only developed toward the end of his life (Askochensky, 1863).

---

12 The score is in the RIII collection.

In order to understand Bortniansky's approach to this task we need to compare his settings with the monodic sources from the ancient chant. Nineteenth-century scholars suggested a variety of possible sources: Razumovsky considered them to have been *Pechatnye notnye knigi Sinoda Irmolog, Oktoikh, Prazdniki* and *Obikhod* of 1772 (The Synodal Scores of Hirmologion, Octoechos, Festive and Ordinary Chants, Razumovsky, 1867:233–5) but only three of the chants are to be found there: *Slava i nyne* [Glory..., Now and ever], *Deva Dnes'* [Today the Virgin] and *Pomoshchnik i pokrovitel'* [God is our refuge and strength]. Metallov (1915:103) and Preobrazhensky (1900) suggested their belonging to the South Russian tradition, but only two of them – *Chertog Tvoy* [Thy bridal-chamber] and *Nyne sily nebesnyya II* [Now the heavenly powers] – have been found in Ukrainian Hirmologions of the eighteenth century.[13] It should be noted, however, that both monodic and harmonized chant are full of variants in different locations over different periods, similar to the Russian folklore. Hence, when comparing Bortniansky's arrangements with certain chants considered as originals, no clear link can be made between any specific chant and a particular arrangement. The aforementioned chants can be offered only as possible sources rather than as exact prototypes; there may be many other similar variants, all fairly similar to Bortniansky's versions. All this suggests that what took place was a generalized adaptation of their most typical features rather than the harmonization of a single original existing somewhere.

It may have been this variability of the chants that provided the principle behind Bortniansky's approach to melodies. He simply cut out the entire melismatic element of the chant and preserved only its framework, which was suitable to the functional-harmonic interpretation. A comparison between Bortniansky's settings and the *partes*-singing tradition shows that he elevated the chant from tenor to upper voice and made it an harmonically active part, which itself defined harmonization. His harmonization was generally based on the *partes*-singing tradition, although he sometimes went much further than four-chord successions of tonics and dominants of relative keys. For example, his setting of *Chertog Tvoy* (Example 14.1) includes modulation in the natural minor-mode dominant key as found in the Ukrainian lyrical songs *Oy ya z rodu chumakuyu* [Oh, I have been a porter/wagon driver from birth] and *Oy siv zapiv* [Oh, sitting and singing]. The muted mode is typical to Bortniansky's harmonizations , often making modality dominate over functionality and giving prominence to secondary degrees.

One interesting example of Bortniansky's work with the sources is that of his piece *Nyne sily nebesnyya II*, in which he synthesized the elements of several quite different versions of a single chant, selecting the structure from one, and the tonal organization from another (Examples 14.2a, b, c).

---

13 See eighteenth-century manuscripts in RGB, f 152, no 75, L 352; no 77, Ll 318, 326; no 78, Ll 125, 148; no 82 L 247; f 379, no 93, L 350.

Example 14.1   Bortniansky: *Chertog Tvoy*

Example 14.2 (a) *Nyne sily nebesnyya*, **anonymous**

Example 14.2 (b) *Nyne sily nebesnyya*, **anonymous (prayer book, 1864)**

Example 14.2 (c) Bortniansky: *Nyne sily nebesnyya II*

Finally, there is a group of his settings characterized by obvious harmonic experimentation (*Angel vopiyashe* [The angel cried], *Slava Tebe* [Glory to Thee], *Da ispolnyatsya usta nasha* [May our mouth be filled], *Telo Khristovo primite* [Receive ye the Body of Christ]). In these Bortniansky went far beyond the limits of the eighteenth-century European major-minor system, lending the secondary degrees the significance of tonal centres, with each represented as a tonality. His piece *Telo Khristovo primite* is particularly characterized by modal harmonic successions, anticipating the late nineteenth-century search for new harmonies (Example 14.3).

Example 14.3   Bortniansky: *Telo Khristovo priimite*

It is also worth noting that although the tradition of settings did not permit textural variety, Bortniansky nonetheless found a way to play with colours. Voice-leading in parallel thirds was still typical for *partes*-singing settings. Preserving this feature, the composer divided the voices, sometimes all three upper ones, doubling each line in the third and achieving the special effect of a clustered choral mass as can be seen in *Deva dnes'* [Today the Virgin] and *Dostoino est'* [It is truly meet].

Bortniansky's settings were an easy target for later criticism from many sides. Adherents of authenticity of the chant felt insulted by his reduction of the melismatic cantillations, not realizing that the laws of monody and of choral music demand different approaches, and that lengthy, undulating harmonizing melodies are simply boring. Attempts at this had been undertaken by Bortniansky's younger contemporary Peter Ivanovich Turchaninov, followed by Alexey Lvov, but those works have a historical significance rather than an artistic or practical one.

Bortniansky was also accused of using dominant harmony by Prince Odoevsky, who was apparently unaware of the *partes*-singing tradition. The Prince was prepared to accept only 'the revered *Dreyklang* on the tonic or, maximum, on the mediant, but by no means on Diapent, as Bortniansky did when his conscience prevented him from over-sweetening the church chant by using the seventh chord'.[14]

Finally, the prosody of Bortniansky's settings elicited perplexity and reprimand from Tchaikovsky when the latter was preparing a new edition of Bortniansky's collected works in 1881–2: 'Here the error against the prosody was so rude that I took the risk of changing the original measure.'[15] Tchaikovsky was not, of course, obliged to know about the old Russian choral practice, which used to ignore prosody (as I noted earlier in regard to the redaction of the concerto by Sarti, who was himself pedantic in its use, see Chapter 10). But instead of taking it at face value, Tchaikovsky should, perhaps, have understood that in the slow tempo of a live performance, accentuation may reside in other than only the score; and that Bortniansky wrote it this way not out of neglect of the prosody but for a practical reason – not to over-complicate the musical text for the semi-educated choristers anywhere in Russia who might have had to learn it.

In 1816, Alexander I issued a decree requiring that 'All that is sung in churches by scores, must be performed according to the printed scores composed either by the director of the Court Choir and the Active State Counsellor Bortniansky himself or by other well-known composers but printed and approved by Mr. Bortniansky.'[16] The same year that Bortniansky began to apply his official censorial stamp 'Permitted to print. D. Bortniansky',[17] saw the publication of *a cappella* choral compositions with Russian texts by Galuppi and Sarti. It appears to have been Bortniansky himself who prepared these editions. The same series also included several works by the

---

14 'почтенный Dreyklang на тонике или, по крайней мере, на медианте (но отнюдь не на Диапенте, как делал Бортнянский, когда совесть ему зазрила подсластить церковный напев септаккордом' (Odoevsky, 1956:308).

15 'Здесь ошибка против просодии была до того груба, что я решился изменить подлинное обозначение такта' (comment by Tchaikovsky in *D.S. Bortniansky, Dukhovno-muzykal'nye sochineniya na polny khor*, Moscow, Jurgenson, 1881, vol. I:78).

16 'Все, что поется в церквах по нотам, должно быть печатное и состоять или из собственных сочинений директора Придворного певческого хора Действительного Статского советника Бортнянского, или других известных сочинителей, но сих последних сочинения непременно должны печатаемы быть с одобрения г. Бортнянского.'

17 'Печатать позволяется. Д. Бортнянский'.

younger contemporary composer P.I. Turchaninov and probably also *Ne otverzhi* by Berezovsky.[18]

At about the same time Bortniansky also undertook a revised collected edition of his earlier choral works. Either Alexander's edict had obliged him to do so, or the composer may have done so out of his own considerations, but the two events coincided nonetheless and the existence of some kind of connection between them is quite possible.

The praxis of collected editions became a feature of the time for two main reasons: the coexistence of contemporary and earlier repertoires, and the advanced technology of music printing. Bortniansky would almost certainly have been aware of Handel's collected edition prepared by Samuel Arnold in 1787–97, as well as of Mozart's complete edition in the early nineteenth century. He may even have known of Beethoven's approach to the publishers Breikopf and Härtel with a similar suggestion in 1810.[19] Indeed, Bortniansky would probably have realized only too well that the era of the choral spiritual concerto was approaching its demise, and after his own death there would be no one to care properly for his legacy. Publication of his secular works composed in the 1770s–80s was probably out of the question because the audiences of the new epoch would have had little appreciation for them; but a future for his choral compositions, which remained within the conservative spiritual repertoire, was secured by the nature of the genre itself. They merely needed to be canonized in printed format because manuscript copies tended to be full of errors and variants and their circulation was no longer appropriate to the new century. Bortniansky undertook the project at his own expense, which his financial circumstances fortunately allowed him to do.[20] Indeed, he is known to have invested a large amount of money in the venture, as can be seen from his heirs' request that Tsar Nikolai I purchase from them the copper and tin engraved plates for the Imperial treasury, which after a long negotiation were finally purchased for a sum far below their true value.[21]

---

18 There is mention of an edition of this concerto by Berezovsky from the beginning of the nineteenth century that could have hardly been published otherwise than by Bortniansky. (Ginzburg, 1968:468)

19 *The Letters of Beethoven*. Collected, trans and ed. by E. Anderson, 1961, vol. 1, no 273 (before 21 August 1810), pp. 290–1.

20 For the engraving of the concertos Bortniansky hired a talented engraver from the Map Depot, Vasily Petrovich Pyadyshev, famous for the exquisite quality and beauty of his work. According to newspaper advertisements, the concertos began selling in 1820. The resulting edition was exact, thorough and, uncharacteristically for the scores at the time, rich in dynamic details. When, in the years 1881–2, P.I. Tchaikovsky edited these concertos for the Jurgenson edition, he based his editing on Bortniansky's own editing and publishing, and Tchaikovsky's work was mainly the addition of a piano arrangement. For a detailed account of Tchaikovsky's redaction see Kuzma, 1996.

21 *Delo po prosheniyu vdovy direktora Pridvornoy pevcheskoy kapelly D.S. Bortnyanskogo o pokupke v kaznu sochineniy ee muzha*. RGIA, f 519, op 9, 1826, no 498.

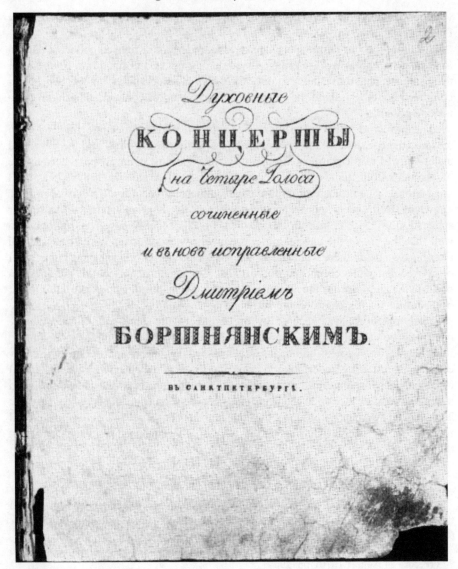

**Figure 14.3   Title-page of the life-time edition of Bortniansky's choral spiritual
concertos**

There is a groundless suggestion by M. Kuzma (1996) that the edition preserved
in RIII (see Figure 14.3) was published posthumously. In her attempts to disprove my
statement that it was published during Bortniansky's lifetime (Rytsareva, 1973:34;
1979:207–8) she postulated that the later publisher had used the title page as a 'piece
of false advertising' (p. 193). However, the recent substantial research undertaken

by N. Ryzhkova in St Petersburg has shown that the collection in question was assembled from the concertos published individually from 1815–18, copies of which are found in RNB and GMMK (Ryzhkova, 2003:55–6).

Public Life

Various sources note Bortniasky's having composed occasional cantatas and hymns in the 1800s–1810s, which by then were obviously replacing the spiritual concerto in secular ceremonies. Derzhavin mentions Bortniansky as the composer of the cantatas *Strany Rossiyskie, obodryaites'!* [Russian countries, cheer!] (probably for the Emperor's visit to Russian army units in Brest-Litovsk, on 16 September 1805); *Sretenie Orfeem solntsa* [Orpheus meeting the Sun] (1811), written on the occasion of Alexander the First's scheduled (but never transpired) visit to the *Beseda lyubiteley russkogo slova* [Society of Russian Literature and Language Lovers]; and *Na priezd iz chuzhikh kraev Velikoy Knyagini Marii Pavlovny* [Upon the return of Grand Duchess Maria Pavlovna from abroad]. Papers from the Academy of Arts mention Bortniansky's hymn (words by Alexander Vostokov) composed for the festive meeting of its members on 1 January 1806. There were probably more compositions of this kind, for the archive of the Court Cappella contains many records of singers accompanying the Emperor's trips, such as when he inspected the Russian troops after the battle at Preussisch Eylau in January 1807, which was followed by his meeting with Napoleon on the River Neman.

As the major official composer, Bortniansky reacted to the current events by composing a popular song, similarly to Handel who wrote 'The Song of Noble London Volunteers' in that critical moment of English history on 14 November 1745. Bortniansky's songs for the masses to commemorate the Patriotic War of 1812 were *Pesn' ratnikov* [Song of the Militiamen] and *Marsh vseobshchego opolchenia* [March of the General Home Guard]. At the beginning of Napoleon's invasion, with the enormous public surge of Russian patriotism, he set to music the poem by Vasily Andreevich Zhukovsky *Pevets vo stane Russkikh voinov* [A Singer in the Field-Camp of Russian Soldiers], which became the emblematic anthem of the war. Zhukovsky, at the time a young member of the Muscovite civil guard, completed the poem 'after Moscow was abandoned by its inhabitants before the battle of Tarutin' as he noted. Even before being published in *Vestnik Evropy* (ns 23, 24), it was already circulating in handwritten form. Soon after first publication it began to appear in various editions, with the text adapted according to the ongoing developments at the front.

The text of the poem expressed the sincere and impetuous style of a young romantic poet-fighter, delighting the readers with its novelty of form, far removed from the familiar pathos and rhetoric of the classical ode. Zhukovsky addressed his contemporaries and comrades-in-arms in a direct and lively style, combining the patriotic epic expression with the informal manner of a hussar drinking song to create an image of a *Boyan* from the Kievan Rus' epoch. Paying respect to his contemporaries, the poet also inserted a modest yet formal eulogy to the Tsar, but only after first praising the great Russian commanders: Svyatoslav Kievsky, Dmitry Donskoy, Peter I, and Alexander Suvorov.

Choosing eight stanzas from this very long poem, Bortniansky composed a song for a soloist (tenor), choir (alti and bassi) and symphonic orchestra in a simple and lively style resembling the popular and democratic hussar ballads. The score of *Pevets vo stane russkikh voinov* was published in 1813 by Dalmas and the piece spread in hand-written copies as well (Example 14.4).

The celebration of victory took place upon the return of the army and the Emperor from Paris in July 1814. The magnificent welcoming ceremony initiated by Maria Fedorovna included Bortniansky's cantata *Na vozvrashchenie Imperatora Alexandra I* [On the return of the Emperor Alexander I], set to words by Peter Vyazemsky and Yury Neledinsky-Meletsky, as well as several other compositions commissioned from Ferdinand Antonolini. The greeting cantatas and dances were performed by the pupils of the Smolny Institute in front of the Palace; the *corps-de-ballet* at one point in the festivities formed the shape of the Imperial monogram. Bortniansky's participation appears to have gone beyond just writing the scores, as follows from a letter to the composer from Maria Fedorovna's secretary, G.I. Villamov: 'Her Majesty the Empress, grateful from the bottom of her heart for your efforts related to the celebration that took place here, has ordered me to present you, my dear sir, with this seal-ring, as a sign of most gracious will'.[22]

Whatever knowledge of Bortniansky's public life that can be gleaned from indirect information, suggests his connections with artists and art connoisseurs. Without any formal application, he was unanimously elected an Honourable Member of the Academy of Arts at a special meeting of the Board of Directors on 1 September 1804 (its future President A.N. Olenin, connoisseur of the arts P.L. Veliaminov and Prince Volzogen were also elected at the same meeting, but only after making a formal application). Soon after, as a sign of his gratitude, Bortniansky presented the Academy with two pictures, as documented by the Academy of Arts. The Academy President, Count A.S. Stroganov, and its director, the sculptor Ivan Martos, were his friends. Stroganov frequently sought Bortniansky's advice when choosing or appraising works of art (Dolgov, 1857:18). Bortniansky himself owned a picture gallery, as ascertained from newspaper advertisements regarding the sale of his possessions after his death. It is thus hardly surprising that there exist numerous painted and sculptured images of the composer (which is revealing not only of his friendship with the artists but also of his wealth). The architects Zacharov and Paulson, commissioned to build and decorate his house, were referred to him by the Academy of Arts. Bortniansky is not known to have had any special interest in

---

22 'Государыня Императрица, приняв со всемилосерднейшею признательностью усердие, Вашим Превосходительством при случае бывшего здесь праздника оказанное, Высочайше повелеть мне изволила доставить к Вам милостивый государь мой, приложенный при сем перстень, в знак всемилостивейшего к Вам благоволения' (RGIA, f 759, op 6, no 1237).

literature, but that he was not indifferent to poetry is clear from his two versified psalms, which can be found in the handwritten collections.[23]

Example 14.4 Bortniansky: *Pevets vo stane russkikh voinov,* **1812**

Family

Bortniansky's family and private life have been poorly documented, leaving much unclear. He had a wife, Anna Ivanovna Bortnianskaya, whom he married after 1808, and who was probably much younger because she outlived him by thirty-two years. Although she had no children, Bortniansky had at least four and there is no indication as to who their mothers were. One child was a daughter (b. mid-1780s), whose married name was Lyashenok; her husband was an 'official of the 14th class'. Their daughter, Maria, was being brought up in Bortniansky's house by the time of his death. Another was an illegitimate son, Alexander Vershenevsky, born in 1801.[24] Bortniansky also had two other daughters who bore his name. The elder was Elizaveta (b. *c.* 1796, in marriage Dolgova)[25] who died in February 1818, soon after

---

23 Bortniansky's versification of the fragment from Prophet Isaiah is found in IRLI.

24 *Formulyarnyi spisok* (RGIA, f 1349, op 4, 1825, no 68, Ll 34–5.

25 Elizaveta Dolgova's age is given according to the record in the Confession book for 1816, where her age is indicated as twenty years old: TsGIA SPb, f 19, op 112, 1816, no 640. Ll 530–1.

the birth of her second son, Vladimir Dolgov, b. 19 December 1817).[26] The younger one was Ekaterina (b. *c*. 1798) whose traces are lost after 1817 when her name appears in connection with the birth of her nephew; her name does not appear in any of the documents belonging to Bortniansky's family concerning their negotiations with the Tsar Nikolai I over Bortniansky's engraved plates after his death in 1825.

Although the fact that Bortniansky's daughters bore his name may indicate their being born from a legal marriage, there were other forms of paternity if noble ladies were involved. There is the example of the above-mentioned diplomat Yakov Ivanovich Bulgakov, who brought up two sons born to him in 1781–82 by a French woman E.-L. Imber (later married to A. Shumlyansky) during his diplomatic service in Constantinople (Kochetkova, SRP, 1988:131).

The mystery surrounding the mother/s of Bortniansky's children somewhat parallels the mystery of Bortniansky's relations with the family of Countess Ekaterina Vasilievna (1761–1829) known in Russian history under three names: Engelhardt (née), Skavronskaya (from her first marriage) and Litta (from her second marriage). Born Engelhardt, she was one of the five sisters famous as Potemkin's nieces/mistresses, 'the beautiful daughters of his sister Marfa Engelhardt [that] formed the first and fairly permanent nucleus of his own – otherwise kaleidoscopic and ambulant – harem.'[27] From 1776 'Katin'ka' was a lady-in-waiting to the Empress and enjoyed her patronage. The young woman was distinguished by her captivating beauty and intelligence, as noted by Baroness Luise d'Oberkirch, Maria Fedorovna's friend, Elizabeth Vigée Le Brun and others.[28] In 1781 she made a brilliant marriage to the wealthy Count Pavel Martynovich Skavronsky (1757–93, mentioned in Chapter 6 as an avid music lover), who had returned from Naples in 1780. In 1784 the Count was appointed Russian ambassador to Naples, but the Countess reluctantly followed him only much later. In the late 1780s she spent much time in Russia and participated in the Empress's 1787 journey to the south. Her own musical interests remain unknown, although there is occasional mention of her name among those whom the fashionable Italian singer Minarelli instructed prior to 1787.[29] Two daughters, Ekaterina and Maria, were born to this marriage in the early 1780s. Their names appear on the titles of the similar collections of Italian ariettas and duos dedicated to both by Carlo Pozzi, Italian harpsichordist, singer and composer, who taught at the Smolny Institute from 1794–97. Later, both were married to distinguished men: Ekaterina – in 1800, to Major General Prince Peter Ivanovich Bagration, future hero of the war with Napoleon; and Maria – to Count Pavel Alexeevich von Pahlen, the Military Governor of St Petersburg (known as the main plotter behind Paul I's

26 The date of Vladimir Dolgov's birth is noted in TsGIA SPb, f 19, op 111, tom 1, 1817, no 185, L 25.

27 George Soloveytchik, *Potemkin: Soldier, Statesman, Lover and Consort of Catherine of Russia*, New York, 1947:170.

28 See H.L. Oberkirch, *Memoirs of the Baroness d'Oberkirch*. London, 1852; Elizabeth Vigée Lebrun, *Memoirs of Madame Vigée Lebrun*. Printed by Lionel Strachiy. New York: George Braziller Inc., 1989 (reprint from 1903).

29 V.G. Orlov to A.V. Orlov, 15 October 1787. RGB, f 219, carton 8, no 8, L 8.

assassination); after her divorce from von Pahlen in 1802 she married General Adam Ozharovsky.

Little is known about the years between Pavel Skavronsky's death in 1793 and Ekaterina Vasilievna's remarriage in 1798. According to two portraits painted by Elisabeth Vigée Le Brun in 1796, she appears to have led an enjoyable life.

In 1797, a new figure appeared in St Petersburg at the court of the new Emperor Paul I, as an ambassador of the Maltese Order. This was the Italian Count de Litta (1763–1839, whose Russified name sounded like Juliy Pompeevich Litta), a Chevalier of the Maltese Order since 1780, who had also served in the Russian navy during the recent Russian-Turkish war (1789–92), commanding a rowing fleet. He conquered the hearts of both the Emperor and the Countess Skavronskaya (who despite her past association with Potemkin was welcomed at the new Court). Paul I accepted Count Litta's suggestion to take the Maltese Order under Russia's wing and made all his family (including his favourite Anna Lopukhina) members of the Order. The following year, 1798, Count Litta accepted the Emperor's suggestion that he marry the Countess Skavronskaya, who was eventually granted the status of a member of the Order (she and Lopukhina were the only women to hold this status). In 1799, in the course of Paul's unpredictable repressions, Litta, who was Vice-Admiral of the Baltic rowing fleet, was fired from his post and exiled for unclear reasons to the estate of his wife. Shortly afterwards, however, he was reinstated with all the respect that Alexander I and Nikolai I were later to accord him too. The Countess Litta was awarded the Order of St Catherine, First Class (1809) and in 1824 she became Stewardess of the Household of the Highest court.

Although outwardly the Countess's biography does not seem to intertwine greatly with Bortniansky's life and work, there are four linking documents, three of which are puzzling.

The first, and the only clear one, is a deed of purchase by Bortniansky of a little yard from the Countess' mother-in-law Maria Nikolaevna Skavronskaya, who was to remain in Italy for the rest of her life. It was Ekaterina Vasilievna who undertook the procedure of selling the yard to Bortniansky by proxy (for the sum of five thousand roubles). The procedure took a considerable time, protracted by the death of the Empress, and was completed only in March 1797, involving an impressive list of witnesses headed by Maria Nikolaevna's relative Count Alexander Sergeevich Stroganov and Count Christopher Sergeevich Muennich, Senator Andrian Ivanovich Divov, Senator Alexey Loginovich Shcherbachev and Senator Andrey Ivanovich Golokhvostov.[30] (The house was situated in the most prestigious Admiralty part of St Petersburg, at 9 Bol'shaya Millionnaya Street, close to the Marble Palace and not far from the Cappella House.)

Two of the other documents relate to the Countess' daughter Maria Pavlovna and grand-daughter Julia. In her first marriage, to Count von Pahlen, Maria Pavlovna gave birth to a daughter Julia (b. 1803) and in 1807 the young woman died. Despite

---

30 *Peterburgskaya palata grazhdanskogo suda. Kniga zapisi kupchikh i zakladnykh na dvory, dvorovye mesta…*: TsGIA SPb, f 757, op1, 1797, no 1030, Ll 6–8.

her mother (and Julia's grandmother) Ekaterina Vasilievna Skavronskaya and Count Litta still being alive, it was Bortniansky who arranged for Maria Pavlovna to be buried at her family estate at Grafskaya Slavianka, near Pavlovsk,[31] and who undertook the guardianship of her daughter Julia.[32] In Russian cultural history Julia von Pahlen remained known as the Countess Samoylova who, after her divorce from Count Samoylov, was a close associate of the renowned Russian painter Karl Brullov, with whom she spent many years in Italy during the 1830s–40s. The legend says that her real father was not Count von Pahlen, but Count Litta, with whom she corresponded a great deal and who left her his fortune, a 'circumstance' that 'explains the typically Italian traits of her face'.[33] Her guardianship by Bortniansky serves only to confuse an already highly confused relationship.

No less interesting is the fourth, later document – a notary receipt (an acknowledgement of dept) from Ekaterina Vasilievna Litta to Bortniansky's daughter Elizaveta regarding a loan of 10,000 roubles from Bortniansky, with interest, on 11 February 1815. This receipt served as Bortniansky's dowry to his daughter.[34] The Countess's loan from Bortniansky is surprising for at least two reasons. On the one hand, her uncle-lover Potemkin's fabulous wealth, as well as Pavel Skavronsky's enormous riches, in addition to the honour she was accorded by Alexander I and the fact of her husband still being alive, suggests that there should have been no reasons for her difficult financial position. On the other hand, had she truly needed money, there were many other sources in addition to Bortniansky, who was wealthy but not the richest man in St Petersburg. The situation thus might be read as her desire to provide the young Elizaveta Bortnianskaya with the interest from the sum.

These documents attest to such close financial and legal interweaving of Bortniansky and the Skavronsky family that one can merely hope that if the story behind it is ever revealed, it will shed greater light on Bortniansky's personal life and make it less of a mystery. In the meantime one can only suggest that his personal life encompassed more than a few tragic losses, like the deaths of one of his young daughters (or maybe both of them); and that his mourning spiritual concertos *Skazhi mi, Gospodi, konchinu moyu* [Lord, make me to know mine end] and *Vskuyu priskorbna esi, dushe moya* [O my God, my soul is cast down within me] may be tentatively considered as his private requiems to those close to him. This might explain why these concertos were never advertised (to the best of my knowledge) in the eighteenth-century sources.

---

31 *Delo po prositel'nomu pis'mu Statskogo Sovetnika Dmitria Bortnianskogo, o predpisanii Grafskoy Slavyanki svyashchenniku, o predanii zemle tela grafini Marii Pavlovny Ozharovskoy pri Slavyanskoy tserkvi.* 9 May 1807. TsGIA SPb, f. 19, op 9, 1807, no 257, Ll 1–3.

32 *Opekunstvo nad maloletney grafiney Yuliey von der Pahlen*: TsGIA SPb, f 19, op 111, tom 1, 1808, no 148, L 395. Tserkov' Zaharia i Elisavety.

33 This legend has been developed in I. Bocharov and Yu. Glushakova, 'Karl Bryullov i teatr', in *Nauka i zhizn'* 1981, no 5:122.

34 TsGIA SPb, f 268, op 1, 1827–35, no 3656, L 12.

Bortniansky's home was full of young people. There were his son Alexander Vershenevsky and grandchildren Dmitry Dolgov and Maria Lyashenok (or Lyashenkova) who lived with him, as well as a girl called Maria who was twenty years old in 1825, and a young woman, Alexandra Mikhaylova, whose relationship to Bortniansky was unknown even to his wife Anna Ivanovna. Three names are listed as the heirs of the composer: Anna Umantseva, Elena Mazileva and Maria Lyashenkova, all possibly related to his Ukrainian relatives from Poltava.

The hesitant signature of Anna Ivanovna Bortnianskaya on certain documents gives the impression that she was not used to writing. After Bortniansky's death she sold the house, the picture gallery and the country home in Pavlovsk. In February 1826 the widow presented Bortniansky's manuscripts, a copper etching and printing plates for some scores (worth an estimated 25 thousand roubles) as a gift to Nikolai I, hoping for partial reimbursement. A year-and-a-half later, after humiliating negotiations with the Emperor, she was presented with jewellery worth 3,000 roubles, and Bortniansky's heirs were paid 5,000 roubles in assignats. The manuscripts and etching were sent to the Court Cappella house, where 'they were listed and placed in their proper prepared place... under the supervision of the director.'[35]

Anna Ivanovna retained possession of Bortniansky's letters and documents. After her death, his grandson Dmitry Dolgov, basing his writing on a brief perusal of these papers, which were apparently part of the material bequeathed to him, wrote a biographical essay on Bortniansky for *Nuvellist* magazine. Dolgov's whereabouts have remained unknown, however, and there is no record of him in the St Petersburg address books of the beginning of the twentieth century.

The aesthetic style of Bortniansky's life encouraged the apocryphal legend that, having sensed he was dying, he called for his singers, who sang his own concerto *Vskuyu priskorbna esi, dushe moya*. His death certificate states that he died on 28 September 1825 of a stroke. Regardless of the accuracy of the tale, its existence confirms the love and respect that his contemporaries felt for this extraordinary man and notable figure of Russian culture. Bortniansky was buried in the Smolensky Cemetery in St Petersburg, but his grave was no longer to be found when, in 1901, people came to visit it following the celebration of the one hundred and fiftieth anniversary of the composer's birth. There is an image of him on the monument 'One thousand Years of Russia' (sculptor M.O. Miklashevsky, 1861, Novgorod), as well as a simple marble memorial in the Alexandro-Nevsky churchyard among the monuments to other great Russian composers. The Russian Diaspora too has erected a stature of Bortniansky, at St Patrick's Cathedral in New York City.

Bortniansky and the Nineteenth Century

There is one circumstance in relation to Bortniansky's publication of his collected edition that has usually passed unnoticed. Thirty-five four-voice concertos that

---

35 RGIA, f 519, op 9 1826–7.no 498, Ll 3–6.

comprised the main corpus of what Bortniansky had published at the time, were not only edited but also revised, of which he informed his audience through the title: _Dukhovnye / kontserty / na chetyre golosa / sochinennye / i vnov' ispravlennye / Dmitriem / Bortnyanskim / v SANKTPETERBURGE_ [Spiritual concertos for four voices, composed and revised by Dmitry Bortniansky, in St Petersburg]. Even a superficial comparison of the eighteenth-century manuscript copies with this printed version shows that he had reduced the appoggiaturas and made the style stricter. Future comparative research into these two versions of style, divided by several decades, might produce interesting results.

Unlike Degtyarev, who, directing himself to the Moscow public, modernized his style by incorporating more Italian and operatic traits in it, Bortniansky adjusted his earlier style to the new fashion of noble simplicity, characteristic of St Petersburg during the Alexandrian era. This was also a step for him toward the new and more ascetic spirit of the church music that the romantic era demanded. Reducing the gallant features did not, nonetheless, prevent his music from being typically eighteenth-century, with its minuetic rhythms. Hence, even his thorough revision failed to save him from later criticism by nineteenth-century Russian musicians.

After Bortniansky's death the position of director of the Cappella was held by Fedor Petrovich Lvov (1766–1836) and then by Alexey Fedorovich Lvov (1799–1870) – father and son. Berlioz, in the paragraphs following his earlier-quoted expression of delight regarding both the choir and Bortniansky, described the further history of the Cappella, in all probability as he had heard it from the younger Lvov:

> After him [Bortniansky] the direction of the chapel was entrusted to Privy Councilor Lvov, a man of exquisite taste and possessed of a wide practical knowledge of the masterworks of all schools. An intimate friend and one of the most fervent admirers of Bortniansky, he deemed it his duty to follow scrupulously in his footsteps. The Imperial Chapel had become a splendid and remarkable institution by 1836 when, after the death of Councilor Lvov, his son, General Alexis Lvov, was appointed its director.
>
> Most connoisseurs of string-quartet music and all the great violinists of Europe know this eminent musician, who is both virtuoso and composer. His talent as a violinist is remarkable, and his latest work, which I heard in St Petersburg four years ago, the opera _Ondine_, which has just been translated into French by M. de Saint–Georges, contains beauties of the highest order: it is a fresh, lively, youthful, and charmingly original work.
>
> Ever since he became director of the Imperial Chapel, General Lvov has carried forward his predecessors' work as regards the perfecting of execution, while also applying himself to extending the already rich repertory of the chapel. This he has done both by composing religious music of his own and by engaging in fruitful scholarly research in the musical archives of the Russian Church, thanks to which he has made several discoveries of great importance to the history of music. (240–41)

Both the Lvovs' activity, however, had some other sides to it too. Bortniansky's death almost coincided with that of Alexander I, which was followed by the famous Decembrists' revolt and Nikolai's reactionary rule. That Nikolai I had little sentiment for either Bortniansky or the Cappella is clear not only from his contemptuous trade with Bortniansky's heirs, but also from the humiliating act toward the institution by appointing Fedorovich Petrovich Lvov as its director. The latter's only connection to music lay in his being the nephew of Nikolai Alexandrovich Lvov and in having participated as an amateur singer at his uncle's gatherings. Before his appointment to the Cappella he was known as a poet and writer, close to Derzhavin and Kapnist though of more obvious Slavophilic orientation, and who had been published under the pseudonym Skhimnik.[36]

It is clear that by the time of his appointment, thirty years after Bortniansky, the criteria for nomination to such a position had changed. It is also clear that there was no major national musician in 1825 who fitted the position, which would thus have had to be filled by some functionary. From 1824–26 many changes in the State apparatus at the Department of Religious Affairs and National Education took place. The Church, seeking a form of protest against a situation in which the Synod was completely subjugated to the Department, found no less a powerful ally than Alexander Arakcheev – one of the most odious figures of nineteenth-century Russian history and the *de facto* ruler of Russia in the late Alexandrian period from 1815 to 1825. In 1824, Arakcheev pushed aside Prince Golitsyn and achieved for the Synod the formal status of an independent department, yet then completely suppressed it. Probably as a result of all this bureaucratic re-shuffling Lvov was appointed to this position in 1826. His rank of Privy Counsellor, one rank higher than Bortniansky's, suggests both protection at Court and probable bureaucratic and management experience.

Lvov's task seems to have been three-fold: to create a model of a well-organized institution, to improve the quality of singing, and to do away with 'Italianshchina'. This 'intimate friend and one of the most fervent admirers of Bortniansky', who 'deemed it his duty to follow scrupulously in his footsteps', started his new activity with a detailed report to the Tsar stating the poor and neglected state of the Cappella as left by Bortniansky. Among the changes that Lvov was most proud of were those of organized book-keeping and record-keeping. He also restricted the education of those singers who were minors, now preparing them only to be office clerks, as well as reorganizing classes according to the formal criteria of age and year of study, and reintroducing corporal punishment, etc. In an attempt to root out Bortniansky's influence, he fired several singers who were Bortniansky's distant relatives, on the pretext of their belonging to the merchant class, who were forbidden to be members of the Cappella according to the new statutes. Considering himself an expert in singing, 'a man of exquisite taste' possessing 'a wide practical knowledge of the masterworks of all schools' (all quotations from Berlioz), he demanded that the veteran singers change their style in order not to become like the 'disfigured' choir of Count Dmitry Sheremetev, which symbolized 'Italianshchina' in his view. Realizing, however, that without proper training a choir cannot exist, he nonetheless played with the idea of hiring the famous Italian tenor Giovanni Battista Rubini for vocal instruction of Cappella singers. His

---

36 *Skhimnik* means a monk having taken vows of *schema* – a Greek religious term for the highest monastic grade in the Orthodox Church, demanding that the initiated person observe the rigid ascetic rules.

struggle to preserve the national tradition was expressed through the brochure he wrote, *O penii v Rossii* (About Singing in Russia, 1834), which deals with church singing and folk song separately. Lvov's talents as an administrator were truly exploited, however, in putting the church liturgical repertoire in order in continuation of the seventeenth-century Church policy of unification (to which Bortniansky had also contributed with his plainsong arrangement). Directly upon his appointment in 1826, Lvov began a campaign of harmonization of ancient chant and its preparation for publication.[37] A committee of the most veteran Cappella singers collected the chants in use at the Imperial court and Peter Turchaninov set them in a four-voice score.

That 'the Imperial Chapel had become a splendid and remarkable institution by 1836 when, after the death of Councillor Lvov, his son, General Alexis Lvov, was appointed its director', can be seen from the *Notes* by Glinka, who, as a reward for his *A Life for the Tsar*, received the position of *Kapellmeister* of the Cappella. An examination held in January 1837 showed that many of the adult choristers, that is tenors and basses, were quite bad and appeared to be almost illiterate in music (Glinka, 1831:182).

The younger Lvov, Alexey Fedorovich (Alexix), was at least a musician, and even a gifted one. Performing as a violinist since the age of seven, he achieved fame as a brilliant quartet player and his violin exercises are still in use in Russia today. He also studied theory and composition and assiduously combined his musical education with both study at the *Institut putey soobshchenia* (Institute of Communication) and work in Arakcheev's military settlements, which obviously contributed to his later efficient management of the Cappella. His musical talents, the success of his national anthem 'Bozhe, Tsarya khrani' [God, save the Tsar], and his father's authority at the Court, made his appointment as director of the Cappella a natural one.

Alexey Lvov continued his father's cause of unification of Russian church music. Realizing that the Court tradition of Russian chant represented only one of a countless number of traditions existing in other places in the vast lands of Russia; and, what was worse, it had already been 'corrupted' through the Italian manner influenced by the Ukrainian singers in the Court Cappella, he decided to collect all the variants in their original neumatic notation (*kryuki*), to compare them and to determine some invariant that would serve as an absolute original to be distributed throughout all of Russia and be confirmed once and for all. His goal, however, included not only an abstract idea for the sake of order, but also to monopolize the entire choral repertoire in Russia. Had his own operas been a success, perhaps he would have been less ambitious in church music reforms; but they were not, despite Berlioz's polite finding that *Ondine* 'contains beauties of the highest order: it is a fresh, lively, youthful, and charmingly original work'.

Alexey Lvov wanted to be like Bortniansky, whom in 1816 Alexander I had made the church music censor for all Russia. What he failed to take into consideration was that the mere issue of a decree does not automatically ensure the people's full obedience to

---

37 *Delo o garmonizatsii i podgotovke k izdaniu drevnikh tserkovnykh pesnopeniy*. RGIA, f 499, 1826–8, op 1 no 2921. See Belonenko, 1983:182.

it. Moreover, the decree might have helped to promote Bortniansky's music to a certain extent, but it had not provided him with a great income. Indeed, three decades later, in the late 1840s, a secular choral praxis had developed and there were many free choirs, especially in Moscow, where they naturally continued the eighteenth – early nineteenth-century Muscovite predilection for choir singing.

Lvov was especially angered by the Moscow choirs, which, using the advantage of being far from the capital sang whatever they liked. Failing to monopolize all the free choirs, Lvov decided to at least control their repertoires through policing. On 5 January 1850 he sent secret letters to the Moscow Metropolitan, Filaret, and the Moscow military Governor-General Count Zakrevsky, demanding that they take rigid measures to ensure that free choirs would not use music without approval from either the director of the Court Cappella or St Synod, and followed this with a catalogue of permitted works. Pretending to cooperate, Count Zakrevsky agreed, merely asking Lvov to give him a list of the free choir managers in order to give the appropriate orders to the authorities.

General Lvov, whose character had been formed in his youth by the Arakcheev military system, became totally obsessed with mastering the free choirs. On 17 October 1851 he presented Zakrevsky with a new project aimed at disciplining them, and for this purpose all the singers were to be housed in isolation, that is barracks. 'All the houses must be managed by four NCOs, a vocal instructor; (all appointed by the Government).'[38] According to Lvov, there also should be a priest and every house must have a signpost such as: 'The house of free choirs, section 1'; 'The house of free choirs, section 2' and so on.'

It took Count Zakrevsky half a year to compose his answer to this delirium. On 18 February 1852 he wrote:

> From the collected information it appears that free choirs consist of people of various professions and ranks (including minors): court personnel serving their landlords, actors from the Moscow theatre, and people occupied in commerce and other trades, for whom singing is a secondary and temporary occupation. It is impossible to determine for such people a permanent abode and even less possible to appoint a mutual house for their residence and submit them to special supervision.
>
> With all my desire to please Your Excellency, I do not possess the means to execute your proposal in regard to introducing order among the free choirs.[39]

---

38 'При каждом доме должны состоять: Надзиратель, четыре унтер-офицера из отставных, учитель пения (все сии лица назначаются от правительства).'

39 'Из собранных сведений оказывается, что вольные хоры составлены из людей разного звания (и малолетних): дворовые люди, находящиеся в услужении у своих помещиков, артисты московского театра, лица, занимающиеся торговлею и разными другими промыслами, для которых пение составляет занятие второстепенное и временное. Определить для таких людей постоянное местопребывание, а тем менее назначить для жительства их общий дом и подчинить их особому надзору представляется невозможным. / При всем желании моем сделать угодное Вашему Превосходительству, я не нахожу средств привести в исполнение Ваши предложения относительно введения порядков в вольных хорах' (RGIA, f 1109, op 1, 1900–1917, no 59, Ll 24ᵛ, 49ᵛ, 58).

Lvov's activity elicited strong opposition also from the Moscow Metropolitan, Filaret, who had organized a committee of experts in the ancient chant in order to examine the scientific validity of Lvov's enterprise. Its members included the fundamental scholar Dmitry Razumovsky. The committee asserted that Lvov had used only some of the manuscripts, which were mostly of Ukrainian origin, and that they were not only not very old, as Lvov had contended, but not old at all; the oldest ones related to the second quarter, while the others – to the last quarter of the eighteenth century, and one of them – even to the nineteenth century, as follows from its paper, script and even its inclusion of services mentioning events from the Petrine epoch (Belonenko, 1983:186).[40] This serves to illustrate Berlioz's report regarding Lvov's achievements in 'engaging in fruitful scholarly research in the musical archives of the Russian Church, thanks to which he has made several discoveries of great importance to the history of music'. With his works on Russian chant, Lvov indeed succeeded in constructing a partial image of himself as an expert, although his works are not considered by serious scholars as a notable contribution. What is true, however, is that Lvov's unfortunate undertaking stimulated a highly useful discussion on Russian palaeography and thus indeed contributed to the science.

The more corrupt side of Lvov's ambitions was no secret to his contemporaries. A.O. Smirnova-Rosset has left various interesting comments in her autobiography, such as that his church canticles were

> ...the most worthless; he made a deal with the Synod and ordered that they be learned throughout the entire lands of Russia, which made him ten thousand [roubles] revenue. Metropolitan Filaret passionately complained that they have spoiled our church singing. Today this singing, conducted by Bakhmetev, is completely spoiled, and music lovers visit Count Sheremetev.[41]

From this and other quotations it can be seen that the Capella's tradition as the Lvovs had wanted it to be (that is maintaining a strict church-music style), and Count Sheremetev's tradition with its para-liturgical tendency (which music lovers preferred and the Lvovs condemned), were two separate poles and Bortniansky's reputation in the nineteenth century was consequently defined by this situation. While the audiences loved Bortniansky, for which the best proof is Jurgenson's commercial enterprise of his collected edition in 1881–82 (to which he invited Tchaikovsky to be an editor), Russian musicians and musical thinkers were more influenced by the Lvovs' canon or rather by the creed that determined their canon.

---

40 See A.V. Preobrazhensky, Documents on the history of church singing in the Court Capella from its archives as well as from the Ministry of the Imperial Court. RGIA, f 1109, op 1, no 58, L 100ᵛ.

41 '...самые негодные, он сторговался с синодом, велел их разучивать по всей России, что дало ему десять тысяч дохода. Митрополит Филарет горячо жаловался, что испортили наше церковное пение. Теперь это пение под управлением Бахметьева совсем испортилось, и охотники ездят к графу Шереметеву' (A.O. Smirnova-Rosset, *Avtobiografia*. Moscow, 1931:295).

Prince Vladimir Odoevsky wrote to Alexey Lvov in 1860, having become indignant by Berlioz's (as well as Fétis's) delight in Bortniansky, and praised Lvov himself as the one who had '…liberated us from a dancing rhythm, so contrary to our church chant, so dangerous for the correct accentuation, and… indicating… mistakes into which Bortniansky had fallen despite his unarguable talent, based on the Western rules, to which he considered he was "obliged to subject himself"'.[42]

In the same year Alexander Serov, probably inspired by the preparations to publish the complete editions of Palestrina's œuvre in Leipzig, noted in his article 'Music, musical science and musical pedagogy':

> The one for whom the only light in the window is that of Bortniansky, will undoubtedly not be at peace with any document of ancient Russian church music.
>
> Russian lovers of church singing, brought up on Bortniansky – the weak echo of the Italians of Mozart's epoch – could greatly contribute to enlightening their taste by listening to the clean colours of Palestrina's music. There lie entire worlds of unearthly sensations – unknown and unachievable in other fields of music… Palestrina wrote the double-choir *Stabat Mater*, in the face of which all the latest compositions on this topic are only profanation of this highly pathetic subject. But, again, the one who would approach this music with the 'contemporary' demands, brought up in theatres and concert halls, will find little consolation.[43]

In 1878 Tchaikovsky wrote to Nadezhda von Mekk: 'I recognize some merits in Bortniansky, Berezovsky and so on, but how little their music harmonizes with the Byzantian style of architecture and icons, with the entire tone of the Orthodox service!'[44]

The row of critical comments regarding Bortniansky's spiritual music is sometimes extended by Rimsky-Korsakov's words that it was 'one big mistake in the understanding of Russian church style'. But the composer had never *written* this as

---

42 '…освободил нас от плясового ритма, столь противного духу нашего церковного песнопения, столь опасного для правильности ударений, и указал ошибки… в которые впал Бортнянский, несмотря на свой неоспоримый талант, на основании западных правил, коим он считал себя "в обязанности подчиниться"' (Odoevsky, 1956:677).

43 'Для кого только и свету в окошке, что Бортнянский, тот, без сомнения, не поладит ни с одним из документов старинной русской церковной музыки. / Русским любителям церковного пения, воспитавшим себя на Бортнянском – этом слабом отголоске итальянцев моцартовского времени, – особенно полезно было бы просветить свой вкус слушаньем чистых красок палестриновской музыки. Тут целые миры надземных ощущений, – в других областях музыки неведомых и недосягаемых… Палестрина написал двухорное "Stabat Mater", перед которым все позднейшие сочинения на эту задачу – только профанация высокопатетического сюжета. Но, повторяю, кто будет подходить к этой музыке с требованиями "современными", возросшими в театрах и концертных залах, тот не много найдет себе утешения' (Serov, 1957:211).

44 'Я признаю некоторые достоинства за Бортнянским, Березовским и проч., но до какой степени их музыка мало гармонирует с византийским стилем архитектуры и икон, со всем строем православной службы!' (Tchaikovsky, 1962:238).

Kuzma wrote (1996:184), referring to Ivanov (1980:7, 142) who actually quoted I.F. Tyumenev's memoirs on Rimsky-Korsakov.[45] All the written mentions Bortniansky by Rimsky-Korsakov are positive, the composer especially liked his *Prostoe penie*, some other liturgical pieces and two concertos (Rimsky-Korsakov, 1923:17).

It should be noted that the accusations of lack of authenticity and spirituality that nineteenth-century musicians addressed to the eighteenth-century spiritual music were to be heard not only in Russia. Both Haydn and Mozart were subjected to such critique. Alfred Einstein commented on this phenomenon long ago:

> The scorn on the part of the nineteenth-century Romantic purists and 'Cecilians' for the church style of Haydn and Mozart is the more comical because their admiration for the church music of the Palestrina period rests upon a historical fallacy. If they had had a better knowledge of the secular music of Palestrina and Lasso and the Gabrielis, they would have had to reject the church music of these masters and their contemporaries also, as being too similar to the secular music and flowing from the same spirit. They regarded as eminently churchly works that in reality were full of an eminently secular symbolism of expression, or at least were full of a symbolism common to both secular and sacred music. If they had known more, nothing would have remained to the Cecilians *à la* Thibaut but to go back to plainsong or the antiphonal chants of the early Christians... If Mozart's church music is to be criticized, then, it must be on the ground not of being too 'worldly', but because it is not worldly enough. (Einstein, 1945:320)

Giving a historiographical explanation Einstein wrote:

> When the romantic nineteenth century began to discover the Middle Ages, not only the Gothic cathedrals and pre-Raphaelites but also what is considered medieval in music – the alleged *a cappella* style of the Gabrielis, Lasso and Palestrina – the church music of the seventeenth and eighteenth centuries became an object of contempt. (p. 319)

The following quotation from Anton Friedrich Justus Thibaut, professor at the University of Heidelberg and Privy Councillor (who also consulted Metropolitan Evgeny of Kiev (Bolkhovitinov) about Russian music (Mazo, 1987:24), and whom Einstein cited), would have been concurred with by many Russian thinkers:

> Thus our more recent masses and other ecclesiastic compositions have degenerated to the extent that they have become purely amorous and emotional and bear the absolute stamp of secular opera and even of that type of opera which is most in demand, that is, downright vulgar opera [What does Thibaut mean? Opera *buffa*?], in which, to be sure, the crowd feels most at home, and people of quality even more so than the common herd. Even the church music of Mozart and Haydn deserves that reproach, and both masters have even expressed it themselves. Mozart openly smiled at his masses... (*Über Reinheit der Tonkunst*, 1824, 1st edn, Chap. VIII. Quoted by Einstein: 319)

This clash in the problems of nineteenth-century understanding of the seventeenth- and eighteenth-century church and spiritual music, can be viewed from another point

---

45 I.F. Tyumenev. Vospominaniya o Rimskom-Korsakove, vol. 2. Moscow, 1954:200.

– the changes in function of this music in post-Viennese Congress Europe. It was not Bortniansky, Mozart or Haydn that nineteenth-century thinkers criticized so severely; rather it was that para-liturgical music had lost its respectable place in the new era of irreversible secularization of European cultural values. The nineteenth-century critics applied to the para-liturgical musical legacy the concept of 'church music', confusing two functionally different genres, and hence, miscriticizing their composers.

In Russia, Bortniansky was the last in line of those who had secularized para-liturgical music, beginning with the patriarch Nikon (regardless of his intentions) who had introduced *partes* concertos into Russia in the mid-seventeenth century. The secularization of this genre was its immanent feature and it lasted as long as the genre itself – during the long eighteenth century. In order to understand why this happened, two questions should be answered: why did para-liturgical music in Russia disappear; and what exactly was it that disappeared – only Russian or every kind of such music?

The answer to the second question can be found in Rimsky-Korsakov's *My Musical Life*, in the following excerpt from the history of concerts of the Russian Musical Society:

> The first of these concerts had taken place in the Spring of 1867 under the leadership of Balakireff and K.N. Lyadoff. The second concert was conducted by Balakireff alone in the spring of 1868. A vast chorus participated in addition to the orchestra. Herewith I reproduce verbatim the rather interesting bill of that concert:
> Sunday, 5 May, 1868, Concert by A. Kologrivoff at the Mikhaylovski Manège.

Part I

1) Introduction to the oratorio of *St. Paul*	Mendelssohn
2) *Gloria Patri* (Chorus without orchestra)	Turchaninov
3) Prayer *Ne perdas* (with orchestra)	Dargomyzhski
4) Funeral March	Chopin-Maurer
5) Excerpts from *Stabat Mater*	L'voff
a)He who without grief and sorrow	
b) O eternal avenger of sin	
6) Symphonic work, with the national anthem	Rubinstein

Part II

1) Introduction to a Biblical Legend [op. 74]	Mendelssohn
2) *Gloria Domini* (Chorus without orchestra)	Bakhmetyeff
3) Introduction to *Fuite en Egypte*	Berlioz
4) Fragment of a Psalm	Bortniansky
5) March for the Coronation of Nicholas I, orchestrated by Rimsky-Korsakov	Schubert
6) *Bozhe, Tsarya khrani* (God save the king!)	

M. A. Balakireff, Conductor

All these choruses of Turchaninoff, Bortnyanski and Bakhmetyeff[46] were nothing but these authors' orthodox canticles performed in Latin because the censor did not permit the performance of orthodox ecclesiastic canticles at concerts, together with profane music. The chorus of oriental hermits, to a text by Pushkin, with the words *Ne perdas* prefixed in order to mislead the ecclesiastical censor, thus came into the class of such quasi-catholic prayers. Rubinstein's symphonic work with the national anthem was but his *Festouvertüre* renamed for a similar reason. Thus, with the help of some masquerading, the ecclesiastic censor with his absurd rules was duped. (Rimsky-Korsakov: 1923:82–3)

Censorship by the Holy Ruling Synod even at the end of the nineteenth and beginning of the twentieth century often rejected spiritual concertos by the new composers, preferring those written a century or more before. Some of the eighteenth-century concertos – among them works by Berezovsky, Degtyarev, Vedel (most often) and even Bortniansky, a former censor himself of Russian ecclesiastic music – were ruled to be inadmissible for performance in church. For example, in the case *O notnykh rukopisyakh Karpenko, Degtyareva i Dubenskogo* [About the music manuscripts of Karpenko, Degtyarev and Dubensky], the prosecutor of the Moscow Synod Office wrote as late as 10 May 1900 that compositions by Degtyarev and Bortniansky are permitted to be printed but not to be used in the church service.[47] In another case, *O notnykh rukopisyakh Vedelya, Degtyareva i Berezovskogo* [About the music manuscripts of Vedel, Degtyarev and Berezovsky], the Supervising Council of the Synod school of church singing concluded that despite these having been the works of composers of fame and, of course, having historical significance, their style is such that it is definitely not desired in the Russian Orthodox Church.[48] All these requests were submitted to the Synod during a period of intensive development of amateur choirs in Russia (in parallel to Germany), and came from musicians wishing to broaden their repertoires by including the eighteenth-century legacy, in which they perceived a genuine artistic value as well as an historical significance.

From the above materials it can be seen that in the nineteenth century the eighteenth-century Russian spiritual concerto as a para-liturgical genre had a place neither in the concert hall nor in the church. At the same time the Western mass had gained a respectable place in concert programmes – a circumstance that the young Russian musicians of the late 1860s exploited in the above-described camouflage tactic. As we can see, the banning body – the religious censor – was the same, but its motivation was different: while in the concert performance it could object to reducing the sacred value of Russian spiritual compositions by their being performed along with secular music, in the church it could object to offending the religious sensitivity of the parishioners by offering music too secular in style. With some variation, this situation continued into the Soviet era. The church repertoire had little changed since the pre-Revolutionary years and church choirs were too apathetic to

---

46　Nikolai Ivanovich Bakhmetev (1807–91), Russian composer and violinist, was the director of the Imperial Court Cappella from 1861–83 and composed church music.

47　RGIA, f 796, op 181, 1900, no 3670, Ll 3–4.

48　RGIA, f 796, op 181, 1900, no 3670 Ll 2–4.

broaden it. In concert practice Russian spiritual music was forbidden as constituting possible religious propaganda, while Western spiritual classics – being alienated by language and belonging to another culture – did not present such a danger. Only one of Bortniansky's concertos was still performed, and even that with new, neutral text by A. Mashistov.

The 'thaw' of the 1960s somewhat liberated this repertoire. The pioneering performance of Bortniansky's, Berezovsky's and Vedel's works as well as some *partes* concertos and even earlier Russian church compositions was undertaken in 1966 by Alexander Yurlov, who directed the same Cappella as Bortniansky.[49] Yurlov's endeavour broke the ice and inspired further performances (by Valery Poliansky and Vladimir Minin in Moscow, Vladislav Chernushenko in Leningrad and Victor Ikonnik in Kiev) and new research.[50]

As to the question of why para-liturgical music in Russia disappeared – the answer should be sought in Russian history, in the aspect of relations between the Church and the State and in the role of this music in the manifestation of these relations. This music had always existed in Russia since the time of the country's Christianization. Among other functions, it served as a ceremonial genre not only for glorification of the secular power, but also to deify it, personifying the Tsar as 'blessed by God to rule the land', thus reflecting 'theocratic absolutism'.[51] The more the tsars became independent of the Church, the more interaction with secular genres the para-liturgical styles revealed. The entire history of *partes* concerto and the following late eighteenth-century spiritual music illustrates this, including its stagnation in the era of Empress Elizabeth, who was much more religious and Church-dependent than her father Peter I and even grandfather Tsar Alexey Mikhaylovich, not to mention Catherine II who followed her.

From the 1720s (the late years of Peter's rule), the church officially became an *instrumentum regni* of the Russian autocracy and a source of State income. The organization of the Synod as a body subjugated to the Senate transferred all management of Church affairs into State hands. Peter even made Metropolitan Dmitry Rostovsky preach against beards (one of the main symbols of Russian Orthodoxy), as well as constituting the Synod functionaries from his own (often non-religious) officers. The same policy continued uninterruptedly into the nineteenth and twentieth centuries: Stalin, a graduate of a theological college and an Okhranka agent (the Secret Police Department in tsarist Russia), kept an eye on the Church, officially

---

49 In 1922 this institution was officially named *Leningradskaya Gosudarstvennaya Akademicheskaya Kapella imeni M.I. Glinki* [Leningrad State Academic Capella named after M.I. Glinka], until 1991, when it received its present name *Gosudarstvennaya Akademicheskaya Kapella Sankt-Peterburga* [State Academic Capella of St Petersburg].

50 While this repertoire carved its way into concert performances, censorship of printed matter remained strict as late as 1979, when my book on Bortniansky appeared without musical examples and the titles of the concertos, presenting only their numbers and keys. (By the time of my 1983 book on Berezovsky this ban had already been rescinded.)

51 See Michael Rywkin, 'Russia and the Former Soviet Union' in *Encyclopedia of Nationalism*, vol. I, San-Francisco, 2000:655.

separated from the State, by forming its cadres from NKVD (later KGB) agents.

At the beginning of the eighteenth century the so-called *Tabel'nye dni* [Table days] were established for the performance of special church services in honour of the tsarist family. The policy of their sanctification was enforced so severely that terrorized priests could be seen wearing panagias with an image of the Empress Anna Ioannovna in décolletée.[52] The profanation of church ritual became so deep that the atheistic Catherine II, who converted to Orthodoxy for much the same reason that Henry IV of France became Catholic, called herself the 'Head of the Greek Church'. She did not object when in the fresco at Mogilev Cathedral, in commemoration of her meeting with the Emperor Joseph II in 1782, the court painter Borovikovsky portrayed her as the Virgin while Prince Potemkin was represented as the archangel Gabriel, and a place was also found for Joseph II (Nikol'sky, 1983:221).

With the expansion of the Imperial family, the number of Table days increased, as did their pomp and grandeur. Maria Fedorovna alone gave birth to ten Grand Dukes and Duchesses. It is clear now how many new panegyric concertos would have been demanded in the 1780s – early 1790s, and consequently what kind of feelings towards Bortniansky the Imperial family may have felt.

By the beginning of the nineteenth century the Church was subjugated to the State to such an extent that in the official vocabulary the very term 'Church' was replaced by the term 'Department of Orthodox Denomination'. Prince A.N. Golitsyn, whom Alexander I had asked to be Chief Prosecutor for the Synod, initially refused to accept the position, feeling it inappropriate to his beliefs as an atheist, but eventually gave in and performed his duties with 'pagan diligence' (Nikol'sky, 1983:206). Any danger from the Church toward the Throne receded to such extent that the earlier need of the State to subjugate the Church and to transform it into a means for glorification of the secular powers became irrelevant. While in the eighteenth century the celebration of Table days had been a means of dissemination of loyal feelings, in the nineteenth century they gradually became a tribute to court and official etiquette. Except for the cathedrals, all other churches performed services on Table days in a week-day way, with fewer candles, without singers and parishioners, early in the morning (Nikol'sky, 1983:223–24).

In 1817 secularization went even further, when the above-mentioned Department was reorganized to include the management of national education and other religious confessions. In the 1830s, Alexey Lvov's national anthem *Bozhe, Tsarya khrani* [God Save the Tsar] (1833) and Glinka's *Zhizn' za Tsarya* [A Life for the Tsar] (1836) firmly imprinted the classical formula of Count Sergei Uvarov's *Orthodoxy, autocracy, nationality*, centralizing the meaning of autocracy from both sides – Orthodoxy (Lvov) and nationality (Glinka), and hammered the last two symmetrical nails into the coffin of Russian para-liturgical music. All that the ruling powers required as 'liturgical' was now under control in the churches, and all that had served as 'para' – was now in the civil institutions and in the theatre. Ritual music had become divided according to the demands of real life and no longer needed any

---

52 *Panagia* is an image worn round the neck by Orthodox bishops.

euphemisms. Russian para-liturgical music ended with the end of the century-old phantom of the Church's threat to the State.

It is hard to predict to what extent Bortniansky's critics would have succeeded in compromising his historical reputation if some Slavophile-oriented anonymous ghost-writer would not have decided to use Bortniansky's name to promote the idea of printing all the *kryuki* Russian chants.

In 1878, when Tchaikovsky failed to recognize the genuine nature of Bortniansky's religious music, the addenda to the *Protocol godichnogo sobrania Obshchestva lyubiteley drevney pis'mennosti* [Record of the Annual Meeting of the Society of Lovers of Old Writings] included an anonymous *Proekt ob otpechatanii drevnego rossiyskogo kryukovogo peniya, rassmatrivaemy v dvukh glavneyshikh otnosheniyakh, v otnoshenii k sostoyaniyu vsekh staroobryadcheskikh tserkvey, i v otnoshenii k sostoyaniyu vsekh velikorossiyskikh tserkvey* [Project for Printing Ancient Russian *Kryuki* Chants, considered in two main relations, in relation to all Old Believers churches and in relation to all Great Russia churches]. The text has been ascribed to Bortniansky and exists in four nineteenth-century handwritten copies; however, neither its autograph nor any references to materials related to Bortniansky have been found and only one copy, known as Vyazemsky's, vaguely indicates its having been copied from an unknown copy that belonged to P. Kachenovsky, who in turn states that he had copied the text from a draft by his teacher, Dmitry Bortniansky (Belonenko, 1983:180; 1986:153–75).

The anonymous author mentions his Italian education and thus transparently identifies himself as Bortniansky, who was the only Russian musician at the time studying in Italy and committing himself to Russian sacred music. He reveals a definite knowledge of the field and expresses his admiration for this part of the musical legacy, seeing in it a great potential for the development of a national school of composition. The main objective of this work was to produce a comprehensive scholarly publication of the *kryuki* chants in order to (1) preserve this vanishing art form as a valuable and genuine national cultural treasure, and (2) make it available for study by contemporary and future musicians, thus encouraging its further development through the technique of counterpoint. The latter corresponds to Glinka's famous reflection: 'I am almost convinced that the western fugue can be united with the conditions of our music through the bonds of legal matrimony.'[53]

The ideas revealed in this *Project* do not contradict Bortniansky's image, considering his enlightened worldview in general and his work on the Russian chant settings in particular. However, the rhetorical and pompous style, masking the author's superficiality and pettiness, does not correspond to Bortniansky's, which, though known only from official documents, is generally elegant and modest. The text of the *Project* reflects a trivial opposition to western European culture, with a negative approach to 'westernization', for example. Such an approach by Bortniansky would have constituted a total denial of his own musical background. It

---

53 'Я почти убежден, что можно связать Фугу западную с условиями нашей музыки узами законного брака' (M.I. Glinka to K.A. Bulgakov, see Glinka, 1977:180)

would also have been inconsistent with his promotion and publication of Galuppi's and Sarti's compositions. The tendentious use of the first person narrative also seems suspicious. Did Bortniansky actually need anonymity at all?

The document became known as *Proekt Bortnianskogo* [Bortniansky's Project], but it did not attract any serious attention until 1900–01, when the commemoration of 75 years since Bortniansky's death and the celebration of the 150th anniversary of his birth, respectively, began to revive interest in this composer among wide circles of Russian musicians and scholars. Authorship of the *Project*, which had already been questioned for some decades, now became a focus of public discussion. Vladimir Stasov, smelling forgery, disclaimed Bortniansky's authorship (1901) while Stepan Smolensky, choir conductor and researcher in the history of Russian church music, argued that only Bortniansky could have been involved in formulating the initial outline of the project (1901). Since that time, the issue of the *Project*'s attribution has divided scholars into two camps, with the controversy remaining largely unresolved. The most fundamental studies to date of the source have been offered by A. Finagin (1927:174–88) and Belonenko (1986:153–75).

Irrespective of the essence of the *Project*, the discussion that its publication provoked around Bortniansky's name turned the attention of the more snobbish musical circles toward the composer, though probably making some adjustments to contemporary fashion and emphasizing his nationalistic strivings. Thus, while the eighteenth century loved Bortniansky for his spiritual concertos, the nineteenth century finally accepted him for his settings of Russian chant, and in the twentieth century his reputation survived due to his secular music. Today Bortniansky is fully recognized in Russia as its major eighteenth-century composer and the research into his work and life – in parallel with eighteenth-century studies in general – has never been so encompassing, as the conferences dedicated to the 250th anniversary of his birth, held at the Conservatories of St Petersburg, Moscow and Kiev in 2001, have shown. However, there is still much to be discovered in the Russian archives as well as in other depositories all over the world, since many documents became dispersed with the flood of Russian emigrants during the 1917 revolution. The more deeply Russian eighteenth-century music legacy will be studied, the more obvious it will become that so many of the traits of later Russian music and musical culture had begun then, and indeed in many ways even earlier; as well as how many links connect it with both the past and the centuries that came after it.

Bibliography

Alexeev, M., (1921) 'M. Berezovsky', in *Posev*. Odessa.

Altshuller, A., Dansker, O. and Kopytova G. (eds), (2nd edn revised, 1996) *Putevoditel' po Kabinetu rukopisey Rossiyskogo Instituta Istorii Iskusstv*. St Petersburg: Rossiyskiy Institut Istorii Iskusstv.

Antonowycz, Myroslaw, (1990) *Ukrainische geistliche Musik. Ein Beitrag zur Kirchenmusik Osteuropas*. Wissenschaftlicher Kongress zum Millennium des Christentums in der Ukraine in Zusammenarbeit mit der Ukrainischen Freien Universität. München.

Asafiev, Boris V., (1927a) 'Ob issledovanii russkoy muzyki XVIII v. i dvukh operakh Bortnyanskogo', in V. Prokofiev, (ed.), *Muzyka i muzykal'ny byt staroy Rossii*. Leningrad: Academia, pp. 3–5.

———, (1927b) 'Pamyatka o Kozlovskom', in V. Prokofiev, (ed.), *Muzyka i muzykal'ny byt staroy Rossii*. Leningrad: Academia, pp. 117–22

———, (1971) *Muzykalnaya forma kak process*, books 1–2. Leningrad: Muzyka.

———, (3rd edn, 1979) *Russkaya muzyka (XIX i nachala XX veka)*. Leningrad: Muzyka.

Askochensky, V., (1856) *Kiev s ego drevneyshim uchilishchem Akademieyu*, part II. Kiev.

———, (1863) *Protoierey P.I. Turchaninov*. St Petersburg.

Bantysh-Kamensky, D., (1836) *Slovar' dostopamyatnykh lyudey Russkoy zemli*. Moscow.

Belkin, A.A., (1975) *Russkie skomorokhi*. Moscow: Nauka.

Belonenko, Alexander S., (1983) 'Is istorii russkoy muzykal'noy textologii', in *Problemy russkoy muzykal'noy textologii (po pamyatnikam russkoy khorovoy muzyki XII–XVIII vekov)*. Leningrad: Gosudarstvennaya konservatoria, Gosudarstvenny Institut teatra, muzyki i kinematografii, pp. 173–94.

———, (1986) 'K voprosu ob avtorstve "Proekta Bortnyanskogo"', in A.S. Belonenko and S.P. Kravchenko (eds), *Russkaya khorovaya muzyka XVI–XVIII vekov*, Proccedings of the GMPI imeni Gnesinykh, 83:153–75. Moscow.

Belyaev, Victor M., (1962) *Drevnerusskaya muzykal'naya pis'mennost'*. Moscow: Gosudarstvennoe muzykal'noe izdatel'stvo.

Belza, Igor' F., (1975) *Mikhail Kleofas Oginsky*. Moscow: Muzyka.

Berkov, Pavel Naumovich, (1977) *Istoria russkoy komedii*. Leningrad: Nauka.

Berlioz, Hector, (1956) *Evenings with the Orchestra*. Trans. and ed., with Introduction by Jacques Barzun at the request of the Berlioz Society. New York: Alfred A. Knopf.

Bessonov, P., (1872) *Praskovia Ivanovna, grafinya Sheremeteva*. Moscow.

Bezsonov, S.V., (1938) *Krepostnye arkhitektory*. Moscow: Izdatel'stvo Vsesoyuznoy Akademii arkhitektury.

Billington, James H., (2nd edn, 1970) *The Icon and the Axe: An Interpretive History of Russian Culture*. New York: Vintage Books Edition.

Birzhakova, E.E., Voinova, L.A. and Kutina, L.L., (1972) *Ocherki po istoricheskoy lexikologii russkogo yazyka XVIII veka. Yazykovye kontakty i zaimstvovania.* Leningrad: Nauka.

Bolkhovitinov, E., (1805) 'Prodolzhenie novogo opyta istoricheskogo slovarya o rossiyskikh pisatelyakh' *Drug prosveshchenia*, part 2, June.

———, (1838, 1845) *Slovar' russkikh svetskikh pisateley, sootechestvennikov i chuzhestrantsev, pisavshikh v Rossii.* Moscow.

Borovik, M., (1971) 'Pro vplivi narodnoy pisni na melodiku A. Vedelya', in *Ukrains'ko muzykoznavstvo*, vol. VI:137–52. Kiev: Muzychna Ukraina.

Brazhnikov, Maxim V., (1972) *Drevnerusskaya teoria muzyki (po rukopisnym materialam XV–XVIII vekov*. Leningrad: Muzyka.

———, (2002) *Russkaya pevcheskaya paleografia*, scientific ed. N.S. Seregina. St Petersburg: Rossiyskiy Institut Istorii Iskusstv.

Brown, Malcolm Hamrick, (1983) 'Native Song and National Consciousness in Nineteenth-Century Russian Music', in Theofanis George Stavrou (ed.), *Art and Culture in Nineteenth-Century Russia*. Bloomington: Indiana University Press, pp. 57–84.

Carpenter, Ellon D., (1983) 'Russian Music Theory: A Conspectus', in Gordon D. McQuere (ed.), *Russian Theoretical Thought in Music*. Ann Arbor, Michigan: UMI Research Press, pp. 1–82.

Chudinova, Irina A., (1994) *Penie, zvony, ritual: Topografia tserkovno–muzykal'noy kul'tury Peterburga*. St Petertsburg: Rossiyskiy Institut Istorii Iskusstv.

Ciechanowiecki (Tsekhanavetsky), A., (1961) *Michał Kazimierz Ogiński und sein Musenhof zu Słonim*. Böhlau verlag Köln Graz.

Cracraft, James, (2004) *The Petrine Revolution in Russian Culture*. Cambridge, Massachusetts, and London: The Belknap Press of Harvard University Press.

Cross, A.G., (1988) 'Early British Acquaintance with Russian Popular Song and Music (The Letters and Journals of the Wilmot Sister)', *Slavonic and East European Review*, 66/1:21–34.

Dadiomova, Volga, (2001) *Narysi gistoryi muzychnai kul'tury Belarusi*. Minsk: Belaruskaya Dzyarzhawnaya Academia Muzyki.

———, (2002) *Muzychnaya kul'tura Belarusi XVIII stagoddzya*. Minsk: Belaruskaya Dzyarzhawnaya Academia Muzyki.

Dashkova, E.R., (1987) *Zapiski; Pis'ma sester M. i K. Wilmot iz Rossii*, ed. S.S. Dmitrieva. Moscow: Moskovsky universitet.

Diletsky, Mikola, (1971) *Grammatika muzykal'na*. Kiev: Muzychna Ukraina.

Diletsky, Nikolai, (1979) *Idea grammatiki musikiyskoy*, publication, transl., ed. and research by V.V. Protopopov, PRMI, vol. VII. Moscow: Muzyka.

Dobrokhotov, Boris V., (1950) *D.S. Bortnyansky*. Moscow-Leningrad: Muzgiz.

———, (2nd edn, 1968) *Evstigney Fomin*. Moscow: Muzyka.

———, (1983) 'I.E. Khandoshkin', in IRM, 3:226–41.

Dolgoruky, Ivan M., (1870) *Slavny bubny za gorami ili puteshestvie moe koe–kuda 1810 goda*. Moscow.

————, (2nd edn, 1890) *Kapishche moego serdtsa ili slovar' vsekh tekh lits, s koimi ya byl v raznykh otnosheniyakh v techenii moey zhizni*, suplement to *Russky arkhiv*. Moscow.

————, (1916) *Povest' o rozhdenii moem, proiskhozhdenii i vsey zhizni, pisannaya mnoy samim i nachataya v Moskve, 1788 goda v Avguste mesyatse na 25 godu ot rozhdenia moego*. Petrograd.

Dolgov, Dmitry, (1857) 'D.S. Bortnyansky', literaturnoe pribavlenie k zhurnalu *Nuvellist*, 18, March.

Dolgova, S.R., (1975) 'Pervaya "Marselieza" v Rossii', in V. Rabinovich (ed.) *Traditsii russkoy muzykal'noy kul'tury XVIII veka*, Proceedings of the GMPI imeni Gnesinykh, 21:181–6. Moscow.

Dolskaya-Ackerly, Olga, (1983) 'The Early Kant in Seventeenth-Century Russian Music', Ph.D. dissertation. University of Kansas.

Druskin, M.S. and Keldysh, Yu.V. (eds), (1956) *Ocherki po istorii russkoy muzyki 1790–1825*. Leningrad: Gosudarstvennoe muzykal'noe izdatel'stvo.

Einstein, Alfred, (1945) *Mozart: his Character, his Work*. New York: Oxford University Press.

Elizarova, Nadezhda A., (1944) *Teatry Sheremetevykh*. Moscow: Ostankinsky Dvorets-Muzey.

————, (1969) *Praskovia Ivanovna Kovaleva–Zhemchugova*. Moscow: Ostanskinsky dvorets-muzei tvorchestva krepostnykh.

Famintsyn, Alexander S., (1995, reprint from 1889) *Skomorokhi na Rusi*. St Petersburg: Aleteya.

Fedorovskaya, Lyudmila A., (1977) *Kompozitor Stepan Davydov*. Leningrad: Muzyka.

Fedosova, E.P., (1991) *Russky muzykal'ny klassitsizm: Stanovlenie sonatnoy formy v russkoy muzyke do Glinki*. Moscow: Rossiyskaya Akademia Muzyki.

Fesechko, Grigory F., (1965) 'Novye materialy o kompozitorakh P.A. Skokove i E.I. Fomine', in E. Gordeeva (ed.), *Muzykal'noe nasledstvo*, vol. II:9–43. Moscow: Muzyka.

————, (1972) *Ivan Evstafievich Khandoshkin*. Leningrad: Muzyka.

Filshtein, Sofia, (1980) 'S velikoyu opasnostiu ot tamoshnego pravlenia', *Muzykal'naya zhizn'*, 24:23–4.

————, (1989) 'Listuvannia D.S. Bortnyans'kogo z kantselyariyu Imperatritsy Marii Fedorovny', in M.M. Gordeychuk (ed.), *Ukrains'ka muzychna spadshchina* (articles, materials, documents), vol. I:80–97. Kiev: Muzychna Ukraina.

Finagin, A., (1927) 'Proekt Bortnyanskogo', in V. Prokofiev, (ed.), *Muzyka i muzykal'ny byt staroy Rossii*. Leningrad: Academia, pp. 174–88.

Findeizen, Nikolai F., (1917) 'Predpolagaemy masonskiy gimn Bortnyanskogo', in *Russkaya muzykal'naya gazeta*, 29, 30. St Petersburg.

————, (1928–9) *Ocherki po istorii muzyki v Rossii s drevneishikh vremen do kontsa XVIII veka*, 2 vols. Moscow-Leningrad: Gosudarstvennoe Izdatel'stvo, Muzsektor.

Fortunatov, Yury A., (1997) 'Kompozitor Osip Antonovich Kozlovsky i ego orkestrovaya muzyka', in *Osip Antonovich Kozlovsky. Orkestrovaya muzyka*, scores. Moscow: OOO Kotran, pp. 417–99.

Galkina, (Sokolova) Alla M., (1973) 'O simfonizme Bortnyanskogo', in *Sovetskaya muzyka*, 10:92–6.

———, (1975) 'Razvitie simfonicheskikh printsipov v russkoy teatral'noy muzyke kontsa XVIII–nachala XIX vekov', Ph.D. dissertation. Moscow: Moscow Conservatory.

———, (1985) 'Kontsertnaya zhizn'', in IRM, 3:242–74.

Gardner, Ivan (Joann von), (1980–82) *Bogosluzhebnoe penie Russkoy Pravoslavnoy Tserkvi: sistema, sushchnost' i istoria*, 2 vols. Jordanville, N.Y.: St Vladimir's Seminary Press.

———, (1980) *Russian Church Singing: Orthodox Worship and Hymnography*. Trans. by Vladimir Morozan, vol. 1. Crestwood, N.Y.: St. Vladimir's Seminary Press.

Georgi, I.G., (1794) *Opisanie tsarstvuyushchego grada Sankt-Peterburga*. St Petersburg.

Gerasimova-Persidskaya, Nina A., (1976) *Patresny kontsert*, scores, publication, ed. and research. Kiev: Muzychna Ukraina.

———, (1978) *Khoroviy kontsert na Ukraini v XVII–XVIII st*. Kiev: Muzychna Ukraina.

———, (1983) *Partesny kontsert v istorii muzykal'noy kul'tury*. Moscow: Muzyka.

———, (1988) 'Avtorstvo kak istoriko-stilevaya problema', in *Muzykal'noe proizvedenie: sushchnost', aspekty analiza*. Kiev: Muzychna Ukraina, pp. 27–88.

———, (1994) *Russkaya muzyka XVII veka – vstrecha dvukh epokh*. Moscow: Muzyka.

Ginzburg, Semen L., (1941) *Russky muzykal'ny teatr 1700–1835*, ontology. Leningrad-Moscow: Iskusstvo.

———, (2nd edn, 1968) *Istoria russkoy muzyki v notnykh obraztsakh*. Moscow: Muzyka.

Glinka, Mikhail, (1963) *Memoirs*, trans. by Richard B. Mudge. Norman: University of Oklahoma Press.

———, (1977) *Literaturnye proizvedeniya i perepiska*, Polnoe sobranie sochineniy, comp. and ed. A.S. Rozanov, vol. IIb. Moscow: Muzyka.

Gorchakov, Nikolai, (1808) *Opyt vokal'noy ili pevcheskoy muzyki v Rossii*. Moscow.

Gourevich, Vladimir, (2003a) 'Tvorchestvo D.S. Bortnyanskogo na stranitsakh Nemetskoy muzykal'noy pressy (1800–1840)', in E.G. Sorokina, Yu.A. Rozanova and I.A. Skvortsova (eds), *Bortnyansky i ego vremya,* Proceedings of the Moscow State Conservatory, 43:137–57. Moscow.

———, (2003b) 'Tipicheskoe i osobennoe v garmonicheskom yazyke proizvedeniy Bortnyanskogo', in E.G. Sorokina, Yu.A. Rozanova and I.A. Skvortsova (eds), *Bortnyansky i ego vremya,* Proceedings of the Moscow State Conservatory, 43:24–34. Moscow.

Gozenpud, Abram A., (1959) *Muzykal'ny teatr v Rossii. Ot istokov do Glinki.* Leningrad: Gosudarstvennoe muzykal'noe izdatel'stvo.

Grachev, P.V., (1956) 'O.A. Kozlovsky', in M.S. Druskin and Yu.V. Keldysh (eds), *Ocherki po istorii russkoy muzyki 1790–1825.* Leningrad: Gosudarstvennoe muzykal'noe izdatel'stvo, pp. 168–216.

Gusarchuk, T., (1995) 'Dvanadtsyat' khorovikh kontsertiv z avtografu A. Vedelya', in M. Stepanenko (ed.) *Ukrains'ky muzychny archiv. Dokumenty i materialy z istorii ukrainskoy muzychnoy kul'tury,* vol. 1:53–67. Kiev.

Gusin, Israil' and Tkachev, Donat, (1957) *Gosudarstvennaya Akademicheskaya Kapella imeni M.I. Glinki.* Leningrad: Gosudarstvennoe Muzykal'noe Izdatel'stvo.

Guthrie, Matthew, (1795) *Dissertations sur les antiquités en Russie.* St Petersburg.

Hinrichs, J.C., (1796) *Entstehung, Fortgang und Jetzige Beschaffenheit der Russischen Jagdmusik.* St Petersburg. (Facsimile edn. Kassel: Barenreiter Verlag, 1974).

Hoch, Moshe, (1977) 'The Jewish Folksong and the Ukrainian Folksong: a Delineation of Musical Communication in Folklore', M.A. dissertation. Tel-Aviv University.

Holman, Peter, (2000) 'Eighteenth-Century English Music: Past, Present, Future', in David Wyn Jones (ed.), *Music in Eighteenth-Century Britain.* Aldershot: Ashgate, pp. 1–13.

Hunt, J. L., (1975) *Paisiello: his Life as an Opera Composer.* New York.

Ilyin, V.P., (1985) *Ocherki istorii russkoy khorovoy kul'tury vtoroy poloviny XVII– nachala XX veka.* Moscow: Sovetsky kompozitor.

Ivanov, Vladimir F., (1980) *Dmytro Bortnyans'kiy.* Kiev: Muzychna Ukraina.

——, (1995) 'Rodovid D.S. Bortnyans'kogo', in M. Stepanenko (ed.), *Ukrains'ky muzychny archiv. Dokumenty i materialy z istorii ukrainskoy muzychnoy kul'tury,* vol. 1:29–33.

Ivanov-Boretsky, M., (1935) 'D. Sarti v Rossii', in M.V. Ivanov-Boretsky (ed.), *Muzykal'noe nasledstvo,* vol. 1:199–207. Moscow: Ogiz-Muzgiz.

Jensen, Claudia R., (1987) 'Nikolai Diletskii's "Grammatika" (Grammar) and the Musical Culture of Seventeenth-Century Muscovy', Ph.D. dissertation. Princeton University.

——, (1992) 'A Theoretical Work of Late Seventeenth-Century Muscovy: Nikolai Diletskii's *Grammatika* and the Earliest Circle of Fifths', *Journal of American Musicological Society,* XVIII:305–31.

Kaluzhnikova, T.I., (1967) 'Intonatsionnye osnovy partesnogo mnogogolosia', Ph.D. dissertation. Moscow: Institut Istorii Iskusstv.

Kantor, Georgy M., (1973) 'A.V. Novikov (Iz istorii muzykal'noy zhizni Kazani)', in E.M. Orlova and E.A. Ruchievskaya (eds), *Stranitsy istorii russkoy muzyki.* Leningrad: Muzyka, pp. 176–82.

Karlinsky, Simon, (1985) *Russian Drama from its Beginnings to the Age of Pushkin.* Berkeley and Los-Angeles.

Kartashev, A.V., (1959) *Ocherki po istorii russkoy tserkvi.* Paris: YMCA-Press.

Kashkin, Nikolai D., (1908) *Ocherk istorii russkoy muzyki*. St Petersburg: Jurgenson.

Kastal'sky, Alexander D., (1923) *Osobennosti narodno-russkoy muzykal'noy sistemy*. Moscow-Petrograd.

Katz, Boris, (1994) 'Ob odnom opyte prevrashchenia bibleiskoy prozy v russkie stikhi posredstvom muzyki', in W. Moskovich, A. Alexeev, L. Allain and S. Schwarzband (eds), *The Bible in a Thousand Years of Russian Literature, Jews and Slavs*, 2:113–20. Jerusalem: The Israel Academy of Science and Humanities.

Keldysh, Georgy V., (1965) *Russkaya muzyka XVIII veka*. Moscow: Nauka.

———, (1969) 'Ob istoricheskikh kornyakh kanta', in *Musica Antica*, Acta scientifica, 2. Bydgoszcz.

———, (1978a) 'Problema stiley v russkoy muzyke XVII–XVIII vekov', in G. Keldysh, *Ocherki i issledovania po istorii russkoy muzyki*. Moscow: Sovetsky Kompozitor, pp. 92–112.

———, (1978b) 'Ital'yanskaya opera M. Berezovskogo', in G. Keldysh, *Ocherki i issledovania po istorii russkoy muzyki*. Moscow: Sovetsky Kompozitor, pp. 113–29.

———, (1978c) 'K istorii opery "Yamshchiki na podstave"', in G. Keldysh, *Ocherki i issledovania po istorii russkoy muzyki*. Moscow: Sovetsky Kompozitor, pp. 130–40.

———, (1978d) 'Polonezy Yuzefa Kozlovskogo', in G. Keldysh, *Ocherki i issledovania po istorii russkoy muzyki*. Moscow: Sovetsky Kompozitor, pp. 141–58.

———, (1983–86) Yu.V. Keldysh, O.E. Levasheva and A.I. Kandinsky (eds), *Istoria russkoy muzyki* (v desyati tomakh), vols 1–4. Moscow: Muzyka.

———, (1983) *Drevnyaya Rus': XI–XVII veka*, IRM, Vol. 1. Moscow: Muzyka.

———, (1984a) 'Puti razvitia russkoy muzyki v poslepetrovskuyu poru (30–60–e gody)', in IRM, vol. 2:65–90. Moscow: Muzyka.

———, (1984b) 'Zapisi i izuchenie narodnoy pesni', in IRM, vol. 2:216–55. Moscow: Muzyka.

———, 1985. 'D.S. Bortniansky', in IRM, vol. 3:161–93. Moscow: Muzyka.

Khivrich, L., (1971) 'Fugatni formi v khorovikh kontsertakh D. Bortnians'kogo', in *Ukrains'ke muzikoznavstvo*, vol. 6:201–15. Kiev: Muzychna Ukraina.

Khodorkovskaya, E., (1991) *Opera-seria v Rossii XVIII v.* Problemy muzykoznania, vol. VI. Muzykal'ny teatr. St Petersburg: Rossiyskiy Institut Istorii Iskusstv.

Kholopova Valentina N., (1983) *Russkaya muzykal'naya ritmika*. Moscow: Sovetsky kompozitor.

Kiknadze, Larisa V., (1975) 'Osobennosti stilya barokko v russkoy muzyke', in V. Rabinovich (ed.), *Traditsii russkoy muzykal'noy kul'tury XVIII veka*. Proccedings of the GMPI imeni Gnesinykh, XXI:32–46. Moscow.

Kompaneisky, Nikolai I., (1908) 'Italianets li Bortnyansky?', in *Pamyati dukhovnykh kompozitorov Bortnyanskogo, Turchaninova i L'vova*. St Petersburg: Vremenny komitet po uvekovecheniyu pamyati nazvannykh kompozitorov, pp. 31–42.

Konechny, Al'bin, (1997) *Byt i zrelishchnaya kul'tura Sankt-Peterburga –*

Petrograda. XVIII–nachalo XX veka. Materialy k bibliografii. St Petersburg: Rossiyskiy Institut Istorii Iskusstv.

Kononenko, Natalie, (1998) *Ukrainian Minstrels*. Armonk, NY: M.E. Sharpe.

Koshelev, V. (ed.), (1994) *Skomorokhi*. St Petersburg: Rossiyskiy Institut Istorii Iskusstv.

Kots, E.S., (1926) *Krepostnaya intelligentsia*. Leningrad.

Krasnobaev, B.I., (1983) *Russkaya kul'tura vtoroy poloviny XVII–nachala XIX v.* Moscow: Moskovsky Gosudarstvenny Universitet.

Kuck V., (1971) 'Novi dokumental'ny dani pro zhittya A.L. Vedelya (Vedel'skogo) u Khar'kovi (1796–1798 rr.)', in *Ukrain'ske muzikoznavstvo*, vol. 6:153–69. Kiev: Muzychna Ukraina.

——, (1995) 'Rukopisna partitura tvoriv Artema Vedelya', in M. Stepanenko (ed.), *Ukrains'ky muzychny archiv. Dokumenty i materialy z istorii ukrainskoy muzychnoy kul'tury*, vol. 1:34–52.

Kukol'nik, Nestor, (1852) 'Maksim Berezovsky', in *Sochinenia*, vol. 2. St Petersburg.

Kurmacheva, I.D., (1983) *Krepostnaya intelligentsia Rossii. Vtoraya polovina XVIII–nachalo XIX veka*. Moscow: Nauka.

Kuzma, Marika, (1996) 'Bortniansky à la Bortniansky: An Examination of Sources of Dmitry Bortniansky's Choral Concertos', *The Journal of Musicology*, XIV: 183–212.

Lapin, Victor, (2003) 'Rukopisnaya versia "Sobrania" Lvova – Pracha (Eshche raz k istorii legendarnogo sbornika)', in G.V. Kopytova (ed.), *Iz fondov Kabineta rukopisey Rossiyskogo Instituta Istorii Iskusstv*, vol. 2:32–52. St Petersburg: Rossiyskiy Institut Istorii Iskusstv.

Lebedev, N., (1882) *Berezovsky i Bortnyansky kak kompozitory tserkovnogo penia.* St Petersburg.

Lebedeva, Antonina V., (1985) 'Khorovaya kul'tura', in IRM, vol. 3:111–31.

Lehmann, D., (1958) *Russland's Oper und Singspiel in der zweiten Hälfte des 18 Jahrhunderts*. Leipzig.

Lepskaya, L.A., (1980) 'Teatral'naya shkola Sheremetevykh vo vtoroy polovine XVIII veka', in *Vestnik Moskovskogo gosudarstvennogo universiteta*, series 8, History, no 3. Moscow.

Levashev, Evgeny, (1973) 'Pashkevich i ego opera "Skupoy"', in *Pashkevich V.A.: Skupoy*, score, piano arrangement, ed. and comments. PRMI, vol. IV:261–2. Moscow: Muzyka.

——, (1980) 'Opera "Sanktpeterburgsky gostiny dvor" i ee avtory', in *Pashkevich V.A., 'Kak pozhivesh', tak i proslyvesh', ili Sanktpeterburgsky gostiny dvor'*. Score, piano arrangement, ed. and comments. PRMI, vol. 8. Moscow: Muzyka.

—— (with A.V. Polekhin), (1985) 'M.S.Berezovsky', in IRM, vol. 3:132–60.

——, (1986) 'S.A. Degtyarev', in IRM, vol. 4:184–208.

——, (1994) *Traditsionnye zhanry pravoslavnogo pevcheskogo iskusstva v tvorchestve russkikh kompozitorov ot Glinki do Rakhmaninova 1825–1917.* Istorichesky ocherk, notografia, bibliografia. Moscow: Nezavisimy Tsentr TekhnoInfo.

Levasheva, O.E., (1956) 'Romans i pesnya. A.D. Zhilin. D.N. Kashin', in M.S. Druskin and Yu.V. Keldysh (eds), *Ocherki po istorii russkoy muzyki 1790–1825*. Leningrad: Gosudarstvennoe muzykal'noe izdatel'stvo, pp. 98–142.

————, (1972) *Russkaya vokal'naya lirika XVIII veka*. Issledovanie, publikatsia, kommentarii. PMRI, vol. I. Moscow: Muzyka.

————, (1984) 'Razvitie zhanra "Rossiyskoy pesni"', in IRM, vol. II:184–215. Moscow: Muzyka.

————, (1985) 'Nachalo russkoy opery', in IRM, vol. III, part 2:5–45. Moscow: Muzyka.

Levin, S.Ya., (1958) 'O russkikh orkestrakh nachala XVIII veka', in *Uchenye zapiski Gosudarstvennogo nauchno-issledovatel'skogo Instituta Teatra, Muzyki i Kinematografii*, vol. 2:405–14.

Lisova, N.A., (1985) 'Sukhoputny shlyakhetsky kadetsky korpus – pitomnik otechestvennykh muzykal'no-instrumental'nykh kadrov', in *Pamyatniki kul'tury: Novye otkrytia*. Ezhegodnik. Leningrad: Nauka, pp. 263–78.

Livanova, Tamara N., (1938) *Ocherki i materialy po istorii russkoy muzykal'noy kul'tury*, vol. I. Moscow: Gosudarstvennoe muzykal'noe izdatel'stvo.

————, (1952–53) *Russkaya muzykal'naya kul'tura 18 veka v ee svyazyakh s literaturoy, teatrom i bytom: Issledovania i materialy*, 2 vols. Moscow: Gosudarstvennoe muzykal'noe izdatelstvo.

Lotman, Yuriy and Uspensky, Boris, (1974) 'K semioticheskoy tipologii russkoy kul'tury XVIII veka', in I.E. Danilova (ed.), *Khudozhestvennaya kul'tura XVIII veka*. Moscow: Institut Istorii Iskusstv, pp. 259–82.

Lozovaya, I.E., Denisov, N.G., Gurieva N.V. and Zhivaeva O.O. (eds), (2001) *Russkoe tserkovnoe penie XI–XX vek*. Issledovania i publikatsii 1917–99. Moscow: Moskovskiy Gosudarstvenny Universitet.

Lvov, Alexey F., (1853) *O tserkovnykh khorakh*. St Petersburg.

————, (1858) *O svobodnom i nesimmetrichnom ritme*. St Petersburg.

Lvov, Fedor, (1834) *O penii v Rossii*. St Petersburg.

Maiburova, K., (1971) 'Glukhivs'ka shkola pivchykh XVIII st. ta ii rol' u rozvytku muzychnogo profesionalizmu na Ukraini ta v Rossii', in *Ukrains'ke muzikoznavstvo*, vol. 6:126–36. Kiev: Muzychna Ukraina.

Manferdini, Vincenzo, (1805) *Pravila garmonicheskie i melodicheskie dlya obuchenia vsey muzyke*. Trans. S. Degtyarev. St Petersburg.

Maret, H., (1875) 'Le cors de Potemkin', *Chronique musicale*, X:13–16. Paris.

Matsenko, Pavlo, (1951) *Dmitro Stepanovich Bortnyans'ky i Maxim Sozontovich Berezovs'ky*. Winnipeg, Man: Ukrainian Cultural and Educational Centre.

Mazo, Margarita, (1987) *A Collection of Russian Folk Songs by Nikolai Lvov and Ivan Prach*, ed. Malcolm Hamrick Brown, with Introduction and Appendixes by Margarita Mazo. Ann Arbor: UMI Research Press.

McMillin A. and Drage C., (1970) 'Curanty: an unpublished Russian Song-Book of 1733', *Oxford Slavonic Paper*, VIII:1–31.

Metallov, Vasily M., (1912) *O natsionalizme i tserkovnosti v russkoy dukhovnoy muzyke*. Moscow.

————, (4th ed., 1915) *Ocherk istorii pravoslavnogo tserkovnogo penia v Rossii.* Moscow.

Mikhaylenko, A., (1985) 'Fugirovannye formy v tvorchestve D. Bortnianskogo i ikh mesto v istorii russkoy polifonii', in *Voprosy muzykal'noy formy*, vol. 4:3–18. Moscow: Muzyka.

Mikhnevich, V., (1879) *Ocherk istorii muzyki v Rosssii v kul'turno-obshchestvennom otnoshenii.* St Petersburg.

Milov, L.V., (2000) 'Rossia pri Petre I' and 'Rossia pri preemnikakh Petra I i v pravlenie Ekateriny II' (parts I, II), in A.N. Sakharov (ed.), *Istoria Rossii: S nachala XVIII do kontsa XIX veka.* Moscow: AST, pp. 9–296.

Mischakoff, Anne, (2nd edn, 1983). *Khandoshkin and the Beginning of Russian String Music.* Ann Arbor: UMI Research Press.

Moleva, N.M., (1971) 'Muzyka i zrelishcha v Rossii XVII stoletia', in *Voprosy istorii*, 11:143–54.

Monas, Sydney, (1983) 'St Petersburg and Moscow as Cultural Symbols', in Theofanis George Stavrou (ed.) *Art and Culture in Nineteenth-Century Russia.* Bloomington: Indiana University Press, pp. 26–39.

Mooser, Robert-Aloys, (1932) *L'opéra comique français en Russie au XVIIIe siècle.* Geneva.

————, (1948–51) *Annales de la musique et des musiciens en Russie au XVIIIe siècle*, 3 vols. Geneva: Mont-Blanc.

————, (3rd edn, 1964) *Opéras, intermezzos, ballets, cantates, oratorios joués en Russie durant le XVIIIe siècle.* Geneva.

Montefiore, Sebag, (2001) *Prince of Princes: the Life of Potemkin.* New York: St Martin Press.

Morozan, Vladimir, (2nd edn, 1986) *Choral Performance in Pre-Revolutionary Russia.* Ann Arbor: UMI Research Press.

Muzalevsky, V.I., (1961) *Russkoe fortepiannoe iskusstvo: XVIII – pervaya polovina XIX veka.* Leningrad: Gosudarstvennoe muzykal'noe izdatel'stvo.

Natanson, V.A., (1960) *Proshloe russkogo pianizma (XVIII–nachalo XIX veka).* Moscow: Gosudarstvennoe muzykal'noe izdatel'stvo.

Nikolsky, Nikolai M., (3rd edn, 1983) *Istoria russkoy tserkvi.* Moscow: Izdatel'stvo politicheskoy literatury.

Nikitenko, A.V., (1904) *Zapiski i dnevnik*, vol. 1. St Petersburg.

Novikova, A.M., (1982) *Russkaya poezia XVIII – pervoy poloviny XIX veka i narodnaya pesnya.* Moscow: Prosveshchenie.

Norris, Geoffrey Arthur, 'The Influence of Folk Music on Russian Orchestral and Instrumental Works of the Eighteenth Century'. Ph.D. dissertation, University of Liverpool.

Odoevsky, Vladimir Fedorovich, (1956) *Muzykal'no-literaturnoe nasledie.* Comp. and ed. G.B. Bernandt. Moscow: Gosudarstvennoe muzykal'noe izdatel'stvo.

O'Douwes, Henk, (1957) 'De Russiche jaren van Gius. Sarti in dienst van Catharina II', *Mens en melodie* 12/5:146–52.

Ogarkova, N.A., (1998) 'The burial ceremony of the Polish king Stanislas-Augustus

Poniatowsky in connection with 'Missa defunctorum' by O. Kozlovsky' (in Russian), in T.Z. Skvirskaya, F.V. Panchenko and V.A. Somov (eds), *Peterburgsky muzykal'ny arkhiv*, vol. II:55–63. St Petersburg: Nauchnaya muzykal'naya biblioteka Sankt-Peterburgskoy gosudarstvennoy konservatorii; izdatel'stvo Kanon.

Oleary (Olearius), Adam, (1986) 'Opisanie puteshestvia v Moskoviu', in Yu.A. Limonov (ed.), *Rossia XV–XVII vv. glazami inostrantsev*. Leningrad: Lenizdat, pp. 287–470.

Orlov-Davydov, V., (1878) *Biograficheskiy ocherk gr. Vl. Grig. Orlova*, vol. I. St Petersburg.

Orlova, Elena M., (1978) 'O traditsiakh kanta v russkoy muzyke', in *Teoreticheskie nablyudenia nad istoriey muzyki*. Moscow: Muzyka.

———, (1979) *Lektsii po istorii russkoy muzyki*. Moskow: Muzyka.

Panareo, Salvatore, (1910) *Paisiello in Russia*. Trani: Vecchi e C.

Pantielev, Grigory, (1983) 'Dvesti let spustya', in *Sovetskaya Muzyka*, 3:74–6.

Petrovskaya, I., (2000) *Kontsertnaya zhizn' Peterburga, muzyka v obshchestvennom i domashnem bytu: 1801–1859 gody*. St Petersburg: Petrovsky fond.

Petrushevsky, V., (1901) 'O lichnosti i tserkovno-muzykal'nom tvorchestve A.L. Vedelya', in *Trudy Kievskoy Dukhovnoy Akademii*, vol. 7. Kiev.

Polekhin, Arkady V., (1983) 'Problemy biografii i tvorcheskogo nasledia M.S. Berezovskogo'. Ph.D. dissertation. Moscow: Institut Istorii Iskusstv.

Popova, Tatiana V., (1977) *Osnovy russkoy narodnoy muzyki*. Moscow: Muzyka.

Porfirieva, Anna L. (ed), (1997–2002) *Muzykal'ny Peterburg: XVIII vek, entsiklopedichesky slovar'*, 5 vols. St Petersburg: Rossiyskiy Institut Istorii Iskusstv; Kompozitor.

Preobrazhensky, Antonin, (1900) 'Bortniansky. K 75-letiu so dnya smerti', in *Russkaya muzykal'naya gazeta*, 40.

———, (1910) *Ocherk istorii tserkovnogo penia v Rossii*. St Petersburg.

———, (1916) 'Ot uniatskogo kanta do pravoslavnoy kheruvimskoy', *Muzykal'ny sovremennik*. February:11–28.

———, (1924) *Kul'tovaya muzyka v Rossii*. Rossiyskiy Institut Istorii Iskusstv, Russkaya neperiodicheskaya seria, izdavaemaya razryadom istorii muzyki, vol. II Leningrad: Academia.

'Proekt ob otpechatanii drevnego rossiyskogo kryukovogo peniya, rassmatrivaemy v dvukh glavneishikh otnosheniyakh, v otnoshenii k sostoyaniyu vsekh staroobryadcheskikh tserkvey, i v otnoshenii k sostoyaniyu vsekh velikorossiyskikh tserkvey', (1878). Addenda to the *Protocoly godovogo sobrania chlenov Obshchestva lyubiteley drevney pis'mennosti*, pp. 1–20.

Prokofiev, V., (1927) 'O.A. Kozlovsky I ego "Rossiyskie pesni"', in Prokofiev, V. (ed.), *Muzyka i muzykal'ny byt staroy Rossii*. Leningrad: Academia, 12–73.

Protopopov, Vl., (1973a) 'Nikolay Diletsky i ego russkie sovremenniki', *Sovetskaya muzyka*, 12:82–93.

———, (1973b) 'Muzyka Petrovskogo vremeni o pobede pod Poltavoy,' in *Muzyka na Poltavskuyu pobedu*. Publication, ed., research and comments. PRMI, vol. 2.

Moscow: Muzyka.

————, (1987) 'Polifoniya v russkoy muzyke XVII–nachala XX veka', in *Istoria polifonii*, vol. V. Moscow: Muzyka.

————, (1989) *Russkaya mysl' o muzyke v XVII veke*. Moscow: Muzyka.

————, (2000) *Russkoe tserkovnoe penie. Opyt bibliograficheskogo ukazatelya. Ot serediny XVI veka po 1917 god*. Moscow: Muzyka.

Pryashnikova, Margarita P., (2001a) *E.R. Dashkova i muzyka*. Moscow: Moskovsky Gumanitarny Institut imeni E.R. Dashkovoy.

————, (2001b) 'Iz istorii notnogo sobrania Vorontsovykh: muzyka v zhizni E.A. Sinyavinoy, v zamuzhestve Vorontsovoy', in L.V. Tychina (ed.) *E.R. Dashkova i rossiyskoe obshchestvo XVIII stoletia*. Moscow: Moskovsky Gumanitarny Institut imeni E.R. Dashkovoy, pp. 169–84.

Raaben, Lev N., (1967) *Zhizn' zamechatel'nykh skripachey*. Moscow: Muzyka.

Rabinovich, Alexander S., (1948) *Russkaya opera do Glinki*. Leningrad: Gosudarstvennoe muzykal'noe izdatel'stvo.

Rapatskaya, Lyudmila A., (1975a) 'Znachenie iskusstva Velikoy Frantsuskoy revolyutsii dlya razvitia russkoy muzykal'noy kul'tury 90-kh godov XVIII veka', in V. Rabinovich (ed.), *Traditsii russkoy muzykal'noy kul'tury XVIII veka*. Proceedings of the GMPI imeni Gnesinykh, vol. XXI:47–71. Moscow.

————, (1975b) 'O zabytom sbornike russkikh pesen – "Novom rossiyskom Pesennike" I. Schnora i T. Polezhaeva', in V. Rabinovich (ed.), *Traditsii russkoy muzykal'noy kul'tury XVIII veka*. Proceedings of the GMPI imeni Gnesinykh, vol. XXI:195–204. Moscow.

————, (1977) 'Vliyanie radishchevskikh tendentsiy v prosvetitel'stve na razvitie russkoy muzykal'noy kul'tury 80–90–kh godov XVIII veka'. Ph.D. dissertation. Moscow: GMPI imeni Gnesinykh.

Ravich, N., (1964) *Dve stolitsy*. Moscow.

Raynor, Henry, (1972) *A Social History of Music from the Middle Ages to Beethoven*. New York: Schoken Books.

Razumovsky, Dmitry, (1867) *Tserkovnoe penie v Rossii*. Moscow.

Ricks, Robert, (1969) 'Russian Horn Bands', *The Musical Quarterly*, LV/3: 364–71.

Rimsky-Korsakoff, Nikolay A., (1936) *My Musical Life*. Transl. from the revised second Russian edition by Judah A. Joffe. Ed. with Introduction by Carl van Vechten. NY: Tudor Publishing.

Ritzarev (Rytsareva, Rycareva, Ritsareva), Marina G., (1973a) 'Iz tvorcheskogo naslediya Bortnyanskogo', in E.M. Orlova and E.A. Ruchievskaya (eds), *Stranitsy istorii russkoy muzyki*. Leningrad: Muzyka, pp. 3–17.

————, (1973b) 'O stile khorovykh sochineniy D.S. Bortnyanskogo'. Ph.D. dissertation. Leningradskaya Gosudarstvennaya Konservatoria.

————, (1979) *Kompozitor D. Bortnyanskiy*. Leningrad: Muzyka.

————, (1981a) 'O zhizni i tvorchestve Maxima Berezovskogo', *Sovetskaya muzyka*, 6:110–16.

————, (1981b) 'O neizvestnom khorovom kontserte M.S. Berezovskogo',

Pamyatniki kul'tury. Novye otkrytia. Ezhegodnik AN SSSR. Leningrad: Nauka, pp. 187–93.

———, (1982) 'Russky khorovoy kontsert v tvorchestve italianskikh kompozitorov, rabotavshikh v Rossii vo vtoroy polovine XVIII veka', in *Musica antiqua. Acta scientifica*, vol. 6:855–67. Bydgoszcz.

———, (1983) *Kompozitor M. S. Berezovsky.* Leningrad: Muzyka.

———, 'Maxim Berezovsky i zabytaya russkaya drama', in *Teatral'naya zhizn'*, 1984, 24:26–7.

———, (1989a) 'Problemy izucheniya russkoy khorovoy muzyki vtoroy poloviny XVIII veka', in V. Zak and J. Chigareva (eds), *Problemy muzykal'noy nauki*, VII:193–204. Moscow: Sovetsky Kompozitor.

———, (1989b) 'Rossiysky khorovoy kontsert vtoroy poloviny XVIII veka: problemy evolyutsii stilya'. Post-doctoral dissertation, Kiev State Conservatory.

———, (1995) 'Yakiv Andriyovich Timchenko (Materiali do biografii)', in M. Stepanenko (ed.), *Ukrains'ky muzychnyi archiv. Dokumenty i materialy z istorii ukrainskoy muzychnoy kul'tury*, vol. 1:68–73. Kiev: Tsentrmuzinform.

———, (2000) 'Chant and Polyphony in Russia: Historical Aspects', in Bruno Bouckaert and Eugeen Schreurs (eds), *The Di Martinelli Music Collection (KULeuven, University Archives); Musical Life in Collegiate Churches in the Low Countries and Europe; Chant and Polyphony*, the Yearbook of Alamire Foundation 4:357–68. Leuven: Alamire.

———, (with A. Porfirieva), (2001) 'The Italian Diaspora in Eighteenth-Century Russia', in Reinhard Strohm (ed.), *The Eighteenth-Century Diaspora of Italian Music and Musicians, Speculum Musicae* series, vol. VIII:211–53. Brepols, Turnhout.

———, (2002a) 'The Legacy of Late Eighteenth-Century Russian Spiritual Music: its Sources and Destiny', in H. Loos and K.-P. Koch (eds), *Musikgeschichte zwischen Ost- und Westeuropa: Kirchenmusik–geistliche Musik–religiöse Musik*. Bericht der Konferenz Chemnitz 28–30, Oktober 1999. Bonn: Studio Verlag, pp. 479–92.

———, (2002b) 'Russian Music before Glinka', in Adena Portowitz (ed), *Min-ad*: *Israel Studies in Musicology Online.* http://www.biu.ac.il/hu/mu/min-ad02.

———, (2003) 'Rethinking Eighteenth-Century Russian Music', in Sh. Burstyn, J. Cohen, Z. Eitan, D. Halperin and D. Tanai (eds), *Orbis Musicae*, Proceedings of the International Conference 'Rethinking Interpretive Traditions in Musicology', Tel-Aviv University, June 6–9, 1999, vol. XIII:99–106. Tel-Aviv: Tel-Aviv University Press.

———, (Forthcoming) *Dukhovny kontsert v Rossii vtoroy poloviny XVIII veka.* St Petersburg: Kompozitor.

Rogger, Hans J., (2nd edn, 1969) *National Consciousness in Eighteenth-Century Russia*. Cambridge, Massachusetts: Harvard University Press.

Rogov, A.I. (ed.), (1973) *Muzykal'naya estetika Rossii XI–XVIII vekov*. Moscow: Muzyka.

Roizman, Leonid I., (1979) *Organ v istorii russkoy muzykal'noy kul'tury*. Moscow:

Muzyka.

Rozanov, Alexander S., (1962) 'Kompozitor Nikolai Petrovich Yakhontov (1764–1840)', in E. Gordeeva (ed.), *Muzykal'noe nasledstvo*, vol. I. Moscow: Muzyka, pp. 11–64 and 447–565.

———, (1970) '"Prazdnestvo seniora", opera D.S. Bortnyanskogo', in E. Gordeeva (ed.), *Muzykal'noe nasledstvo*, vol. III. Moscow: Muzyka, pp. 9–26 and 411–57.

———, (1975) *D.S. Bortnyansky. "Sokol"*. Publication, piano arrangement, research and comments. PRMI, vol. 5. Moscow: Muzyka.

———, (1976) 'Frants-German Lafermier, librettist D.S. Bortnyanskogo', in E. Gordeeva (ed.), *Muzykal'noe nasledstvo*, vol. IV. Moscow: Muzyka.

———, (1978) *Muzykal'ny Pavlovsk*. Leningrad: Muzyka.

Rozenberg, A., (1975a) 'O russkom proizvodstve dukhovykh instrumentov v XVIII veke', in V. Rabinovich (ed.) *Traditsii russkoy muzykal'noy kul'tury XVIII veka*. Proceedings of the GMPI imeni Gnesinykh, vol. XXI:164–80. Moscow.

———, (1975b) 'Muzyka okhotnich'ikh fanfar v Rossii XVIII veka', in V. Rabinovich (ed.) *Traditsii russkoy muzykal'noy kul'tury XVIII veka*. Proceedings of the GMPI imeni Gnesinykh, vol. XXI: 187–94. Moscow.

Rubtsov, Feodosy A., (1964) *Osnovy ladovogo stroeniya russkikh narodnykh pesen*. Leningrad: Muzyka.

Rudakova, Evgenia N., 1947. *D. S. Bortnyansky*. Moscow.

Rytsareva (*see* Ritzarev)

Ryzhkova, Natalia, (2003) 'Istoria izdania dukhovnykh kontsertov D.S. Bortnyanskogo', in G.V. Kopytova (ed.), *Iz fondov Kabineta rukopisey Rossiyskogo Instituta Istorii Iskusstv*, vol. 2:53–66. St Petersburg: Rossiyskiy Institut Istorii Iskusstv.

Seaman, Gerald R., (1958) 'E.I. Fomin; 1761–1800', *Monthy Musical Record*, 88/985:21–6.

———, (1959) 'Russian Horn Bands', *Monthy Musical Record*, 89/993.

———, (1962) 'Russian Folk Song', *The Slavonic and East European Review*, XLI.

———, (1967) *History of Russian Music. From its Origins to Dargomyzhsky*, vol. 1. Oxford: Basil Blackwell.

———, (1973) 'The Rise of Russian Opera', in Egon Wellesz and Frederick Sternfeld (eds), *The Age of Enlightenment, 1745–1790*. New Oxford History of Music, vol. VII:270–80. London: Oxford University Press.

Serov, Alexander N., (2nd edn, 1957) 'Muzyka, muzykal'naya nauka, muzykal'naya pedagogika', in *Izbrannye stat'i*, v. II:187–216. Moscow: Gosudarstvennoe muzykal'noe izdatel'stvo.

Schidlovsky, Nicolas, (1983) 'Sources of Russian Chant Theory', in Gordon D. McQuere (ed.), *Russian Theoretical Thought in Music*. Ann Arbor, Michigan: UMI Research Press, pp. 83–108.

Shcherbakova, Maria N., (1997) *Muzyka v russkoy drame. 1756 – pervaya polovina XIX v.* St Petersburg: 'Ut'.

Shreer-Tkachenko, A.I. (ed.), (1981) *Istoria ukrainskoy muzyki*. Moscow: Muzyka.

Shteinpress, Boris S., (1970) 'Muzyka Gaydna v Rossii pri zhizni kompozitora', in G. Edel'man (ed.), *Muzykal'noe ispolnitel'stvo*, vol. 6:276–306. Moscow: Muzyka.

Skrebkov, Sergei S., (1969) *Russkaya khorovaya muzyka XVII–nachala XVIII veka*. Moscow: Muzyka.

————, (1980). 'Bortnyansky – master russkogo khorovogo kontserta', in *Izbrannye stat'i*. Moscow: Muzyka., pp. 188–215.

Smolensky, Stepan V., (1901) 'Pamyati D.S. Bortnyanskogo', *Russkaya muzykal'naya gazeta*, 39–40:946–55.

Sokolova (Galkina), A.M., (1997) *Kompozitor Osip Antonovich Kozlovsky*. Moscow: Kotran.

Sorokina, E.G., Rozanova, Yu. A. and Skvortsova, I.A. (eds), (2003) *Bortnyansky i ego vremya*. Proceedings of Moscow State Conservatory, vol. 43. Moscow.

Sosnovtseva, I., (1984) *Mel'nik-koldun, obmanshchik i svat*. Score. Reconstruction, ed., piano arrangement, research and comments. PRMI, vol. 10. Moscow: Muzyka.

Spiegelman, Joel, (1973) 'Style Formation in Early Russian Keyboard Music', in John Garrard (ed.), *The Eighteenth Century in Russia*. Oxford: Clarendon Press.

Stählin, Jacob von, (1769) 'Nachrichten von der Musik in Russland', in M.J. Haigold, *Beilagen zum Neuveranderten Russland*, vol. 1. Riga – Mietau; facsimile with research, commentaries and index by Ernst Stöckl, Leipzig: Edition Peters, 1982.

————, (3rd edn, 1830) *Podlinnyye anekdoty o Petre Velikom, sobrannye Yakovom Shtelinym*, in 4 parts, part 2. Moscow.

————, (1868) 'Zapiski o Petre III', in *Utro*. Moscow.

————, (1935) 'Izvestia o muzyke v Rossii', translation by M. Shtern, comments by T.N. Livanova, in M.V. Ivanov-Boretsky (ed.). *Muzykal'noe nasledstvo: sbornik materialov po istorii muzykal'noy kul'tury v Rossii*, vol. I. Moscow: OGIZ-MUZGIZ, pp. 94–198.

————, (1935) *Muzyka i balet v Rossii XVIII veka*, translation by B.I. Zagursky, ed. and preface by B.V. Asafiev. Leningrad.

————, (1990) *Muzyka i balet v Rossii XVIII veka*, translation and comments by Konstantin Malinovsky. Moscow: Iskusstvo.

Stasov, Vladimir V., (1900) 'Sochinenie, pripisyvaemoe Bortnyanskomu', *Russkaya muzykal'naya gazeta*, 47:1230–43.

Stepanenko, Mikhail B., (1995) 'Sonata dlya skripki i chembalo Maxima Berezovskogo', in M. Stepanenko (ed.), *Ukrains'ky muzychnyi archiv. Dokumenty i materialy z istorii ukrainskoy muzychnoy kul'tury*, vol. 1. Kiev: Tsentmuzinform, pp. 6–8.

————, (2003a) 'Nevidomiy tvir D. Bortnyans'kogo', in M. Stepanenko (ed.), *Ukrains'ky muzychnyi archiv. Dokumenty i materialy z istorii ukrainskoy muzychnoy kul'tury*, vol. 3. Kiev: Tsenrmuzinform, pp. 15–16.

————, (2003b) 'Tvorchist' Timofiya ta Elizaveti Bilograds'kikh (poshuki i znakhidki)', in M. Stepanenko (ed.), *Ukrains'ky muzychnyi archiv. Dokumenty i materialy z istorii ukrainskoy muzychnoy kul'tury*, vol. 3. Kiev: Tsenrmuzinform, pp. 28–34.

Stolpyansky, Pavel N., (1989) *Muzyka i muzitsirovanie v starom Peterburge*. With commentaries by A. Rozanov. Leningrad: Muzyka.

Swan, Alfred J., (1973) *Russian Music and its Sources in Chant and Folk-song*. London: John Baker.

Taruskin, Richard, (1984) 'Some Thoughts on the History and Historiography of Russian Music', *The Journal of Musicology*, III:321–39.

———, (1997) *Defining Russia Musically: historical and hermeneutical Essays*. Princeton: Princeton University Press.

Tchaikovsky, Peter I., (1962) *Pis'ma, Polnoe sobranie sochineniy*, vol. 7. Moscow: Muzyka.

Thrane, Carl, (1901–02) 'Sarti in Kopenhagen', in Oskar Fleischer and Johannes Wolf (eds), *Sammelbände der internationalen Musikgesellschaft*, Dritter Jahrgang. Leipzig, pp. 528–38.

Tikhomirov, M.N., (1968) *Russkaya kul'tura X-XVIII vekov*. Moscow.

Tooke, William, (3rd edn, 1801) *View of the Russian Empire during the Reign of Catherine the Second and to the Close of the Eighteenth Century*, 3 vols. Dublin: P. Wogan.

Tsekhanavetsky, (Ciechanowiecki) A., (1993) *Mikhail Kazimir Aginsky i yago 'syadziba Muzay' u Slonime*. Minsk: Byelarus'.

Ugryumova, T.S., (1975) 'U istokov russkoy liricheskoy opery', in V. Rabinovich (ed.), *Traditsii russkoy muzykal'noy kul'tury XVIII veka*. Proceedings of the GMPI imeni Gnesinykh, vol. XXI:142–63. Moscow.

Uspensky, Nikolai D., (1968) *Obraztsy drevnerusskogo pevcheskogo iskusstva*. Leningrad: Sovetsky kompozitor.

———, (1971) *Drevnerusskoe pevcheskoe iskusstvo*. Moscow: Sovetsky kompozitor.

———, (1975) 'A Wreath on the Grave of Dmitry Stepanovich Bortnyansky', *Journal of the Moscow Patriarchate*:63–78.

———, (1976) *Russky khorovoy kontsert kontsa XVII – pervoy poloviny XVIII vekov*. Leningrad: Muzyka.

Vasilchikov, A., (1869) 'Semeystvo Razumovskikh', in *Osmnadtsaty vek. Istorichesky sbornik, izdavaemy Petrom Bartenevym*, book 2. Moscow.

Vassiliades, Evangeline, (1977) 'Overture and Symphony in Eighteenth-Century Russia'. Ph.D. dissertation. New York University.

Vernadsky, G., (1961) *The Origins of Russia*. Yale University Press.

Vertkov, Konstantin, (1948) *Russkaya rogovaya muzyka*. Moscow-Leningrad: Gosudarstvennoe muzykal'noe izdatel'stvo.

Vetlitsyna, Irina M., (1977) *Fomin, E.I. Yamshchiki na podstave*. Score. Ed. and research (with Yu.V. Keldysh). PRMI, vol 6.

———, (1987) *Nekotorye cherty russkoy orkestrovoy kul'tury XVIII veka*. Moscow: Muzyka.

Vladyshevskaya, Tatiana F., (1975) 'Partesny khorovoy kontsert v epokhu barokko', in V. Rabinovich (ed.), *Traditsii russkoy muzykal'noy kul'tury XVIII veka*. Proceedings of the GMPI imeni Gnesinykh, vol. XXI:73–112. Moscow.

Volman, Boris L., (1957) *Russkie pechatnye noty XVIII veka*. Leningrad: Muzgiz.

Volynsky, J., (1971) 'Dmitro Bortnyansky i Zahidna Ukraina', in *Ukrains'ke muzikoznavstvo*, vol. 6:216–22. Kiev: Muzychna Ukraina.

Vorotnikov, P., (1851) 'Berezovsky i Galuppi', in *Biblioteka dlya chtenia: zhurnal slovesnosti, nauk, khudozhestv, promyshlennosti, novostey i mod*, vol. 105, part 1, section of arts, January:103–22. St Petersburg.

Vsevolodsky–Gerngross, V.N., (1913) *Istoria teatral'nogo obrazovania v Rossii*, part 1. 1913.

———, (1960) *Russkiy teatr vtoroy poloviny XVIII veka*. Moscow.

Vytvyts'ky, Vasyl, (1974) *Maksym Sozontovych Berezovs'ky: zhyttya i tvorchist'*. Jersey City: M. P. Kots Publishing.

Whaples, Mariam Karpilow, (1958) 'Eighteenth-Century Russian Opera in the Light of Soviet Scholarship', in *Indiana Slavic Studies*, vol. II:113–34.

Wilmot, Martha and Catherine, (1934) *The Russian Journals of Martha and Catherine Wilmot*. Ed. the Marchioness of Londonderry and H.M. Hyde. London: Macmillan and Co.

Yampolsky, Izrail M., (1951) *Russkoe skripichnoe iskusstvo*, Leningrad: Gosudarstvennoe muzykal'noe izdatel'stvo.

Yasser, Joseph, (1949) 'References to Hebrew Music in Russian Medieval Ballads', *Jewish Social Studies* XI:21–48.

Yazovitskaya, Eleonora E., (1956) 'Kantata i oratoria. S.A. Degtyarev', in M.S. Druskin and Yu.V. Keldysh (eds), *Ocherki po istorii russkoy muzyki: 1790–1825*. Leningrad: Gosudarstvennoe muzykal'noe izdatel'stvo, pp. 143–67.

Yurchenko, Mstislav S., (1985) 'Ukrains'ki folklorni traditsii v tvorchosti Maksima Berezovskogo', *Narodna tvorchist' ta etnografia*, 4:18–26.

———, (1986) 'Neizvestnye proizvedenia Maksima Berezovskogo', *Sovetskaya muzyka*, 2:99–100.

———, (1989) 'Maxim Berezovsky v Italii', in M.M.Gordeychuk (ed.), *Ukrains'ka muzichna spadshchina, stat'i, materialy, dokumenty*. Kiev: Muzichna Ukraina, pp. 67–79.

Zabolotnaya, Natalia V., (1983) 'Tekstologicheskie osobennosti krupnoy kompozitsii patresnogo pis'ma', in A.S. Belonenko (ed.), *Problemy russkoy muzykal'noy textologii (po pamyatnikam russkoy khorovoy muzyki XII–XVIII vekov)*. Leningrad: Gosudarstvennaya konservatoria, Gosudarstvenny Institut Teatra, Muzyki i Kinematografii, pp. 152–74.

Zalusly, A., (1999) *Vremya i muzyka Mikhaila Kleofasa Oginskogo*. Minsk: Chetyre chetverti.

Zemzovsky, Izaly, (1967) *Russkaya protyazhnaya pesnya: opyt issledovania*. Leningrad: Muzyka.

Zhakova, V., (1962). 'Maxim Berezovsky', *Muzykal'naya zhizn'*, 1:3.

Zguta, Russell, (1978) *Russian Minstrels: A History of the Skomorokhi*. Oxford: Oxford University Press.

Zielinsky, Jaroslaw, (1917) 'Russian Hunting Music', *Music Quarterly*, III:59–69.

Index